The Cicero Spy Affair

The Joint Free
Public Library
of
Morristown
& Morris Township

THE CICERO SPY AFFAIR

German Access to British Secrets in World War II

RICHARD WIRES

Perspectives on Intelligence History
David Kahn, Series Editor

Westport, Connecticut
London

Library of Congress Cataloging-in-Publication Data

Wires, Richard, 1930–
    The Cicero spy affair : German access to British secrets in World
War II / Richard Wires.
        p.   cm.—(Perspectives on intelligence history, ISSN 1525–9544)
    Includes filmography.
    Includes bibliographical references and index.
    ISBN 0–275–96456–6 (alk. paper)
        1. Bazna, Elyesa, 1904–1970.   2. World War, 1939–1945—Secret
service—Germany.   3. Espionage, German—Great Britain.   4. Spies—
Germany.   I. Title.   II. Series.
D810.S8B399   1999
940.54'8743—dc21   98–50249

British Library Cataloguing in Publication Data is available.

Library of Congress Catalog Card Number: 98–50249
ISBN: 0–275–96456–6
ISSN: 1525–9544

First published in 1999

Praeger Publishers, 88 Post Road West, Westport, CT 06881
An imprint of Greenwood Publishing Group, Inc.
www.praeger.com

Printed in the United States of America

The paper used in this book complies with the
Permanent Paper Standard issued by the National
Information Standards Organization (Z39.48–1984).

10 9 8 7 6 5 4 3 2 1

Copyright Acknowledgments

The jacket photo of Sir Winston Churchill with Sir Hughe Knatchbull-Hugessen is
used with permission of the Imperial War Museum. The jacket photo of Adolf Hitler is
courtesy of the U.S. Holocaust Memorial Museum.

Every reasonable effort has been made to trace the owners of copyright materials in this
book, but in some instances this has proven impossible. The author and publisher will
be glad to receive information leading to more complete acknowledgments in subsequent
printings of the book and in the meantime extend their apologies for any omissions.

For
Marion Siney

Contents

A photo essay follows page 142.

Preface

In the extensive literature about espionage affairs and intelligence activities during World War II the episode known as Operation "Cicero" has gained prominence and popularity, because of its remarkable character and ironies. For more than four months during the winter of 1943–1944 the valet of Britain's ambassador in neutral Turkey photographed secret papers that his employer failed to safeguard properly; by selling his undeveloped films to a representative of German intelligence in Ankara for a reported total of $1.2 million the servant became history's then most highly paid spy. The access to one of its opponents' most important embassies marked Germany's outstanding achievement in an otherwise poor record of secret service work. But little came of the success. Many of the documents were extremely valuable, but the dictatorship never used the information effectively; the enterprising spy escaped being caught but soon discovered that his money was mostly counterfeit. References to the affair have become a staple of intelligence lore, usually with emphasis on the most sensational elements and often with little regard for the actual facts, but there has not yet been a full and objective account of the episode. A careful and comprehensive analysis of the available evidence and troublesome issues is needed, not only to identify and counteract the distortions and misconceptions so commonly found but also to examine the extraordinary events and conflicting views within their larger historical context.

My interest in the affair began with the first published accounts of both the espionage and counterfeiting operations, and it continued over the years because of reminders through travels and other contacts. While staying with friends one summer in rural Austria I visited the nearby caves at Redl-Zipf, where the forgery team had been hurriedly moved. On later occasions I often toured the lake and river region, where crates of bogus notes were abandoned in the war's final weeks. During early visits to Turkey I stayed at the now-replaced Park Hotel in Istanbul, where so many foreigners in World War II carried on their intrigues. I saw too the Çelik Palace Hotel in Bursa, which the spy had been expanding when word came from the Bank of England that his British banknotes were forged. When the former "Cicero" belatedly published his own account of the espionage, stressing how a young German secretary's defection to the Allies had threatened his safety, I discovered that she and I shared a Cleveland background and ties. Also, during an intelligence assignment in Munich, where the frustrated ex-spy later died, I acquired a professional appreciation of the Cicero case's many oddities and ironies. Then the controversy over the affair that erupted in Britain in the 1970s revealed the lack of consensus about what had happened. Only later did I consider preparing a detailed study of the episode, still surprised that no one else had yet taken on the task, but learning too that a degree of obscurity best suited many people.

The activities and operations of spies and intelligence agencies are understandably shielded in official secrecy, necessary for security but also readily invoked for less commendable reasons—the habit creating a mystique that conceals failures and encourages conjecture and rumor. Such factors are present here. The sources available for inquiry into the Cicero affair are substantial, despite the many gaps. Some documents, like reports of the intelligence service that ran the operation, have disappeared; other records, such as items covering the investigations of a security leak, remain closed. But sizable bodies of diplomatic messages exchanged between the British and German embassies and their respective capitals provide a helpful substitute. In particular they permit an understanding of the powers' opposing policies and of the difficulties that each side experienced. There are useful memoir accounts by the three Germans most directly involved in buying and analyzing the spy's films. Although each writer had self-serving motives for publishing his book, and all distorted the facts to suit their separate intentions and views, the different perspectives and insights tend to complement one another. For his part the spy too belatedly recorded his experiences; his recollections are untrustworthy, though they are the sole testimony touching upon certain activities. Especially when he discusses his thoughts and self-image, and also when others do the same, their exact words reveal much about the individuals. Comments by the victims of the spying have been meager. Given the circumstances and embarrassment of the affair, few British participants have made public statements helpful in reconstructing it.

Since the complete story of the espionage case involves more than the activities of the spy and his contact, a particular aim in this study has been to present and discuss the affair in a comprehensive way, enabling readers to understand both the international context in which it unfolded and the background developments that affected it. The spy operation occurred at a time when Nazi leaders wondered where and when the Allies would launch their next attacks against the continent. They learned that Britain wanted a campaign in the Aegean and then the Balkans, if it got cooperation from Turkey. Receiving the spy's photographs at this critical juncture gave Berlin a potential advantage in adjusting its policies and defenses. Of great significance too in the Cicero affair were the personal antagonisms and jurisdictional disputes among Germany's top party leaders and security officials. Full understanding of the handling and outcome of the spy operation is impossible without taking into account such bitter and wasteful rivalries. Essential also is knowledge of the Nazis' highly secret project for counterfeiting the British currency that paid the greedy spy. All these components have been integrated into the discussion where the explanations seemed most appropriate.

Reconstruction of the case to reveal its character and dimensions has been made difficult not only by the gaps and discrepancies in available information but also by the various claims and controversies that have colored its interpretation. Therefore the task of assessing the reliability of surviving reports and witnesses must include testing the tenability of conflicting theories and arguments drawn from much the same body of evidence. In the main text only the most significant of the unresolved questions and disputed points have been discussed in full; less important instances of differences in information and opinion have been covered in the notes. No attempt has been made to call attention to specific errors in popular books, however, although one could cite numerous false or misleading statements and tendentious claims. But the major shortcomings of the purportedly accurate film *Five Fingers* have been identified, because of its wide distribution and impact. Throughout the examination process the goal has been to emphasize the most sustainable findings, develop a sound account of the events, and indicate clearly areas where the existing knowledge does not allow a definitive conclusion.

Several matters about style also require mention. Wartime code names have been placed in quotation marks when first introduced but thereafter appear without them. I have left all financial figures in the original amounts, explaining where needed the equivalencies in other wartime currencies but not attempting to update or interpret their present values. Italicizing familiar foreign words—Führer, Luftwaffe, Gestapo, Abwehr—has been considered unnecessary. In initials designating various British and German organizations no periods have been employed. Such punctuation for German terms is not appropriate; the pattern for British agencies is apparently mixed. Thus I have opted for one form: SS, RSHA, and SD, for example, or MI6, SIS, and JIC. Other abbreviations, like OSS, are treated similarly.

A number of people have made valued contributions to the content and shaping of this book. Of exceptional help have been the encouragement and advice of Marion C. Siney throughout the development of the project and its several drafts. Her skills and scholarship in the field of diplomatic history, personal acquaintance with the late British ambassador involved in the affair, and her perceptive suggestions resulted in many improvements and new insights. Frank Brenchley in London kindly answered my questions about the British embassy in Ankara; at the beginning of his distinguished diplomatic career, during the spy episode, he served on the embassy staff. Another retired ambassador, Sir Donald Hawley, explained unfamiliar terms. Through queries in Turkey, retired General Zeki Ozdilekcan was able to provide information for me about the Çelik Palace Hotel in Bursa and its history. Also, from Lutz Kempner in Germany I learned about the later futile efforts made by Cicero to enlist Robert Kempner's legal help.

Others have assisted in the locating of records and sources. I am indebted to friends and colleagues Rosanne Marek and Nancy Turner of Ball State University, Marion Siney and Patricia Beall in Cleveland, Eric Farnsworth and Johannes Williams in Washington, and Jonathan Strickland Coleman in North Carolina for tracking down troublesome details and references. Of great help in London have been Brian Jensen and especially James Hobbs; Dirk F. G. Douglas and Sabine Coates, working in Munich, verified points of information. I wish to express appreciation as well to others who facilitated my work in a number of ways: W.R.M. Michel, Maurice Fooks, and the late Anthony Ellery in Britain, and Morton M. Rosenberg, Dirk Lindemann, and James E. Blount, Jr., in the United States. Without their interest and concern my tasks would have been more difficult and perhaps impossible.

The courteous assistance of the archivists and librarians at many research institutions and universities is acknowledged with special gratitude. Various members of the professional staffs of Britain's Public Record Office, the Newspaper Library at Colindale in London, and the National Archives II outside Washington helped locate materials in their collections. On repeated occasions I drew upon the research librarians of Case Western Reserve University, Ball State University, and the University of North Carolina for their expert skills in finding items not readily available. But a complete listing of the many university libraries and records depositories that over the years have provided services and information would be much longer.

For their help in locating the photographs that appear in the book, I want to thank Rosemarie Nief, Institute of Contemporary History and Wiener Library (London); the staff of the Still Picture Department, National Archives II (Maryland); Ian Carter, Photograph Archive, Imperial War Museum (London); Alice Meyer, Droemer Knaur Verlag (Munich); and Angelika Steinacker, Picture Press Bild- und Textagentur, *Stern* Syndication (Hamburg).

To all these people I am grateful for their guidance and patience. Their contributions have added immeasurably to my understanding and coverage, and to my efforts to achieve accuracy in this study.

There are aspects and details of the Cicero affair that will surely never be known. Some doubts and uncertainties will understandably persist about those points where the testimony is either suspect or inconsistent and thus allows interpretations to vary. Nor will even general consensus on the nature of events and their consequences prevent the continued sensationalizing of the episode by some, or weaken the steadfast belief in alternative theories or explanations by others. The purpose in undertaking this needed study has been to assemble the available evidence, identify in the course of a comprehensive narrative important issues that have produced disagreement and controversy concerning the affair, and offer closure to some past disputes and credible solutions to questions that remain.

1 The "Notorious" Case

The Cicero affair has long held a prominent place in the espionage lore and literature of World War II. Since the time the awkward episode first became public knowledge five years after the conflict ended, it has produced embarrassment and fascination because of both its previously unsuspected existence and then its sensationalized coverage. Before long even the serious dimensions of the enemy spying that actually occurred at the British embassy in neutral Turkey were overshadowed by false reports and imaginative tales lacking a sound basis in fact. Most extravagant were the early and often repeated claims that British documents relating to D-Day, the Allied landings in Normandy known as Operation "Overlord," had reached Berlin through the undetected German spy who had worked as valet to the careless ambassador. No such loss took place. Yet such fanciful versions added to the story's notoriety and appeal, leading to official admissions in Parliament and an entertaining Hollywood film (which drew worldwide audiences), until the mixing of truth and exaggeration created confusion and a legend. Neither the affair itself nor the related context need fictional embellishment, however, for even the undistorted tale provides colorful and compelling drama.

Over the years, authors of sober studies and popular narratives alike have found superlatives not merely apt but nearly inescapable in describing the famous occurrence. It has been called "perhaps the most spectacular single incident" in wartime intelligence work and "the greatest spy coup" of the entire war; the man responsible has been regarded as an "agent of stellar rank," "the most successful spy of the war" and possibly "the spy of the century"; the documents he photographed had an "incalculable value," because his copies gave full and "last-minute information on the most secret plans" of one side to its opponents; the money he eventually received lent him the distinction of having been "paid more than any other spy in history" until that time. These and other observations and assessments scarcely overstate the character and significance of the affair.

Neither the passing of a half-century nor the extensive and continuing commentary on the episode has brought full consensus concerning the interpretation of various records and testimony in the case. Disputes have involved not only details but the very essence of the affair, which some British writers later argued must have been controlled by London as part of an unrevealed scheme to mislead German leaders, though little credible evidence has ever been cited to support a deception thesis. Such areas of controversy and doubt have arisen and been sustained because many of the essential documents were destroyed or sealed, and because public disclosures were kept to a minimum. Yet the time has come when the troublesome issues stemming from exaggerated claims, official reticence, and conflicting opinions must be reexamined and the most sound positions identified.

* * *

During World War II there were few places where international intrigue was practiced with more spirit and determination than in Istanbul and Ankara. Although its general interests and sympathies lay with the Allied cause, Turkey remained neutral and kept ties to both sides until summer 1944, when Germany's waning power allowed a break in diplomatic relations. Before that time Axis military control of areas on the nation's borders—Greece, many Aegean and Mediterranean islands, and Bulgaria—had always posed a serious threat of German invasion or bombing. Meanwhile, both its carefully maintained nonbelligerency and its key geographical position between German-occupied Europe and the Allied-dominated Middle East made the country's commercial hub and political capital centers of intense competition and espionage.

The diplomatic struggle carried on by rival ambassadors, chosen for their prominence and skills—Britain's Sir Hughe Knatchbull-Hugessen and Nazi Germany's Franz von Papen—was backed and supplemented by the clandestine efforts of countless intelligence and security agents. Every major power and information-gathering unit valued the nation as a listening post, vied there for influence and gain, and built up confusing networks of informants and analysts to deal in secret data. Monitoring of the aims and activities of allies and friends was as common as the surveillance of foes and suspect strangers. Ankara's own secret service tried, with mixed success, to watch the multitude of foreigners who for whatever reason found themselves in Turkey. Certainly by the mid-war years the success of any extended spy or undercover operation depended on its total isolation, allowing no market for the flourishing trade in rumors and gossip, shielding the project's existence even from associates whose eagerness might overcome their discretion or whose changing self-interest might outweigh old loyalties. But if the purposes behind most of the foreigners' intelligence activities were indeed serious, there nevertheless also existed at times an atmosphere of adolescent games, even comic opera, with the worried local authorities often functioning simply as referees or observers. Some of the players in the intelligence competition were experienced professionals; many were recently recruited amateurs with more enthusiasm than knowledge or training. Awaiting a chance to join the roster of performers was an ambitious valet who thought he could outwit them all.

Elyesa Bazna had only recently been hired by Sir Hughe. He would not have been engaged had his employment record been investigated with proper care, and the ambassador's further lack of prudence allowed the new servant to become a spy. From late October 1943 until March 1944 the valet photographed many papers that his employer removed from embassy offices for study in his residence; the spy quickly bargained for the sale and delivery of his undeveloped films to the Germans for £15,000 sterling, or about $60,000, per roll. Few people at the German embassy ever knew of the secret arrangement, basically only the intelligence officer who was his contact, Ludwig Moyzisch, and the ambassador who reviewed the arriving reports and assigned him the name "Cicero," because his material was so eloquent. Certainly the information losses came as the war entered a critical stage. The espionage itself occurred during a period of top-level conferences held in Moscow, Cairo, and Tehran to plan future Allied strategy; items copied included vital messages and analyses as the British ambassador struggled to get Turkey's cooperation in the conflict. The Germans at times got detailed knowledge of British and Allied intentions within days of when issues and policies were discussed. For such extraordinary information the spy apparently received a total of about £300,000 sterling, or $1.2 million, over the more than four months of his career in espionage.

Much of the affair's fascination has derived from its ironies, which have given the entire situation a character that borders on the comic. Indeed the popular motion picture made soon after the spying became known treated its basic components with wry humor. Britain's pride in its wartime intelligence efforts and clever deception schemes was embarrassingly undermined by realization of what the enemy had managed in Turkey. Attitudes were shaken also by awareness of altered values and principles. The failure of an aloof ambassador of the traditional school to follow careful procedures for safeguarding valuable documents highlighted the discomforting differences between old-fashioned concepts of gentlemanly diplomacy and a newer world of pragmatism, of gaining every possible advantage by any means available. Still another element of irony arose through misjudgments and disdain. Even after the ambassador came to suspect a leak, leading to the arrival of outside specialists to tighten embassy procedures and controls, the true character of the security breach went undiscovered. The British believed that they had handled the situation effectively and thus remained complacent, unaware that losses continued, for it seemed unthinkable that the culprit could be the seemingly dull Turkish valet. In the end only the spy's mounting fear of being caught and his accumulated wealth caused him to curtail his filming and then to resign his position. He walked away a free man.

Overshadowing even Britain's false sense of security was the paradox of Berlin's intelligence failure. Despite their windfall of enemy secrets the Germans never profited from the information that they obtained so easily from Cicero, because of their own feuding and inflexibility. The handling of the data became caught up in long-standing personal rivalries, especially the bitter competition between Foreign Minister Joachim von Ribbentrop and ambitious young Walter Schellenberg of the Sicherheitsdienst (Security Service, or SD) over control of foreign intelligence. Such jealousies also dominated the evaluation and impact of the material. Some at first thought that it all seemed too good to be true. But no Nazi leader was initially, or ever fully, prepared to believe that ultimately the Allies would win: the spy's information was reviewed but not greatly valued, because it ran so deeply counter to fanatical views. Thus the most successful spy of the war carried out his daring espionage for naught. Nor did Moyzisch ever realize that a new young secretary in his own office spied for the Americans before defecting. He himself proved as vulnerable to enemy spying as the enemy ambassador whose secrets he so happily bought. The Americans, for reasons of rivalry and pique, for several months refused to reveal to their British ally what they were learning. Such situations illustrate well the complexities, cross-purposes, and confusion encountered in intelligence work.

Then too there was a final irony, which many have felt gave the entire tale a just ending. The spy had required the Germans to pay for his photographs in Britain's respected and stable currency; their own money was not trusted. But he never questioned where they got such a seemingly inexhaustible supply of the banknotes, discovering to his chagrin only at the war's conclusion that nearly all the funds he had received were bogus. The highest-paid espionage agent yet known to history had routinely been given British notes that the German regime had been printing as part of a huge, official counterfeiting scheme. He therefore found himself not merely stripped of his wealth but deeply in debt, after being held responsible for defrauding those to whom he had been passing his worthless money.

Nowhere in the story were there winners. The unusual twists that separate the affair from other espionage cases help to explain why it is sometimes regarded with humor. Many have found a certain comic element in seeing proud diplomats and intelligence agents fooled, narrow-minded officials willing to sacrifice a great advantage in information to pursue their personal hatreds and pettiness, and a clever rogue whose illusions and gullibility lead to his being cheated and humiliated. Nonetheless, even such ironic humor is tolerable only because of another characteristic of the affair, easily overlooked: its surprising lack of any violence to either the participants or innocent outsiders. With no instance whatsoever of bodily injury, and without such dire consequences as battlefield casualties resulting from compromised data, the affair lacked the bitter self-reproach and tragedy so often associated with spying.

The intriguing fragments of the full story appeared over the years in a variety of forms. They have been carefully investigated and elaborated; they have been grudgingly acknowledged as fact by some and promptly dismissed as insignificant by others; they have been widely sensationalized and romanticized. From such pieces and arguments the truth may emerge.

In 1950 Moyzisch first brought the case to public light, in a book called *Operation Cicero*. Held and questioned repeatedly by the Allies for many months after the war, though never charged with any crimes, he also gave testimony at Nuremberg during the lengthy series of postwar trials. Soon after the last important hearings he produced his sensational narrative, supposedly to counteract rumors and speculations about the episode and such matters as the counterfeiting scheme, and insisting that he remembered events with the "greatest distinctness" and detail. Undoubtedly the interrogations and court examinations had helped preserve his recollections of experiences: "I happen to be the only person who knows all the facts of the case." He assumed that the spy, whose real name he never knew, must surely have died; his survival had seemed "unlikely in the extreme" after they parted. But he would be proved wrong. Cicero had indeed lived, and investigations for his own book showed a number of significant errors made by Moyzisch. From the beginning, Moyzisch's editors had detected how he had deceived his readers and had doubted his overall trustworthiness. To offset the expected criticisms the publisher got Papen to contribute a postscript affirming the essential story.[1]

Through carefully phrased assertions and key omissions Moyzisch had deliberately misrepresented his Nazi affiliation and his specific function at the embassy. Although formally listed as a commercial attaché, and though he repeatedly indicated that he worked for Ribbentrop and the Foreign Ministry as part of the regular diplomatic staff, he belonged in fact to a special foreign intelligence service. The concealment took several forms. Thus he wondered if handling a spy was "really part of an attaché's job"; Moyzisch had worried, he wrote, about pursuing such contact, since "our official authority was, of course, the Auswärtige Amt"; nevertheless "one could trust" the foreign minister "not to back up his own people." (That observation occurred when he ran afoul of his real superiors and sought a protector.) Certainly Moyzisch was neither a diplomat nor responsible to Ribbentrop's ministry, but he liked to see himself in that role. In fact he worked for a Schutzstaffel, or SS, structure called the Reichssicherheitshauptamt, or RSHA (Reich Security Central Office), headed by SS General Ernst Kaltenbrunner under Heinrich Himmler's supervision, and specifically for the SD, which operated as the RSHA's Amt, or Department, VI to gather foreign intelligence. Moyzisch throughout his posting in Ankara during 1941–1944 was therefore responsible to Walter Schellenberg.[2]

While occasional slips in Moyzisch's logic and wording alerted careful readers, the book's postscript by Papen made clear his deception. Papen explained that he had stipulated upon his appointment in 1939 that he not suffer from any interference by the Gestapo. "Once the war had broken out, it was difficult to resist demands that the intelligence service of the secret state police should be represented in Ankara, and in the end I had to give way." Moyzisch therefore answered to Papen for basic administrative purposes, but the ambassador insisted that Moyzisch "took no part in the diplomatic affairs" handled by the embassy; Papen never saw Moyzisch's routine exchanges with Berlin—"Nor would they have interested me." Nevertheless the two worked well together. "I am glad to be able to say that my former attaché, faced with an extraordinarily complex situation and in a frequent conflict of loyalties, always did his best to be guided by his own common sense and fairness, no less than by the carefully considered interests of his country."[3]

There are also instances where the information in Moyzisch's book differed from his responses in postwar interrogations. During the Nuremberg war crimes trials, Robert Kempner, a prosecutor for the United States, studied what Moyzisch had revealed. The attorney's article about the spy affair, rather sensational in tone but based on the deposition statements, appeared at the same time as the book. Because of the narrow material he used, Kempner included errors and misjudgments acquired from Moyzisch, but there were differences in facts too.[4] Such points of discrepancy in what Moyzisch wrote for the public and reportedly said to Allied officials must be weighed with care. It is not a case where one version or the other can be taken as the truth.

When starting to write, Moyzisch had contacted Papen about his project. The former ambassador, whose postscript was decidedly reserved, later claimed that he had initially opposed publication to avoid embarrassing his former British counterpart. Having satisfied himself that the text "described the case with complete fairness," he withdrew his objections but planned to write his own memoirs, "in the interests of historical accuracy," for he wanted to correct several misleading points and false impressions left by Moyzisch. In his postscript he questioned the author's ability to read English texts well enough to assess the spy's material; he also claimed to have exploited the information in ways Moyzisch had neither fully understood nor reported. Two years later the ex-ambassador's lengthy autobiography, *Der Wahrheit eine Gasse* (1952, issued in English as *Memoirs*, 1953), elaborated upon his recollections of the espionage affair. Even more self serving than most such personal disclosures, the account passed over some awkward points but stressed the author's decency and innocence. He took particular pains to show his strong opposition to Nazism and his cleverness in trying to promote reason and peace. With respect to the Cicero case Papen sought substantial credit for benefiting from the spy's information, despite disagreement with Ribbentrop and Hitler over the war's course.[5]

Schellenberg offered a third perspective of the affair, that from within SD headquarters and Berlin's top circles, which is especially useful on processing the material from Cicero. Like many well-educated young men without employment prospects, Schellenberg had been an early member of the Nazi Party, enthusiastically making its security service his career. Despite his youth he rose rapidly to head the SS foreign intelligence office; he even gained Himmler as a protector, an important strength given the bitter rivalries among the party and capital elites. With help from his superiors he intrigued to undermine Ribbentrop, at times using the Cicero case as leverage. Because of his place in the dictatorship's power structure, he was later tried and imprisoned. Schellenberg would nearly complete his informative memoirs, *The Labyrinth*, before dying from liver disease in 1952. Postwar interrogations and the preparation of his trial defense helped him recall a wealth of detail, his statements and recollections being largely corroborated by other sources, and his continued pride in his lost achievements prompted keen observations about the defeated regime. Schellenberg's comments on the spy affair both extended and modified the version proffered by Moyzisch. He confirmed that Moyzisch had been his "assistant" and served the SD in his assignment: "Moyzisch and I had always worked on the very friendliest of terms."[6]

Moyzisch's claims piqued wide interest in Britain even before his book appeared in English. Although the publisher of the translation cautioned readers that the account told only part of the story and suggested that further revelations might alter early perceptions, the few public statements issued at the time tended to acknowledge the basic elements of the incident. British official comment on the affair has always been so limited, however, that eventually a body of comforting speculation arose about Cicero. Some writers later began to argue that London must surely have identified the spy in Ankara and used the situation to deceive the Germans by channeling false data through him. Since the nature and weight of available evidence failed to support such a theory, most analysts challenged it, producing an unexpected renewal of comment and debate about the episode after a quarter-century.

In 1947 Sir Hughe retired. Two years later, before the affair became known, he published his memoirs, entitled *Diplomat in Peace and War*. It seems reasonable to assume that he had meanwhile become aware of postwar interrogations that revealed the outlines of the wartime espionage. Neither his autobiography nor other postwar writings made reference to the spy incident, and he issued few comments about what happened, but those remarks must be noted. In mid-January 1950, when a London newspaper first carried the story, repeating foreign coverage, the revelations brought denials from Knatchbull-Hugessen and left the Foreign Office silent. The former ambassador told a journalist that "the backbone of the story is certainly true," a leakage had indeed been noticed and stopped, but that there was "a great deal of imaginative treatment" in the tale currently being told. Noting that the "whole business, as far as intense activity was concerned, took place in a period of about six weeks," he declared that the espionage ended upon its discovery, the valet being discharged or having quit. He recalled that the man's name was Elias but had forgotten his surname. In a further comment the diplomat said, "He was vetted by the Embassy, of course, before being taken into British employment" and had held an earlier staff position. About three weeks later the ambassador complained that much of the story was "highly-coloured nonsense" and that the publicity had become a little trying. Especially resented was the tale that he had once provided a piano accompaniment to his valet's operatic selections: "All of which is absolute poppycock"—"Can you imagine anything more absurd?"[7]

By keeping his remarks somewhat vague and dismissive, the retired diplomat implied that the entire matter had little importance, an attitude that at the outset served to satisfy many people, although he spoke from scant knowledge and unclear memory. Thus he noted that the spy had been a Turkish clerk pressed into service as a valet; he also seemed to think that during the war Moyzisch had deserted his country and ended in disgrace. The errors are important only in showing that Sir Hughe had still not familiarized himself with the case. That he made no further statements seemed to suggest either that there was nothing more to be said or that some question of security required continued discretion.

Meanwhile the publicity and curiosity generated by Moyzisch's book forced the British government to investigate the situation and claims. The results became known in the House of Commons in mid-October 1950 during a question period. On 18 October the foreign secretary, Ernest Bevin, admitted the substance of the story, that the valet had photographed "a number of highly secret documents" for delivery to the enemy, but his allusion to D-Day plans, Operation Overlord, was too careful to be comforting. (In fact he might correctly have reassured Parliament that the Overlord secrets had not been compromised.) Bevin openly criticized Knatchbull-Hugessen without specifically naming him. He declared that the espionage could not have occurred had the diplomat "conformed to the regulations governing the custody of secret documents" and that new instructions had been issued to prevent similar leakage. Despite his emphasis that no papers had actually been stolen, only copied, he agreed that the information had reached the enemy. His statements appeared immediately in the press, *The Times* heading its brief report with the words "Betrayal of War Secrets," while more detailed accounts included key names.[8] The discomfort and pain of Sir Hughe must have now become acute.

For over thirty years both government officials and former embassy staff treated the embarrassing affair with dignified silence. That no high-ranking intelligence officer came forward quickly to refute the story represented telling evidence that the incident had occurred largely as reported and without mitigating factors. Under the circumstances it is surprising that one British writer, Anthony Cave Brown, later claimed that London must have initiated or come to control the spy's activities.[9] Yet Cave Brown relied less on proof than on conjecture and could not explain details of the deception. His thesis and arguments must still be examined, however, because they began to appear in other accounts. Final confirmation of the spy's success eventually came in discussion of the "notorious" case in Britain's multivolume semiofficial history of its wartime intelligence services and their operations. Despite the authors' tendency to minimize the affair they concluded that luck alone prevented "the appalling national disasters" that might have resulted.[10]

Sensationalized accounts of the affair early established an exaggerated version of the spy's accomplishments, one that has never entirely disappeared. Moyzisch himself had introduced such overstatement by claiming that Cicero had managed to steal vital military secrets about D-Day. That and other significant errors continue to be repeated, because later writers have drawn upon material that they wrongly assumed was reliable or whose popular appeal they found irresistible.

But the source of many familiar and indelible misconceptions about the affair was not a book but rather a witty and imaginative motion picture.

Hollywood was quick to recognize the entertainment potential of the story revealed by Moyzisch. Darryl F. Zanuck as head of production for Twentieth Century–Fox acquired the film rights to the book. Zanuck's personal interest in the project ensured that planning proceeded rapidly; a working script was finished by spring 1951. Responsibility for the production fell to a gifted director, Joseph L. Mankiewicz, who developed it with his characteristic style and quality. The result was a sophisticated and exciting film, which was released early in 1952 with international stars James Mason and Danielle Darrieux heading an excellent cast, and it enjoyed both critical and box-office success. Yet the screenplay for *Five Fingers* was far from factual. While the documentary-type adaptation retained the basic situation, proclaiming its truthfulness and highlighting its ironies, the spy's glamour and his espionage achievement were enhanced. In particular the film showed theft and delivery to the enemy by Cicero of the Normandy invasion plans.[11] Countless viewers among the acclaimed production's worldwide audiences undoubtedly accepted the cinematic treatment as accurate.

The shooting of location scenes for the film brought the ex-spy out of hiding. By then he was in deep legal and financial trouble for having spent his counterfeit money. Any hope that the director might cast him in the production, or perhaps pay him a consulting fee on the film project, ended in the disappointment that a less desperate man would have foreseen. Over the following years he nevertheless came up with new schemes to publicize and alleviate his plight.

Hans Nogly was intrigued by the man who telephoned him in Munich in the early 1960s and identified himself in poor English as a foreign businessman, Elyesa Bazna. Nogly became curious but remained wary when the visitor from Istanbul claimed to have been the famous Cicero and indicated that he now wanted to publish his story. Nogly thought it worthwhile to meet him at the Vier Jahreszeiten Hotel, as the caller suggested—in the lobby, since as it turned out the man could by no means afford a room there—listening calmly as the Turk sought to ingratiate himself while outlining his book proposal in French. But the journalist doubted that the "short, bald, thickset, elderly man" could have been the daring spy. "His eyes, then and later, were the only thing about him that suggested that here was a man capable of being dangerous, crafty, and of shrinking at nothing." He produced a child's green composition book, saying that it contained his life story, and seemed anxious to have his work published. He therefore asked if Nogly would oversee the project, to draw attention to his situation and finance his lawsuit against Germany for having cheated him. Despite his initial misgivings, Nogly looked into what he heard from Bazna, eventually losing his skepticism. Most decisive to his involvement was a critical test: Nogly insisted on verifying the claimant's identity by arranging a reunion with Moyzisch. The meeting, seventeen years after their wartime association, proved more awkward than dramatic, since neither man discovered much of importance to say to the other. But Moyzisch indeed confirmed Bazna's role.

I Was Cicero appeared early in 1962 in Germany. Nogly had wisely preserved the terms and manner in which the former spy told about his life and grievances in the exercise book and in their conversations. "I have a mighty fine opinion of myself"; "In that notebook I have made myself out to be a great hero and an even greater patriot." Despite some occasional self-deprecation and critical self-analysis, always sounding more contrived than convincing, readers are unlikely to sympathize with the author, consumed by his grandiose dreams and sad delusions, switching his tone between bravado and humility, unaware how his admissions reveal his greed and amorality. But his account at least clarified confusion over his real name. Bazna appears to have called himself by a number of names, probably more to play out the changing roles he imagined for himself than to hide his identity, and he was often remembered by wartime contacts under the surname Diello. There have also been various renderings of his given name—Elyea, Elyasa, Elias, Eliaza, Eleazar, Elysea, Ilya, Ulysses—which in some instances may reflect the games he enjoyed. Recognizing the underlying importance of his romantic fantasies and effective role-playing is essential to understanding his character. His success as a spy was due to his mastery of the actor's art.

Bazna's book was shaped by Nogly. In addition to the much needed editing and restructuring of the original material, unsuitable as it was for publication, Nogly introduced fictionalization and special research to flesh out the account. Conversations supposedly remembered were rendered verbatim, situations and events underwent some rearrangement to enhance impact and excitement; documents allegedly recalled came in fact from archives; developments never known to the spy provided the basis for speculations. Yet the volume also offered previously unavailable evidence, for to verify and complement the spy's tale two important participants in the affair had been traced, and printed transcripts of various taped interviews had resulted. The accuracy of the material must be accepted on faith. One omission, however, is noteworthy. Even though he had managed to stage the identification meeting, Nogly apparently received no further cooperation from Moyzisch, whose reactions to the investigators' new data never appeared. He preserved the silence he had adopted after release of his own book.[12]

* * *

Intelligence operations are by nature seldom well documented officially. The reluctance to commit details to paper, preserve reports, or
to open or release files is pervasive. Occasionally other records provide
a useful alternative, however, illuminating at least certain aspects of
secret activities. That is true in this case. Thus while recollections by
participants in the affair are too self-serving and exaggerated to be fully
trustworthy, documentary sources can be used for partial corrobora-
tions, even though the files of the intelligence service apparently failed
to survive the final bombings and fighting of 1945. Papen's telegrams
to his superiors in the capital allow identification of some documents
and papers that were photographed by Cicero.[13] Fragmentary references to the Cicero material also appeared in the minutes of military
briefings. Where documents from the archives of Germany and Britain
help most is in analyzing their policies. Understanding Britain's strategic aims and regional goals during the critical winter of 1943–1944
is essential in evaluating the potential and real impact of German espionage. To place the origins of the affair in historical context it is
necessary first to examine the unusual setting and circumstances in
which the events occurred.

2   Turkey and the Powers

By autumn 1943 Turkey had maintained neutrality through four difficult years of World War II. Its foreign policy from the outset had combined the pursuit of long-standing national goals, expediency, and an
acute awareness of its vulnerable position amid the struggles of power
blocs. Although Turkey's general interests and sympathies lay with the
Western democracies, the war had seen its borders and coasts menaced
by Italian and German forces, which controlled its continental neighbors and most nearby islands, while Soviet strength and intentions
remained deeply suspect to Turkish leaders. Now the war had entered
a new phase. Allied victories in the Mediterranean produced a series
of conferences in which leaders debated their operations for 1944 and
often discussed Turkey. The initial events in the Cicero affair occurred
in late autumn against this background of fresh planning. Subsequent
developments in the case unfolded as Britain pursued a new effort to
persuade Turkey to enter the conflict as an active ally. Under such
circumstances Cicero's spying and the information he obtained, if effectively used, were of great potential value to Germany's government and
military. To understand just how the espionage case fitted into the situ-
ational context of the war and diplomacy it is necessary to identify the
outlooks and representatives of the nations concerned.

In the late 1930s the reformers who created the Turkish republic
after the Ottoman Empire's collapse in World War I sought to adjust
Ankara's policies to the realities of Europe's new power structure. The
death of revered President Kemal Atatürk in November 1938 had elevated his longtime colleague Ismet Inönü to head of state without altering Ankara's wariness of the Soviet Union or its vacillation between
the Western powers and Nazi Germany for ties and support. Thus appointment of Sükrü Saracoglu as the new foreign minister had signaled

Map 1
Turkey and Its Neighbors in World War II

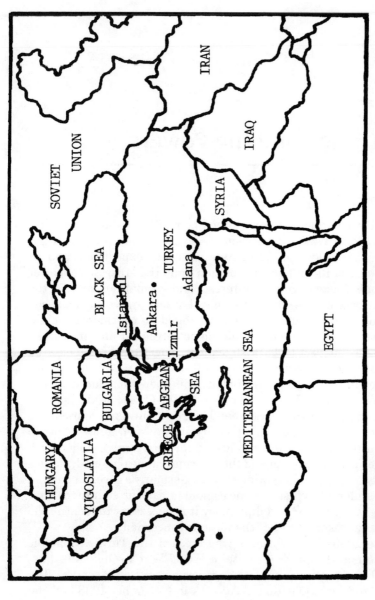

During 1943–1944 all of southeastern Europe was controlled by Axis forces. Italy and Germany occupied Greece, Albania, and Yugoslavia; Bulgaria, Romania, and Hungary had joined the Axis. But the Western Allies dominated the Middle East and North Africa by mid-1943. Soviet armies advancing westward soon threatened to overrun the Balkans. Their country's position amid the three powerful blocs caused Turkey's leaders great anxiety in deciding upon their safest course.

a likely pro-Western alignment; the counterbalance of Numan Mene-mencioglu as the ministry's permanent under-secretary pleased the pro-German advocates. If subsequent adjustments in foreign policy reflected factional strengths and influence patterns, shifting with world events, they nevertheless adhered to a broad consensus concerning the nation's fundamental goals. All its leaders remained committed to obtaining every possible advantage with minimal risk—protecting the republic from old enemies and pursuing its various territorial ambitions.[1] Yet the prospects for expansion were slight. Turkey's known designs upon parts of neighboring Syria and Iraq met strong opposition from the resurgent Arabs. Nor was there much chance of regaining Cyprus from the British government, of extending the Bulgarian border northward, or of forcing Italy to abandon the Mediterranean islands lying off the coast. But rapidly changing international conditions encouraged Turkish politicians to consider all foreseeable possibilities.

During 1939 Turkey gradually aligned itself with the Western powers as the continent moved toward World War II. Behind its decisions lay traditional fears of Russian encroachments, and also newer anxieties about Italy's dreams of adding to its existing empire. Turkey by late summer 1939 also distrusted the Germans as allies of Rome and then of Moscow. The unexpected Nazi-Soviet pact in August had intensified Ankara's deep suspicions: Turkey therefore reacted quickly to assure itself of friends in the West. Following the outbreak of hostilities Ankara concluded an alliance in October that called for joint Anglo-French-Turkish action if the Mediterranean region or the Balkans became areas of war operations. In the negotiations Turkey had won excellent trade and financial concessions from the West while stipulating that it would not fight the Soviet Union. Then, following the disastrous Allied defeats in spring 1940, the Italian attack on Greece, and Nazi conquest of the Balkans, the alarmed Turks found themselves isolated and nearly surrounded: Bulgaria had meanwhile joined the Axis, Germany occupied Greece and the Aegean; and Italy held islands off southwest Anatolia.

Under such circumstances Ankara had stayed out of the war, despite its 1939 treaty and commitments. In June 1940 the nation declared itself a nonbelligerent while still acknowledging its special ties with Britain. Turkey also reached accommodations with Germany: in June 1941 it concluded a ten-year treaty of cooperation, which might have been an alliance had there not been last-minute qualms in Ankara. Kept well informed by Turkish leaders and understanding their predicament, London accepted the inroad by the persistent Germans, undoubtedly heartened by Turkey's stipulation that its prior obligations took precedence. Open satisfaction reigned in Turkey just a few days later, when the Soviet Union fell victim to sudden Nazi attack and seemed destined for destruction. Some people even expected that a German victory would enable Turkey to acquire new border areas. Meanwhile the see-saw fighting in Libya and Egypt and in the Mediterranean remained a cause for concern until the British victory at El Alamein in late 1942 turned the balance in that theater. By May 1943 the Allies had cleared the Axis from North Africa. Nonetheless, swift German occupation of Italy after its capitulation in September showed the determination of Berlin to hold the European continent.

Throughout those difficult years cautious leaders in Ankara followed military reports but took no action. Only one political change of significance took place: Saracoglu became prime minister after his predecessor's death in July 1942. Initially he retained his old post, but Menemencioglu soon succeeded him as foreign minister. Their different outlooks posed few problems. Despite a willingness to hear rival arguments and proposals, the Turks maintained a guarded neutrality, played each side in the war against the other, thought hopefully of a Soviet defeat, and regarded their policy as both prudent and promising. Ankara was still watching and waiting in late 1943.

Trade and finance issues had meanwhile remained a special difficulty. German economic interests had predominated in the 1930s, but with the coming of war Ankara had sought closer ties with the Allies. A Turco-German trade treaty was allowed to lapse in August 1939. Yet despite much hard bargaining and some key agreements, Britain and France could not satisfy Ankara's demands for markets and weapons. In July 1940 Turkey therefore accepted a new and complicated commercial accord with Berlin for 1940–1941. Britain countered with an improved trade and payment agreement in November. Tensions persisted as each nation pursued its own objectives: Turkey bargained for assured outlets for all its exports and reliable sources of industrial goods while manipulating trade policies to protect its neutrality; Britain promoted sales of its products to offset costly preemptive buying designed to keep vital commodities from reaching the Axis; Germany needed certain mineral ores and was forced to make unrealistic supply commitments and substantial purchases of agricultural items it did not want.

The prize in this economic warfare was the control of Turkish chromite, essential for high-grade steel and therefore to all armaments; German heavy industry was totally dependent on imports of the ore. Although Britain had contracted to purchase all of Turkey's chromite exports for two years, capping other agreements denying the Germans access to any ore supplies, the economic planners in London had shortsightedly not covered the 1943 output. In autumn 1941 Berlin arranged an agreement to supply war materials in exchange for large chromite shipments over two years starting in January 1943. Circumstances by 1943, however, brought new complications: Germany had proven to be an unreliable trading partner, because of its own military needs in fighting the Soviet Union. Turkey nevertheless honored some of its export obligations and continued to earmark a sizable amount of its chromite production for shipment to Germany; Anglo-American efforts to deplete its ore stocks through expensive purchases, and to halt other deliveries, were frustrated by Ankara. Yet shipments remained well under contract levels, due to mining capacity and transport problems. While the agreement for 1943 had called for shipping 90,000 tons of ore, the Turks sent fewer than 47,000 tons, arguing that Germany had failed to provide Turkey with the goods it had promised.[2] The dispute over Turkey's trade policy in general and chromite shipments in particular would stay unresolved until drastic action by the Allies the following spring. Meanwhile it contributed to Anglo-Turkish friction over other issues.

Turkish leaders worried constantly about the inadequacy of the nation's defenses in the early 1940s. Although the army had been considered strong by prewar regional standards, the war had demonstrated the need for quick movement and air power; the military now found itself largely outmoded. Turkey's army had about fifty equipped divisions in 1943. Its infantry was judged effective and had sufficient rifles, and its artillery units were also in reasonably good shape, but armor was scarce and largely outdated, and few planes or antiaircraft guns were available. Thus the greatest need was for expensive tanks and planes. No one doubted the superior fighting spirit and quality of the ordinary Turkish soldiers, which certainly helped deter invasion, but the shortage of modern weaponry weighed heavily against any provocative Turkish actions. Early in the war Ankara had expected arms from its Western allies, and later it hoped Germany would be a source. Obviously, however, neither side would rearm Turkey without assurance of its full assistance; trust and confidence in the Turks were undermined by their own caution; and in general neither the British nor Germans had any weapons to spare. Britain had nevertheless done its utmost to accommodate the Turks. Yet the armaments issue by February 1944 would bring Anglo-Turkish relations to their lowest point.

* * *

The emphasis and intensity of the pressure exerted on Ankara by the British and the Germans reflected their relative strengths at any given time. Britain's relations with Ankara were therefore marked by an underlying resignation from mid-1939 until early 1943. Although expecting political cooperation and military assistance from their ally, and anxious to limit its trade in strategic items, government leaders in London understood the policy of nonbelligerency. Their aim was simply to preserve ties until Britain became stronger and Turkey's active help in the war could be most useful. During those years Germany had won such impressive gains in the region that it sought to persuade Turkey to join its side. Berlin's ability to deal from a position of power produced some concessions from Turkey. But neither adversary could pry Ankara away from its cautious stand.

To a considerable extent the frustration resulted from the fact that the ambassadors representing the rival powers were opponents of great intelligence and resourcefulness: Britain's Sir Hughe Knatchbull-Hugessen and Nazi Germany's Franz von Papen. Each possessed both wide experience and unusual skills, albeit of different kinds, and they shared some similarities in their backgrounds. Most noteworthy was that each had served his country in the former Ottoman Empire and therefore had a good grasp of past events there and old attitudes. Nonetheless, more significant were the differences in their characters and roles: Knatchbull-Hugessen was a diplomat respected for his professionalism and personal manner; Papen had a reputation for intrigue and being less than trustworthy. Certainly the assignment of two such remarkable men to Turkey showed the nation's great importance to the opposing powers.

Sir Hughe had been born into an old and distinguished county family in March 1886.[3] Educated at Eton and then Balliol College, where Anthony Eden became his friend, he had sought a foreign service career, in 1908 passing the required examinations and joining the Foreign Office's junior staff. At a time when the Diplomatic Service was still separate and its trainees unpaid, he was able in October 1909 to obtain special assignment to Constantinople as an attaché with salary. He came to know Ottoman Turkey from several years of living and working there. In 1912 he had married a young woman—Mary Gordon-Gilmour—whose father became a general, for his next assigned duties were back home, in the Foreign Office. During World War I he had dealt with questions of economic warfare and then been in his country's Paris Peace Conference delegation.[4] After the war, when inexperienced diplomats were finally paid, Knatchbull-Hugessen had several postings in Europe, learning procedures and rising to important positions. Then had come assignment as ambassador to China, just before that country was attacked. In late August 1937 his car was strafed by a Japanese plane; Knatchbull-Hugessen spent over a month hospitalized in Shanghai, recovering from his bullet wounds. The need for further convalescence had led to his recall and departure for home at the end of the year.[5] Sir Hughe became Britain's ambassador to Turkey in late February 1939.

The new representative was a man of considerable charm and culture. A gifted linguist, at ease with his varied obligations, he handled comfortably the formal procedures imposed by diplomatic life and showed a flair for its social aspects, while also making time for private thoughts and pursuits. Known for his wit and sense of humor, setting forth his views in clever short verses, he was amused by the Foreign Office's more rigid and stodgy ways.[6] Knatchbull-Hugessen could also laugh at himself—useful for someone nicknamed "Snatch." But he took a serious interest in the arts, had notable talent as a painter and creator of pen-and-ink drawings, and enjoyed music and playing the piano for relaxation.[7] His love of music was to provide unusual circumstances and opportunities for the valet who was a spy.

Observers reasoned correctly that the assignment of such a respected senior diplomat indicated London's view that Turkey held a critical place in the development of both regional security and strategic trade. The new ambassador's arrival at a time when Ankara was entering its post-Atatürk era had allowed for adjustments and new beginnings. Sir Hughe helped to guide Turkey back to its traditional pro-British policy and to undermine its commercial ties to Germany before the outbreak of World War II and military setbacks of 1940. He had good relationships with government leaders, finding both Inönü and Saracoglu pro-Allied in outlook, but he understood their worries and caution.[8] Sir Hughe counteracted Papen's influence and intrigues, something he managed because Saracoglu kept him well informed, and worked especially to limit the Turkish concessions to Germany. Meanwhile Turkey's press and informed opinion generally continued to favor the Western Allies.[9]

No change in Ankara's policy could be expected, however, until the British military situation had been improved. Sir Hughe so advised the foreign secretary, his old friend Eden from college days, when he briefed him in December 1942. Churchill ignored the caution early in 1943, when he insisted on meeting with Inönü and planned a trip to Turkey. He and senior military personnel journeyed to Adana soon after the end of the Allied leaders' meetings in Casablanca, acting against the advice of his foreign secretary, who believed the visit was doomed to failure—as Churchill indeed discovered for himself when the Turks' fear of Germany kept them firm about building up their military before any involvement. His unforeseen setback in personal diplomacy caused annoyance with Eden and a brief period of coolness in their relationship.[10] In mid-1943, however, following the victories in North Africa and with the collapse of Italy imminent, the prime minister and some other British leaders began to insist that Ankara finally commit itself to helping the Allies in concrete ways. That fall Britain launched an ill-fated attack to seize key Aegean islands. The altered situation required Knatchbull-Hugessen to press for fulfillment of alliance obligations and other forms of military cooperation, which Ankara remained reluctant to undertake. Those were the circumstances when Cicero first approached the German embassy with his filmed documents.

Papen, in the other camp, had been born into the Catholic nobility of Westphalia in 1879 and had served in the German army from 1896 to 1918. With the family estate entailed to an older brother, he had chosen a career in the cavalry, starting as a cadet-page at the imperial court, then rising rapidly from regimental duty to important posts: service with the General Staff during 1911–1913 and then as military attaché in the United States and Mexico for two years. Involved in a major scandal, Papen was declared *persona non grata* by Washington and was expelled in late 1915. After duty on the western front, in mid-1917 he joined German units helping Turkey fight the British in the Palestine sector, staying there until the war ended. His last task was repatriation of German troops caught by their ally's collapse.[11] In the 1920s he entered politics through the Center Party and was briefly chancellor of the Weimar Republic during the confusion of its breakdown in 1932. As vice-chancellor in the coalition cabinet he had helped arrange for Hitler, he soon found himself outmaneuvered by the Nazis and nearly killed in a violent purge, but Papen then was offered diplomatic posts as the regime sought to project a greater respectability. His assignment as ambassador to Austria ended when Germany early in 1938 invaded and annexed its neighbor.

Few contemporaries and scholars have spoken of Papen with anything but criticism and disdain. As a French diplomat commenting on his political image in the early 1930s has said, "He was reputed to be superficial, blundering, untrue, ambitious, vain, crafty, and an intriguer."[12] Knatchbull-Hugessen too had little good to say about Papen. Observing that his name "was universally connected with all that was sharp and disreputable in diplomatic dealings," the envoy thought of him as an "artful dodger" who appeared to be "quick and clever on the surface" but who also caused "grave doubts" about his substance or depth, for "there was something terribly professional about his charm" with all its "virtuosity which bespoke considerable practice." Papen's store of "charm could be turned on and intensified at will—not always with the desired result in the case of the Turks."[13] They regarded his smoothness with suspicion.

Papen's appointment as ambassador had long been resisted by Turkey. Ankara's reasons included Papen's close identification with Nazi policies, concern about his reputation for plots and scheming, and the Turks' memory of how Germany tricked them into World War I. The proposed envoy's military service reminded them of that grievance. Only after a year of negotiations did Ankara in late April 1939 welcome the nominee as the new ambassador. "Even then he was received with scant enthusiasm," recalled Knatchbull-Hugessen later, though the German diplomat had quickly stressed Berlin's peaceful intentions.[14] During his first years Papen's main effort shifted from trying to prevent Turkey from entering the war as an enemy to courting it as a partner. Only with the Allied resurgence of spring 1943 did Papen change again. Thereafter his aim reverted to keeping Turkey from aiding or joining the enemy. What he learned from the Cicero papers proved a great help.

Papen built many contacts among the Turks. A sizable element among Turkey's military officers and government officials saw friendship or alliance with Germany as an expedient course. Their views had nearly prevailed in the 1937–1938 period, although Berlin had then proven cautious. They were pressed again during 1940–1941 with the ambassador's full support, but Papen had been too assertive, causing Inönü and others to react against the pressure. Menemencioglu and those sharing his outlook persisted, however, and continued to urge cooperation with Germany. Still, most of Turkey's leaders recognized that their nation's interests were incompatible with Berlin's other pursuits: the secret backing of Arab causes and radical groups, political loyalty to Italy and its imperial schemes in the Mediterranean, the military pact with Moscow during the critical years of 1939–1941, and control of the Balkans and nearby coastal islands. Berlin and its ambassador labored hard to reassure and court the suspicious Turks. Papen's last major success produced a treaty on the transit of armaments concluded in September 1942. The agreement in fact represented an attempt by Germany to buy Turkey's continued nonbelligerency with more unrealistic promises.[15] Thus while Papen won some friends and concessions, he failed to alter Ankara's basic point of view, grounded as it was in Turkish self-interest.

A special problem plagued the ambassador during his entire tenure. Through his political intrigues Papen had made powerful enemies among the Nazi hierarchy and party stalwarts. Most important were the foreign minister, Joachim von Ribbentrop, his immediate superior, and the propaganda minister, Joseph Goebbels, both close adherents to party principles. Of critical importance in the Cicero affair was Ribbentrop's jealous hatred of the ambassador: he would distrust almost anything the diplomat endorsed. In addition, Ribbentrop's sister was married to the second-ranking embassy official, Albert Jenke, and the ambassador obviously wondered what stories were reaching Berlin through them. Another high-ranking aide was also close to Ribbentrop, Hans Kroll, Papen's nemesis, whose private reports often contradicted his own.[16] As an early precaution Papen had distanced himself from such party informants on his staff by rejecting the ambassador's residence in favor of the seized Czech legation and greater privacy.[17] Nonetheless, the antagonism and plots persisted. In February 1942 a bomb exploded near the Papens in Ankara. The bomber's death prevented identifying those responsible, but some observers thought agents of the ambassador's own government were involved. Four months later influential friends thwarted a Nazi effort to have him recalled from his post. He was also suspected during 1942–1943 of having contacts with Americans about possible terms for peace: his accusers were correct but lacked evidence.[18] Yet Papen had protectors, headed by Hitler himself. Also, the networks of traditional conservatives in both his ministry and the military helped shield him.

As representatives of opposing powers, the two ambassadors met rarely before the war and never after the start of hostilities. On special occasions, like official receptions marking Turkey's National Day on 29 October, the government carefully separated all wartime enemies.[19] Still, each envoy remained alert to the other's actions and plans: Knatchbull-Hugessen met secretly with Saracoglu, Papen would confer with Menemencioglu. It was still impossible, however, to foresee all problems. In that sense Papen gained an important advantage from the Cicero papers he saw.

* * *

Britain's top government leaders in the months following the Churchill-Inönü meetings at Adana in late January 1943 continued to assume some commitment to action by Ankara. Without any full mutual understanding of the viewpoints raised at the conference, however, there soon arose major difficulties over joint planning. The visits of British military commanders not long after the meetings probably increased the Turks' fear of pressure. Certainly their approach remained one of watchful waiting to see exactly how the war developed and whether conditions would somehow offer any greater benefits. By late spring Ankara's arguments citing lack of military preparedness and vulnerability to bombing attacks began to strike the British as mere stalling. Sir Hughe noted that the discord marked the start of a long period of trouble with Ankara.[20] Yet no hurdle seemed able to deter London from moving ahead along the lines already chosen.

During the summer and autumn of 1943 the British pursued an independent course of action designed to alter dramatically the Aegean and Balkan situation that so concerned them. At best a highly risky undertaking, the campaign became what has justifiably been called a military disaster, one with varied and deep repercussions. In various ways the issues and events connected with this episode of the war effected and confirmed a final change in the balance of power within the alliance. With the failure of its effort in the Aegean, Britain had to abandon real hope of influencing Turkey to enter the war and of saving the Balkans from the ambitions of Moscow, since the whole region was of little interest to Washington. By revealing itself incapable of mounting and executing successfully this demanding operation, Britain was forced to accept American leadership in determination of strategic plans. Under the circumstances it is understandable why so many bitter words have been used in assessing the reasons and responsibility for the failure of the campaign.[21] Certainly it is much easier to identify the problems than to explain why they occurred or remained unsolved.

One of the principal concerns of Churchill and many other British leaders was to prevent Russian domination of the Balkans in the post-war period. They knew their success in upholding this traditional British policy would depend on how the military situation unfolded. A bold campaign by the West seemed to be the answer, and obvious restiveness in Italy after the Allies won control of Africa in spring 1943 presented a special opportunity. It appeared possible that some Axis-held islands in the Aegean could be seized with minimal effort and be used to pressure the Germans in southeastern Europe through a number of means. Perhaps the Allies could force the enemy to abandon its exposed positions in Greece, open the whole Balkan peninsula and especially the oil fields of Romania to air attacks, and persuade Turkey to declare war and start a land front against the Axis. Whatever immediate advantages they might cite, British leaders also wanted to reduce the postwar power of Moscow, a concern not shared by their principal ally.

During the mid-summer weeks of 1943 the profound differences between British and American views on prosecuting the European war became an open quarrel. American planners were not interested in any undertakings that did not lead directly to the defeat of Germany. They had no patience with what they considered to be sideshows, even suggesting that the British were using dilatory tactics, and they seemed not to appreciate the need to anticipate postwar problems. Despite their persistent efforts to win cooperation, the most the British could obtain was the freedom to proceed on their own.

Britain had worked on plans to carry the war into the Aegean since May, but conditions changed continually before action began in September. The main problem was the lack of sufficient air cover, especially from nearby bases, to protect ships and landing forces from enemy air attack. Repeated British pleas for more air support during September and October failed to alter the previously adopted American stand. The Americans at first withheld the units for planned operations in Western Europe but soon needed them for the new campaign in Italy. Certainly the surrender and invasion of Italy in September altered the whole matter of resource allocation, but none of their obvious and unsolved problems deterred the British from going on with their military and naval plans.

Germany, meanwhile, acted with decisiveness and boldness to protect its position in southeastern Europe. While the deteriorating situation throughout the Mediterranean had already forced defensive adjustments, such as transferring units to Rhodes to bolster its ally's garrison, the prospect of total Italian collapse created the need for independent action. Germany had no intention of opening its southeastern flank to easy air attack or invasion by the Allies. Hitler refused to follow the advice of his top commanders to withdraw from at least the most exposed positions; he personally made the decision to hold the Aegean. It proved to be a wise commitment that cost the Germans little and served them well both militarily and politically. Through the autumn they showed how significant a sense of determination could be in dealing with an unprepared enemy. Thus Berlin did not hesitate on 8 September to implement its Operation "Axis" to take over Italian positions when Italy surrendered to the Allies.

At the time these opposing plans were taking form, the Aegean area had been quiet for more than two years. Italy's entry into the war in 1940 had made the Aegean a zone of naval conflict with Britain.[22] Fighting spread in October, when Italy attacked Greece from Albanian bases, and increased greatly in intensity during spring 1941 as the Germans came to the rescue of their hard-pressed ally. British aid to Athens failed to save Greece or Crete, and by the end of May the Aegean was firmly controlled by Italian and German forces. For the next two years the war in North Africa kept the British busy, and nothing more could be done. Yet memories of earlier events undoubtedly rankled the British and perhaps misguided their decision in 1943 to carry operations back to the island region.

Rhodes was the key to control of the Aegean. Largest of the Italian islands, it had good airfields, bases the British would need for close air support. The British, however, never had a real chance of seizing the island with the men and resources available to them. Germany had placed 6,000–7,000 men on Rhodes since the beginning of 1943, and the confused Italian force of about 35,000 accepted control by the Germans. Failure to gain easy control of Rhodes by persuading the local Italian commanders to resist the Germans was a serious handicap to the British, perhaps a critical block. A later analysis concluded that when Rhodes "was captured by the Germans it was the time for the abandonment of the Aegean operation completely or the recapture of Rhodes first."[23] Neither of those steps was taken; instead the island was bypassed. That proved to be a costly mistake indeed.

Both sides raced to occupy other important positions. In mid-September small British units took Cos, Leros, and lesser Italian and Greek islands. Cos also had airfields and was undoubtedly the most valuable prize after Rhodes. Realizing the serious threat a continued British presence posed to them, the Germans attacked the British forces, first with heavy air assaults and on 3 October by a full invasion. The British were taken totally by surprise but resisted fiercely before Cos fell. Leros was the next objective of the Germans. They used aircraft to hamper British efforts to reinforce the island, then on 12 November landed troops, which after four days of fighting took Leros from its defenders. Losing Leros provided the final blow to Britain's campaign. There was no alternative but to withdraw units from other islands and acknowledge the enemy's continued dominance in the region.

That the operation became a military and political disaster cannot be denied. From the beginning almost everything went wrong for the British and revealed problems previously unrecognized or merely ignored. Among the major causes of failure were the inadequacy of planning, absence of interallied cooperation, an outmoded command structure, and lack of sufficient men and air support at crucial stages. The losses in manpower, ships, and planes were high. Germany enjoyed valuable advantages over Britain: its supply and communications routes were shorter, and its purpose and objectives were clearer. Nor did its defense deplete other fronts. Except for a parachute battalion brought from Italy, only units already stationed in Greece and the Balkans were deployed in the operations; the Luftwaffe used obsolete planes unneeded elsewhere. The failure of the British scheme left the Aegean in German hands, and a backwater. Germany controlled the area until the Russian advance drove the Axis from the region at the end of 1944.

Allied policy was redefined after the setback in the Aegean. There were to be no more daring adventures or risky gambles in that part of the world. The new strategy was described by Air Marshal Sir John Slessor in one of his analysis reports: "The best service we in this theatre can perform for Overlord [the Normandy invasion] is really to create hell in the Balkans by any means, air, land, and sea, that can be made available without embarking on major operations involving bridgeheads that have to be covered and supplied."[24]

In a statement prepared aboard the USS *Iowa* in November 1943 the Combined Chiefs of Staff made their decision quite emphatic. They noted that "the Balkan-Eastern Mediterranean approach to the European fortress is unsuitable" for major military operations, that all efforts should be directed toward the primary goal of defeating Germany, and that "our experience shows that the acceptance of limited objective operations, however attractive in themselves, invariably requires resources beyond those initially anticipated." Instead Germany must be made to weaken itself defensively by having to tie down substantial numbers of its forces in the Balkan area. This goal could be achieved by limiting Allied efforts to supplying guerrillas, staging occasional commando attacks, and bombing those targets in the Balkans considered to be of vital importance. There was but passing acknowledgment of Churchill's longstanding political aim in the region. "We agree that it is desirable to bring Turkey into the war at this time but this must be brought about without diversion of resources that would prejudice our commitments elsewhere."[25]

The policy statement affirmed what the Combined Chiefs of Staff had already advised in late October about the value of teaching Bulgaria a "sharp lesson" by opening a sustained bombing attack. Through such a campaign they hoped "to promote resistance in Bulgaria and possibly bring the country out of the war." Since Germany could scarcely afford to accept the collapse of its satellites, it would be forced to occupy them, and such further dispersal of its manpower suited the general Allied aims.[26]

Sofia was panicked by the first raid on 14 November and two more before the end of 1943. The psychological effects on the previously quiet and almost defenseless capital were much worse than the actual destruction and casualties, until a devastating raid occurred early in the new year. The several bombings affected the Cicero affair in two important ways. Nervousness during the first raids helped justify a German embassy secretary's transfer to Ankara, where she secretly worked for American intelligence and helped identify the spy her supervisor paid. Also, for still skeptical Germans the staging of the heaviest raid exactly as scheduled according to the compromised documents showed that information found in Cicero's photographs was indeed sound.

* * *

The many vacillations and evasions in Turkey's conducting of its foreign policy had by late 1943 undermined respect for its government's trustworthiness. At times both sides in the war considered its leaders guilty of bad faith, extortion, or concern only with pursuing narrow national interests, for material gain at little cost. In the initial periods of the conflict the country's friendship meant so much to the rival belligerents that its motives and tactics were accepted; the Allies had been content that Ankara had resisted the early German offers. Now Berlin was on the defensive and could no longer expect Turkey's help. The British did. Yet Ankara seemed unwilling or unable to abandon the noncommittal policy it had followed since 1940. It failed to grasp that though it continued to hesitate and make exorbitant demands, the value of its bargaining power had waned and would soon all but vanish. Not until after Turkey finally realized in spring 1944 its dangerous isolation as Soviet armed forces neared the Balkans did change occur. By then it was too late.

Developments in the Cicero affair occurred against this background of a showdown over the participation issue—Britain's firm insistence on fulfillment of old promises made by Turkey—a prolonged dispute in which Ankara exasperated its ally and lost all prospect of earning post-war benefits. Cicero throughout the most crucial period of Anglo-Turkish contention supplied a flow of information to Germany. Certainly Papen's possession of British papers became a factor of indeterminate but real value in his pressing of German arguments with Turkey's leaders.

3   The Volunteer Spy

Among the basic principles recognized by all modern intelligence agencies are suspicion of those who volunteer their services and distrust of information they obtain too easily. The individuals are generally adventurers, crackpots, or infiltrators sent by opponents: the material is probably unimportant, planted, or falsified for some deception. Common sense and experience have given such guidelines so much authority that professional agents and analysts often dismiss or mishandle the occasional exceptions. Even then, error in judgment seldom has a major impact on the course of events. The doubts and reactions of many top officials in Berlin with respect to Cicero and the photographs he provided were to have great significance. Yet given the circumstances in which the spy first appeared and offered his films, the caution and disbelief which followed seemed reasonable and sound.

* * *

Elyesa Bazna was born on 28 July 1904 in the small Balkan town of Pristina (Prizren) in the western Ottoman Empire.[1] Because his landowning father not only identified with Turkey but also taught privately the Muslim religion, the family moved several times as the declining Ottoman state lost its outlying regions through successive defeats, settling in Constantinople just before World War I destroyed all remnants of empire. While some relatives profited from career opportunities the 1918 peace and revolution made possible, Bazna rebelled at school discipline and took advantage of the turbulence in occupied Constantinople, finding temporary work with a French military transport unit, where he learned to drive. There followed other jobs and repeated troubles with the police over thefts of weapons and cars, crimes that were neither patriotic nor political in nature. Finally another incident and his cumulative record led French authorities to sentence him to three years' detention in a penal labor camp in France. Released under Turkey's revised peace treaty, he worked briefly in a Marseilles truck factory.

Returning home, Bazna held a succession of jobs before ending as a *kavass*, or servant, to foreigners. The term applies to any servant, regardless of assignment, and it carries a certain stigma. But such employment proved to be his most steady occupation; his skill with cars and knowledge of French got him work as a valet-driver, while the vicarious life of wealth appealed to his snobbery. His employers came primarily from diplomatic circles, and Bazna worked in Ankara when the inland city became the republic's capital. For seven years he served the Yugoslav ambassador and then the American military attaché for a short time.[2] During this period he married, fathering four children before the couple drifted apart, the marriage finally ending in divorce. Meanwhile Bazna had also taken singing lessons from a German professor. Later the newly trained baritone recalled feeling that "music became my consolation" and left him "consumed with ambition" to achieve fame as a singer. Considering himself ready to perform, Bazna quit his current job and persuaded the Union Française to host a formal recital in Istanbul, but the concert failed financially. Despite favorable notices, the Turkish public had showed little interest in hearing the European classical music he selected. Bazna returned to being a *kavass*.

The most important phase of his life began midway through the war.[3] In the latter part of 1942 he took a job in the home of Albert Jenke, a prominent German businessman, long resident in Turkey and temporarily appointed to Germany's embassy staff, promoted early in 1943 to the rank of minister and made assistant to Papen. Bazna eventually fell under suspicion by the Jenkes. "I did not shrink from poking my nose into my employer's correspondence, both private and official," he would later acknowledge, and he secretly took photographs of some of the letters he found. His habit of prying had by then become a compulsive vice. It now included camera experiments to hone skills acquired in years of taking family pictures; in a brazen prank he even photographed himself reclining on the couple's sofa.[4] The pictures were supposedly intended only to impress his wife with his bravado and daring, but one day he noticed that someone had searched his trunk, and shortly afterward he was dismissed. The valet remembered being offended at the time, because he did not yet consider himself a spy.

In April 1943 Bazna sat in the lobby of the Ankara Palace Hotel. As the city's best establishment despite rather old-fashioned furnishings and creaking floors, it seemed to him a "desirable background" and good place to relax, playing the gentleman with his black coffees and sweet liqueurs while reading the international newspapers. Giving expression to pretensions and fantasies by sitting in fashionable hotels was indeed a favorite and frequent indulgence. Bazna on this occasion was reviewing his life—"the boring, stupid, contemptible life of a *kavass*." He was thirty-eight years old, a relatively short man but not yet overweight, quite ordinary in appearance, notable only for his dark and piercing eyes, or perhaps for his premature balding. Despising himself as a failure yet eager for money, he then hit upon a scheme: "Why not set up as a spy? The idea fascinated me and would not let me go. I made up my mind that I would do it, and sell my services more dearly than anyone else did. I made up my mind to be the greatest spy of all." Such postwar statements cannot be given much credence. That his life took the direction it did actually rested upon opportunities he could not have foreseen.

Before long he answered a newspaper advertisement and began working for the first secretary of the British embassy, Douglas Busk, for whom Bazna looked after the car and handled some heating repairs then especially needed in the household.[5] Mrs. Busk was expecting a baby, which later was born in Istanbul. Two points about the employment interview are significant in the spy affair. The issue arose of how well Bazna knew English and whether he could read it. He claimed to have understood the diplomat's questions, simple and oral, but admitted that otherwise he had great difficulties with the language. Bazna answered all queries in French. The second and more critical matter involved his background. Busk asked him to write out something that the applicant thought was intended only to determine whether he could write, but which he rendered as a form of biographical sketch, not mentioning his recent job with Jenke. Perhaps Busk was too preoccupied and anxious to get help; he apparently neither checked nor investigated Bazna's vitae. The valet's next employer, the ambassador, was to assume that he had been vetted. Another factor of importance followed. Mrs. Busk, upon her return, brought a nursemaid—a young woman just over thirty, named Mara. In time she became the valet's mistress and an unwitting accomplice in his first spying. Throughout the many months that he remained with the Busks he pried into their affairs, but only near the end did he claim to have photographed any official papers, for a major part of Bazna's incentive was to show off to his attractive admirer. A romantic by nature, the impressionable Mara was induced to believe that he worked for the Turkish secret police, on a covert assignment. Subsequently she helped him when he sought to get access to more and better information.

Bazna saw little advantage in staying with Busk. "It became clear to me that I could not get what I wanted in the Busk household. My objective was the British Embassy itself." The idea may have developed because an unexpected opportunity became available early that autumn. All the city's domestics knew that the British ambassador was seeking a new valet, a coveted job, and it occurred to Bazna that his employer could give him the inside track. Upon the completion of various tasks for the Busks, he was no longer needed; he also managed to convince Mara that their affair required separate jobs. Telling her the Busks would surely disapprove of their secret involvement, Bazna asked her to speak to Mrs. Busk, who perhaps influenced her husband to suggest Bazna for the vacant post. Busk in any event took the valet a few days later to see Knatchbull-Hugessen. He left the meeting after presenting Bazna and receiving some papers from the ambassador, who then asked Bazna about previous jobs, learning only what Busk had been told. The brief interview ended with Bazna being hired upon his employer's recommendation. He was to start at once. A British intelligence official working in wartime Turkey who knew the ambassador thought it seemed "incredible" that the man was being employed by the British despite being warned about him by the Turks. Presumably he referred to reports that the Turkish security service had given to his colleagues. Years later Sir Hughe would recall believing that the servant's credentials must have been verified before his initial employment by another diplomat at the British embassy.[6] Yet circumstances indicate that neither Busk nor the ambassador had checked Bazna's statements or discovered his background.

Whether the fledgling spy ever copied any papers while working for Busk has been cast in doubt by people who knew the diplomat. He was a conscientious person who would not have brought official documents to his home. If the valet did pry and take photographs at his residence, which itself seems likely, the items involved would have been private letters or records. Still, the spy's account must be noted. Most of the photographs Bazna initially sold to the Germans supposedly came from the Busk residence during the autumn. He claimed that he had already learned how to get into his employer's locked desk, where important papers were kept. One evening when the couple went out he again sought to impress his mistress, by taking items he removed from Busk's briefcase back to the kitchen, where he had been keeping his camera concealed in an unused saucepan. The papers were purportedly those Sir Hughe had given Busk at Bazna's job interview earlier that day. Standing on a stool the valet photographed each page placed on the table under bright light, afterward returning the documents and putting the camera back in its hiding place, the experiment having shown him that the simple method worked but took too much time. Mara witnessed the entire procedure but revealed nothing to the Busks.

Even after Bazna had started his employment with Sir Hughe he reportedly retained access to Busk's secret papers. During an evening when the Busks were once again away, he returned to visit Mara and repeat his prying, claiming to copy a list of Britain's agents and contacts. Bazna identified the date of this occurrence as 25 October, the night before he approached the Germans.[7] Thus the photographs were presumably among those he submitted for his initial sale. Whether he really knew the papers' contents is questionable, given his admitted problems understanding the language, although cognates and simple words would have been familiar. Both the incidents and details he described illustrate the type of dramatic reporting that makes Bazna's narrative about his espionage exploits so suspect as a source of facts and insights.

Despite his pretense of having carefully planned his espionage venture, Bazna never explained why he then waited many months and did no filming until October, when he suddenly became active in photographing items to sell. Also undermining his claims of having calculated everything that subsequently occurred is the fact that he could reasonably have expected neither an extended nor especially lucrative career in spying. Even at the time he approached the Germans he had only three rolls of film and could not be certain of continuing access to British papers through either his past or current jobs. Once having taken at least some photographs, he had to act quickly, for the value of his product depended on a timely sale. He set the price high in case it proved impossible to copy more papers. Supposedly he never hesitated in his resolve or doubted the acceptance of his offer. He would simply contact the Germans through an official who, he knew, was influential in the embassy and regime; yet because their currency was undesirable he would demand to be paid in stable and spendable British pounds. He also realized his attitude and manner had to be fully convincing: "I should have to approach them confidently." To gain their attention and trust he felt it "absolutely vital" to present himself as a cold and experienced spy.[8] It became a role he enjoyed.

Bazna thought he could work through Jenke, not only because of his previous employment by the minister but also because he knew the diplomat had special connections, Inge Jenke being the sister of Ribbentrop. He remembered her as "a nervous, ambitious woman in her middle forties," difficult to serve and please. His description of reestablishing contact with Jenke by first requesting to see his wife seems odd and contradicts Papen's recollection that the spy had telephoned him. Jenke had told the ambassador one day that a former servant had called him with a proposal to sell information to Germany. The offer had been refused, but the caller had proved persistent. Papen thought the matter had little significance—"It seemed to me that a spy who offered his wares by telephone was hardly worth taking seriously"— and he left the whole situation in Jenke's hands. They apparently agreed to let the Security Service, or SD, handle the affair if the calls continued. Papen later explained that with the strong likelihood of the man being simply an *agent provocateur* he preferred to spare the military intelligence staff and instead burden the SD.[9] Bazna may therefore have chosen to appear in person at the embassy and ask for Frau Jenke because he had already been rebuffed perhaps more than once in telephone calls to Jenke. That he would later exaggerate the daring and directness of his approach was characteristic of his self-image. Yet his account is useful.[10]

After dark in the early evening of 26 October Bazna visited the big German embassy compound on Atatürk Boulevard, where the gate porter still recognized him. When the man telephoned Frau Jenke she permitted Bazna entry. He walked to the building where the Jenkes lived, and a *kavass* had him wait in the drawing room. At first Frau Jenke listened to him with little patience, Bazna using French, for he indicated having come to the Germans for money. Only when he hinted at his purpose and his employment in Britain's embassy did she suggest that her husband ought to see him. Jenke also seemed disdainful as his ex-valet spoke of his regard for Germany. He became more interested, however, when photographs were mentioned. Bazna did not reveal that he had brought two rolls of film with him or explain why he wanted to be paid in British pounds. The Jenkes were clearly surprised upon hearing his prices—£20,000 for two initial rolls and £15,000 for each subsequent roll—and by his willingness to try the nearby Soviet embassy. Jenke said that any decision and money had to come from Berlin; Bazna agreed to wait several days and to telephone on the 30th. At that point Frau Jenke supposedly mentioned Moyzisch to her husband: they concurred, in German, that he should handle the matter. They asked the visitor to wait, and she telephoned him. Jenke seemed to suspect that the servant had understood their German. He also made clear his distaste for both espionage and the man who had offered to spy.

By referring the spy to Moyzisch, Papen and Jenke created a situation that soon exacerbated old problems. The antipathy between Papen and Ribbentrop was largely personal, but the involvement of Moyzisch fed the foreign minister's hatred and fear of the SD and its ambitious head. In this conflict the issues were jurisdictional, and the ultimate stake was power. Thus the espionage operation saw the Foreign Ministry and SD head Walter Schellenberg vying for precedence and exclusive control. From the outset the information acquired from the valet would reach the capital through the competing channels: Moyzisch found himself answering not only to Papen and the foreign minister but also to Schellenberg and others at intelligence headquarters in Berlin. Certainly such a position was not enviable. Nor was it unexpected that the suspicious and stubborn Ribbentrop disagreed with others about the spy and his material. All these factors complicated the whole affair. Yet it must be noted that had the volunteer spy been turned over to the Abwehr, the military intelligence service riddled with opponents of the dictatorship, Cicero would not have remained active for long before his espionage was betrayed by some informant.

Moyzisch was by birth an Austrian. A rather slightly built man with dark hair and alert eyes, quiet and diligent by nature, he had been a member of the Nazi Party and a journalist in his native land, had then joined the intelligence service, and had begun his assignment at the embassy two years earlier. He lived in the compound but was already in bed when Frau Jenke's telephone summons brought him to the minister's quarters at once.[11] Upon his arrival she indicated that her husband had retired, wanted him to interview the man waiting in the drawing room, and would expect a full report immediately in the morning. Moyzisch then listened to the stranger's story, told in what he later called poor French. When he declared the man's price out of the question, there was only a smile, followed by a comment that other buyers could be sought. Moyzisch learned only that he claimed to hate the British. He refused to give his name and allowed Moyzisch four days in which to consult his superiors. On 30 October the man would telephone Moyzisch's office at 3:00 P.M. and identify himself as "Pierre." (Bazna chose the name because the embassy's Yugoslav gate porter who had admitted him was Peter.) He would ask if a letter had come for him: a positive response would mean they would meet that night at 10:00 near the tool shed at the rear of the compound grounds. Moyzisch would then receive two rolls of film for £20,000, but he must understand that each future roll would cost £15,000. The visitor asked that the building be darkened as he left and whispered quickly that he was the ambassador's valet.

In the morning Moyzisch prepared a memorandum covering the situation, reported to Jenke as directed, and accompanied him to inform Papen of the night's events. After receiving Moyzisch's oral and written reports, Papen told him to draft a signal to Berlin, with which Moyzisch soon returned. The ambassador made minor changes in green ink (his personal mark), and they discussed the valet and his stipulations. Moyzisch related that he tended to believe the man, although a ruse was possible, that he wanted money and hated the British. Papen signed the dispatch summarizing what had occurred and the spy's terms, its text being encoded at once; the radio message went off before noon, its content restricted solely to Ribbentrop. Among the details that it provided the foreign minister was the fact that his brother-in-law had once employed the man. The intelligence officer believed everyone thought that because Papen was involved the offer would be rejected, the "animosity" between the ambassador and foreign minister being "unbridgeable," but also because it was always difficult to get Ribbentrop to make timely and clear-cut decisions.

Ribbentrop got the ambassador's telegram about midday on the 27th. He reportedly showed great annoyance that Jenke had referred the matter to Moyzisch and his enemies in the SD rather than calling in military intelligence. Under the circumstances he had to consult Schellenberg and on 28 October instructed a personal aide to telephone him.[12] Schellenberg agreed to meet at once with a ministry official, Horst Wagner, who informed him of the offer and message from Ankara. Uncertain about how to proceed, Ribbentrop had also told his representative to seek advice from Schellenberg—perhaps to compromise him later if there was a trap. Noting that payment would cover films only upon delivery, and trusting in Moyzisch, whom he regarded as "intelligent and experienced," Schellenberg felt the valet's proposition could be accepted with a minimum of risk. Doing so would also keep the Soviet Union out of the running as a buyer. Wagner therefore reached an agreement with Schellenberg and quickly reported back to Ribbentrop. The minister apparently chose to protect his position against any outside encroachment: risking money from the ministry's limited resources for the trial purchase, he dispatched the first of the payments probably in sound currency. That conclusion is supported by the mixed small denominations of the notes sent.[13] Thereafter the SD bore the costs, and nearly all the funds paid to Cicero were counterfeit.

Meanwhile the valet took stock of his new position in order to increase his supply of films to present for sale.[14] The British ambassador's residence was a large building next to the embassy in a compound in the Çankaya hills. Originally the structure had served as the chancery, but changing space needs had caused the functions of the two main buildings to be reversed some years earlier, leaving the ambassador's old office and safe intact.[15] It was there that Sir Hughe still liked to work. On the ground floor were the staff's living quarters and the big kitchen, above which was the spacious office kept as a study, to which papers were brought from the chancery in violation of security rules. The separate bedrooms and baths of the ambassador, his wife, and their daughter were on the top floor. Once the valet realized the strict routine, with such activities as Sir Hughe's twice-daily baths, he weighed the possible opportunities and time constraints. It seemed safest to pry only when Sir Hughe was away from the study or house. Then he might risk using one of the two staircases to take documents to his room for copying; he noted small places along the route where if necessary he could conceal anything he might be carrying. There seemed nothing about the physical premises that would impede his spying.

Other household staff performed their duties with little close association. Their separate work locations and schedules, combined with their desire for privacy and concern with personal affairs in leisure hours, helped keep the valet's activities secret. Bazna clearly did not like the butler, Zeki: "He regarded everything below the level of his own elevated nose with complete contempt." Thus he gave no notice to the other servants. The vain Manoli Filoti took great pride in his role as chef and considered himself to be Lady Knatchbull-Hugessen's right hand. While he kept an eye on other members of the staff and had a room in the house, he spent most nights in a city apartment with his family. Another servant, Mustafa, who served meals, was "a carefree, submissive, cheerful, unreflective sort of person," who never questioned things.

Bazna maintained that he got keys to Sir Hughe's safe and security boxes prior to 26 October, when he first approached the Germans. Having noticed the importance attached to the keys, which the ambassador always kept with him, he had purchased a big piece of wax and awaited a chance to make good impressions. Knatchbull-Hugessen one morning had left the key ring on his bedside table while Bazna drew the bath. The valet had just taken impressions of the three keys, cleaning them with one of the ambassador's silk handkerchiefs and replacing the ring on the table, when the ambassador returned to the room to get them. Bazna still held the handkerchief, but his explanation that it needed laundering aroused no suspicion in Sir Hughe. The valet later said that he might have been caught had the diplomat not been so proper and taken the time to put on his robe. Perhaps the security slip occurred because the ambassador was still unused to his new valet or because he was distracted by other thoughts and problems. A locksmith friend soon provided Bazna with keys from the impressions.

The spy later implied that he felt no nervousness while waiting to telephone for an answer to his offer. Everyone was quite busy, because 29 October was the republic's National Day, marked with receptions and a parade. That morning the ambassador seemed in a good mood, telling his valet about Turkey's troubles keeping the Germans and Britons apart at various functions, especially since using French alphabetical order put Allemagne and Angleterre very close to each other. An unexpected joke caught the servant by surprise: Knatchbull-Hugessen asked if the *kavass* wanted to take a little present to the German embassy. Bazna relaxed only when the ambassador explained that the Turkish holiday was also Papen's birthday. During the day Bazna claims to have taken his first photographs in the residence, while the ambassador attended President Inönü's formal reception.[16] He used his duplicate key to remove two telegrams from the red boxes on his employer's desk and photographed them on a window sill, using natural light.

Late that same afternoon Papen called in Moyzisch to say that Ribbentrop had accepted the offer. The ambassador warned that "every precaution" was to be exercised. A courier would arrive with the money before noon the following day, and a report was expected immediately upon receipt of the documents. Realizing that any film had to be developed quickly and secretly, Moyzisch established a lockable darkroom in the basement of the embassy. Although an amateur photographer, he knew little about developing film or making prints, particularly the necessary enlargements. He found a code clerk who had been a professional photographer before the war and who now instructed him at first.[17]

Having worked on Turkey's holiday, the valet was free the next afternoon, 30 October. He spent time with Mara while waiting to make his telephone call. He boasted to her of having photographed papers in the embassy residence the day before. When "Pierre" telephoned at 3:00 P.M. sharp, the intelligence officer himself answered, Moyzisch's secretary sensing it was secret SD business. Moyzisch told him there were letters waiting, confirming their meeting that evening, and then reported the contact to Papen. The ambassador urged him to be extremely careful, for there could be no scandal, and warned him he would be repudiated if necessary. Papen then produced the courier's bundle of British notes—in £10, £20, and £50 values—which Moyzisch found so bulky that he questioned Berlin's judgment.[18] He counted the £20,000 and wrapped it in the large front page of La République lying on the desk. Moyzisch locked the package of money in his office safe, reclaiming his secretary's key for a period but returning it a week later when called to Berlin. Thereafter she kept her key regardless of what was in the safe. Nonetheless, security breaches in his own office would become a problem early in the new year, when a second secretary came to work.

Emboldened by his success the preceding day, the spy tried a more dangerous feat that evening while the ambassador and his family were at dinner. He removed several documents from the boxes, reclosed them, took the papers to his room, and used an improvised apparatus and strong light to copy them, but upon returning upstairs heard the ambassador using his telephone. In fear, he walked slowly down the hall. There had been no reason for the diplomat to open the boxes, however, and the papers concealed under the valet's jacket went unnoticed. After his call the ambassador returned to dinner, and the servant quickly replaced the items. Bazna decided not to take this third roll of film to his meeting later that night with Moyzisch: "I was too superstitious." Those photographs had caused enough risk for one evening.[19]

* * *

Of the many uncertainties and difficulties in this case that long worried Berlin, none was more fundamental than determining the spy's motives. Why had he taken photographs of British papers and then appeared at the German embassy to offer them for sale? Answering the question was critical: volunteer spies are seldom trustworthy. Schellenberg and others therefore insisted that the matter be pursued with vigor by Moyzisch. Given the spy's personality, it proved to be a frustrating and lengthy task. Moyzisch's superiors added to their problems by never quite accepting the obvious explanations, and they continued to probe for some obscure motive they thought was eluding them.

Money was Bazna's basic aim: "For me nothing existed but my obsessional greed for money."[20] Although he fixed no specific sum as a goal, not knowing how long his luck would hold, he acquired more than he could ever have foreseen. His dreams of a life of great wealth and comfort merely took new forms as the weeks and months passed. Probably even his stipulation that he be paid in British currency, a requirement that puzzled the Germans and was never really explained, reflected Bazna's image of the money that best suited a future gentleman. Bazna recalled his reaction upon seeing the initial £20,000: "If there was anything I wanted at that moment, it was not this sum of money which I had long regarded as my own, but more money and still more. Much more." Later he agreed with little fuss to sharply reduced prices for his photographs; by then he was so assured of affluence that he could patronize his clients. As the early lust for money subsided, other motives, always present, become clearer in explaining his thinking.

Spying enabled the resentful servant to satisfy a yearning to exercise power and control. Because he believed knowledge of secrets gave him importance, feeding his need for respect, he derived pleasure from the ability to manipulate people, for instance by prying into their affairs. Thus he justified spying in part because he considered the Knatchbull-Hugessens too proud and aloof toward him: "If I were not treated with proper respect, I got my own back," and "this conceited idea made me smile." In a similar way he imagined himself controlling great events: he not only was "in the know" about major developments but held a "nightly colloquy" with top world leaders. When they encountered blocks and frustrations, he claimed some responsibility for their setbacks, however insignificant they considered a valet. Moyzisch was correct that the servant's ego and delight kept him spying long after he had accumulated a fortune and faced increased danger from the British.

Another important factor was Bazna's quest for thrills and excitement. Espionage to him was a great adventure. Moyzisch noted his strange bravado, how he "boasted about his dangerous work as if it were a schoolboy's prank," reveling in deceiving the British. He showed off his audacity to women. Thus he encouraged the admiring but gullible Mara to believe he was an undercover agent. "I was the secret service personified—cold-blooded, supercilious and, above all, secret. . . . I felt like a hero in a spy play." But his life of deception also took a toll: "I was as changeable as the weather. Moods of depression and exhilaration followed each other in rapid succession." With his vanity requiring an audience to know and appreciate his daring, Bazna played the same role for the Germans, seeking to appear an experienced spy who succeeded through boldness. Privately he saw himself as competing in a heady and glamorous game and beating the odds. Photographing secret papers "became a sort of nervous stimulation for me, a kind of drug that I required to enable me to go quietly to sleep," and "I played with danger" but "believed it impossible" to be caught. Pretense or risk figured in all his fantasy images—wealthy gentleman, famous singer, secret agent, business leader—since conceiving each part was sham or high adventure.

In order to appear in a better light he also invented other motives, one created to mislead the Germans and another for his memoir, both devised to suggest that his actions had been more than base and venal. Bazna told Moyzisch that his father had been shot and killed by an Englishman in Albania. His listener had been impressed by the story, "deeply moved" for a moment and even feeling a "fleeting sympathy," perhaps because the tale was offered simply and without detail. During another meeting the spy spoke of a hunting incident but refused to say whether the sportsman had been a diplomat. Later he stated that his father had hated foreigners and added, "I hate them even more than he did." Now he was seeking revenge. Moyzisch thought that "it seemed a fairly plausible story, and I was prepared to accept it at face value," having some idea about blood feuds in the Balkans. "Yet there was an element of cheap melodrama about it that left me feeling slightly skeptical." He was right to be doubtful. Bazna's father had died a natural death, and he admitted concocting the tale to amuse himself by playing a role for the Germans.[21]

In his memoir Bazna stressed his patriotism—his contribution to keeping Turkey safe and neutral. "I felt myself to be champion of the Turkish cause, though an uninvited champion," blocking Britain's schemes to force the country into war. Not only had he "objected violently" to such Allied plans, but he had hoped his "little countermeasure" would thwart Moscow's aims. In his imagination he thought himself an idealist helping Ankara find means to delay commitment to a belligerent role. Still, he acknowledged that his actions had been disreputable and futile. "All I could do was to take my photographs," a "mean and shabby" step, for his activities would not change how things went: "Had I once imagined that I could hold up the course of events?" The patent falsity of such rationalization of his opportunism and greed failed to embarrass him.

Because the Germans long sought some hidden grievance or passion to explain his behavior, they remained reluctant to give full weight to Cicero's real motives. Although most officials in time came to understand his avarice and weaknesses, realizing he was prone to storytelling, they continued to worry about having failed to grasp something significant. That underlying doubt contributed to their initial slowness to trust the valuable information he was about to provide.

* * *

The participants' accounts of the beginning of the spy operation seem reliable within limits. Their points of disagreement have only minor significance; their melodramatic claims and touches can be disregarded. But the outlines of how a combination of negligence and opportunism made possible espionage are clear from the texts. Despite the need for tightened security under wartime conditions, especially in a neutral country where the intelligence services of many nations vied for information, there lingered an old-fashioned complacency among senior diplomats. The servant who took advantage of the situation was in hidden ways unusual—crafty, determined, given to mythomania and lying, self-important, greedy—generally capable of assuming whatever role or deception best suited his current ambition. Bazna nevertheless did not appear likely to become an outstanding spy when he contacted the Germans, nor indeed would his espionage have long gone unreported had he not been referred to Moyzisch and the small, special department known for closed ranks and firm loyalty that he served. Amid all his vain claims of calculation and control, Bazna never acknowledged that he had also been just lucky.

4 Selling the Secrets

During a brief period at the end of October and in the first week of November, lasting patterns in the spy affair took shape. The contacts between the valet and Moyzisch acquired a form they would retain, Schellenberg organized the validation and processing of the information arriving from Cicero, and the eager spy found that Sir Hughe's routine helped him pursue his purpose. In the following weeks the servant continued to perfect his espionage methods, encouraged by the lax security, but there were uncertainties and problems of which he remained unaware. After the conclusion of three film transactions within a span of just seven days. Moyzisch was called to Berlin, where caution and interdepartmental conflicts combined to produce a break in the film purchases. Meanwhile Bazna proceeded with copying British papers. It never occurred to him that the Germans would question the ease and speed with which he worked and think that he might be a planted British agent and his films therefore a ruse. From his standpoint the whole affair seemed to go smoothly from the outset.

* * *

The place for the initial rendezvous had been chosen well. A remembered hole in the wire fence at the rear of the embassy grounds allowed entry, and bushes concealed the tool shed where they would make contact. Neither man trusted the other, the intelligence officer suspecting a trap or robbery of some kind, the spy perhaps an attack, even an attempt at blackmail to obtain the films without paying. Bazna's sudden appearance from the shadows therefore startled the nervous Moyzisch. When they reached the building where Moyzisch had his office, each wanted to see what the other had; Moyzisch opened his safe to show the money, while the spy displayed the rolls of film. Bazna watched as the German counted out the £20,000. The latter returned it to his safe, took the two rolls of 35-millimeter film to his darkroom, and left the spy locked in his office. Moyzisch feared the night watchman might come upon him.

Moyzisch was gone longer than the expected fifteen minutes, because the photographer had to explain each step; upon confirming that the films showed documents he left the assistant waiting outside the darkroom and rejoined Bazna. The man appeared to be "neither impatient nor irritated" and had been merely smoking. Moyzisch paid him and tried unsuccessfully to get a signed receipt, a transparent ploy which prompted him to admit, "I must say that at that moment I felt slightly ridiculous." A "curiously sneering and triumphant tone" supposedly came into the spy's voice as he stuffed the package of currency under his overcoat and set a second meeting for the next evening: "À demain, Monsieur. À la même heure."[1]

Throughout the night Moyzisch reviewed the fifty-two photographs of British papers and reports. Following instructions from the code clerk, who then left, he himself had produced the enlargements. The few he spoiled were torn into pieces and flushed down a toilet. Moyzisch's claim to have understood the documents and absorbed their importance was exaggerated, in the opinion of Papen. He rightly questioned whether Moyzisch's command of English had been really sufficient.[2] But the intelligence officer undoubtedly puzzled over the first material in an effort to determine its significance. He concluded that the items were of "incalculable value" and that the price had been reasonable. In the morning, disheveled and unshaven, he went to Papen's office and waited, the ambassador's secretary frowning at his appearance. There he reportedly discovered that he had only fifty-one photographs, a figure the secretary verified by counting them face down, so he retraced the route from his own office building, finally spotting the missing item lying near the main gate.[3] There is no way of knowing if he had really been so careless as to let a photograph fall and blow away, or had just invented the story to make his account a little more dramatic.

The ambassador was deeply impressed by the photographs and reasonably sure that the documents were authentic. "Form, content and phraseology left no doubt that this was the genuine article." The messages conformed to what he knew of British policy and still used oddities like "Angora" despite the change to a modern spelling.[4] "I realized that we had come upon a priceless source of information." He inquired about security and learned that only four people knew about the situation—they themselves and the Jenkes. None of the secretaries or the photography assistant had been informed; nor were any of the military intelligence staff told of anything; still the ambassador ordered a re-check of his own embassy's local servants and employees. Papen kept the set of prints and said he would notify Ribbentrop. He then stated that the spy needed a code name that he would not himself know. "Pierre" was suitable for his contacts with Moyzisch but not for the exchanges with Berlin. Papen thought of the documents' eloquence and chose the name "Cicero." "It seemed a happy nickname." Notwithstanding Bazna's bragging and claims to the contrary, he remained unaware of his wartime code reference, at least until the publicity over Moy-zisch's revelations.[5] Early that evening the ambassador conferred with Moyzisch and Jenke to review the situation from various angles. Moy-zisch dutifully took notes on the various points he was expected to pursue with the enigmatic Cicero.

At 10:00 P.M. he went to the tool shed and met Cicero again. Return-ing together to Moyzisch's office, where the spy first made sure the drapes were closed, he accepted a scotch and relaxed. When he deliv-ered two more rolls of film, including the one previously held back, the intelligence officer had no money for payment; Cicero agreed to wait until their next meeting to collect his £30,000. Moyzisch tried to put him further at ease by saying Berlin had liked his earlier films; he complimented their technical quality and raised various questions about the procedures used. All he learned was that Cicero had long liked photography, wanted to replace his Leica, and that, the spy in-sisted, he had no assistant. Clearly he disliked being questioned. Before parting they agreed about security measures—appointments would take place a day earlier than mentioned on the telephone and at pre-arranged places in the old city—both conditions being stipulated by the spy.[6]

After their transaction Moyzisch drove the valet from the embassy in an Opel borrowed from a friend, since his own old Mercedes was being repaired. The spy hid in the dark interior of the car. Before being dropped off he pointed out the exact place where they would meet for the next exchange. Moyzisch just a few days later arranged to purchase the big Opel, newer than his own car, to use for their meetings, because it looked like many cars in Ankara. During the day he continued to drive his Mercedes, which was familiar to people in the city.[7] A pattern later developed whenever he met the spy at night, Cicero slipping into and concealing himself in the rear seat of the Opel, then later jumping out while it slowed but did not stop. The car was always in motion through the darkened streets as they made their exchanges and talked.

Moyzisch developed the rolls' forty exposures and left them to dry in his darkroom, spending some of the time playing cards at the Jenkes' flat, where he had noticed lights from a party, then returned to make enlargements and study them until nearly daybreak on 1 November. After several hours' sleep Moyzisch returned to the embassy and took the second batch of Cicero's photographs to the ambassador.

There are some discrepancies between the Moyzisch and Bazna recollections of the first two meetings. One uncertainty involves just when Bazna requested and got his new camera; a similar issue concerns whether Moyzisch honored his demand for a revolver. Bazna reports that at their first meeting on 30 October he asked for film and a new Leica. To get the camera he lied that the one he was using was borrowed and had to be returned to its owner. He wanted nearly the same type, since that would avoid problems of adjustment, and a continuing supply of new film in exchange for each exposed roll. His explanation that his being seen or remembered making such purchases would be dangerous was of course quite reasonable. In fact, he had long owned his own camera and invented the story simply to obtain a more recent model. Moyzisch agreed that the valet had asked for a new camera, which he gave him in due time; he placed the request during their second, or 31 October, meeting. The spy said he also asked for a revolver at their first meeting and received it during the second, 31 October, meeting, but his purpose may have been only to impress his contact or readers with the dangers of his work. Moyzisch mentioned that during at least one later meeting the valet carried a revolver but strongly implied that he had not given it to Cicero.[8] Of course an evasion might be expected on such a point. In any case, the weapon was never used.

Pierre telephoned Moyzisch again five days later and left a message with his secretary inviting him to play bridge at 9:00 P.M. on 6 November. Therefore the third delivery would occur that same night, 5 November, at the location the spy had identified earlier. At the street corner the driver found him making a "melodramatic and quite unnecessary signal" with a flashlight before he got into the rear seat. While driving around they exchanged the £30,000 already owed and another roll of film, for which payment also had to be delayed, the spy always hiding to avoid bright lights. All attempts at questioning by Moyzisch brought forth only a few brief statements. Moyzisch claimed that Cicero did tell him, however, that he was Albanian and not Turkish. Asked why he hated the British, he said that an Englishman had shot his father many years earlier. Afterward he slipped out of the car into the darkness. Moyzisch developed the roll's twenty shots, made enlargements, and in the morning briefed Papen.[9] This was the last delivery for some time, because Moyzisch was summoned to Berlin and supposedly had to remain there for two weeks. His curious failure to devise some method by which to contact the spy, and in a case like this to forewarn him of a problem, was but one of the things that would bring censure upon him from his superiors. Cicero learned by his repeated attempts to reach him by telephone that he was unavailable, but nothing more. He would not receive payment for his fifth roll of film until mid- or late November.

Details concerning how the first films were handled in Berlin have been obscured by Moyzisch's false claims about his status, and by limited accounts. Moyzisch misled readers of his book by implying that as a minor diplomat he deferred to Papen during the period of the earliest trial purchases for all necessary official reports to Berlin. The information reached the capital and rival units of government through two channels, however, and the competition for control, the differences in assessment of the situation, became critical. But throughout the operation a single person, Maria Molkenteller, prepared the translations in most common use.

Papen insisted on his prerogative as ambassador to examine on a continuing basis all the material from Cicero. For security reasons he wrote the telegrams to the Foreign Ministry covering the start of the operation and incoming data. Only later, after Moyzisch received specific orders to withhold the photographs from the diplomat (but chose to disregard the instruction), was Papen perhaps less informed.[10] Meanwhile two further disadvantages hampered the Foreign Ministry in preliminary evaluations of the affair. Ribbentrop's personal suspicions and attitude outweighed any different opinions his subordinates might have formed about Cicero; what advice his documents expert, Friedrich Gaus, gave him remains unclear; Foreign Ministry officials also lacked the intelligence technicians and secret financial resources available to the SD. Therefore in the end both practical factors and Ribbentrop's adverse reaction to information of a kind he refused to accept psychologically gave the SD the dominant position in handling the spy affair.

Moyzisch sent copies of all the arriving materials and full accompanying reports to the SD, where his already informed superiors awaited them. Even though Papen had kept for personal forwarding to Ribbentrop a set of enlargements from the first transaction, and most likely from all other batches as well, delivering the original film and any further Cicero information to the intelligence service was clearly Moyzisch's own task. He could not ignore his real job. Nor could time be wasted when the document analysts and photography experts needed the texts and negatives immediately in order to apply their scrutiny and tests. Certainly, as the spy operation continued it became Moyzisch's practice to send vital data to the SD at once in coded messages, and supporting film by the next courier plane.

Schellenberg realized as soon as he saw the first documents the necessity of organizing a system both for analyzing the films and their content and for anticipating problems that might develop in Berlin.

While enthusiastic about a chance to demonstrate his effectiveness and thereby further his career and personal schemes, he still remained wary of traps; he devised a methodical and self-protecting approach to determine whether the material was genuine. He later outlined the basic steps. One involved an attempt to authenticate the documents, and possibly break one or more of the enemy's codes, by matching the papers with known radio transmissions. Copies of all the printed texts were therefore given to General Fritz Thiele in the High Command's code section for close comparison with its recordings of signals. Schellenberg's other tasks pitted him against Ribbentrop. Immediately upon learning that they disagreed about the spy's credibility and his photographs' worth, he intensified his plans to safeguard his reputation and prevail in any showdown. He intended to get all the key information directly to Hitler via Himmler rather than let the foreign minister thwart or control its use. Toward that end he asked various experts to formulate questions he might have to answer for Hitler in order to appear thoroughly informed about all aspects of the operation and its potential worth. With the jurisdictional struggle with Ribbentrop promising to remain a bitter contest of wills Schellenberg meanwhile needed an expedient working basis.

Given their long and mutual antipathy, Schellenberg and Ribbentrop had to consult through an intermediary. The responsibility for liaison fell to one of the foreign minister's aides, Gustav Baron Steengracht von Moyland, a personal friend who held the official rank of state secretary. Steengracht immediately reached an important agreement with Schellenberg: the intelligence service would cover the cost of all further payments to the spy. Only if requested would the Foreign Ministry contribute any of its funds; apparently it was rare for Schellenberg to seek any such assistance. His own department's printing of the counterfeit pounds gave him unlimited resources, of course, and the ministry officials never questioned how he met the mounting expenses. Schellenberg sent a package with £200,000 to Moyzisch by a special courier, who arrived on 4 November; the £30,000 that Moyzisch paid Cicero on the night of 5 November came from those German forgeries.[11] Berlin later sent more such money to Moyzisch. Except for minor sums paid under unusual arrangements, Bazna received only bogus notes during the following months. Chance had placed him in contact with the one agency in Berlin that never needed to worry about meeting his high financial demands.

By 6 November five rolls of film were in German hands. It is impossible to determine how many separate documents had been copied in the 112 exposures, since some messages and other items would have exceeded a single page. Nor is there any way of verifying all the information that was revealed in the early photographs. That substantial losses did occur, however, is evident from documentary sources. Sir Hughe's position meant that he was always kept well informed about major developments affecting the region and about current issues or conflicts among the principal Allies. Much more significant is the fact that the espionage began just as the Moscow Conference of the Allied foreign ministers met during 19–30 October to discuss the many differences that had arisen over policies and future plans. A sizable number of photographs in Cicero's first three deliveries gave background data assembled for the conference or analyzed the problems arising for Britain during the lengthy sessions and arguments.

Certain of the British documents are identifiable from Papen's telegrams describing them. One item was a Foreign Office memorandum dated 7 October dealing with Britain's long-term policy toward Turkey. Papen translated the paper into German and transmitted it on 5 November. He also had a copy of Knatchbull-Hugessen's list of fifteen questions to ask Eden at Cairo before they met there in early November with Menemencioglu to discuss joint plans. Among Sir Hughe's queries was one that always caused Britain trouble: "It is useless for me to give the Turks assurances about Russia as long as Russia itself gives none. Can I possibly say something to satisfy the Turks to the effect that we will not allow Russian influence in this part of the world?" Papen reported other information as well that undoubtedly came from Cicero. Both he and Sir Hughe recognized that the greatest concern of the Turks was over the designs of the Soviet Union on their sovereignty. That anxiety allowed Papen to spread additional fear about an Allied secret agreement sacrificing the rights of Turkey in favor of wartime unity.[12]

Some points as to content recalled by Moyzisch and perhaps even by Bazna appear to be credible, within limits, suggesting broadly what Berlin learned from the British secret papers in the first deliveries. Other memoirs are less helpful. Papen recorded no details about the early materials, but Moyzisch wrote of the ambassador's "considerable astonishment"; Schellenberg was equally unspecific about content but noted that Berlin found the initial documents "breath-taking."[13] Such reactions were justified.

Moyzisch described in general terms the first documents he got from Cicero. Unable to organize the messages according to value, since all were marked as secret in the top left corner, he decided to arrange them instead by date, finding that most were recent and none over two weeks old; each showed the dates and times of sending and receipt. All were signals exchanged between London and the embassy giving Foreign Office instructions or answers to queries. "Many of them were reports concerning political and military matters of the utmost importance." Moyzisch claimed that he foresaw in the references to the Allies' determination and capabilities the coming destruction of the Third Reich. One paper detailing the infiltration of British air personnel into Turkey had especially surprised Papen, because the activities exceeded his own estimates. Several items summarized the total deliveries of American weapons and equipment to Moscow during the preceding months and years. There was a Foreign Office analysis, for the ambassador's eyes only, indicating Soviet insistence on a major second front and suspicion of Anglo-American delays in mounting it. How accurately he remembered and reported the more specific items is debatable, of course. Moyzisch later related only that the second group of photographs he processed dealt with the conference in Moscow. He did not describe the content of the last twenty shots.[14]

There is little in the spy's commentaries on what he photographed that was new or could be trusted. Both the speed with which he worked and his minimal English undermine his smug claims about what he knew of content. In most instances he merely amplified Moyzisch's text so as to make his own more dramatic.

Bazna's first detailed description of a document concerned an incident early in his employment by Busk. The diplomat supposedly often brought files home from the embassy for further study. Usually he was meticulous about security, but on this occasion he had been called away suddenly and seemed distracted: Mrs. Busk was giving birth to their daughter in Istanbul. He slipped a file into his desk and neglected to lock the drawer; the valet was able to take it to the cellar to read, striking the hot water pipes at times to pretend that he was making repairs. Bazna would claim that the material dealt with Churchill's pressure for a military commitment from Turkey—information about building airfields, opening the Black Sea supply route, and delivering war matériel; Inönü's reply to the proposals was cautious and raised concerns about the intentions of Moscow. The valet decided, "as I obtained this overall view of the world situation while working on the central heating system," to help keep his country neutral.[15] His story is curious, however, for two reasons. Its placement early in his narrative suggests an editorial contrivance to inform readers about political conditions and promote a better image of the author. Also, why did a man who had resolved to spy not have his camera ready to copy the papers? Nothing he allegedly saw in the file reached the enemy.

The admission in Bazna's account of photographing in the Busks' kitchen is revealing: "I had no time to read the documents I had photographed. I discovered their contents only later." Bazna's book sometimes extended remarks by Moyzisch. Through archival research Nogly had located a list giving figures for American war aid to the Soviet Union, and they represented it to be what the valet must have copied. The same British memorandum also mentioned the current Moscow

Conference and the determination to obtain Turkey's war help. In another instance of specificity Bazna claimed that he copied from among Busk's papers a roster of British agents working in Turkey in an open or secret capacity. It appears most unlikely that any such master listing would have been compiled, however, and especially odd that the great value of acquiring such a list was not emphasized.[16] The obvious conclusion is that Bazna's descriptions of what he copied are valueless.

Having gambled that the first photographs might be worth their price, the Germans were surprised by the data found in Cicero's films, a factor that increased their worry. On one hand the information appeared to be so valuable that its provider could not be ignored; on the other hand, its quality seemed so exceptional that the source had to be regarded as suspect. No one could risk misjudging the man or his work. Therefore, attempts to reconcile their conflicting reactions and views kept the Germans occupied during the following weeks while the enterprising Cicero pursued his spying, unaware that his credibility was far from accepted.

Bazna in three deals in just a week had earned £65,000. Unconcerned that he had not yet received payment for the third delivery and confident that arrangements for further sales were satisfactory, he sought to ensure a regular inventory while making his espionage safer. Unfortunately, only Bazna could describe how he managed to obtain and copy Knatchbull-Hugessen's secret papers. He divulged something of his methods to Moyzisch during their meetings, and the SD officer revealed them in his postwar statements. The spy's own later account of events, confusing in chronology and sensational in tone, clarified only certain matters while raising new problems. If his claims about several points must be questioned, however, other assertions appear credible, providing an outline and useful details of what occurred.

Sir Hughe's preference for working in the study of his residence rather than in an office in the protected main embassy building created the conditions that made possible the spying by Cicero. Important official documents that were always carefully guarded in the chancery became vulnerable in the ambassador's home, especially when they were kept overnight in the secretary's safe or in a leather despatch box in the diplomat's bedroom. Although the portable containers were called "boxes," the embassy term, they were more like common attaché cases: made of wood and covered in leather, they were about the size of American legal paper and six inches deep, allowing documents inside to lie flat. The lock was on the side. Their usual contents were papers referred to as the "print" or file copies of signals to and from embassies. Other items were sometimes present.

Early in his employment Bazna acquainted himself with the routine followed by the ambassador's private secretary, "Miss Louise," in handling the messages and papers carried to his home for Sir Hughe to examine. Any items requiring his personal attention arrived at the residence in red boxes, which were stored in the safe protected by the secretary, who each afternoon placed in a black attaché case those papers the ambassador wanted to review after office hours. She put any other unfinished work in the office safe until the following day. The safe itself was not a sophisticated model, but the careful secretary kept the key by day and the ambassador took it at night, when an elderly guard watched the office door. The old man often dozed off while on duty, and a whistling noise from ill-fitting dentures signaled his slumber. Meanwhile the black box remained in the ambassador's bedroom during the night, locked except when the diplomat was using its contents, and it was returned to the secretary in the morning when she arrived.[17]

Despite the precautions, the removal of documents from the embassy did not conform to standards of common sense or to formal regulations for safeguarding vital papers, especially in wartime. Foreign Secretary Bevin made that point clear in his criticism of the ambassador in his statement to Parliament in October 1950. Nevertheless Sir Hughe's negligence stemmed less from any particular acts of carelessness than from a general outlook toward security found among many old-fashioned diplomats, unprepared for the altered realities and complexities of World War II intelligence. Awareness of espionage existed, but problems were approached with false confidence and inadequate measures.

Knatchbull-Hugessen's attitude with respect to security was revealed in an incident in early 1943. William Sholto Douglas, Air Commander-in-Chief for the Middle East with headquarters in Cairo, visited the Knatchbull-Hugessens in Ankara on business. London wanted him to arrange for British air defense installations in Turkey. When his guest arrived at the embassy, the ambassador asked if he was carrying any secret papers in his briefcase, explaining his reason for inquiring: "You'd better let me have it to lock away in my safe for the night. Too many of our servants seem to be spies." When he was asked why they were not dismissed, "the Ambassador's reply was made with all the aplomb that we think of as typical of the Foreign Office": they were actually good servants, "and in any case any others we might get would also probably be spies." After the war when the Cicero affair became known, Douglas remembered the explanation.[18]

Bazna found himself treated with cordial indifference by his employer, who was a gentleman at all times, but at first Bazna distrusted the imperturbable manner of Sir Hughe. To test how much the ambassador really noticed, he hid one of his unfinished pen drawings for three days; the diplomat failed to note its disappearance or then to observe that it had been returned to his dressing table. Bazna had more concern about the alertness that he detected in Lady Knatchbull-Hugessen. He might know the ambassador's general whereabouts, but she moved freely around the house and might endanger him if she became suspicious or appeared suddenly. As a form of cover he usually carried a duster about with him. Nevertheless, he made the most of his opportunities. From the time the ambassador was awakened at 7:30 each morning, in a bedroom only he used, his routine was tightly scheduled and seldom altered. There were morning and predinner baths and various changes of clothes, which kept the valet busy; meals eaten at home took little time; each morning and afternoon the diplomat worked at his desk in the study, with his secretary nearby. While the spy risked a few ventures during their brief periods of absence, chancing quick access to papers, he worried that any variation in timing might lead to his being caught.[19] Two of the ambassador's habits sometimes gave him safer periods in which to copy papers.

After lunch the diplomat "used to play the piano in the drawing-room" in order to relax. The *kavass* in his book reported that during such times he might have access to Knatchbull-Hugessen's papers. But Sir Hughe later told a journalist that there was no piano at the embassy and denied in particular that he had once accompanied his servant while Cicero sang. (That incident supposedly occurred in mid-December and will be considered in context.) More serious was Bazna's claim that Knatchbull-Hugessen used sleeping pills. The spy said he noticed a bottle on the bedside table and learned that his employer relied on its contents after having worked on papers late at night. Sir Hughe denied the practice and cited the matter as one of the untrue stories about Cicero.[20] If he did indeed use such tablets, he certainly made the spy's work easier.

Suitable opportunities would have been insufficient had the valet not possessed duplicate keys, but his ability to open the black and red boxes from an early date, and the question of when he gained access to the safe, are separate issues. Bazna would claim he made wax impressions of three of the ambassador's keys, believing them to fit the safe and both types of boxes, but his account differs in important details from that given by Moyzisch, according to whom the keys to the boxes were satisfactory after Berlin provided a better copy of one of them. Exactly when Bazna got a key to the safe is uncertain. Despite his assertion that the impressions he made in late October produced a key to the safe, made by his friend, it seems likely that Bazna was lying or that his copy was imperfect and failed to work. That supposition is supported by the fact that he admitted seeking help later in getting some different keys. Moyzisch recalled being given wax impressions for two complicated safe keys in about mid-December. The duplicates were made quickly in Berlin, and, he said, they gave Cicero entry to the diplomat's safe. Bazna agreed about the approximate date of the request but claimed that the copies were needed for a more difficult black box being used by Sir Hughe.[21] Such discrepancies cannot be resolved, but Moyzisch's version is likely to be true. Probably Bazna wanted to emphasize his own resourcefulness and give the impression that from the beginning he had outwitted the British.

Familiarity with his employer's routine and absences allowed the valet to improve his photography. While much of his filming was done quickly and under varying conditions, he created a better means for working in his embassy room, building a quadripod for use when time permitted. He screwed the camera to a metal ring, secured and held up by four metal rods, and, using a hundred-watt bulb, laid papers below it for photographing. When the components were not needed they blended into the room's furnishings: two rods became part of boxes he made and attached to the wall in order to hang towels and laundry, the others were fitted into the wardrobe to hold clothes, and the metal ring seemed to form part of an ashtray where artfully made burn scars helped hide its markings.[22] Exactly how he managed the photographic processes requires a detailed and separate discussion, however, because his skeptical buyers questioned the quantity and quality of his early photographs. That issue had indeed become part of a major investigative effort by Berlin to determine whether the source and his material could really be trusted.

* * *

It may seem strange that after 5 November an extended interruption occurred in German communication with the spy while Moyzisch answered questions in Berlin. Given the extraordinary ease with which seemingly valuable documents were being obtained, however, there was widespread worry that the enemy had mounted some purposeful deception. The information being received from the spy was largely political intelligence, important for knowing the enemy's problems and broad intentions, but difficult to verify through specific events. Berlin therefore focused upon learning everything possible about Cicero, and grew impatient with the overworked Moyzisch. He had yet to find out much about the valet himself or his motives and methods, and he could not be certain that even the little he did learn was to be trusted.

Finding accurate answers to the numerous questions put to Moyzisch and to analysts about the photographs and their contents became essential; the Cicero business provided a new element of contention within the feuding hierarchy. To understand fully the unexpected break in contact with the spy that risked the operation's success, it is necessary to look closely at both the confusing structure of German intelligence services and the bitter struggles for power and prestige among senior officials, and then to examine how the critical issues in the spy affair reflected and fed those conflicts. For more than two months such factors strongly influenced reactions to the data and how the case was treated.

5 Germany's Intelligence Labyrinth

Cicero's contact in the embassy was not affiliated with the primary intelligence service in Germany. That circumstance, which came about accidentally from his unorthodox method of approach, proved significant. Had a connection been established with the usual agency, his activity would probably have soon been reported to the enemy and terminated, for that organization had long been penetrated and compromised. Moyzisch represented a newer and tighter foreign intelligence unit, the Sicherheitsdienst (SD), or Security Service, staffed and administered as a component of the expanding SS. Although such control and handling afforded better concealment of the spy's presence and identity, it created serious problems in acceptance and use of information, for the operation developed against a background of both jurisdictional conflicts and personal antagonisms.

There were too many powerful figures not only within the SS but also in the older intelligence service and government ministries who deeply resented the SD's growing role and its clearly ambitious and ruthless young head. Walter Schellenberg intended to gain control of the entire field of foreign intelligence, engaging repeatedly in dangerous intrigues and power struggles to advance his authority and designs, and characterizing the confusing milieu through which he steadily rose as *The Labyrinth*, the apt title of his memoirs. Schellenberg's aspirations and enemies provide context indispensable to explaining the varied reactions of high-ranking officials to the Cicero documents.

* * *

A certain amount of rivalry among the intelligence agents and services of a nation is understandable, and even healthy when it leads to more or better information. Too much competitiveness destroys effectiveness by dissipating energies in petty squabbles and jealousies. The security and intelligence services of the Third Reich were a maze of confused jurisdictions. In part the situation mirrored the personal conflicts among the leaders of the regime, for everyone wanted his own operation—often called an information service or a research department—if only to investigate his rivals, but in part it also reflected a basic principle of totalitarian rule. "The maxim that all authority should be unreliable" holds that subordinates should be kept "uncertain and busy so that higher-ups are not threatened."[1] Professional jealousy and mutual suspicion serve a useful purpose, whatever their cost in inefficiency or productivity; concentrated power and unlimited freedom are highly dangerous. These notions were perhaps nowhere applied with greater skill and effectiveness than in the field of security and intelligence work.

Heinrich Himmler stood at the top of the security system in the Third Reich. He has always been something of an enigma—more diligent than imaginative, more crafty than brilliant—but he succeeded in the scramble for power. Within a few years he transformed the SS organization from Hitler's bodyguard into a huge elite force; at the same time, the hardworking Himmler acquired new responsibilities that made the SS the indispensable instrument of tyranny.[2] His most ambitious subordinates—Reinhard Heydrich, his chief deputy in the organization, and Schellenberg, anxious to oversee all foreign intelligence—always coveted greater opportunities. Heydrich had created the special Security Service within the framework of the SS. "The S.D.'s initial *raison d'être* had been investigation and discovery of hostile elements within the ranks of the Nazi Party," but it soon expanded into other areas of intelligence work, circumventing Hitler's order that the Nazi Party and its units, like the SD, must not conduct intelligence activities.[3] Despite the restriction, the SD would become in the end Germany's sole intelligence service.

Increasingly dissatisfied with his role as second in command, Heydrich intended at some point to supplant Himmler. It made administrative sense to Heydrich to coordinate his superior's assortment of titles and powers. Finally in September 1939 he succeeded in having established under his own supervision the Reichssicherheitshauptamt (RSHA), or Reich Security Central Office, and in incorporating most of the previously separate functions in the elaborate new RSHA structure.[4] Some components, like the various kinds of police, were state organizations, the Secret Police (or Gestapo) becoming Department IV under Heinrich Müller. Other divisions had been created to serve the party, the old SD being split between RSHA Departments III and VI. Amt III, or SD Inland, was essentially the old domestic information organization, now headed by economist Otto Ohlendorf; Amt VI, or SD

Ausland, handled matters concerned with foreign intelligence activities, under the supervision of Heinz Jost. Heydrich himself kept close control of all SD work: his official title in 1939 was Chef der Sicherheitspolizei und des SD (Chief of Security Police and the SD), and his SS rank was lieutenant general. Thus Himmler remained Reichsführer SS, but he had now allowed a subempire to be created in the form of the RSHA, under Heydrich.

Yet the effective centralization Heydrich envisioned for the RSHA was never really achieved. The individual units had been independent too long and now opposed both authority and coordination; the rivalry between the Gestapo and the SD was deep and continuing; even the head of the whole structure soon lost interest, pursuing newer goals. Heydrich's neglect led to the further entrenchment of self-serving attitudes and policies well before his death in June 1942. All that resulted from his grand organizational project was an unwieldy bureaucratic amalgam of party and state groups. Only when opposing some common enemy could the RSHA leaders abandon their competition to become temporary allies; even then, they retained their mutual distrust and sometimes hatred of one another.

Soon Department VI presented serious problems, in part because its director, Jost, refused to develop his division as aggressively as Heydrich wanted.[5] Trouble had been developing for some time, but it was one of Jost's unscrupulous assistants, Major Alfred Naujocks, who caused the SD's leaders to be removed. Suspected and probably guilty of having engaged in illegal financial deals, Naujocks found his affairs being investigated by zealous Gestapo agents. Heydrich became most outraged over other charges against Naujocks, probably evidence that he had spied on Heydrich's private life. One of Naujocks's most secret projects, a counterfeiting scheme, later figured prominently in the Cicero case. Heydrich vented his wrath over both past and new issues by at last dismissing nearly the entire top leadership of Amt VI.

Schellenberg had probably intrigued to exacerbate the situation and became the beneficiary of the shakeup in SD Ausland. At the time he was barely past thirty but had already been marked as a young man of ability and promise—one who possessed all-consuming ambition, dedication to hard work, intelligence, surface loyalty, charm, no deep moral principles, and a particular gift for intrigue. Previously he had headed a department dealing with counterespionage in the internal security system, but direction of foreign intelligence remained his goal, and he had learned how to impress the right superiors by guile and sound work. Schellenberg had certainly discovered the importance of professional alliance with Heydrich: "The development of a whole nation was guided indirectly by his forceful character."[6] He moved ahead quickly with his protector's help, and later with Himmler's aid as well, but he also incurred jealousy, and his guardian's enemies became his own. Nor could he ever be sure when Heydrich might turn against him for slight cause.

He later described his appointment in his often ingenuous style. Early in 1941 Heydrich had sounded him out about taking over and reorganizing Department VI operations. By June 1941 the "inexcusable conditions," professional failings, and "personal irregularities" had led Heydrich to a "ruthless purge." Müller wanted the whole department dissolved and necessary functions transferred to the Gestapo. Heydrich instead made Schellenberg the acting head. Schellenberg later described his feelings: "The new task excited me. . . . On the one hand, I was very happy to have received finally the assignment for which I had waited so long. On the other, I was somewhat oppressed that it had been brought about by such a sad failure. . . . I was more than ever convinced that only a complete reconstruction of the department would be effective." Thus the paranoid Schellenberg had the accounts carefully audited to protect himself, because he knew of the SD's suspect financial state. He was sure that Heydrich watched him closely, that most of the staff resented his appointment, that people were waiting for him to fail, that the bitter Müller was conspiring against him. "I realized now to what depths of hatred, envy, and malicious intrigue men are capable of descending."[7]

Immediately Schellenberg set to work on the range of Amt VI's difficulties. Ideal solutions were seldom possible, due to the awkwardness of the foreign intelligence service being administratively in a structure essentially designed for police and internal security purposes. One constraint arose from its organizational problems—"overlapping bureaus and agencies which resulted in duplication, waste, inefficiency, and inevitable personal and professional jealousies"—complicated by shortages of specially trained personnel. Some of the staff owed their positions to party service; others had ability but busied themselves solely with pedantic research. Few had the skills and experience needed for the kinds of projects assigned to the department.[8] Another source of troubles was that Schellenberg posed a threat to many people, not only rivals in the RSHA, who resented his new power, but also those with services or roles that Schellenberg wanted to take over and integrate. His running jurisdictional disputes with colleagues, plus conflicts with the Foreign Ministry over rights and priorities, engaged all his attention and energy.

Throughout the time Schellenberg labored to restructure and expand his department he also struggled to supply the kind of sound foreign intelligence that Heydrich demanded of him. He knew that he would be made a scapegoat if he failed in his central task. Two inherited issues required his immediate efforts: Soviet capabilities, and Japanese intentions. In autumn uncertainties about both had suddenly become critical. Heydrich had appointed Schellenberg on the very day that the Nazis attacked the Russians. His intention was clear. Despite reporting by both the Abwehr, or military intelligence, and the SD, using a variety of sources, Germany's information on Russia was never adequate to meet its changing needs. Schellenberg remained ever vigilant to ensure that he not be held responsible and that all blame be cast on the Abwehr. Nevertheless, Hitler's rebukes of military intelligence when his campaign faced unexpected conditions in 1941 put Schellenberg under heavy pressure to submit impressive data and thereby justify the SD. Like his rival, he found that more and better information had little usefulness if the facts and analyses did not reinforce the dictator's views. Schellenberg nonetheless placed great importance on his agents in key listening posts, like neutral Turkey. Moyzisch's presence and duties reflected the continuing and deep anxiety about the military situation on the southern flank and about direct prospects in Russia. Finding out what Tokyo intended to do was another top priority for Schellenberg's small department. Still, the young acting director thought he could be satisfied with his initial performance and achievements. Missteps had been relatively few and minor, just enough to keep him nervous about his job, while the affairs of the department were soon running smoothly. He enjoyed his control of major intelligence work.[9]

He was nevertheless disturbed by a falling-out with the unpredictable Heydrich in late summer, one that threatened his new position and ambitions. Himmler had meanwhile become his protector, however, undoubtedly to keep Heydrich in greater uncertainty, and he forbade any change in Schellenberg's assignment. The head of the SS also allowed Schellenberg direct access at any time, bypassing Heydrich, a privilege explained by the fact that Schellenberg needed Himmler's help in dealing with government ministries. Schellenberg welcomed his influence with Himmler, "which I was never tired of exerting to the utmost," and intrigued against Heydrich and Ribbentrop. It seems likely that Heydrich agreed to Schellenberg's request in autumn 1941 for personal control over Department VI's separate budget so Schellenberg might somehow entrap himself. Schellenberg knew the danger but remained pleased: "This was an unexpected success, putting me a step further on the road toward the realization of my aims."[10]

Meanwhile, Schellenberg proceeded with extreme care concerning a particularly worrisome project. During 1939–1941 a group of skilled workers in Amt VI's technical laboratory, already makers of fake passports, university degrees, driver's licenses, and other types of documents, struggled also to counterfeit British currency, in a scheme Hitler had sanctioned. The undertaking had always been controversial even within the RSHA and was therefore fraught with political as well as technical difficulties. Schellenberg knew his bitterest enemies monitored both the operation and his responsibility for overseeing how the currency was distributed by the SD. Certainly at that stage the acting department head could not anticipate how the troublesome counterfeiting scheme would figure in his handling of the war's most successful spy case.

In September 1941 Heydrich assumed the additional position of Protector of Bohemia-Moravia. Some think that the appointment was arranged by Himmler and others to dilute his growing power; meanwhile, he continued as administrative head of the RSHA but became less involved in routine operations. It is not surprising that by spring 1942 he was worried about where he stood. Early in June, Heydrich died of wounds sustained when Czech nationalists attacked his car. There was a period of uncertainty in the RSHA units after his death, because no new head was named immediately. Hitler asked Himmler himself to assume authority until a permanent replacement could be found; the result was a further increase in the closeness between Schellenberg and Himmler.

On 30 January 1943, the tenth anniversary of the regime provided the occasion for various changes in leadership of the Third Reich. Schellenberg was able to become regular head of Department VI and but for his youth might have headed the RSHA. That appointment went instead to a man Hitler himself selected for the post, SS General Ernst Kaltenbrunner, a fellow Austrian and a fanatic follower from the early days. There is unanimous agreement that his crude manner concealed a "remarkable vacuity" that made him totally ill suited for intelligence work. Certainly Schellenberg agreed; he would have preferred almost anyone else as his immediate superior. Kaltenbrunner in turn disliked his young subordinate, because he owed his position to the long-hated Heydrich, but as long as Schellenberg enjoyed the protection of Himmler, Kaltenbrunner found himself blocked. Schellenberg was therefore finally confirmed as full director of the intelligence service on 24 February.[11]

To the determined leaders of the RSHA, the continued independence of the Abwehr posed an especially difficult challenge. Formed originally as the counterintelligence branch of the military services, it had evolved into a broad secret service, one both responsible to and protected by the military chiefs of staff.[12] Himmler knew that any interference in military matters by his men was forbidden by Hitler. Such restrictions had seldom deterred his ambitious subordinates—Heydrich, Müller, and Schellenberg—in their competing quests for personal power. Over the years they found many ways to harass their common rival, because the stakes involved were basic—SS exclusive control of all security and intelligence operations of the Reich.

Admiral Wilhelm Canaris had become head of the Abwehr in 1935. To the end of his life he remained a strange and enigmatic figure, fatalistic, indecisive, opposed to the regime but never involved with the conspirators he sheltered.[13] His ambiguous attitude and curious behavior played into the hands of his enemies during the struggles for power that plagued the intelligence services. Canaris eventually fell victim as much to his own personality and professional inefficiency as to his rivals in the RSHA.

Jurisdictional disputes were inevitable as all the intelligence services expanded. Many problems centered on the Abwehr's role in counterespionage and the RSHA's responsibility for internal security. A series of talks beginning in 1936 had failed to resolve the key issues.[14] An agreement signed on 1 March 1942 gave advantages to the SD but lacked consistent enforcement when Heydrich's death soon afterward altered things. Himmler did not press concerted action against the Abwehr, yet there is no question that 1942 saw what Schellenberg called the "climax" of the anti-Abwehr campaign by his department and colleagues. Hitler was annoyed that military intelligence was failing to provide sound information and analyses concerning the capabilities of the Allies. Heydrich and Müller kept files and merely awaited the right moment to move against the Abwehr and Canaris. Schellenberg served as Heydrich's liaison with Canaris while he intrigued against the Abwehr. Still, Himmler thought Hitler was not yet ready to assign a unified intelligence service to Heydrich and the RSHA, and Heydrich's death in June temporarily postponed any showdown. Schellenberg was undoubtedly disappointed by the unexpected turn of events and hypocritically continued to profess personal friendship for Canaris. He was zealous to learn everything possible about espionage management, and he knew how much he profited from their contacts. The Abwehr meanwhile placed part of the blame for its failings on disruptions caused by the dead SS leader.

Schellenberg thought of 1943 as the "penultimate pause" in the SS move against Canaris. Certainly few things were going well for the Abwehr, and the various leaders of the RSHA were gathering materials for a final contest. An Abwehr agent was arrested at the end of 1942 on currency violations, and no effort was made to protect him; he told the Gestapo enough to provide new leads against Canaris and his aides, prompting a long and thorough investigation.[15] It was the kind of close scrutiny that the careless Abwehr leaders could not afford to let continue. Yet Canaris unwisely allowed the situation to drift until it became a disaster.

For some time the Abwehr's central administration (Department Z) had harbored active anti-Nazi conspirators. Canaris was not personally part of the group, but he nevertheless gave it protective cover, provided it with sources of information and means of communication, and accepted passively its existence and aim, thereby endangering himself and the whole Abwehr staff. Heading the conspiracy were his own deputy chief, Major-General Hans Oster, and the latter's civilian assistant, Hans von Dohnanyi, an attorney connected with other opposition circles. Dohnanyi and some other suspects were arrested in April; Oster was merely forced to resign at the end of 1943.[16] Not until the following summer did the authorities come to realize the full dimensions of the conspiracy against the regime.

Nor was the continuing Gestapo investigation the only source of SS pressure. Aware of Hitler's increasing annoyance at the Abwehr's failures to provide useful military intelligence, Schellenberg in autumn 1943 complained to Himmler, charging that Canaris had deliberately concealed foreknowledge of Italy's defection and surrender. He presented a dossier "with absolute proof of Canaris' treachery," gathered by his agents. Himmler said only that he would keep it until the "right opportunity" arose to bring the matter to Hitler's attention. Frustrated by his superior's strange and unexpected caution, Schellenberg concluded that Canaris must have known "something incriminating against Himmler, for otherwise there is no possible explanation of Himmler's reaction to the material which I placed before him."[17] The reason was probably less dramatic, for Himmler knew that military leaders like Field Marshal Wilhelm Keitel continued to support Canaris firmly, lest they lose control of all intelligence operations. There was no denying, however, that a showdown was near.

German ministries and agencies that dealt with foreign relations and intelligence also felt pressure and competition from the ambitious new director of Amt VI. An insufficiency of knowledge of the enemy following the attack on the Soviet Union forced the service to demonstrate quickly its usefulness. Heydrich therefore had allowed Schellenberg to develop contacts with other government offices; he needed a flow of information to impress Himmler and especially Hitler. Schellenberg had welcomed the opportunity to extend his influence, but he made mistakes through being too eager, encroaching on the private preserves claimed by top Nazi leaders. In general, he had resolved most problems of working with the government ministries and units without detriment to his operations and goals.[18] Recurring problems with Ribbentrop and his Foreign Ministry, however, produced a power struggle. Not only was the SS anathema to the conservative office and diplomatic staffs, whose ties to the Abwehr were old and close, but also trouble arose from the unpredictable nature of Ribbentrop's moods and behavior. Disdained for his arrogance and stubbornness, the incompetent Ribbentrop still kept Hitler's unflagging support. As the number of friendly and neutral countries steadily dwindled, reducing the role of his ministry, he became even more fanatical and assertive of his importance. Heydrich had forewarned his new head of foreign intelligence to expect tough times in all his dealings with Ribbentrop.[19] That is exactly what came about.

Trouble with the Foreign Ministry had long-standing sources. The regime's racial policies and agitators had long created difficulties for the ministry in neutral countries. During the war additional conflicts arose over attitudes toward the dictatorship's allied and client states. In many instances the military authorities, Foreign Ministry, and party organs followed different approaches. Romania became the focus of sharp Ribbentrop-SS conflict during the autumn of 1942. The awkward situation emerged just as Himmler and Schellenberg were pursuing a showdown with the minister. Schellenberg explained later that he and Himmler thought some sort of negotiated peace was possible, but they knew Ribbentrop would oppose any feelers or talks because he believed so fervently in Hitler's total victory; they began to conspire that fall to have Ribbentrop ousted from his position by Christmas. Himmler even mused that his replacement might be Papen. Presumably an attempt to persuade Hitler to try negotiations would follow. Instead, Ribbentrop had managed to convince Hitler that he and not Himmler was correct in the Romanian situation. Himmler suddenly found himself out of favor and on the defensive with Hitler. By the time Hitler realized that he had misjudged the issues in the controversy, Himmler had lost his nerve. Schellenberg thought he had simply tired of continual intrigue and decided against challenging Ribbentrop. Himmler even failed to back a high ministry official who had openly accused Ribbentrop of spending special government funds to help pay for his family's lavish living. Schellenberg thought his superior nevertheless kept back the most damaging evidence that had been assembled against Ribbentrop.[20]

The inevitable result of all such conflicts and intrigues was a lingering antipathy, which the minister manifested in his official opinions and actions. One example was Ribbentrop's suspicion and rejection of intelligence reports that the SD claimed were reliable. Schellenberg ran into particular opposition, because he invested his personal credibility in the endorsement of Cicero. Given their past hostility, the Cicero information provided an exceptional opportunity for the vindictive Ribbentrop to criticize and undermine his enemy.

One manifestation of the jurisdictional antagonism between the Foreign Ministry and the RSHA involved primary access to intelligence forwarded from embassies.[21] Routine reports from agents with a diplomatic cover, like Moyzisch, had always caused problems regardless of the information's nature. In the Cicero case, Papen's awareness of the vital documents and insistence on seeing all the photographs before they were transmitted to the capital produced special and lingering difficulties. Moyzisch found himself under firm instructions from his superiors to withhold items from the ambassador; the diplomat meanwhile was expected to enforce fully the handling procedures demanded by Ribbentrop. Despite some complications from their long-standing and widely known quarrels, Ribbentrop and Papen agreed completely about their right to evaluate all political information. In the end the SD officer quietly modified his orders, and the ambassador at times employed some of the Cicero data on his own. The basic conflict never came to resolution, and it helped prevent the spy's achievement from having greater impact.

Cicero's information always had dual destinations in Berlin. Each principal in the embassy immediately conveyed by telegram important matters to his superior, as extracts; photographic items and accompanying reports of any kind followed by the regular diplomatic pouch and courier plane. Moyzisch forwarded the original films and his answers to constant questions to SD headquarters, where Schellenberg organized all the material for his memoranda and briefings for Kaltenbrunner. Through Schellenberg's special access he also kept Himmler informed. Himmler in turn decided how to bring oral and written intelligence analyses to the attention of Hitler. At the same time SD technicians were subjecting every photograph to careful scrutiny to detect any signs of trickery, and cryptanalysts were comparing their telegraph recordings with the printed texts to determine if any British codes could be broken.

Papen's telegrams and comments were earmarked for Ribbentrop. Few people in the Foreign Ministry knew about the secret source (though one who did was an anti-Nazi who subsequently copied a range of documents and delivered them at intervals to an American agent he could meet abroad, thereby starting one channel through which the British received a warning of leakage). Key Foreign Ministry business was always presented to Hitler by Ribbentrop. Since Ribbentrop remained skeptical about the spy's credibility, however, he treated most of the information obtained from Cicero with caution. Hitler therefore must have received conflicting opinions about the value of these documents.

From the outset of the case, the issue of priority in handling the new data produced a contest of wills and odd incidents. Ribbentrop insisted that under an old agreement with Himmler only he could present political information to Hitler. In his estimation, nearly all the Cicero items dealt with matters of foreign policy. Early in November 1943 a high ministry official reminded Kaltenbrunner that Ribbentrop had authority to screen SD reports; Kaltenbrunner agreed with Ribbentrop's aide but remarked that sometimes the Führer demanded immediate and direct reports from the SD.[22] Obviously, neither the definition of political content nor the issue of reporting channels was settled.[23]

Because of his diplomatic cover, and as noted, Moyzisch found himself between two masters. Kaltenbrunner ordered him to forward everything without showing any material to the ambassador; upon reporting his new instructions the agent was confronted by an angry Papen. "I refuse to tolerate such a procedure. You are my subordinate, and I require you to show me in the first instance all the material that passes through your hands." Papen prevailed less because of any formal agreement or support from Ribbentrop than because of his determination and past working relationship with Moyzisch. Still, he later claimed, some items must have been withheld from him.[24]

That the feuding persisted and was probably heightened by the spy case can be seen in a later exchange. A telegram postdating the Cicero affair by several months reveals how Ribbentrop pursued his ministry's right. Papen had relayed a copy of a political report that Moyzisch had sent directly to Schellenberg and some days later received a sharp response from Ribbentrop: "This action is totally objectionable and intolerable." Moyzisch was to present "all information of a political nature which comes to his attention" to Papen first, the ambassador deciding its disposition, since Moyzisch "under no circumstances may forward such a political report as his own" directly to the SD. In closing the minister asked that the ambassador "forthwith lecture Herr Moyzisch about the intolerable nature of his action" and proper duties.[25]

Ribbentrop's vehemence undoubtedly stemmed from an earlier humiliation involving Moyzisch. Near the beginning of the Cicero operation the foreign minister had summoned him to Berlin to make a personal report. Intercepted en route upon Kaltenbrunner's order, the agent was interrogated first by his own superiors, the experience reminding him where his official ties lay, while Ribbentrop seethed in bitter frustration. The episode had an importance far beyond interagency rivalry, however, and it formed part of investigations to understand and evaluate the spy.

6   Questions and Doubts in Berlin

Bazna's photographs gave rise to both excitement and doubts when they reached Berlin. Only a tightly restricted circle received the intelligence reports and had some idea of how such information had been obtained. Some officials accepted the material rather quickly and with few reservations, because it represented the kind of dramatic success they wanted; there were those who believed more readily in the authenticity of the content than in the messages' clear implications for their regime and country; others considered the circumstances and papers far more critically and advised proceeding with utmost caution. Too often the reactions reflected little more than the belligerent egos and tangled missions of those who headed the nation's complex array of competing power structures. "An objective analysis of the operational data was out of the question where rival cutthroats were vying for position and prestige."[1]

Efforts to determine the trustworthiness of the documents they had purchased occupied German officials for an extended period, but their various approaches did not resolve all doubts. Papen and others who examined the photographs concluded that the dispatches conformed in style and content to practices and interests identified with the British. Cipher analysts sought to match the printed items with recordings of enemy radio signals. Because many of the texts dealt with broad policies and planning, information not susceptible to immediate verification, there were few instances in which actual events proved the material's value. One such opportunity arose in mid-January, however, when an air raid on Sofia occurred just as had been indicated. While it removed many surviving misgivings, it happened fairly late. Meanwhile there were concerted attempts to ascertain if the spy himself was truthful and indeed capable of doing everything he claimed. Fears that he was a trained agent or an unwilling instrument of enemy intelligence prompted a succession of investigations of the man and his photography work. Underlying much of the uncertainty was a profound respect for the British secret services' reputation and their ability to mount such a clever ruse.[2]

* * *

Moyzisch soon found himself bombarded by both the SD and the Foreign Ministry with specific and repeated questions about Cicero. Who was the man, and why did he spy? How did he obtain access to the documents and manage to take the pictures? What were his skills in photography, and where had he learned them? Did he work alone or have help? In retrospect Moyzisch felt that he answered, "generally quite plausibly," almost all the questions that had arisen, but explanations he thought credible were not sufficient for others, or necessarily true. Given the insistence on immediate and full data that only he could provide, Moyzisch drew upon his conversations with and his impressions of Cicero, who concealed his identity behind a number of half-truths and fanciful tales. Since the men became neither friends nor close, never shaking hands until their final parting, the talks yielded few details of much worth.[3] The intelligence officer proved oddly unimaginative about pursuing even discreet investigations to gain more concrete and reliable facts. Perhaps the explanation lies in his growing workload, his basic position as a processor rather than developer of information, or a fear of somehow frightening or compromising the valet. It is hardly surprising that his superiors wondered about his ability to handle the situation or that they continued their inquiries when his reports failed to satisfy them.

Berlin wanted complete personal data about Cicero—his name, background, character, habits, and views. Moyzisch first checked with Jenke, but he apparently chose protective vagueness, claiming not to recall the servant's real name so long after employment (which he implied had been some time earlier). Bazna was nevertheless sure Jenke in fact remembered his name; that first night both he and his wife supposedly spoke to him using his given name. It seems unlikely indeed that they had forgotten it, and Schellenberg noted also the aloofness and disdain shown toward intelligence matters by Jenke, who had quickly distanced himself from the entire operation. Did he perhaps hint privately to his brother-in-law to be suspicious? Such a simple caution to Ribbentrop would help explain the latter's coolness. Meanwhile Moyzisch made further vain efforts to elicit from Cicero his name. Especially strange was his failure to tap the gossip network among household staffs to learn the valet's identity. In the end his postwar confession—"I never knew his real name"—revealed a key area of shortcoming.[4]

Misreporting the spy as Albanian arose from Cicero's fictions and Moyzisch's false assumptions. Having heard stories of the valet's provincial childhood and thinking at least their setting true, the intelligence officer never questioned his ethnic background.[5] Perhaps he considered it more understandable for an outsider to lack national loyalties and sell information; he apparently never heard the man's postwar rationalizations that he had spied to protect his country's neutrality. Moyzisch may have had still another reason for thinking the spy Albanian: because Cicero chose to use French in their contacts, it came as a surprise when Moyzisch heard him speak Turkish fluently. Apparently he convinced himself that reliance on French stemmed from necessity rather than affectation. Berlin, however, seemed satisfied about the spy's ethnic origins as reported by Moyzisch: its primary interest lay in determining if Cicero's tales of youthful experiences explained his actions. It is nevertheless clear that Bazna's nationality was misidentified; he considered himself Turkish in both culture and outlook. Awareness of their error would not have altered the Germans' thinking to any great extent, however, unless knowing he was a Turk had underscored pure greed as his motive.

Moyzisch also relayed his observations about the appearance and character of Cicero. His physical descriptions were accurate, if too dramatic at times, except for overestimating his age. Moyzisch thought the man to be in his early fifties, but Bazna was in fact only thirty-nine in the autumn of 1943. Undoubtedly his receding hairline and his facial features misled the intelligence officer. With respect to the spy's character and ambitions, however, he was an astute judge. The impressions that he later reported sending to his superiors, perhaps subsequently polished, captured well the man's social pretensions and aspirations: "I think he's an adventurer. He's vain, ambitious and sufficiently intelligent to have raised himself out of the class into which he was born. He doesn't belong to that class any more, but then he doesn't belong to the class above either, which he both loathes and admires."[6]

A curious insecurity seemed to force the Germans into seeking more complicated reasons behind Cicero's aims and activities than in fact existed. Their reluctance to accept relatively simple explanations clearly affected their assessments in three areas of particular concern— the spy's motives, access to papers and choices for filming, and camera skills.

Analysts rightly believed that discovering the spy's motivations would help them greatly in evaluating the man and his material. Some convincing basis for his activities—revenge, conviction, adventure, avarice, hatred—might validate his behavior and photographs. Instead their caution increased, because Cicero engaged in games and fantasies. While it should have been obvious that greed played the central role in his scheming—and if freely admitted it would probably have satisfied most doubts—the spy's ego and mythomania led him to invent other more fanciful and flattering tales. Perhaps the badgering for details encouraged his willingness to lie. Even when the Germans' initial interest in whether an Englishman had killed his father in Albania waned because of discrepancies in Cicero's stories, there remained a deep suspicion that some key to his personality still eluded them; Moyzisch would afterward write of the spy's "obscure motives," and Schellenberg would confess that he never fully grasped Cicero's purpose.[7] Their inability to explain his behavior in terms of some concrete or psychological reason, aside from his cupidity, left the two frustrated, and disadvantaged in dispelling others' lingering uncertainties.

How a valet got access to the ambassador's papers and evaluated their significance caused further difficulties, given doubts that embassy security could be easily breached. It was hard to accept that such important papers were routinely carried to the residence or that the ambassador could be even briefly lax about his key.[8] At the same time, officials questioned how the valet repeatedly seemed to select only the generally most valuable items to film; both the matter of ready access and the surprisingly high quality of the copied documents fed fears of an enemy trick. For that reason Berlin sought to ascertain what languages Cicero spoke or read: the critical issue was whether he knew enough English to choose the papers he would photograph. Proving fluency in the language, given his denial, would also point to a deception. Yet the answers were as simple as some came to believe: the ambassador regularly kept nearby a batch of troublesome items for further study or to draft replies; the valet might indeed recognize their security headings, but he had only to photograph everything time allowed. In effect the ambassador himself had selected the items.

While the spy knew French and something of other languages, including German (from his singing of an operatic and *Lieder* repertoire), a misjudgment by the Germans clouded their estimate of him: Moyzisch reported that the man understood English. Cicero certainly knew some basic English and could spot a designation like "secret" as a cognate of the French, but he had neither time nor knowledge enough to sort and weigh the documents he filmed. On one occasion Cicero submitted a copy of something the SD found puzzling, pages reporting household expenses; the Germans decided the spy must know English and was cheating them. Moyzisch thought he was attempting to be paid for photographs he knew to be worthless by claiming not to know English. The intelligence officer described with pride how the spy finally admitted lying, and he recalled that they held subsequent conversations in that language. His own modest ability in French and English makes his account far from believable, but Schellenberg accepted and repeated Moyzisch's conclusion. Actually, the language issue was simply not important. While congratulating themselves on having thus exposed the spy's alleged falsehood, the pair also added to their other problems, for they now wondered if their discovery had increased chances of an enemy deception.[9]

Meanwhile, the whole question of Cicero's filming methods was being checked. Both his degree of proficiency with a camera and his claim to be working alone became elements of concern. The view persisted that the superior skill evident in the photographs indicated professional training or help and therefore made more likely the existence of an elaborate trick. Clearly, one question was crucial: could such an individual on his own take the photographs he was selling? Skepticism among the Germans prompted various efforts to determine an answer. First, there were repeated queries about the spy's photography equipment and exact procedures, which Moyzisch attempted to answer with whatever details he obtained in his conversations with the valet.[10] Of special concern was the spy's initial insistence that he used no tripod but instead held each paper under a lamp with one hand while operating the camera with the other. To do so without considerable wobbling seemed unlikely and the method far from compatible with the sharpness of his early photographs. Unresolved doubts about his veracity and camera expertise therefore led to a more thorough laboratory analysis of the photographs.

Soon after forwarding the first deliveries, as noted above, Moyzisch had been hurriedly summoned to the capital, and Schellenberg had the existing five rolls of negatives and 112 prints of documents examined by technicians. Their conclusions covered various points: all the film stock came from standard commercial products, some sort of photographic floodlamps with portable reflectors had been used, the lens had been quite strong and set at a small stop, the estimated distance between the camera and documents had been four feet, each of the photographs had been focused perfectly but slightly underexposed, and all texts were fully legible once enlargements were made. In summary, they believed that the photographer was an expert who had probably been rushed. Despite a broad accuracy in nearly all respects, the analysis failed to answer satisfactorily the question of whether the spy worked alone or had assistance. As Moyzisch noted concerning the initial doubts, "It seemed improbable though not impossible that one person could have taken the photographs unaided," but the point continued to worry Berlin.[11]

About mid-December, one photograph in particular alerted Moyzisch to trouble. The enlargement clearly showed a thumb and index finger holding the typewritten documents, and he recognized a signet ring that the spy habitually wore on his forefinger. From the positioning it appeared impossible that he could also have worked the camera with his other hand in the manner he had repeatedly described as his filming method. Moyzisch realized that inspection of the photograph would bring renewed pressure from Berlin. Either the spy had lied about his procedures or he had a collaborator; each alternative added to old uncertainties about his and the films' genuineness. The intelligence officer soon had "endless worry and trouble"; his superiors "began inundating me with telegrams" about investigating. "It all nearly drove me frantic."[12]

Appearance of the two fingers on the print led Berlin to send a photography expert to Turkey by special plane to stage and witness an interrogation. The man knew French and had prepared a sizable list of technical and procedural questions for Moyzisch to memorize. He installed a microphone in Moyzisch's office so he could listen in an adjoining room to how Cicero responded to the queries. Moyzisch after some persuasion got the spy to come once more to his office and then tried to seem natural as he questioned him in French. The session went well and produced detailed results, the expert concluding that the photographer was unusually skilled and might generally do everything himself, although the fingers showed that someone had helped on that occasion. In his opinion it remained "most improbable" but not a "physical impossibility" that the agent worked alone. Moyzisch never saw the investigator's report, but apparently it satisfied Schellenberg. The head of the SD wrote later that "from the beginning" he had been sure "one or more" people worked with Cicero to take the films. When his technicians' analyses reinforced that conclusion, he felt only that the findings made the spy a liar but did not cloud the genuineness of the man's photographs. Moyzisch also believed that the spy worked with someone, but he too considered the point unimportant, for he harbored no real doubts about Cicero. Instead he admired his "supreme skill" with a camera and the "superb job" he had usually done.[13] After a while Berlin dropped the matter. Further inquiries into technical questions seemed unlikely to alter opinions about the spy, and the focus of argument shifted to content rather than methods and means.

Moyzisch remained the only source of what became known about Cicero. Answering the barrage of questions put to him, often repeated because his information was sketchy and not trusted, left him feeling frustrated and at times irritable. Underlying his anxiety was the intelligence service's threat that officers abroad whose performances were unsatisfactory might be reassigned to military duties. At one point during Berlin's stream of messages concerning the spy, he supposedly suggested, exasperated by the questioning, just asking the British about their embassy servant.[14] Nevertheless it seems odd that he learned so little, so lacked ingenuity in fulfilling his investigative task, and described the spy simply as an enigma. As a result the information that he sent to Berlin was sparse and on some topics also quite misleading.

* * *

Effective use of the enemy reports and plans received through Cicero depended upon convincing Hitler that they contained reliable data and ought to influence his views. But even when his initial caution about the material was partly overcome, there was no modification in his direction of the war. One reason was the conflicting advice he received; more important was a prevailing state of mind. In theory the intelligence précis and analyses could reach him through two channels, the Foreign Ministry and the RSHA, but the old feuding and jurisdictional disputes at the highest levels caused problems. Because position and circumstances gave the advantage of regular contacts to the foreign minister, whose attitude combined pettiness and refusal to envision anything but total victory, the thrust of the spy's information was presented neither willingly nor objectively to the dictator. The intelligence service could to some extent proceed independently, but Kaltenbrunner had chronic difficulties with Ribbentrop, who insisted that only he and his ministry could process data dealing with foreign relations—which, as noted, Ribbentrop considered to cover nearly everything from Cicero. Quarrels over precedence affected assessments of the source and his documents but scarcely determined final decisions; rejection of the information and its implications despite wide acceptance of its authenticity stemmed from ideological blindness. Hitler and party loyalists could simply never afford to acknowledge the coming disaster that the stolen secrets showed was in store for the regime; they had to challenge and ultimately ignore the Cicero items.

To gain firsthand knowledge, Ribbentrop ordered Moyzisch to come to the capital. The intelligence officer's later narrative of his trip was misleading, however, particularly with respect to its time span and some of its interviews. His deception in details was part of his overall pretense that he was really a diplomat, victimized by interference from the service that actually employed him. Why he described the absence as lasting well over two weeks is less clear. While extending its duration to such a lengthy period allowed a degree of drama, troublesome questions resulted, especially why so long an interruption in deliveries from the spy had been tolerated. Because aspects of the story may be true, his version has some value, but its falseness on certain points cannot be ignored.

On 6 November Papen gave the intelligence attaché a signal from Baron Steengracht, a young state secretary in the Foreign Ministry and a close friend of the minister, saying Ribbentrop expected him to arrive by plane in Berlin on 8 November. Steengracht ordered him to bring all original film, enlargements, and any other material that dealt with Cicero. The next day he took the night train to Istanbul, where he had a reserved seat on the morning courier plane. During a refueling stop in Sofia he was instructed to continue instead aboard a special plane that Kaltenbrunner had arranged for him. According to his account, Moyzisch therefore reached the capital late in the day on 8 November, remained for fourteen days, and then left on 22 November to resume work on the 26th. The trip may in fact have begun sooner than indicated and was probably briefer, apparently ending much earlier than the date given. Moyzisch must have been back in his office on or about 11 November, since he noted that he reported at once to Papen: on 12 November the ambassador began his own trip to Berlin and was beyond reach until 3 December. The schedules of both men were determined by new developments: Menemencioglu returned from the Cairo talks on 10 November. Papen made his journey to reassure his superiors that Turkey continued to resist all pressure; Moyzisch would have been needed to obtain Cicero's information on enemy reactions and further steps. In the ambassador's absence, Jenke submitted a long report concerning the situation on 15 November, which contained some material that had probably come from Cicero during the previous few days.[15] Bazna made no reference to a nineteen-day lapse in his contacts with Moyzisch. Nor is it believable that the eager Schellenberg would have allowed such a long break.

That Moyzisch misrepresented what occurred is clear too from his total omission of Schellenberg's role. At no point did he mention his immediate superior by name or indicate his participation in any of the talks. Instead he focused solely on Kaltenbrunner, as a supposed outside meddler. Perhaps the object of his lengthy description of the episode was merely to create drama or arouse sympathy by claiming an entrapment between the suspicious foreign minister and the powerful security chief. It is possible that the real purpose of his disingenuousness was to conceal the fact that he was undergoing evaluation and reprimand for his failure to discover more information about the spy. He was well aware of official impatience with his record in the case. Whatever elements of truth there may be in his account of the Berlin trip, it is worthwhile relating his version of what happened in the capital.

Moyzisch pretended in his account that he had no prior awareness of the power clash in Berlin: only when informed of the "fierce struggle," which soon took on a "violent nature," did he realize his problem. Then supposedly he understood why Kaltenbrunner had provided the special plane. But in fact Schellenberg had urged Kaltenbrunner's move. Upon learning of the summons through a radio message from Istanbul, he had quickly enlisted help from Kaltenbrunner to frustrate any scheme being hatched by the foreign minister. While such ready cooperation was somewhat unusual, Kaltenbrunner knew of the Schellenberg-Himmler campaign to oust Ribbentrop, whom all three regarded as an enemy. Schellenberg's presence at various meetings cannot be doubted, despite the evasions offered by Moyzisch.[16]

Immediately upon arrival, Moyzisch said, he was taken directly to Kaltenbrunner's office, where four unnamed experts examined the Cicero material he carried. It seems clear that Schellenberg was there as well. For nearly three hours the group questioned Moyzisch and made recordings of what he said. Meanwhile, the five rolls of film and 112 photographs were taken away, subjected to close inspection, and analyzed by the SD team; a report was returned at once. Moyzisch thought the documents' genuineness was accepted by Kaltenbrunner. After some time, Moyzisch would claim, he and Kaltenbrunner were left alone. The chief of security services explained his determination not to let Ribbentrop take credit for the spy operation, although the foreign minister would probably continue to argue that the material was being planted, and he noted that it was essential for Kaltenbrunner himself to insist that such valuable data be evaluated objectively and used. Therefore he intended to see Hitler and have the entire Cicero affair assigned to his departments. Kaltenbrunner acknowledged sending the £200,000. He told Moyzisch to take all future funds from him alone, obey only his orders, and remember that the foreign minister hated him and Papen both.[17] The latter warning was to prepare Moyzisch for Ribbentrop's wrath when they finally met.

In an understandable precaution, Kaltenbrunner's investigators had already sought to determine whether it was reasonable for the enemy ambassador in Ankara to possess critical information. The inquiries made about Sir Hughe and his character concluded just what Foreign Ministry officials had already known: London placed unusual confidence in the veteran ambassador and his vital role in strategically important Turkey. Kaltenbrunner nevertheless considered that discovery original enough to insist that Moyzisch draw the diplomat's special prominence to the attention of Papen. The instruction suggests how little the crude Kaltenbrunner and his largely doctrinaire SS assistants understood about foreign affairs and diplomacy.

Kaltenbrunner also insisted on an appraisal of Cicero. Following that profile, the visitor allegedly added, "I'm entirely convinced the man is genuine," skirting the issue of trusting his information. When he mentioned that an Englishman had perhaps killed the spy's father, Kaltenbrunner became furious at Ribbentrop, who supposedly had gotten that report from Ankara but had not shared it. After Moyzisch repeated the gist of his talk with the spy, he was told to check further into Cicero's story.

At the conclusion of their meeting Moyzisch asked his superior to telephone Ribbentrop to explain the delay in his arrival. Kaltenbrunner agreed and confirmed an appointment for the next evening on 9 November. Enjoying his advantage, he instructed Moyzisch to be certain to tell Ribbentrop that they had already discussed the operation. He was amused when the nervous Moyzisch counted the photographs in preparing to leave, for Kaltenbrunner was to keep the entire briefcase of material until the next day shortly before Moyzisch's appointment, when two men brought it to Moyzisch with strict orders to stay with him.

Despite the unsatisfactory results of their several investigations into Cicero's identity and activities, most German officials in time accepted the photographed documents as genuine. Those closest to the spy operation were first to be convinced. Moyzisch had come to believe in Cicero by the time he went to Berlin during the second week of November. He considered him, regardless of all his tales and pretensions, to be authentic. Papen initially worried about a hoax but soon offered cautious reassurance to Berlin. Following his inspection of "the content and circumstances" of the material, he thought it possible to conclude "with the greatest probability" that the proffered documents were reliable, bearing in mind that "deception is nevertheless not excluded."[10] Moyzisch related that similar views were expressed by Jenke. Leaders in the capital proceeded more cautiously, but Schellenberg and Kaltenbrunner soon concurred that the material could be trusted. Both Moyzisch and Schellenberg argued that the spy's untruthfulness about himself and his methods did not invalidate the reliability of his films; they eventually decided to take an expedient course that separated assessments of the vain and crafty Cicero from those of the British papers. Undoubtedly their attitude was influenced to some extent by eagerness for a major intelligence coup and by antipathy for the troublesome foreign minister.

Ribbentrop remained the principal and most intransigent opponent of trusting Cicero. Wary from the outset of a situation that seemed too good to be true, he suspected an enemy trap, though he welcomed certain reports and wanted credit if the source proved useful. The cause of his doubts and immovability lay not in any sort of reasoned judgment but rather in a slavish loyalty to the regime and a dogged pursuit of old antagonisms. Despite his ministry's loss of importance as the war spread, Ribbentrop retained ready access to Hitler, protecting his own special rights and censoring the information he conveyed. His insistence that only he could channel to Hitler matters dealing with external relations led him to counter all attempts by SD officials to present foreign political intelligence on their own. Because it was also his practice to avoid giving Hitler bad news whenever possible, "describing the source of all such reports as untrustworthy," the prospects revealed in Cicero's photographs were not weighed or argued with much realism. Papen managed to bypass him, but Hitler rebuffed him when he raised broad policy issues. The ambassador understood the early doubts, "that for some time the whole thing was regarded as a clever ruse on the enemy's part," but not the foreign minister's obstinacy.[19]

Old antagonisms helped form Ribbentrop's attitude and wary approach. He looked upon all the other principals in the affair—Papen, Schellenberg, Kaltenbrunner, and Moyzisch—as enemies, and he was sure that the leaders of the SS were actually conspiring against him. His long-standing hatred of Papen also colored his thinking, for the parvenu minister not only envied the former chancellor's prestige but also doubted his commitment and loyalty to the regime, by his own standard of fanatical Nazism. Ribbentrop monitored the ambassador's activities through special reports from Ankara without ever getting sufficient information to move against him, but his frustrations made him ill disposed to trust anything the ambassador might endorse. Ribbentrop even harbored hostility toward Moyzisch, over an episode earlier in 1943. Archbishop Francis Spellman of New York had visited the region during May to learn more about the Balkans and Middle East. Papen thought that through the cleric he might gain access to Franklin D. Roosevelt, a channel for queries to Washington about terms for negotiating peace. Ribbentrop had twice rejected any such contact with Spellman, but the ambassador disregarded him. Moyzisch served as intermediary to arrange for a German Catholic attorney to approach the archbishop on behalf of Papen. Ribbentrop intervened forcefully to prevent any meeting, however, and he still remembered the involvement of Moyzisch.[20]

The interview set for 9 November did not take place. Kaltenbrunner's two men who brought the briefcase of materials to Moyzisch's hotel had been ordered not to be separated from Moyzisch. Upon arriving at the Foreign Ministry the three saw Steengracht and another official, Günther von Altenburg, who both examined Moyzisch's photographs and seemed convinced the British documents were genuine. Steengracht said that other information Berlin had received agreed with an item in one of them about Allied decisions reached at Casablanca. He thought that the material was too important to have been released in a trick. Then the officials informed Moyzisch that the foreign minister could not see him (perhaps because he had not come alone). He was to remain available in Berlin for a future meeting, until which time they would keep his photographs.

Two days later, on 11 November, Moyzisch was summoned to meet another official of the Foreign Ministry, Rudolf Likus, in an annex building. Likus took him to see Ribbentrop. In the car en route, Likus warned him that Ribbentrop was in a foul temper: he was more certain than ever that the Cicero documents were a British trap, remained furious over Kaltenbrunner having outmaneuvered him, became enraged if Papen's name was mentioned, and held a deep grudge against Moyzisch over the Spellman affair. Under no circumstances should Moyzisch contradict him on any point or use Papen's name during the interview.

At the meeting the three sat around a conference table. Moyzisch observed how pressure had aged the minister who, he learned, considered himself greater than Bismarck. Ribbentrop queried the visitor about the documents, obviously not accepting their authenticity, and asked about conclusions reached by Jenke. Moyzisch answered that Jenke believed them genuine and added that Papen did also, forgetting Likus's warning and provoking Ribbentrop's wrath. The only thing the minister wanted to believe was that Moscow and the West had developed a rift over strategic issues. He appeared unable to overcome his misgivings and fidgeted with the material, finally tossing it on his desk. At one point he asked Moyzisch if he could really handle the Cicero case or should be replaced. Likus finally intervened to ease tensions, suggesting that Moyzisch focus on learning whether Cicero worked alone, an approach approved by Ribbentrop. Moyzisch was at last curtly dismissed but told to remain at the minister's call in Berlin. It mattered little that an anxious Cicero would be worried by his absence; in fact it may have been Ribbentrop's intention to destroy the whole contact.[21]

Although he had talked with Moyzisch before his subordinate saw the foreign minister, Schellenberg later had a fuller session with him, discussing the whole operation and trying to analyze Ribbentrop's aims and motives. Schellenberg thought the spy's material was worth the "tremendous expenditure" despite the credibility problems created by Cicero. He agreed with Moyzisch that discrepancies in the man's stories had only "incidental importance," because the documents "spoke for themselves" and conformed to the general picture of developments that Schellenberg had already formed. He admitted that Cicero's varying tales about himself made it harder to convince others, especially Hitler, of the spy's usefulness. Schellenberg believed that the significance of the information made it imperative for him to encourage its effective use, because of the serious implications for Germany: "I told Moyzisch that I still hoped to be able to carry through the peace plans which I had discussed with Papen."[22]

Despite the fact that Cicero had been given no forewarning of his absence, Moyzisch later said, he was required to remain in Berlin for two full weeks. He saw the foreign minister only once. In blaming the long delay on Ribbentrop, who on 22 November ordered his return to Ankara at once, Moyzisch again struck a note of falseness; Kaltenbrunner could readily have outmaneuvered the minister had a key subordinate been so detained by Ribbentrop. Actually, however, by then the visitor had probably returned to his post. Soon the contest for control of the spy's information was being conducted on other grounds. Moyzisch said that he departed by train that night as unusually heavy British air raids were destroying many blocks in the central administrative quarter of Berlin. Not until October 1945 would he touch German soil again.[23]

Meanwhile, lapses of security in Berlin fed such widespread rumors and speculation that Moyzisch feared for the operation's safety. A sizable number of officials in both the Foreign Ministry and the RSHA knew something about the new source of information. While there were probably some leaks from both departments, it seems likely that most career diplomats and analysts followed their training in discretion but that the party's enthusiastic amateurs hinted and boasted. Moyzisch reported discovering that important public figures and party leaders attending a social affair in suburban Berlin in mid-November all seemed to have heard of the informant and expected him to add details about Cicero. He refused, but lack of specific facts only encouraged various tales and theories. Some considered the spy an obvious British double agent; others thought that Nazi propagandists had simply created the man. No supposition was too outlandish. One story maintained that Cicero undoubtedly was the special friend of a homosexual British diplomat and so learned secrets. Competing to acquire or claim inside knowledge of the operation, the rumormongers apparently gave little thought to how they endangered the real source.

Perhaps another indication of widespread awareness among the capital's elite of both Moyzisch and the nature of his operation was the special invitations he received. He was asked to see Rashid Ali el-Gailani, the former Iraqi premier, and the Grand Mufti of Jerusalem to discuss regional issues and prospects. Those occasions may not have resulted from his Cicero role, of course, but Moyzisch was otherwise hardly a prominent political or social figure. More specific evidence was his invitation to tea with the Japanese ambassador, Hiroshi Oshima, and that diplomat's remark revealing knowledge of the spy. It is understandable that Papen became "really angry" upon hearing Moyzisch's reports of such incidents.[24] The objective was to establish the genuineness of the spy's information; gossiping and bragging about the still uncertain situation was highly foolish. No harm or adverse effects seem to have resulted from the loose talk, however, and the rumors probably subsided as new topics and events made their impact.

Information supplied by Cicero became available within Berlin's highest official circle. Schellenberg had insisted on receiving the negatives quickly, so that his technicians could make copies for a distribution list presumably approved by Kaltenbrunner.[25] Although Moyzisch's original reports apparently failed to survive the war, there remain some summaries of the intelligence data he forwarded, plus a substantial number of scattered references to the material, often fragmentary but showing that it was communicated to top German leaders. Ribbentrop reportedly showed the first documents at once to Hitler.[26] Nonetheless, identifying officials who mentioned the information does not necessarily establish that they accepted it as authentic or considered it in planning. While most apparently did come to believe the intelligence trustworthy, they seldom proved willing or able to grasp its full meaning, the dictator himself not letting the reports alter his outlook.

One of the earliest indications of how quickly the Cicero items circulated is evidence that the Propaganda Ministry's head received compilations within just two weeks. Joseph Goebbels alluded to the new source in his diary entry for 13 November: "I have received confidential information which enables me to appraise the Moscow Conference." After noting the differences between the Soviet and Western approaches to various issues, he concluded that "on the whole England and America got the short end of the deal," but he expressed gratification that the British and Turkey had reached no accord on bases. Another diary entry a week later, citing "a number of authentic reports" received, confirmed the denial of air bases.[27] There seems little doubt where such items came from.

High military and naval officials also got pertinent information at an early date. One researcher has found a reference to the Cicero data, for instance, in the 12 November entry in the Naval Staff diary. General Hans Speidel confirmed early knowledge of the results of the Tehran Conference. There are other instances as well.[28]

That Hitler had conversations about the spy is supported in references of late 1943. Papen spoke to him of Cicero: "I also gave details of a new source of information which was to prove of the greatest possible value to us in the coming months."[29] Documentary evidence comes from records of a December conference that dealt with the military situation. In referring to special reports the dictator said, "I have mostly studied through these documents. There is absolutely no doubt that the attack in the west is coming in the spring." He thought there might neverthe-less be distractions elsewhere—the Balkans, the French coast along the Bay of Biscay, or Norway. Both the wording and context of Hitler's remarks would indicate that recent Cicero films prompted his conclu-sion about the assault. Foreign Ministry records confirm that he had been sent the material.[30] Yet opinion about whether Hitler ever fully trusted Cicero's reports has remained divided.[31]

* * *

It seems remarkable that Moyzisch never developed more accurate in-formation about Cicero during their long association. With the spy vol-unteering almost nothing about himself and resenting all questioning, the intelligence attaché's task was difficult and prolonged, but his find-ings were inadequate. His ultimate defense to his superiors, and one Schellenberg raised too, was that personal details were unimportant, only the documents carried weight. Also, several points about his visit to the capital seem to be questionable. It is not unlikely that the real purpose of the summons was to reprimand him for his lack of initiative in learning more about the spy. He also omitted any mention of Schel-lenberg, even though given their thrust and content some remarks that he attributed to Kaltenbrunner would more aptly have been made by Schellenberg. Nor did he indicate that Papen too was in Berlin during part of the same period; he could not have briefed the ambassador upon his return as he said. Finally, it appears implausible that he would have been kept away from Ankara for a period of nineteen days at such a critical time. Thus the suspicion arises that for dramatic effect Moy-zisch adjusted many aspects and details of the episode.

Eagerness for an intelligence coup undoubtedly influenced how sen-ior officials in the security service evaluated and presented the mate-rial. Another factor was their antipathy toward the foreign minister, who blocked any extension of their powers. Yet neither the photographs nor repeated arguments convinced Ribbentrop and some others to trust the information completely. Meanwhile, the repercussions of his un-necessary stubbornness in the lengthy jurisdictional quarrel over han-dling the spy's films were harmful. Still, it is unrealistic to expect such dedicated and determined Nazis to have admitted that victory was a chimera and catastrophe quite likely. The resulting conflict over the import and appropriate use of the enemy secrets became more obvious and significant as the ambitious spy entered his most productive period.

7 Operation Bernhard

Bazna's insistence that the huge sums he demanded be paid in British currency posed no real problem for his contact's superiors in Berlin. Nothing in fact could be easier or cheaper to satisfy than just such a request: through the circumstance of having been referred to an SD agent, he had stumbled upon a deep financial resource. The only difficulty was that the willing providers dealt in fake money. Perhaps he ought to have become suspicious when the amounts he sought were not seriously challenged, but he remained unaware until after the war that nearly all his notes were bogus. His self-importance and greed probably convinced him that his pleased employers felt that his services warranted the outlay. Yet the over-confident and trusting Cicero became the biggest and most publicized victim of the Nazis' wartime scheme to counterfeit enemy currencies.

Operation "Bernhard" evolved as a secret project of the SD's Section F. Its success combined elements of audacity, coercion, and ingenuity in overcoming technical problems, and the quality of its specimens and the magnitude of its production were impressive. In the beginning, Nazi leaders planned to circulate large quantities of the worthless money in order to undermine the British and other economies. Later necessity forced them instead to use the counterfeit notes to finance critical purchases in neutral countries and also intelligence operations in foreign and occupied areas—such as paying someone like Cicero.

Schellenberg came to control the distribution of all the counterfeit pounds, like those supplied to Moyzisch. The manner in which he acquired and oversaw the forgery project illustrates well the nature and pattern of power struggles at the top echelons of the regime. Only through his responsibility for both the Cicero and Bernhard operations can the spy affair's financial dimension be understood. The huge amount reportedly paid to Bazna never strained the counterfeiting scheme. Despite a number of crises, the activities of Operation Bernhard continued until almost the end of the war. At that point the reluctance of a supervisor and some prisoner-workers to destroy all traces of their project and artistry led to discovery of the enterprise by the victors.

* * *

Alfred Naujocks was the mastermind behind the forgery scheme, which had first been named Operation "Andreas."[1] He was a "typical product of the S.S.-Gestapo, a sort of intellectual gangster," educated, determined, and ruthless, and he certainly had a rather curious career.[2] Naujocks at the beginning of the war headed the SD's document-forging and special projects section in Berlin. In 1939 he found himself in unfriendly competition with the similarly young and ambitious Schellenberg. Naujocks's proposal in late summer 1939 to counterfeit British pounds was undoubtedly intended to gain favor with Heydrich and thwart his principal rival. He argued that circulation of fake bank notes—German planes were to drop them over Britain—would create confusion and instability in enemy lands. Any such undertaking required Hitler's formal permission, even for planning. After carefully reviewing his subordinate's idea, Heydrich submitted the necessary memorandum, and Hitler conditionally approved the scheme in November, specifically forbidding, however, any copying of dollars.[3]

A successful effort at counterfeiting required that solutions be found for many critical problems. Difficulties were all the greater since British pounds were to be duplicated. Bank of England notes of higher denominations used during the early 1940s retained the basic design and white background familiar since the mid-1850s; the current issues were "still printed by letterpress from electrotypes." Now, however, there were new safeguards. Early wartime changes affected primarily the £1 note and paper replacements for coins, but counterfeiting the notes of larger value—£5, £10, £20, £50—still posed an array of major difficulties.[4] Even the highly qualified technical personnel in Naujocks's SD workshop were hard pressed to surmount them. There were countless problems in producing the proper paper, developing the ink, engraving acceptable plates, numbering the notes, identifying the signers, and in general turning out a product that could pass close scrutiny. Under the circumstances it is not surprising that the SD spent well over a year carrying out experiments.

As Naujocks and others later explained, an investigator checked past counterfeiting schemes to ascertain the most common difficulties and pitfalls; careful analysis of British notes identified at least 160 distinctive features; and a team of highly skilled engravers, sworn to secrecy, worked in three shifts to create plates. Duplicating Britain's linen-based paper had kept two German paper mills busy; Turkey itself supplied the pure linen needed. Even when the Germans thought their ink samples perfect, the color in the actual printing was not quite right; chemical imitation of Britain's local water became necessary. Giving notes an appearance of reasonable age required allowing a little ink seepage from printed lines into surrounding areas. Mathematicians figured out the serial numbering system. All these activities took more time than Naujocks had anticipated (the watermark problem, solved in mid-February 1941, being among the last major hurdles), and the annoyance of Heydrich with both the delays and the supervisor mounted. Finally, in late spring 1941, enough samples were ready for product tests. Agents submitted small quantities of the notes to various banks in neutral countries with specific requests that they be inspected to determine their genuineness.[5] Eventually officials decided that the £5 and £10 notes could be considered usable.

During its eighteen months of existence Operation Andreas produced about £500,000 in acceptable counterfeit notes.[6] It fell victim to power struggles within the SS, however, and in mid-1941 the project came to a temporary halt. Naujocks had incurred the wrath of Heydrich: he had apparently made sound recordings when Heydrich visited a Berlin bordello (the Salon Kitty) and had also violated financial laws. Evidence of illegal gold and currency transactions was produced as the means first to break Naujocks to the lowest rank in the SS and then to post him to the new Russian front, where some at least hoped he might be killed in action. That was not to happen; Naujocks not only knew too many state secrets to allow him to be exposed to capture but also still had powerful allies and protectors in the SS.[7] Heydrich meanwhile worked out his anger and frustration against Department VI. He replaced Major General Heinz Jost as administrator, removed various other subordinates, and let Operation Andreas become largely inactive.

From the beginning the counterfeiting scheme had been controversial within the upper echelons of the RSHA. SS administrators often held attitudes or aligned their stands on the basis of old antagonisms and personal interests. Heydrich's support of the plan tempered the opposition, because everyone knew he coveted advancement and wanted to succeed Himmler. He was not a man to be crossed. Nonetheless, at least three department heads—Otto Ohlendorf of Amt III (domestic intelligence), Heinrich Müller of Amt IV (Gestapo), and Heinz Jost of Amt VI (foreign intelligence)—worked in secret against the project. Schellenberg had meanwhile pursued his own subtle intrigues against Naujocks and others, with protection first from Heydrich and then as the new favorite of Himmler. He inherited the counterfeiting scheme in June 1941, when the attack on Russia began and Heydrich made him head of Department VI on an acting basis. For nearly a year he followed his superior's orders about the extent and future of the project, but he was fearful of making mistakes or being entrapped, and it was a time of little progress for the counterfeiting plan. His main task was to decide on occasional uses of the notes already printed. Activity increased only when Heydrich's successor, Kaltenbrunner, instructed Schellenberg to expand the operation. Thus he found himself fully responsible for the troublesome project, shielded by Kaltenbrunner and Himmler, badgered by Ohlendorf and Müller, and having to complete its reorganization and a major expansion.

During 1942 the counterfeiting scheme was reconstituted as Operation Bernhard. Heydrich had started to restructure it in late summer 1941, but after his appointment in September to govern Bohemia-Moravia the plans tended to languish, with little work done, and his death the following June left Himmler and his advisers to set their own course.[8] There were certainly compelling reasons to revitalize and improve the whole operation given the new military conditions, both failure to defeat the Soviet Union and the formal entry of the United States into the war, developments that by prolonging the conflict would require more expedient approaches and measures. Heydrich had already reassigned production aspects of the project to Naujocks's former assistant, Bernhard Krüger, a major who now directed the forgeries section, VI F 4. (It was from Krüger's name that the operation had been given the code name Bernhard.)[9] His involvement provided valuable continuity during a period of administrative change. Schellenberg had broad supervisory responsibility for the project, controlling all distribution, but he remained cautious, being only the temporary head of Department VI. Not until early 1943, when Himmler confirmed Kaltenbrunner to oversee all RSHA activities and Kaltenbrunner regularized Schellenberg's post, did Schellenberg become comfortable about expanding Operation Bernhard and spurring Krüger's production efforts.

Much had to be done. A year had passed, key personnel from Operation Andreas were now unavailable, and many of the records of the earlier effort had been destroyed or mislaid. To give Krüger a larger and better protected work space, Block 19 was constructed at the Sachsenhausen concentration camp north of Berlin, and within the following year he required Block 18 also. The move to the camp was dictated not only by secrecy but also by the nature of the new work force. Government ministries and banks had refused technical assistance to even an official counterfeiting operation. Therefore the SD had turned to political prisoners and concentration camps to find men skilled in engraving and printing; as a result, the project's forty or so workers formed a highly diverse group, including many Jewish prisoners. In time another hundred men, carefully selected, were added to the team.[10]

Meeting the growing demand for counterfeit pounds soon placed a heavy burden on the production workers. The printing of notes in small but common denominations (£5, £10, and £20) could barely keep pace with orders.[11] When instructions came to prepare counterfeit £50 notes, certainly conspicuous in both value and any large quantities and therefore risky, Krüger had to create plates of exceptional quality. They were finished in September 1943, and soon thereafter production began.[12] He also worried about diminishing supplies of the pure linen without which his paper could never pass close inspection.

A certain amount of variation in printing remained unavoidable, and notes had to be monitored continuously for production flaws. The checking went beyond basic acceptability, since the quality of individual notes would determine their use. The more likely it was that bills would be subjected to immediate and rigorous scrutiny (in neutral countries they would be submitted quickly to bank experts or returned to the nation of supposed origin), the less useful they were for circulation through any obvious or readily traceable channels. Thus all notes were assigned to one of three categories: top-grade bills were earmarked for purchases in neutral countries and expenses in foreign intelligence operations; medium-quality production could be used with care in occupied areas for certain transactions and to pay informants and collaborators, who dared not present enemy currency in banks; and notes with slight imperfections were set aside for minor deals, where flaws could be risked.[13]

Counterfeit pounds were not Krüger's only kind of assignment. Himmler had the idea of circulating caricatures of British postage stamps, a scheme no one else considered worth the effort, and hard-pressed Sachsenhausen workers had to prepare various samples. Their overprinted wording and design changes were intended to suggest that political and secret opposition movements existed at home and in the colonies. Their sole value lay in short-term propaganda. Schellenberg and others delayed action, and the project was soon forgotten by Himmler.[14]

A major new challenge came when Kaltenbrunner ordered the counterfeiting of American dollars to supplement the supply of pounds. Krüger thought the plan had come too late in the war to help Germany. Complicated preparations nevertheless began during the autumn of 1944, and the first $100 bills were produced early in the following year. They appeared to be satisfactory specimens, and Kaltenbrunner was pleased with this new technical feat. Shortly thereafter Himmler let them be run, and about 5,000–6,000 notes were printed. They were less skillfully made than the pound notes, however, and the war ended before a set of much better plates could be put into use.[15]

Meanwhile, the production operation was proving too efficient. Before long, Krüger was concerned that output, with runs of 400,000 notes a month, would reach the total Himmler had set. Since he wanted to avoid being reassigned to a military front, and the prisoners feared for their lives, the participants conspired to slow operations and create more work.[16] Part of the production was arbitrarily called substandard, and some of the finest notes were hidden in large wooden crates. Those boxes would give away the scheme at the war's end.

Distribution of the counterfeit notes presented nearly as many difficulties as did the technical aspects, and it proved to be unexpectedly dangerous, because zealous Reich police officials charged with enforcing strict currency regulations were kept unaware of the operation. The original plan to drop the specimens over Britain had been abandoned even before full production began.[17] Then the problem became one of how the money might be used safely in neutral or occupied countries. There was firm opposition from military occupation authorities, the Gestapo chiefs, and government finance managers to anything threatening economic stability. They were especially concerned about encouraging the black market and undermining their nation's own currency. Yet the SD was so critically short of foreign monies for its intelligence work that it eventually undertook secret sales and made common use of the fake British pounds.[18]

The SD used two methods of circulation. A simple but risky expedient was to spend the currency on purchases in neutral countries; a safer arrangement was to sell the worthless notes to unsuspecting buyers, for authentic currencies. Many people were willing to pay large amounts of their own money for the pound notes, and the approach developed into a lucrative system, purchasers being forced either to keep the bogus notes hidden or to reexchange them secretly. Problems arose from Hitler's ban on distributions in occupied countries, an order increasingly ignored as channels multiplied, and from illegal transactions attracting Gestapo interest and investigation. Distribution was arranged through selected intelligence agents and German businessmen, who sold the notes on a commission basis. Some SD agents engaged carelessly in black market activities; some German entrepreneurs drew attention to their new fortunes.

Italy became the major field for clandestine sales, partly because it was an ally rather than an occupied area, partly because it offered easy access from Germany; in the confusion surrounding its surrender in 1943, there were many anxious buyers for the notes. One key figure there was Friedrich Schwend, an expatriate businessman with international connections, whose obvious profits angered Müller and Ohlendorf. Schellenberg more than once had to seek help from Kaltenbrunner. Still, the scheme was too useful in meeting operating expenses to be stopped. The head of SD intelligence in southeastern Europe, Wilhelm Höttl, later acknowledged that his department "had acquired a very large capital at a very small cost" by pursuing such arrangements during 1943–1944.[19]

Another important use for the British pounds was to disarm resistance groups, by buying up weapons they received from the Allies or acquired themselves. Werner Hartmann handled such deals in Yugoslavia. The partisans often needed cash and did not know the buyers were enemy agents. Similar purchases in Italy reduced the arms available to the resistance after Germany occupied its former ally. Counterfeit notes also helped create a German intelligence network there and finance Mussolini's rescue from the new government.[20]

Providing field agents with operating funds had been an early use of the bogus notes despite the serious risks involved in the practice. Agents using them in neutral countries might find themselves suddenly exposed; those caught in enemy territory learned that possession of fake notes identified them as spies or saboteurs; those using inferior specimens faced dangers that made their missions almost suicidal. Britain's discovery of fake currency led or contributed to the apprehension of a number of intelligence agents sent by the Germans. The cumulative evidence from such incidents helped convince London that Berlin itself stood behind some sort of counterfeiting scheme.[21]

Schellenberg was nevertheless persuaded by his advisers in 1943 to make greater use of the improved counterfeit notes. Yet he still would not act without Kaltenbrunner's approval, and that meant that both Himmler and Hitler had to authorize the SD's use of bogus money in field work. Hitler raised no objection as long as the fake pound notes were not circulated in occupied Europe.[22] That restriction was first circumvented and then simply ignored as time passed. A curious postwar comment by Schellenberg about the subsequent SD operations reveals much about him: "I used the notes myself for the financing of enterprises abroad where I knew that I had to deal with cold-blooded and mercenary businessmen."[23] He obviously believed that such qualities were not attributable to himself, merely a dedicated official. His description may well, however, have been meant to include one individual of note: Cicero, to whom Schellenberg authorized and supplied payments. Their eventual total must have impressed him with the greed and cunning of the spy who demanded such huge sums.

Awareness of the German forgeries in 1943 prompted the British government to act. To avoid causing alarm and instability, the reason for its new measures was concealed behind other concerns. Therefore the spokesman for the Cabinet told Parliament that "to provide an additional handicap to those who may contemplate breaches of exchange control and other regulations" the Bank of England would cease issuing notes above £5. In this way the government expected to isolate notes circulating abroad and make both tax evasion and black market trading more difficult.[24] While such goals seemed reasonable and worthwhile, the true purpose was to protect the integrity of high-value notes in domestic use and to identify all currency coming from outside the nation so as to subject it to the most careful scrutiny. Those acquiring notes of large denominations abroad would have to prove the legitimate nature of their currency holdings; they would nevertheless not be told that quantities of counterfeit pound notes were in circulation and subject to confiscation.

* * *

The significant question of whether Moyzisch knew he was paying Cicero in batches of fake British pounds cannot be answered conclusively; evidently the initial payment did consist of genuine notes.[25] Yet he had good reason to suspect something was wrong, given his superiors' ready approval of later expenditures, the vast supply of notes, and his close contacts with colleagues in the capital who knew the source of the seemingly unlimited funds. Among those SD officials was the coordinator of political intelligence for the Balkan region, Höttl, whom Heydrich had dismissed during his extensive departmental purge but whom Schellenberg had rehired. Höttl and others knew all about Operation Bernhard from working closely with Schellenberg.[26] Still, there would have been no specific reason to apprise Moyzisch of the scheme in order for him to fulfill his duties. Moyzisch's whole attitude also seems to suggest that he was not anxious to share in the secrets and intrigues of the high SD officials. Several occurrences concerning the money he handled should have aroused and sustained the suspicions of anyone in his position, but he later claimed to have been satisfied with various assurances given him.[27]

During his visits to Berlin he admitted having heard "hints and rumors" about the printing of British pounds for secret uses. While maintaining the fiction that he was a diplomat and that the "Wilhelmstrasse," or Foreign Ministry, sent his funds, he had heard the counterfeiting stories in his own department. Queries to colleagues and superiors had all met with firm denials.

He would also tell of undertaking a favor for Cicero about a month into the spy operation. A bit earlier the valet had asked for £5,000, to be paid in American dollars, which he wanted for a special investment and could not risk getting himself; Moyzisch had withheld the sum from Cicero's payments and approached the embassy's own bank. The manager replied that the timing was good: an Armenian businessman going abroad had requested sterling for his American dollars. The exchange was made without problems. A short time later the bank manager telephoned Moyzisch in distress to report that the pounds were counterfeit: the notes had passed to a Swiss businessman who had taken them to Britain and learned they were bogus. Tracing them back to Ankara had been quite easy. Moyzisch notified Berlin, which supposedly told him that the notes sent to him could not have been counterfeit and that either a switch had been made or there had been a swindle. To avoid a scandal Moyzisch was instructed to draw upon embassy funds to reimburse the Ankara bank and to conclude the matter quietly. In later relating the incident he again implied that the Foreign Ministry had issued the orders to protect its diplomatic mission. The ministry and Papen probably knew nothing of the episode or the SD's handling of it. Under the circumstances it seems highly likely that the bank's reimbursement simply consisted of more counterfeit notes, good enough to pass scrutiny at the local level.

Moyzisch claimed that he nevertheless remained suspicious, picking random samples from each bundle of notes in his safe, finally extracting a total of nearly £10,000.[28] He took the notes to the Istanbul bank used by the German consulate-general and requested a careful check, explaining that the currency had to be verified as genuine. He learned in due time from the Turkish manager that the British notes had been found to be good. So, Moyzisch said, he no longer worried about the money that Berlin sent. In fact his account indicated that the manager had reported back in only a few days, making a thorough check unlikely; the forgeries were clearly good enough to pass such inexpert inspections.

Given his official position and own comments about his several experiences, it is impossible to believe that Moyzisch failed to grasp the real situation but was convinced that the quantities of enemy currency were indeed genuine. The truth would appear to be that though he harbored strong suspicions, he decided against being too inquisitive and thereby risking his position, and to continue to distribute the money. Moyzisch undoubtedly felt that he owed his loyalties to himself, his organization, and his government rather than to the greedy Cicero.

Operation Bernhard continued long after the conclusion of Operation Cicero, but by early 1945 the project was no longer safe at Sachsenhausen—the possibility of air raids and even ground attack was too great—and Himmler therefore decided to close down the SD's forgery scheme. Krüger persuaded him that instead it could be transferred to Austria, there to continue making currency and false credentials for the Nazis' use. Hitler also agreed. Personal antagonisms and departmental rivalries persisted even at that late stage, however, and the relocation took place amid deliberate harassment and frustrating delays. Kaltenbrunner gave instructions about the transfer to Ohlendorf, who let old hatreds shape his actions, Krüger at the time being absent from Sachsenhausen. Krüger's assistant, SS-Lieutenant Hansch, commanded the convoy of trucks that moved the men and equipment to Mauthausen concentration camp near Linz, where the workers suffered during winter conditions in makeshift housing until Krüger arrived and moved them to Redl-Zipf, where extensive caverns had been chosen to accommodate the Bernhard project. Krüger installed the men and equipment in a long tunnel known as Gallery 16. Not until April was printing resumed.[29] By then it was too late.

Himmler soon issued a new order to Krüger: obliterate all evidence of the operation. Records and all supplies of notes and paper were to be burned, plates and dies sunk in the deep nearby lakes, and all the prisoners sent to the main camp to be killed. Krüger delegated the tasks to Hansch. He himself disappeared, with a large quantity of sound money obtained through black market dealings and sales of forged personal documents and passports.[30] Only long afterward was he found and questioned by investigating reporters.

For three days everyone burned supplies of the poorer notes and many records of the operation. Hansch then decided against assuming responsibility for the total destruction that Krüger had ordered. Instead he had the plates and best notes, already crated, loaded on three trucks for transport to the "Alpine Fortress" area, where diehard supporters of the crumbling regime talked of holding out in a mountain redoubt. Kaltenbrunner had already established new headquarters at Alt Aussee. The small convoy was beset with mishaps. When one truck broke down, Hansch had all its cases of money thrown into the Traun river; within days the boxes would break open and huge quantities of notes would float away. When another truck had trouble, Hansch gave its cargo to an army captain and got a Wehrmacht receipt. Kaltenbrunner instructed him to continue with the last truck, but jammed roads ended his journey near the Grundlsee. There Hansch encountered a naval research unit that had been working on secret projects in the nearby Toplitzsee area. With aid from the navy personnel the remaining cases were thrown into the lake. Hansch had meanwhile ordered the workers at Redl-Zipf taken for their own safety to Ebensee. There the arriving Americans soon liberated them.[31]

In the end the "Alpine Fortress" failed to materialize, and French and American forces swept across southeastern Germany into Austria's rugged lake area. A number of high-ranking SS officers who had relocated there, in some cases because they were Austrian by birth and knew the region, were caught in the massive Allied roundup of prisoners. Kaltenbrunner was taken into custody in the Alt Aussee area;

Höttl later swore he saw the infamous Adolf Eichmann there.[32] The man who had organized the extermination of Europe's Jews was nevertheless among the top officials who managed to escape.

* * *

The American counterintelligence officer in Austria who telephoned Major George McNally at Allied Headquarters in Frankfurt startled the military investigator with his report. Even in the shocking world of defeated Germany in May 1945, the incidents he related seemed hard to believe. A German army captain had just surrendered a truck loaded with crates of British money; nearby, Allied troops and local civilians were gathering more notes floating in an Austrian river. After rushing to Austria and verifying the facts, McNally notified the British, who dispatched a Bank of England official at once. Already McNally had calculated that the truck, each of its twenty-three big boxes holding neatly packed notes and a manifest, had carried a total of £21 million. Britain's wartime realization that the enemy had been counterfeiting its currency now turned into a nightmare.

McNally and a British team began a lengthy investigation into the astonishing dimensions of Operation Bernhard. The German had said that the truck had broken down near Redl-Zipf. A check of that area revealed the network of underground tunnels where the presses and equipment were. There were no plates, records, or supplies of paper. Tracing the workers from the project to Ebensee concentration camp, they learned that the men had survived but had now scattered, although Ebensee's camp registers listed their names and old addresses. About a third of the 140 workers were eventually located. Oskar Skala was found in Czechoslovakia: the former head bookkeeper's personal notebook would prove invaluable in sorting out the story.[33]

An extraordinary tale it was. The investigators ultimately concluded that nearly nine million British notes in denominations of £5, £10, £20, and £50 and with a total face value of about £140 million, or $564 million, had been printed and inventoried.[34] Accounting for their disposition posed great difficulty. After tabulating the load in the truck and confiscating the finds along the river, estimating the notes destroyed, and spending two months unsuccessfully diving in the Toplitz-see to recover the many boxes reportedly dumped there (information still considered suspect), no one could safely account for notes representing about two-thirds of the face value.[35] From recorded evidence and testimony the researchers estimated some distribution figures, although no one knew exactly how many notes had been circulated or were still hidden, and for years the counterfeit notes continued to surface around the world. It was thought that perhaps about £1.5 million ($6 million) had gone to Turkey for use there or in nearby regions.[36]

Only later would it be learned that many of those bogus notes had been used to pay the war's most daring spy.

* * *

When the war ended the British government realized immediately that it had to act quietly but decisively to protect Britain's currency and postwar economy. After 1943 the sole note larger than £1 still being issued was the "white fiver," or traditional £5 note. Subsequently the old high-denomination notes gradually disappeared from circulation as banks withdrew them; government officials announced that they would no longer be legal tender after designated dates. Discovery of the magnitude of the counterfeiting scheme affected the £5 note as well, forcing release in autumn 1945 of a replacement issue, similarly designed but with features that readily distinguished the notes from any German copies. They now contained a thin metal thread, employed a different system of serial numbering, and had thicker paper with an altered watermark.[37]

Too many people knew or had heard something about crates of foreign money dumped into Austrian lakes during the war's final days for the stories to be forgotten or easily discredited. Various attempts at underwater explorations at Toplitzsee proved unsuccessful but added to speculation. Then the Hamburg illustrated weekly *Stern* decided to probe the entire story and in 1958 located Krüger and others. The magazine got official permission to dive at Toplitzsee and had special equipment designed and built. Success came in summer 1959, after much dangerous work. Over a dozen cases filled with counterfeit money were recovered from the lake; others had to be left, because they were too deeply embedded in mud. Also recovered were the plates, account books, and other records of activities.[38] While the findings confirmed the persistent tales, making a sensational new story, the notes themselves had no special value.

Over the years the counterfeiting deception took in victims of all sorts, the eager and the reluctant, the legitimate and the disreputable, the careful and the unthinking, many convinced by their transactions or banks that the currency was authentic. Often the notes had passed through several owners and banks before their falseness was spotted; tracing the sums back through the system left many parties blameless but poorer victims. Although certainly not among the innocent holders, Bazna too was identified through his spending of large numbers of the worthless notes on his business ventures in Turkey; the banking records led directly to him. His life of wealth and comfort did not last for long.

8   Cicero's Outstanding Period

Cicero achieved his greatest success during December 1943 and the early weeks of 1944. Moyzisch was certain the spy's accomplishments during this period of critical developments would establish beyond question his credibility in Berlin: "Never before and never again did he deliver so much or such important material." Almost every northbound courier plane took fresh films of secret papers, surely meaning that "there could no longer be the slightest doubt about his genuineness."[1] Papen was more realistic about the attitudes of leaders in Berlin. Nevertheless, the spy's information was valuable because of its detailed coverage of a series of major Allied policy conferences and of Britain's subsequent efforts to persuade Turkey to abandon its neutrality and finally commit itself to active participation in the war. Ankara's steadfast resistance to such pressures soon brought about the worst period in its wartime relations with the exasperated British.

Throughout the weeks and stages of frustrating negotiations, Cicero provided more than enough evidence to let Germany counteract some moves and adjust its military thinking. In the end the Turks' own intransigence held Britain off and shaped events: Ankara, for reasons entirely of its own, acted in the manner most favorable to Germany. To understand the nature and scope of the issues and the significance of the spy's work it is necessary to look at both his continued activities and the goals being pursued by the opposing powers. The first phase of the situation covered development of a new Allied military plan and Turkey's rejection in mid-December of the resulting demand for a direct contribution.

* * *

Knowledge of his employer's routine and habits had confirmed that the spy's initial methods of operation were generally sound. Each day began with the valet bringing orange juice early in the morning; usually it followed a predictable schedule as to the diplomat's office hours and ordinary meals, and it ended with the ambassador's late-night study of papers in his bedroom.[2] December brought conditions that assisted Cicero's work. His employer was busier than ever, appearing at times distracted by and even upset over unfolding events. The difficult negotiations occasioned more frequent meetings away from the embassy, increased the number of reports and signals he needed to read or prepare, and exhausted him both physically and mentally. Undoubtedly he also became even less alert to security. Bazna in consequence had little trouble in copying an impressive number of items in December. Two elements in his later story about his activities produced denials, however, while another explained his greater access to the ambassador's safe.

The spy was to report that the diplomat often relaxed by playing the drawing-room piano after lunch. At such times the valet might pry into office papers, if the secretary was out, feeling safe as long as he heard the music. Bazna described one occasion when he entered the drawing room, bringing juice to his employer, and spontaneously began to sing a familiar passage from Wagner; an impromptu concert supposedly followed. The spy told of then photographing a number of papers while the diplomat continued to play. As already noted, Sir Hughe denied ever having accompanied Bazna, but he erred in adding that there had been no piano at the residence in Ankara.[3] The unusual tale was certainly the kind that Bazna might well have invented to satisfy his vanity. That he did entertain Moyzisch one night at a German friend's home is true; Moyzisch recalled the valet's pride in his voice and the way that music seemed to transform his face as he sang from *I Pagliacci*.[4] The incident with Knatchbull-Hugessen, however, may well be apocryphal. Although the whole matter lacks real significance, it captured popular imagination and lingered, contributing perhaps to other forms of innuendo.[5]

According to Bazna his nocturnal spying was made easier by Sir Hughe's use of sleeping pills. His description of one December incident stressed the point. Quietly entering the dark bedroom to extract papers from the black box, he noticed an empty water glass on the bedside table, a reassurance that the diplomat "had taken his sleeping pills as usual." He then copied the items in his own room. As he returned the documents to their case he knocked the glass to the floor; it broke, causing his employer to stir but not awaken. No problem arose in the morning, the ambassador thinking that he himself was responsible, and the valet removed the pieces. Knatchbull-Hugessen denied having

Map 2
Western Turkey and the Aegean Region in 1943–1944

Bulgaria and Romania were allies of Germany and Italy. Greece and nearly all the islands off Turkey's western coast were controlled by the Axis. Britain in autumn 1943 attacked but could not hold the islands of Cos and Leros. Istanbul lies on the European side of the Bosporus. Its vulnerability was a major factor in policy decisions.

used any sleeping aid, when the spy story emerged in 1950.[6] It seems reasonable to assume, however, that his statement was incorrect. Not only would long hours and stress have made normal rest difficult, but clearly the depth of sleep made him unaware of nearby sounds. It was not a question of one night or the truth of the broken glass tale, but of the spy's work on many nights. Bazna was such an egoist that he might well have claimed still greater daring, but in fact he mentioned the risk-reducing pills to Moyzisch. That an ambassador who kept valuable papers overnight at his bedside would not want to admit compounding his carelessness by using sleeping tablets is wholly understandable.

At this time the spy also acquired his own keys to the safe. Until mid-December he appears to have used sometimes the diplomat's keys while Sir Hughe was asleep. With his own set he was able to copy papers from the safe at other times as well. Having earlier provided a better key to unlock the black boxes, Schellenberg now again called upon his technicians in the SD, sending the spy a special wax and instructions for making impressions. Bazna apparently took them, while the ambassador slept, some time about the second week of December. For protection the wax was shipped in a special wooden box, Schellenberg then expediting creation and delivery of the keys to Ankara, where the spy reported back that they were a perfect fit.[7] He now believed that his opportunities for access to the ambassador's papers had few limits.

Film purchases from Cicero resumed in November, when Moyzisch returned from Germany with new instructions. There are discrepancies in the accounts, however, which leave the exact date uncertain. Moyzisch's statement placing him back in his office on 26 November referred to reporting at once to Papen about the trip.[8] In fact, however, the ambassador was himself away from Ankara from 12 November until 3 December, according to evidence from reliable records. Fortunately, the date of Moyzisch's return is not critical. What is important was the beginning of the valet's most valuable spy work.

Pierre, who during his contact's absence had telephoned repeatedly, succeeded in reaching Moyzisch the day he returned. As usual they spoke in French and arranged to play bridge: their code meant a meeting that same evening at their last rendezvous point. There Moyzisch discovered the spy using a flashlight to make "childish signals" to attract his attention and seeming in the "best of spirits" upon learning that he had been the reason for the Berlin trip. Cicero claimed to have taken many films, exposing some to daylight rather than risking keeping them. He offered one spoiled roll to Moyzisch, who refused to pay for it. They then drove to an apartment borrowed from a friend of Moyzisch, an embassy press attaché named Seiler; there Cicero seemed pleased with both himself and the comforts. The owner had left sandwiches and wine, and afterward there were fine cigars as well. Obviously Moyzisch wanted a relaxed atmosphere, to encourage Cicero's conversation. He paid him £15,000 for a roll delivered before his trip, exchanged fresh film for rolls he now received, and once more refused to pay Cicero for the ruined roll. Slipping it back into the spy's pocket, Moyzisch felt a gun, and Cicero then explained: "I don't intend to let them catch me alive." Moyzisch wondered if the dramatic words, repeated later that evening, would help convince doubters in Berlin. He told the spy frankly of his orders to learn more about his father's death. Cicero clearly resented being queried, but he gave a few details about how an English hunter had killed the beater by careless shooting, an account that would be forwarded in Moyzisch's report. Cicero left on his own rather than return by car with Moyzisch.[9]

The spy's background and motives were not Moyzisch's only special or pressing problem following his return to duty at the embassy. He had to reimburse the local bank that had discovered that the British notes he had exchanged for dollars at the valet's request were counterfeit. He also had to satisfy Cicero's urging for a partial payment in jewels. There were renewed inquiries from Berlin about how the photographs were being taken. Many rolls he now developed revealed that the spy had worked hurriedly: shots were out of focus and difficult to read. Then came the delivery with the exposure showing two fingers, at which point the photography expert arrived to evaluate the valet's skills and claims. Meanwhile, Bazna's lie about having to return a borrowed camera got the desired German response. Berlin, in its eagerness for quality photographs, had quickly provided a compact but more powerful Leica. Schellenberg also sent better darkroom equipment for Moyzisch. Totally useless, however, was the SD's shipment of a large package of books about real and fictional espionage cases that it thought might guide Moyzisch in dealing with the valet.[10]

December also proved awkward because of two orders conveyed to Moyzisch. In the first, he was specifically instructed not to show Papen any items received from Cicero and to give him absolutely no information. Moyzisch decided not to obey the directive, however, and discussed the whole situation with Papen. Toward the end of the month their arrangement got him into trouble when Papen's local use of the spy's material revealed that Moyzisch had disregarded his superiors' orders.[11] Even more significantly, Sir Hughe was alerted to the possibility of leakage. The other order involved cutting to £10,000 the payment for each acceptable roll, probably to limit circulation of bogus currency; the measure may have been prompted by Moyzisch's recent exchange trouble with the bank. Moyzisch again took the valet to his friend's apartment to inform him, hoping a convivial atmosphere would help, and was surprised to get no argument from Cicero. It was on that occasion that the spy sang for his contact.[12]

After a lull during the first week of December, by mid-month there were meetings "every second or third day," as the spy produced a steady flow of new films. Their routine seldom varied, the valet entering and leaving the slowly moving car on outlying dark streets, exchanging films for payments, and the driver returning to his office to work as late as necessary. Moyzisch became exhausted from having to do everything himself—maintaining contacts, processing films, typing reports, encoding signals, answering queries, and trying to avoid the jurisdictional feuding in Berlin. At times he was irritable, and he understandably became furious upon learning that Cicero once used Sir Hughe's private telephone to call him (because it was independent from the embassy switchboard). Had he been caught he planned to explain that he was calling a girlfriend. The foolish daring added to Moyzisch's mounting concern about Cicero's carelessness and display of wealth.[13] He knew that he must soon take some firm step. Meanwhile, he grew increasingly excited about the quantity of material he was handling. Bazna remained solely interested in his rapidly expanding wealth, however, and never realized until later his full achievement as Cicero. Any sense of satisfaction the men shared would be suddenly shaken, when one of their rendezvous became a dramatic car chase.

* * *

Britain began to press Turkey to enter the war as one of Churchill's goals for autumn 1943. The country's position was discussed repeatedly during a sequence of important meetings—the late October conference of Allied foreign ministers in Moscow, Anglo-Turkish talks in early November at Cairo, the Big Three conference at Tehran starting in late November, and Anglo-Turkish talks again in Cairo during December. Still, at every stage the prime minister encountered formidable obstacles to the implementation of his ambitious ideas and military plans. Roosevelt and his staff showed no interest in opening a major southeast European front, but Churchill proved persistent in his arguments for involving Turkey; Stalin gave a degree of encouragement, provided the prime minister could handle Ankara. Thus the task of arranging and defining any Turkish role in the war became Britain's problem, to pursue and resolve on its own.[14] In the event, there was simply no overcoming Turkey's caution, despite months of negotiations, and this aspect of Churchill's strategic concept ended in total failure. Supplying the enemy with photographs revealing Britain's secret position papers and changing assessments throughout the bilateral talks became Cicero's most significant achievement.

Eden made little headway on the Turkish question in the meetings at Moscow. The Americans continued to express little interest in either the region or Turkey's role; the Russians objected to any campaign detracting from a new western European front. Churchill nevertheless pressed his ideas in messages to Eden. He envisioned control of key Aegean islands, despite setbacks in the current fighting, and then Balkan landings under air cover. Churchill obviously worried about the future of southeastern Europe if the area fell to the Russians. Yet his vision and supporting arguments were too ambitious. Nothing concrete emerged, but a protocol drafted by Eden calling for coordinating the policies of Moscow and London toward Ankara was approved and formally signed on 2 November, before the conference adjourned.[15]

Churchill remained determined to force a Turkish commitment before the end of 1943. Menemencioglu was therefore invited to meet Eden in Cairo for joint staff discussions on 5 November. Despite illness, Menemencioglu skillfully countered all the arguments advanced by Eden, refusing any promises. He insisted that his own government would make any decision about entering the war; he sought to know what his country's precise military role and tasks in the operation would be; and he wanted assurance of protection if lending air bases brought retaliation. Eden recalled that even in "three days of ding-dong argument" the British failed to dispel the notion that London had made some secret deal with Moscow. In the end the ministers agreed only that Ankara would soon give its ally a formal answer. Eden thereafter held a more realistic view than did Churchill about the stand to be expected from Turkey; he observed that "no one can be so deaf as a Turk who does not wish to be persuaded."[16]

On 19 November the Foreign Office conveyed the results of the Moscow Conference to Sir Hughe. The ambassador opposed the quickening of pressure by London and thought it potentially disastrous to bring Turkey into the conflict, given the uncertain state of military conditions.[17] Nevertheless, he followed his instructions. Menemencioglu raised the familiar points with Knatchbull-Hugessen. He indicated that Turkey could not act until the Allied land attack in western Europe had succeeded, since the Turks would not antagonize Germany without being convinced that an Allied victory was reasonably assured. Such a timetable meant that mid-summer 1944 was the earliest likely date for participation. While the foreign minister had "expressed himself in very definite terms," he stressed that he did not speak for his government, although he would approach others "with a view to confirming this undertaking." Sir Hughe reported that he still hoped to obtain an earlier commitment date from Ankara, yet he seemed satisfied with the conditions he had been given: "At least this would permit us to prolong the enemy's present state of uncertainty."[18] He had not yet realized, however, that no delay was acceptable.

Roosevelt and Churchill met Stalin at Tehran on 28 November. Churchill's opening remarks focused on the "biggest problem" of obtaining

solid assistance from Ankara: it might involve the lending of its airfields under cover of a benevolent neutrality, declaring war on Germany
and attacking Bulgaria along their border, or joining the conflict without undertaking any specific action. The prime minister expected Rome
to fall soon and worried about a long lull in the fighting before Overlord
began during late spring. He estimated that three divisions could clear
the islands in the Aegean, using Royal Air Force squadrons and several
flak regiments for Turkey's air protection, and insisted that all the
needed units and resources were available. Stalin and Roosevelt, however, opposed any delay in Overlord as a result of Churchill's plan.
Stalin made clear that the others must persuade Turkey to join the
war. Churchill observed that Ankara would be mad not to act so as to
please both Moscow and the West; the premier reminded Churchill that
neutrals like Turkey might prefer madness to fighting.[19]

In subsequent discussions the prime minister and his advisers returned to the troublesome topic. Churchill repeated his arguments, and
Eden reviewed his talks with Turkey's stubborn foreign minister in
Cairo. Although Stalin continued to offer some political support, he
declared bluntly that all such questions were minor, second to mounting the Overlord operation. Finally Churchill undertook himself "to
persuade or induce Turkey to enter the war before Christmas," since
the neutral country was Britain's ally, and he also expressed willingness to accept something less than full belligerency at the outset. Inönü
would therefore be asked to meet Roosevelt and Churchill when they
were once again in Cairo. Churchill declared that if Inönü declined to
travel abroad he would go to Adana instead. At that juncture he believed he had done rather well, "having got all I had thought it right to
ask, and with fair hopes that it would not be insufficient."[20]

Sir Hughe meanwhile extended to Inönü the Allied leaders' invitation to Cairo.[21] Wary of being presented with preset decisions, the president made clear his reservations, accepting only when assured of open
discussions. On 3 December a special train carrying the official party
as well as Knatchbull-Hugessen quietly left Ankara; at Adana the
group transferred to Roosevelt's personal plane. It arrived in Cairo on
4 December. During the following days Churchill pressed his plan vig-
orously. Yet Inönü displayed great caution, because his military staff
was clearly still impressed by German might. On 6 December the prime
minister nevertheless drafted an optimistic memorandum for his chiefs
of staff concerning the substance and timetable for what was called
Operation "Saturn": Ankara's maintenance of its current policies to
mislead Berlin; speedy preparation of airfields by British personnel in
civilian clothes so that during the first half of February fighter squadrons could land; concerted air and naval attacks to disrupt German
defenses and protect Turkey during the period of greatest danger; de-

velopment of all plans needed to seize Rhodes before the end of February, when the landing craft would be needed elsewhere; and Allied warnings of massive retaliation to intimidate the Bulgarians. The British considered the deadline for Turkey's active involvement to be 15 February.[22] After that Allied efforts had to be concentrated on making Overlord a success.

Turkish leaders continued to insist on huge amounts of military supplies and equipment before risking a break with Germany. Their stand was firm. The Turks clearly worried about Soviet plans: with no illusions about Moscow's goals to control the region, they thought it best to wait and watch, hoping that time would reveal Stalin's full ambitions and prospects. After lengthy discussions and fruitless efforts to overcome the Turks' fears, the Cairo meetings therefore ended without achieving the Allies' aims, although Turkish involvement in the war remained open to further negotiation. Inönü agreed only to explain his country's intentions in a note during the coming days, to compile and submit lists of its specific military needs, and to prepare a number of air bases for possible later use by the British.

Knatchbull-Hugessen subsequently reported with frustration and dismay not only the foreign minister's purported acceptance "in principle" of the proposals but also the obvious equivocating and temporizing in Ankara. Their relationship soon deteriorated. Menemencioglu sent the formal answer on 12 December: the Allies' inability to provide adequate arms and supplies in time meant that the country could not be ready to participate in any campaign by the proposed mid-February date.[23] The response both disappointed and angered the British leaders, because they realized how deliberately the Turks were engineering their demands to avoid involvement. Sir Hughe's suggestion of suspending friendly relations with Ankara was nevertheless rejected by Eden. In his frustration the ambassador probably meant a cooling-off period in which the Turks would be forced to ponder the full implications of being without protectors and isolated. His superiors were too committed to pursuing their set objective and timetable. The prime minister and foreign secretary therefore considered any such step too provocative during a tense period when they still hoped for some form of agreement.[24]

Turkey's negative response to the plan advanced at Cairo was certainly not taken as final by Britain, but it ended the least acrimonious phase in the talks. Thereafter Knatchbull-Hugessen continued his unpromising efforts to effect some resolution of the conflict, in keeping with London's instructions. Churchill had fallen seriously ill with pneumonia while returning from Cairo, but from Tunisia he badgered the foreign secretary to stand absolutely firm with Turkey: Ankara must "be left under no illusions" that failure to act now would mean the "virtual end of the alliance" with Britain. "Making impossible demands is only another way of saying no." Yet he himself seemed unwilling to accept that point; instead, the existing strains in Turkey's ties with the Allies were soon exacerbated. "It is difficult to say where the rights and wrongs of what followed really lay," observed Sir Hughe later, but "at this moment . . . we entered upon the most difficult period in our relations."[25]

How much about British military aims and Turkish resistance did the Germans manage to learn? The answer must be that there was little concerning Britain's objectives and the frustration of its timetable that Berlin did not find out rather quickly through the spy's filming. Papen's insistence on seeing at once everything that Moyzisch got from Cicero indeed provides the best means of identifying the many documents sent to Berlin. His communications with the Foreign Ministry referred to the content of a number of Sir Hughe's papers that were compromised. Also, Jenke handled at least some of the reports during the envoy's absence in Berlin.[26] Not all the copied British documents were cited or summarized in their telegram dispatches, since complete items from every roll would follow by the next courier plane, and varying amounts of time elapsed between the documents' dates and the film deliveries, but evidence shows that a substantial body of knowledge reached the Germans through the valet's secret work. The photographs were not only valuable in themselves but also allowed verification of information being volunteered by the friendly Turkish foreign minister or obtained from other sources.

Several of the early items gave Papen and Berlin sound insight to how Britain viewed Turkey's role in the prosecution of the war, but they apparently learned about the talks between Eden and Menemencioglu at Cairo before getting details of what had prompted them. Papen later indicated that nearly a month elapsed before he learned about the decisions at Moscow: the information was sent to Sir Hughe in a Foreign Office telegram of 19 November, which Cicero had been able to photograph. He also saw Knatchbull-Hugessen's reply to it.[27] By that time Papen knew a great deal about the Cairo talks as well. In preparation for the foreign secretary's meetings the British ambassador had drawn up a paper headed "Long-Term Policy towards Turkey," which had been obtained and copied by Cicero in time to elucidate the tenor of discussions. In it Sir Hughe urged Eden to take a strong stand with the Soviet Union about Turkey. He believed Moscow was determined to gain control of the Straits shipping route, neutralize Turkey permanently, and demand Turkish border lands in order to reduce Turkey to vassal status. Ankara in his opinion would not solely rely on British support but would sow discord between the two allies.[28] Soon the Germans also learned that the Cairo talks had found the Turks standing firm. After examining all the material, Papen was able to exploit the Turks' fears during his official conversations.

On 7 November he had a long discussion at his own request with Saracoglu to counteract the pressure he knew was being brought on Menemencioglu. He was told that the talks then being held in Cairo were going well from the Turkish standpoint and that it seemed the British no longer expected the country to enter the war. Still, any setback or change in Allied plans might easily produce new efforts to bring Turkey into line or into the war. He reported to Berlin having described "the serious consequences of any deviation" from the Turkish policy of neutrality. Saracoglu had assured him that no change was foreseen by Ankara.[29] The warning from Papen had been issued in terms the Turks could clearly not ignore.

Menemencioglu returned to the capital on 10 November. Having telephoned Papen the next day to allay the diplomat's fears, he proposed a meeting, allowing himself time to report first to Turkish officials. The reassured ambassador quickly told his superiors that the immediate crisis had been overcome. During their 12 November talk, the foreign minister insisted that Eden had made requests, not demands, which Menemencioglu had countered, and he said that his responses in Cairo had been approved by the government. That night Papen left for Istanbul, and then Berlin to report. After he reached the capital on 15 November there arrived a telegram from Jenke with updated news on recent events: "well-known sources of intelligence" made clear that Turkey had stood firm against all attempts at intimidation.[30] Cicero's efforts therefore allowed the Germans to rest easy about Cairo. Certainly the fact that Papen remained away until early December confirms their lack of anxiety.

Papen took care of both official and personal business during his stay in Germany. He immediately briefed Hitler on the new situation and explained also how a valuable source called Cicero was getting information. There were discussions as well with Ribbentrop and others about the looming threat, but no one showed any interest in rethinking the whole war; therefore, Papen later recalled, he determined to pursue peace on his own. On the evening of 22 November his house in the capital was destroyed by bombs. The occasion was also remembered for another reason: Papen would have to explain several months later how at the Hotel Esplanade that night he had met a distant female relative named Vermehren. Soon she somehow obtained permission for travel to Istanbul, where her husband served in the Abwehr headquarters; the Vermehrens' subsequent defection late in January was to have repercussions beyond what anyone might have expected. There was another raid the following night, but Papen's delayed train was eventually able to leave. He stopped for several days in Hungary before returning to duty at the embassy.[31]

When on 3 December Papen got back to his post he did not yet know that the group headed by Inönü would leave that day for Cairo. In reporting his return to Ribbentrop he noted no substantial change in the country's policy, although he intended to see Menemencioglu to verify what he surmised; he then reviewed the items in recent information from Cicero that he found most important. The material revealed a more serious situation than previously realized. It confirmed that Germany would have to maintain military strength and flexibility in the Balkans to counter planned British raids against airfields and transport routes, and even to prepare Thrace against an attack. Papen emphasized that Turkey's policy had therefore become crucial, even before he learned anything about Inönü's journey to Cairo. By the next day he knew of the trip and talks, yet he passed on assurances from Turkish officials that the nation's policy remained unchanged. During a long consultation with Saracoglu on 6 December he invoked the dangers that the country might face from German-Bulgarian military strength and firmness.[32] Papen also played on the Turks' fears of Moscow to promote caution toward Britain. Privately he believed that his interventions were mere reinforcement. In a delayed analysis of a Cicero document sent to the capital four days earlier he argued that Turkey's evasive tactics to avoid entering the war meant that the Cairo meetings would not produce much agreement. He noted that quick delivery of all the Allied arms being demanded was impossible, that to train men in their use would require further time, and that binding assurances from Moscow about future relations seemed unlikely. Papen foresaw the Turks playing the West against the Russians and getting Roosevelt's help against Britain.[33]

About the beginning of the second week in December, Cicero ended a brief silence and requested a meeting. The Moyzisches had a dinner invitation, so the meeting was an hour earlier than usual, to exchange two rolls of film and money, after which Moyzisch picked up his wife. Following their engagement he returned to his office and spent the night developing the new films. To his surprise the photographs purportedly showed the "complete minutes of the entire conferences" at Cairo and Tehran, clearly an inflated description of what the material contained. He immediately typed a provisional report for the ambassador, Moyzisch and Papen both remaining busy throughout the next day drafting the necessary long signals to their respective superiors. Papen realized that due to American and Soviet opposition there would be no major Balkan campaign but that Britain planned a lesser operation in the Aegean, if Turkey would cooperate. If Moyzisch greatly exaggerated when he wrote of having received the complete minutes of the Allied meetings, some denials of that claim may be misleading too, for instance, British assertions that the spy material "did not include the proceedings of the Allied conferences." Such wording seems to imply that no information about the planning talks had been lost. It was not necessary to have verbatim records in order to grasp the salient points. Moyzisch that evening again met Cicero. This time there was only one roll and just a few exposures, but one of them confirmed that Inönü had been in Egypt for secret, high-level talks.[34]

Menemencioglu briefed Papen about Cairo on 9 December. Although the decision at Tehran to bring Turkey into the war had been presented, Inönü had found understanding and sympathy from Roosevelt, raising his confidence at critical moments, when Churchill and Eden insisted on a commitment. The British had threatened to curtail their weapons deliveries, since continuing to equip Turkey if it did not join the war would feed Moscow's belief that the arms would later be used against the Soviet Union. Menemencioglu thought that there had been no discussion of the future of the Balkans at Tehran but that there had been instead a more limited focus on the expected coming invasion of northern France. Nor did he foresee any landings in the Balkans without protective air cover from bases in Turkey; American views, in his opinion, ruled out any British action simply to seize the needed airfields. He anticipated increased pressure on Turkey and perhaps economic sanctions as well. Papen appeared satisfied with the information obtained in his long conversation with Menemencioglu.[35]

On 12 December Papen told Berlin that a further Cicero report on the Cairo talks would reach Ribbentrop on 17 December. Two days later he submitted his own analysis of nine points in what he identified as the final proposal made at the close of the meetings. The first four points dealt with complete preparation of Turkish airfields by 1 February, or by 15 February at the latest; if by 15 February the Turks had not accepted twenty British squadrons, Britain would cease arms shipments and leave Turkey isolated. Receipt of an affirmative answer from Ankara would lead to the start of "Accolade," or attacks on enemy-held islands. The remaining five points covered details of Britain's naval plans, an attack toward Salonika to come later, and the Bulgarians' probable shifts of their troops for defense. Papen concluded that there was little likelihood of Accolade: Turkey would continue to temporize, and without its airfields nothing would be attempted.[36]

Papen soon knew through Cicero the exact content of Menemencioglu's formal note to Knatchbull-Hugessen. The text of the 12 December answer was among four Cicero reports he sent on 18 December by courier plane. His immediate telegrams confirmed that Menemencioglu had not misrepresented its content: Turkey had asked for some 248,000 tons of equipment and forty-nine air squadrons rather than seventeen to twenty. Another of the documents revealed that during a conversation at Cairo the British ambassador had told a Soviet diplomat observing the meetings that Turkey was to be drawn into the war involuntarily if necessary. Knatchbull-Hugessen thought the country's rearming might even have the desirable effect of provoking the enemy into taking some action that would force involvement by Ankara. The third Cicero item was for the prime minister; in it the ambassador reported failure to get any reduction in the amount of equipment Ankara was asking. Knatchbull-Hugessen set forth three possible steps, for Churchill's consideration: breaking off relations at once, continuing to seek agreement by 15 February according to the original plan, or extending the compliance deadline. A fourth telegram contained Sir Hughe's summary of the arguments, which represented either deliberate stalling or sincere Turkish concerns and fears.[37] The last item had been sent to London just five days before Papen was able to report having seen it.[38]

Moyzisch described in detail another document copied by Cicero about this time, a handwritten draft of a report being prepared by Knatchbull-Hugessen covering the full extent of relations with Turkey. Since the ambassador intended his analysis to be comprehensive, he had made many neat changes in the text, developing a sober and realistic assessment of the situation. The paper included discussions of Britain's pending aims and plans, the determination of the Turks to guard their neutrality, and the strong influence Papen was exerting on the nation's policy. Moyzisch did not date the document or its delivery, except to place it some time in December. The item might have been a draft of any of a number of reports.[39]

Ankara's firm resistance to abandoning or compromising its neutrality needed no encouragement and little underscoring by intimidation from Papen. He had long recognized the prevailing antiwar mood and now, thanks to Cicero's spy work, viewed the maneuverings of the Turkish government with interest but not alarm. Under British pressure, a Turkish concession like the replacement of Fevzi Çakmak as head of the General Staff was to be expected.[40] Yet by rejecting Britain's core proposals Turkey had successfully bargained for time, and there was no reason to think its outlook would or could be changed; Cicero's espionage would provide a continuing check. Papen therefore looked with at least cautious satisfaction upon the state of affairs in mid-December.

By that time an incident had occurred during a meeting one evening that frightened the spy and his contact, and left the Cicero operation's future in doubt. The valet had telephoned that afternoon and entered Moyzisch's car as usual, exchanging a roll of film for his payment, and also giving Moyzisch a small package he was to open later. Soon the German noticed a large dark car following them, always keeping a steady distance despite his increasing speed and turning with him each time he maneuvered through Ankara's dark streets. During the chase the spy sat hunched in the back seat, "deadly white" and "sweating heavily," so fearful that he even chewed his nails at times. That Cicero had a gun worried Moyzisch. He finally managed to elude the pursuer, let Cicero tumble out of the moving car after turning a corner near the British embassy, and reached his office without further trouble. Too nervous to develop the film, he locked it away, but he opened the package, which contained a piece of wax. There were imprints of "two complicated keys" to the ambassador's safe. Moyzisch then sought to relax, driving to a nightclub in his old Mercedes. His later description of the chase was lengthy, constructed to stress its thrills and excitement, and placed to mark a changed pattern. Thus Moyzisch in retrospect came to consider the incident a "turning point," because after it major problems arose in the Cicero affair.[41]

Bazna gave the episode even more dramatic weight than did Moyzisch. After he had rolled out of the car onto the ground "and found myself lying flat on my face in the shadow of a garden fence," he had seen the pursuer's car speed past. "For a fraction of a second I thought I saw a face in the faint light of the instrument panel." Admitting that his imagination might have been overactive, and even though the driver was only "a shadow crouching over the steering wheel," he reported noticing "a young, smooth, expressionless face." The whole story about having seen the mysterious driver under such circumstances was an obvious fiction, however; it was intended to foreshadow his later claim of having recognized the same man. Upon reaching his room he changed into his working clothes before another servant visited him there, providing an alibi in case of suspicion, and he would even claim that soon he calmed down enough to take photographs that very night. This was supposedly the time when the drinking glass was broken.[42] While that story in itself may possess some element of truth, its occurrence on the same night as the car pursuit is highly unlikely; the idea clearly was to emphasize the spy's control and daring.

Moyzisch never found a "satisfactory solution" to the chase incident but was "inclined to think" the pursuer was Turkish. He doubted that the unknown driver had been a British agent, because Cicero reported that all was calm and that he had gone on working. Nor did he think the pursuit some sort of joke or game. Although uncertain just why the Ankara police or Turkish security service would follow his Opel, especially at dangerous speeds, Moyzisch recalled visiting the Jenkes, where a guest from Turkey's Foreign Ministry commented about his careless night driving. Thus he thought perhaps the Turks had indeed chased the car. The most important point in his mind, however, was that his passenger was not known.[43]

A young woman later employed as Moyzisch's assistant secretary, reporting on his affairs to the enemy, indicated that an American intelligence agent had driven the pursuit car. It remains unclear whether his interest lay specifically in Moyzisch or just the mysterious car, not knowing who was driving it, curiosity perhaps turning to suspicion when the German car sped up and took evasive action. Members of the Allied security units operating in the country undoubtedly knew Moyzisch's real function but had no reason in mid-December to suspect him of any association with a British embassy spy. Neither Moyzisch nor Bazna mentioned any repetition of such an incident, surveillance of the German was not initiated, and nothing linked the episode with espionage by Germany until 1944. Thus it appears the chase incident was probably coincidental; its main significance therefore is in the psychological effect it exerted on the pursued.

* * *

Britain had in general remained satisfied with Turkey's policy of neutrality until mid-autumn 1943. By then the Mediterranean had been cleared, Italy had renounced the Axis, and some further Allied action seemed desirable. Churchill's initial gamble on a campaign first in the Aegean and then in the Balkans nevertheless came to frustration, due to the defeats in the Aegean islands. His determination at Tehran to bring Allied pressure on Turkey to cooperate militarily succeeded only in part: persuading Ankara was to be Britain's responsibility. Churchill never doubted the correctness of his position with respect to southeastern Europe: "I regard the failure to use otherwise unemployable forces to bring Turkey into the war and dominate the Aegean as an error in war direction which cannot be excused by the fact that in spite of it victory was won."[44] Given the great strength of his conviction, it is hardly surprising that Churchill refused to accept as final the Turkish stand elaborated in mid-December and therefore ordered his representatives to persevere in efforts to alter it. Cicero too would remain busy in the second half of December.

9 The Contest for Turkey

Turkey's formal answer on 12 December rejecting the British proposals at the Cairo Conference failed to satisfy Churchill. British officials tried in vain for another seven weeks to persuade Turkey to enter the war or provide major assistance by 15 February. With Churchill unwilling to accept the setback to his regional strategy, and with little flexibility in Ankara's stand, the protracted negotiations produced a mounting coolness without advancing the British aims. Certainly it is difficult to explain Churchill's persistence in challenging such a firm attitude. Turkish leaders were clearly determined to avoid precipitate action, hoping that time would clarify both Germany's ability to defend its conquests and Stalin's designs on nearby regions, worries that kept them from committing men and resources to accommodate Britain. Nor were they convinced that the British had not reached some secret accord with Moscow at the expense of their own interests. Under the circumstances Ankara chose to dissemble, posing a mix of reasonable and contrived objections that left the British frustrated and angry.

Knatchbull-Hugessen bore the burden of obtaining some agreement. He worked conscientiously despite his personal misgivings about the policy, but he extracted only a few concessions from Ankara. Through nearly all the extended discussions, Cicero's films kept the Germans remarkably well informed about how the issues were unfolding. Quickly regaining his confidence after the mysterious car chase, the valet continued to produce a flow of information and accumulate more money, although his open spending and the mode of his personal life posed potential problems. Only during the last part of January did he fall silent, when the British began to check for leakage. While Bazna's alarm and inactivity would prove to be temporary, they ended his most productive period as a spy, though not before he had contributed substantially to obstructing Britain's plans.

* * *

Churchill remained a forceful advocate of prosecuting the war through further action in the Aegean. Better informed and more objective officials, including the ambassador and Eden, foresaw difficulties with the proposed timetable, realizing how it rankled the Turks and rushed preparations for an assault. A modification of expectations and a slower approach came too late; by then trust had been undermined and relations had deteriorated.

Turkish leaders insisted that they had never acceded to the terms or schedule outlined at Cairo and had every right to reject them in their formal response on 12 December. They still assessed the overall military situation with both concern and caution. While recognizing the Allies' general ascendancy, they refused to underestimate the formidable German presence in their region, and always there were the Soviet Union's aims to take into account. During the many weeks of stalled talks London could never induce Soviet leaders to reassure Turkey. Moscow's policy throughout the winter puzzled outsiders, because it seemed to welcome an uncooperative Turkey: in fact, the neutral's attitude not only blocked a British campaign and future Western influence in a region the communists themselves coveted but also fostered an isolation rendering Turkey more vulnerable to Moscow's own intimidation and claims in postwar years.[1] Against this background, Ankara's patently spurious arguments and inflated demands served an immediate purpose but damaged Turkey's image and standing.

The wrangling over military equipment and supplies involved both the validity of stated needs and estimates of delivery times. Long convinced that Turkey's armed forces were neither absorbing nor yet trained to use even the material already provided, the British had nevertheless promised at Cairo to furnish an additional 58,900 tons. They still expected to bargain over any final figures and schedules that the Turks would offer as counterproposals. Ankara calculated its essential needs at 248,000 tons, and thereafter the swollen figure would be unaltered. When London directed the total be accepted in order to call Ankara's bluff, an approach Knatchbull-Hugessen disliked, the Turks merely countered that deliveries would be impossible by the February deadline. They noted that only two ports were well shielded, Iskenderun and Mersin, and that both required lengthy transshipment over a single-track railway. The impasse made unnecessary the discussion of difficulties like training time.[2]

Protection against land attack and bombing became another focus of contention. Despite expressed fears of an invasion along their Balkan border, by Germany alone or with Bulgarian help, the Turks in private never considered that prospect very likely. Limited bombing raids, however, did appear probable. Britain had already improved many airfields, and Turkish pilots were being trained by the RAF, but an earlier notion of basing forty-nine squadrons of British planes in Turkey had to be discarded as unfeasible. Now air defense by from seventeen to twenty units was offered instead. Turkish leaders declared that figure inadequate, emphasizing the vulnerability of western Anatolia: the country's ports and rail system, major population centers, and military posts all stood exposed. Nevertheless, Britain could not increase the allocation of air support for Turkey. Stalemate was the result.[3]

The issue of accepting a large number of British technicians caused continuing disputes, partly because the very presence of so many British specialists in civilian clothes—described in documents as "infiltrators"—would be interpreted as reflecting a strong commitment by Turkey to enter the war, and partly because there was considerable suspicion in Turkey as to their actual purpose. Turkish leaders still remembered how German commanders had tricked their nation into World War I: they now made certain that all Britons were kept under close watch. Britain estimated that 2,000 infiltrators were needed to prepare the airfields and a system of radio stations to guide aircraft; Ankara insisted that 250 was the maximum number it was willing to accept without discussion of each specific assignment. The disagreement helped to fuel what Knatchbull-Hugessen called a "sharp passage of arms" with Menemencioglu during a long and spirited meeting on 18 December. The ambassador thought he prevailed, but it soon became clear that Ankara would still question the need for every Briton and would hold down their total number.[4] Yet the apparent softening of Turkey's stand had a hidden importance: Papen's awareness of the shift, revealed by his subsequent protest to Menemencioglu, worried the foreign minister, who in turn alerted Knatchbull-Hugessen to the possibility that a leak existed in Ankara.

Another reason for Sir Hughe's difficult sessions with the obstinate foreign minister on both 18 December and the following day was Turkey's refusal to authorize a visit by regional commanders of Britain's three armed services. Since the ambassador had apparently not expected the rejection, there was a "somewhat heated argument" over the point, followed by repeated efforts to work around the differences. Ankara turned down a series of proposals involving lower-level officers before finally permitting a small delegation to come in January. It was clear that the Turks considered any major staff talks as tantamount to accepting British aims for joint war plans. Not until late December could Knatchbull-Hugessen convey to the Foreign Office the final conditions for receiving the British military mission.[5]

Meanwhile Britain adopted a contingency objective in the Aegean region. The adjustment recognized that the time for preparing any action was rapidly dwindling, reflected Eden's reactions to Sir Hughe's reports and his own talks in London with the Turkish ambassador, and accepted the fact that the obstacles to early agreement could not be surmounted.[6] On 21 December the Foreign Office forwarded to Knatchbull-Hugessen a message that had been prepared by the chiefs of staff, advising him that the foreign secretary concurred in the proposal, which outlined an alternative goal to be pursued if the British could not bring Turkey into the war by 15 February. The original report was intended for General Dwight Eisenhower, to keep his command staff informed. The military leaders expressed willingness to meet Ankara's legitimate demands, adhering if at all possible to the set timetable, but they wanted British technicians in any event to continue the infiltration, an approach that ruled out any break in relations. A reasonable delay in involving Turkey could be tolerated if necessary, but in the meantime the Germans must be made to worry. Therefore, Knatchbull-Hugessen was informed, "our object is to get Turkey into the war as early as possible and in any case to maintain a threat to the Germans from the eastern end of the Mediterranean, until Overlord is launched."[7] The ambassador soon found Turkey unresponsive even to the creation of appearances meant to deceive Germany about its enemies' next moves.

Negotiations with Ankara made no progress during January despite the presence of the British military mission.[8] The group, headed by Air Marshal Sir John Linnell, arrived at the beginning of the year, spent fruitless weeks seeking common ground, and finally withdrew on 3 February, when Churchill acknowledged its failure to make progress in the deadlocked talks. Even though the discussions had been purposefully extended in order to mislead the enemy, Cicero's spy work made the truth clear to the Germans, who gradually saw their position improve, and concern about an immediate Anglo-Turkish military assault dissipate.

Knatchbull-Hugessen and the military mission focused on the original terms during the early January talks, Churchill calling for the familiar points in a message to Eden, but Sir Hughe had no illusions about winning a commitment to war or full assistance short of war from Ankara. He knew it was more realistic to pursue the "alternative objective" of maintaining the prospect of a joint military action.[9] Yet to be convincing and tie down enemy forces, the threat required Turkey to show close cooperation in efforts pointing to some likely future campaign. Ankara proved unwilling to create more than token appearances, however, arguing that any miscalculation might still provoke Germany. Even the announcement of Marshal Çakmak's retirement on

12 January lacked real significance. Replacement of the elderly hero with pro-German sympathies had been expected, a change welcomed by the British but never pressed for by them, and it seemed necessary as Turkey took steps to modernize its armed forces. It signaled no shift in policy.[10] Meanwhile, however, many revealing messages concerned the scheme to demonstrate a continuing threat. Discussing the need to keep Berlin guessing about coming operations, some British telegrams mentioned the code word "Overlord" and made clear its general meaning: for instance, one referred to "attacks elsewhere, e.g., Overlord."[11] Germany learned its broad sense through Cicero.

Lack of measurable progress on any major issue led to another heated meeting between Knatchbull-Hugessen and Menemencioglu on 15 January and, in its aftermath, to two long but unhelpful letters from the foreign minister.[12] Menemencioglu was by now disdained by the British as too pro-German. Stubborn at times and subtly evasive at others, the foreign minister seemed to Eden to be shown "at his worst" in reports from Sir Hughe on the difficulties he caused, whether by raising obstacles or quibbling over words. Even in Turkey there was a feeling that he sometimes did as he wanted rather than follow the prescribed lines of Turkish policy. London, however, could see no acceptable means to force Menemencioglu's removal.[13] Knatchbull-Hugessen also expressed annoyance at lack of support from his colleagues, whether American, Soviet, or representatives of occupied countries in the Balkans.[14]

By the second half of January it was clear that Britain could not achieve its Turkish aims. Therefore, when Churchill suggested to Eden on 14 January that the military mission be withdrawn, the foreign secretary agreed, and Britain decided to show Menemencioglu and other Turks that its anger was indeed substantial. Sir Hughe's suggestion of making one final offer met rejection by London.[15] Yet the ambassador's memoirs were misleading in their careful moderation: "Even if we could use the Turkish bases, we did not necessarily expect Turkey to join in actual hostilities"; and, "No blame was to attach to Turkey if she decided to answer in the negative." The diplomat seemed to regret the shift in attitude toward Ankara that had developed since the proposals for cooperation were first framed. Britain did indeed blame Turkey. Knatchbull-Hugessen acknowledged that "we made no attempt to conceal our disappointment" with the Turks.[16] A temporizing policy had kept Turkey neutral despite Britain's many weeks of continuous pressure. The country's leaders failed to realize in full, however, that their bargaining position had rapidly been losing value, that they were overplaying their hand and exasperating their friends, and that their approach would produce not the kinds of benefits they wanted but instead a dangerous isolation. Thus at the beginning of February began the coolest period yet in Britain's wartime relations with its ally.

Papen was kept fully informed of Anglo-Turkish difficulties by both Menemencioglu and the latest films from Cicero. Although the photographs continued to serve as a check on the foreign minister's statements, Papen need not have worried in any case about major concealments or deception; the minister respected him as "le dernier grand chevalier du Reich" and felt that the interests of their two countries had at least temporarily a common goal.[17] While the ambassador therefore followed Britain's efforts through some of its own documents, gratified by its admissions of frustration, he also learned regularly from Menemencioglu about how the difficulties were being created. Thus there was no necessity for him to exert pressure upon Menemencioglu until late December, when he detected a weakening of resolve on a key issue. Papen's registering of a formal protest over the matter would become the catalyst for special security investigations conducted by the British.

Menemencioglu was pursuing a risky and unrealistic course during the winter of 1943–1944. His schemes affected both sides. He explained to Papen that gaining six months' time would help their countries by allowing the Germans to stabilize their eastern front and thereby force delays in launching the Allies' planned attacks. Secretly, Menemencioglu was hoping to extend his country's borders at minimal cost, as the German-Bulgarian side weakened. He therefore undermined Papen's initiatives for peace. Menemencioglu was gambling that with continuation of the war Turkey could acquire land from Bulgaria when its neighbor lost the protection of the Germans. His subtle references to reaching some form of clear "understanding" with Britain have been seen as hints aimed at obtaining that promise, but he overestimated both Germany's ability to hold its eastern lines and Britain's patience with his temporizing.[18] Therefore Menemencioglu misjudged his nation's bargaining value and the necessity of committing it to timely support of the Anglo-American war effort. Inönü and Saracoglu had a much sounder grasp of the changing situation and feared losing the backing of the West against Moscow. Menemencioglu continued to exert his influence to delay basic decisions, however, until his bankrupt policy forced his resignation in mid-June. Ironically, it was the Germans who caused his downfall.

Turkish leaders had carefully placed their needs for equipment at a high and exaggerated level in order to delay the necessity of making any military commitment until mid-1944. Knatchbull-Hugessen's argument that deliveries of even these large amounts could still be effected as originally scheduled had been anticipated, however, and figures on the capacity of internal transport systems to handle them had accordingly been deliberately underestimated by Menemencioglu. The foreign minister explained to Papen when they discussed matters on 18 December that his deception gave the Turks another way to buy time. He also told Papen that there was a strong possibility that Britain might use force by surprise, seizing Turkish airfields, and that Inönü had therefore issued orders to protect Turkey against any such action. Nonetheless, he cautioned Papen that evidence of German-Bulgarian countermeasures would make Britain even more determined. In reporting the conversation to Berlin, Papen stressed the gravity of the Anglo-Turkish breach and its uncertain outcome. Germany consequently needed to prepare for any eventuality in Turkey.[19] Meanwhile, the friction he described was turning worse daily.

Menemencioglu told the German ambassador about a stormy week just past, during which the breaking of relations had twice seemed near, when he conferred again with Papen on 24 December. The foreign minister had asserted to Knatchbull-Hugessen that he would not accept a planned démarche by the Big Three acting collectively. Nor would he allow the top commanders of the three Allied military services in the Middle East to come for detailed discussions, or even accept visits by their deputies and staffs. Only a fourth British proposal, made after several days, gained Menemencioglu's approval: a small group of officers might be sent for more or less routine talks. The foreign minister told Papen he had pointedly made clear to Knatchbull-Hugessen that Turkey would accept the risk of a rupture and would resist any surprise attack. In his view such risks were no greater than those of joining the war. From Cicero material he received later in December, Papen learned the arrival date of the British mission.[20]

As the year was ending, the controversial question of using the spy's information arose openly and brought many problems. Moyzisch dramatically called the incident his "greatest" crisis; it caused him "no end of trouble" with his angry superiors in Berlin. Just before Christmas one of the spy's photographs revealed that Turkey might soon reach accommodation on certain of Britain's top concerns—the issues involving construction and manning of radio aircraft-guidance stations in European Turkey and the acceptance of more military specialists and technicians in civilian clothes. Given the seriousness of the situation he saw developing, Papen acted immediately, and on 30 December he protested strongly to Menemencioglu, warning him of the consequences such action might produce, even air attacks on Istanbul. The ambassador's claim that his information had come from someone's loose talk—an effort not to reveal the real source—struck his listener as transparently false. Papen obviously knew enough of the facts to threaten Turkey with counteraction and reprisals if it helped Britain. While the foreign minister advised Papen not to be worried, suggesting that he had been misinformed, he suspected how the Germans might have acquired their knowledge. Within just a day Menemencioglu briefed Knatchbull-Hugessen and mentioned a possible leak. The latter's message in early January to alert Foreign Office officials that Papen knew a good deal about specific elements in Britain's secret talks with the Turks was itself copied by Cicero and delivered to the Germans almost at once.[21]

Moyzisch understandably feared the reaction in Berlin. He knew everyone at SD headquarters would realize that Papen was using the information being supplied by Cicero and that he had disregarded orders from Kaltenbrunner prohibiting him from showing Papen any of it. It was impossible to withhold the photograph or negative, however, and he simply had to await the expected trouble. In the event, and though he reported soon getting an official reprimand, stipulating "gross breach of discipline in disobeying strict orders" from superiors, the situation never produced any personal consequences, and despite their effect and significance the developments seem not to have been the great crisis he alleged. Moyzisch merely closed his later account of the incident by again claiming to have been a diplomat and blaming his problems on Ribbentrop: "One could trust him not to back up his own people."[22]

Papen later complained about the lack of direction for handling the information being supplied by Cicero: "At no time did I receive from either Hitler or Ribbentrop any instructions on the general policy to be pursued. . . . I was left entirely to my own devices." Having decided to assume personal responsibility and act upon what he was learning, Papen was able to justify his actions to Ribbentrop, explaining his reasons for intervening promptly despite the risk of compromising the spy. Even later Papen remained certain that the material sometimes required independent judgment, however regrettable the dangers, and he rejected criticism of his behavior expressed by Moyzisch and others: "I therefore maintain that I was right in doing what I could."[23] Certainly insights to the enemy's secret activities lacked practical value without effective use of the knowledge to affect policies and developments. Yet the incident caused Sir Hughe to tighten embassy security and thereby reduce Cicero's access to his documents.

At their final meeting of the year on 30 December, the foreign minister assured Papen that there were no changes in policy. Menemencioglu told him the government looked upon the military mission's visit as routine; that its presence would not be regarded as secret had indeed surprised Sir Hughe. He also confided that no radio direction-guiding stations would be allowed in European Turkey and that runways at airfields were being obstructed by barbed wire and vehicles. The explanation given to British officials had been preventing landings by the Germans, but the real fear was an attempt by Britain to seize the airfields.[24] By the year's end Cicero's information had therefore obviously helped the Germans reinforce the principles of policy that Turkey had set for itself.

Cicero continued to furnish the Germans with British documents during most of January. Among them were exceptional texts that enabled Papen and Berlin to follow the stormy Anglo-Turkish negotiations in detail and with satisfaction. Despite now somewhat longer intervals between the papers' dates and Cicero's deliveries, the picture of unfolding developments was nevertheless both timely and complete, as is evident in Papen's telegrams to the foreign minister in Berlin. To limit the number of people at the ministry who had access to the material, Papen was now instructed to direct reports personally to Ribbentrop, although the change implied neither a special concern nor any heightened involvement on the minister's part.[25] Cicero became much less active later in the month, suspicions of a leak having brought tighter security measures at the embassy, and thus his most productive period ended in January. Yet until then the secret information he provided had the greatest of value.

About midday on 6 January Papen analyzed in a telegram to Berlin material from Cicero that he had just received. One particular item, though two weeks old, was especially useful: a Foreign Office telegram to the ambassador dated 21 December and bearing the "Bigot" restriction—the highest security level—providing Knatchbull-Hugessen a copy of the message that Britain's chiefs of staff had given Eisenhower about their military aims. It declared that Britain intended "to maintain a threat to the Germans from the eastern Mediterranean until Overlord is launched" and conditions changed. Papen rightly concluded that the code word stood for a major action to be executed from Britain. The spy's information also showed that negotiations would continue, despite all the problems, to follow the original timetable for occupying Turkish air bases. British leaders discounted any counteraction by the Axis. While the Turks were not to be told about Allied plans until they entered the war, Papen surmised that there would be no campaign in the Balkans, although it appeared that the British hoped to control the sea lanes using their Turkish airfields.[26] Berlin had therefore learned through its spy not only the broad nature of Overlord but Britain's intent to maintain a threat in the region even without help from Turkey.

In a second telegram on 6 January, the German ambassador reported a further conversation with Menemencioglu, one revealing continuing deadlock with Britain. After summarizing current developments, the foreign minister had answered Papen's direct question about the Allies' operational plans by admitting that he knew no particulars, because Eden had refused at Cairo to reveal them, a secrecy that remained a source of rancor. Upon also learning that thus far Moscow had not attempted any coercion of its own, Papen had himself evoked that constant fear.[27]

During the middle of January, Papen again grew worried. Despite assurances from various Turkish officials he wondered if they might be misleading him, if their resistance to British demands was still strong: the continued presence of the British mission could not be ignored. On 18 January, when he and his wife gave a dinner party for Saracoglu, there seemed to be no problem.[28] But a short lapse about this time in deliveries from Cicero gave him no way of verifying from documents what was happening. Another source of concern was his continuing need to reassure Ribbentrop that the spy and his information were reliable. Ribbentrop was clearly following the struggle over Turkey's course of action, though not taking much part; he even asked Papen whether there were any contingency plans to liquidate Cicero.[29] Where he got that melodramatic idea is not known.

Papen showed relief from his anxiety on 19 January, when he reported both a meeting with Menemencioglu and also new information from Cicero. The foreign minister had declared that the talks with the British found each side repeating the same arguments, as Turkey held firm on its existing stand, but he had further important word on Soviet policy. Moscow's ambassador had reminded him officially on 17 January that only Britain had demanded Turkey's early involvement during the conference at Tehran. Moscow, he had asserted, took no position on the current issues: while his government hoped the Turks would enter the war, they alone must decide their future, and how they dealt with the British was their concern. Ankara was too wary and realistic to trust the Russians, but Papen thought their attitude would strengthen its resistance to Britain. He also noted that Menemencioglu seemed to need rest.[30]

The ambassador's telegram to Ribbentrop about the latest Cicero material stressed four points. Most significant was confirmation that Anglo-Turkish agreement appeared to be impossible: Ankara still insisted on receiving all the stipulated equipment before risking war, but Britain would not discuss even partial delivery until it was allowed to infiltrate 2,000 men, a proposal that continued to meet firm rejection by the Turks. Despite the deadlock Britain was determined not to break relations with Ankara over these issues. Therefore, Papen concluded, Turkey would temporarily remain neutral, Britain would open no major Balkan front, and London could pursue only some lesser objective. Papen's second point concerned a statement made by Menemencioglu to Knatchbull-Hugessen about a future possible step by Turkey: it might join the war two weeks after Allied landings in the west had proven successful. Third, he reported that London was asking Washington to support its efforts. The fourth point dealt with the matter of a leak, whether there might be a spy. Menemencioglu had reported Papen's protest against building the special radio stations to Sir Hughe, resulting in a check of his embassy, but Knatchbull-Hugessen had concluded that the security breach involved the Turks and not Britain.[31] Papen realized from the British message that his intervention with Menemencioglu had not thus far endangered Cicero.

Ribbentrop referred to the recent reports from Cicero when he contacted the ambassador on 22 January. He suggested that Papen find a suitable time and means to assure the Turks that it was clear they need not fear major British steps against them. In effect, he was urging the diplomat to use the secret information that there would be no break in relations regardless of how the talks went. Three days later Papen reported passing that assessment to the head of the secret police, without having indicated how the Germans could be so certain, and noted that his choice of channels meant that Inönü would be informed. The next day he notified the foreign minister that the latest Cicero material revealed sharp argument by Knatchbull-Hugessen with Menemencioglu over the rejection of more specialists and the tracking stations. Certainly, in Papen's opinion, that outcome could be credited to his own forceful protest, and it also confirmed that he had not been misinformed by the Turkish official. British documents now showed that Sir Hughe regarded the situation as hopeless but planned to continue the negotiations in order to keep the Germans in doubt about Turkey.[32] The subterfuge was futile, given the espionage leak and the subsequent departure of the military mission. Papen and Moyzisch were so confident at the end of January that they both took holidays in Bursa.

* * *

Authentication of the documents based on actual developments mentioned in them was rarely possible. Most information available to diplomats dealt with broad policies and strategic aims, which were neither immediately nor specifically verifiable. Such high-level and long-range insights provided little help to officials in Germany, who were still trying to evaluate the truth and worth of the data. In December, however, they had received one item that could indeed meet Berlin's rigid tests: a document outlining a new bombing offensive and identifying the initial target and date of attack.[33] The corroborating incident did not occur until more than ten weeks after the spying started, however, and using it to validate the source meant responsibility for much killing and destruction.

By the end of 1943 the three German satellites in southeastern Europe knew what Allied planners had in store: they had been warned that they would share the mounting attacks and the ultimate defeat of the side they had joined. Among the photographs of papers the Germans studied in December were minutes of military staff talks held by Allied leaders at Tehran agreeing on a new bombing campaign. While there had already been some raids in the southeastern region, those projected for early in the new year would be heavier and directed against the capitals, cities that were wholly unprepared for any effective air defense.

Sofia was to be the first objective, in raids on 10 January. The city not only lacked antiaircraft guns but also had an inadequate siren system; even previous smaller raids had therefore produced widespread terror among its inhabitants. (One of the frightened was a nervous young secretary working in the German embassy, Cornelia Kapp, who later transferred to Turkey and played a significant role in the spy affair.) Berlin nevertheless chose to use advance knowledge of the next raids to test the spy's trustworthiness and thus did nothing to forewarn or protect Sofia. The bombings occurred as scheduled. "Several thousand people were killed, water and electrical connections were broken, many homes and buildings were reduced to rubble, and fires broke out all over Sofia." Winter conditions and panicked flight added to conditions that left the city paralyzed for a week. No one knew when the bombers might return.[34]

Moyzisch and Papen later took pains to dissociate themselves from the callousness of Berlin over Sofia. The former noted that doubts "about the genuineness of the documents were dispelled once and for all and in a singularly ghastly manner" by the devastating raid. He added piously that "one is apt to forget that what is really at stake is the lives of human beings" in handling such information. Yet he had been curious enough to try to telephone the German legation in Sofia; he had had trouble getting through at first due to the bombing. The ambassador later maintained that the material foretelling the raid had been withheld from him, having been forwarded directly by the intelligence officer. Perhaps that was true, since the document apparently dealt with military intelligence of which he had no direct need. Still, he obviously wanted to show that he had been kept ignorant, that otherwise he would have caused difficulties over the matter. Schellenberg would wrongly claim that advance notice had indeed been sent to the Bulgarians: "The city was thus forewarned in ample time, though there was nothing much we could do to counter the attack."[35] Perhaps the kernel of truth in his comments is that some military commanders or units were told to expect the bombing.

Occurrence of the raid as scheduled helped to quiet most skeptics and bolster claims of the spy's credibility. Only a few who had committed themselves strongly to challenging the source continued to resist trusting his information and to think that even the air attack had been leaked to help authenticate some bigger enemy scheme to deceive them.[36] To such doubters, one instance of demonstrated accuracy did not validate all the reports, nor would any amount of proof diminish their faith in achieving a final victory. Even the belated conversions and adjustments in attitude that occurred came too late, however, since improvements in embassy security were already reducing the spy's output.

A mistaken claim by some popularizers of the Cicero story has held that the spy's work allowed German experts to break at least one vital communication code. The contention implies a greater loss than just the photographed documents, for cracking a cipher system would permit access to a continuing quantity of data from intercepted radio signals, affecting the integrity of every transmission sent in the compromised code. In reality, the accomplishments of Berlin's cryptology teams proved to be disappointing.

In theory it seemed possible to use Cicero's material to break a cipher: the British messages bore notations of transmission dates and times, the signals were routinely recorded by Germany's communications intelligence listening posts, and cryptanalysts comparing the texts and recordings in Berlin could theoretically determine how the codes in question had been constructed. For experienced help Schellenberg sought out professionals. He submitted copies of the printed documents to General Fritz Thiele of the Chiffrierabteilung, or Cipher Section, of the Military High Command for special comparisons of all the available evidence. Despite learning that only items of small importance and some length were transmitted in reuseable codes, Schellenberg still described the experts' minor success as a "tremendous achievement," his fascination with the technical process giving rise to similar enthusiasm among his top staff. Schellenberg also asked for help from the Foreign Ministry. Analysts in its deciphering office, "Pers Z," under people like linguist Adolf Paschke and head mathematician Werner Kunze, confirmed the broken texts' limited value and that Britain's major communications were encoded by one-time pad or cipher, which prevented the Germans from applying it elsewhere.

It was Moyzisch who began the later exaggeration of the cryptanalysts' success with the stolen documents—"The only practical use to which they were put was by the cipher specialists"—having believed overstated reports he had received or heard from headquarters in Berlin. Other writers drew upon his ambiguous remarks, however, and often supposed or imagined a breakthrough. Schellenberg's memoirs and careful postwar studies reveal that analyses of the Cicero photographs produced no access to primary codes and did not compromise other British texts.[37] Consequently the assertion that the spy's material had an ancillary but significant usefulness in the field of cryptology is unjustified.

* * *

During December noticeable changes occurred in Cicero's conduct. He was now more confident and relaxed, open to friendly conversation except on personal matters, and clearly proud of success and wealth. Bazna in his own book wrote of dreaming that "the smartest of the smart" would patronize a new hotel he planned to build at Bursa. With Moyzisch, he was clearly cautious. Without giving his contact any details, he claimed to have considered every eventuality and to have made his plans, including a life of luxury abroad. Moyzisch recalled that "sometimes his attitude reminded me of a child's exuberant excitement on Christmas Eve." He soon found the spy so "entirely self-assured" that he feared some careless mistake; and indeed the valet was jolted from his "cocksureness" by the car chase later that month.[38]

Meanwhile a further danger to the operation arose from the spy's purchases and habits. He began to appear at times in expensive clothes, though he said he wore them seldom and with discretion, and to pamper himself with professional shaves and manicures, which might be noticed by anyone who was observant. There were also numerous costly gifts of clothing and perfumes for his mistress and a relative. Jewelry became a special indulgence. When Cicero appeared wearing "a large and flamboyant gold wrist watch," his contact persuaded him to surrender it for safekeeping until the spy could store it "with his other jewelry" in Istanbul. On another occasion Cicero asked if Moyzisch would pay him his £15,000 in diamonds and other precious stones. Although concerned that even he would arouse suspicion by buying gems, the German agreed to purchase "a couple of thousand pounds' worth" from some discreet Turkish merchants, since he could pretend the items were intended for his wife.[39]

December brought the order to cut the spy's payment per roll to £10,000. While no explanation was given for the instruction, it had arisen from neither a shortage of false notes nor the poor quality of his films; perhaps it was imposed to control his extravagance. Berlin also wanted to reduce the overall amount of counterfeit money going into circulation, and it had no way of ascertaining how much currency was being spent by Cicero. Having caught the valet in an expansive mood, Moyzisch mentioned the new price during their evening at Seiler's; to his surprise the change evoked no complaint.[40] The explanation must lie in the spy's confidence in accumulating further wealth without major difficulties.

Still unsolved was the spy's problem of hiding his money from the embassy staff and his mistress. He knew that she had searched a house they had just rented. One possibility was to conceal the notes under a loose stone beneath the embassy's basement steps, but he thought someone might find them, whereas he liked having the money where he could enjoy seeing it often. At first he had spread the big old-style notes as evenly as possible on the floor under the yellow carpet in his room in the servants' quarters. In time he took a bank deposit box, but he still kept some money in his room.[41] Therefore he panicked when a security check began, first placing the notes that were still on hand in the hiding place under the basement steps, then transferring them to safety in the bank.

His personal life underwent a disruption too. Mara had many appealing qualities, despite her heavy smoking and fondness for whiskey, but her jealousy annoyed Bazna.[42] When their relationship deteriorated through a series of quarrels, the valet concluded that "she had outlived her usefulness" and ended the affair, though she maintained her loyalty and protected his secret. For several months she had accepted his sudden wealth without question and enjoyed the small house he rented for their personal life. His claim that he privately called the retreat in the Kavaklidere hills the "Villa Cicero" was only a fanciful tale he later invented to show that he knew his cover name and how clever he had been. When Mara came to realize that he was a handsomely paid German spy she made no fuss, but Bazna no longer trusted her and especially safeguarded his British notes. He seemed surprised by her fidelity. On one occasion she told him of overhearing Busk mention that the Germans must have some good source of secret information. Also, during January she took the Busk baby to the embassy, passing the visit off as a routine outing but in fact alerting Bazna about the arrival of British security men. She had heard Busk tell his wife that a team had been sent by London to check things. In both instances her warnings helped him protect himself.

The final break came in the new year. One cause was the appearance of a younger woman, Esra, whom the valet soon used to provoke his mistress. When she implicitly threatened to reveal his activities, hoping to hold on to her lover, he slapped her and decided she was dangerous. In the meantime Mrs. Busk was preparing to return to Britain with the baby and wanted Mara to accompany them. Given what had happened and the opportunity now open, she decided to leave. Bazna learned much later that she had married and moved to America.

Before long Esra became Bazna's new mistress.[43] Having done well in commercial studies, she had been sent to find work in the city by her father, a distant cousin of the valet. Esra was attractive and fair, showing her Greek background, and had impressed the *kavass*. Her simple devotion made her a welcome audience. Boasting one night after showing her the sights of Ankara, he told the impressionable girl how he got his money. She wanted to assist him, and during her brief stay at the embassy she indeed helped him discover the arrangement of the fuses so that he could deactivate a new electric alarm installed on the study safe.[44] Neither needing nor wanting to work with anyone, he convinced her that she "was not intelligent or quick-witted enough" to contribute much help, though making clear that she might become his mistress: "Vainly and stupidly I took advantage of her love." Unable to remain at the embassy, where no job had been found for her, she moved to the rented house. During the final period of Cicero's spying Esra too remained loyal and silent.

* * *

Neither the difficulties nor the eventual coolness in Anglo-Turkish relations by early February 1944 can be attributed to the espionage activity. Cicero nevertheless provided the Germans with substantial and timely information on the lengthy negotiations until Britain improved security in late January. Although the spy's frequent reports showed little need for intervention, because of Turkey's own intransigence, Papen subtly influenced the talks by underscoring the known anxieties of Ankara, adroitly reminding Turkish leaders of the military strength of Germany and the threat from communism. Without Turkey's help, it became unlikely that Britain would risk undertaking a Balkan attack: in Papen's opinion the spy had furnished "indisputable evidence" that such immediate aims had been blocked. Of course there might always be a new crisis or shift in plans, yet Papen had every reason to be satisfied with the state of affairs from the German view: "The first round in the battle over Turkey's entry into the war has undoubtedly been won by us."[45] Time had shown that even his decision to use the secret information at what he considered to be a crucial juncture in the negotiations had not compromised the source or led to catching the spy.

10   Searching for an Agent

Establishing how and when British authorities learned about and then dealt with the embassy leakage is complicated by the gaps and discrepancies in available information and by a basic disagreement over what the Cicero affair had represented. The reluctant postwar consensus that the spy had escaped detection and caused substantial harm was challenged in the mid-1970s by several writers who argued that the valet had been discovered quite early and had been used to deceive the enemy. Their contentions of British control of the situation as part of a broad deception aimed at Berlin gained considerable attention. Former intelligence officials denied the spy operation had been managed, however, and influential analysts were quick to reject the revisionist claims. Still, the questions underlying the controversy are fundamental: When did the possibility of espionage first arise? What was then done? Had the spy been effectively controlled? Given the array of assertions and opinions that are now readily found, it is essential not only to identify the most trustworthy evidence and credible view of what occurred, but also to explain why the deception theory is unsound.

* * *

Officials at the embassy clearly suspected a leak before obtaining any confirmation of its existence. London received a warning in mid-December from Washington about a report from neutral Stockholm: the Americans had learned through the Hungarian legation there that Germany had information about the current Cairo talks. British representatives sought a further explanation from the State Department, but background details were unavailable until late January. It developed that on 4 December, Hungarian diplomats in Stockholm had received a report via Budapest in which the Hungarian consulate-general in

Istanbul summarized the Cairo talks about the war. The information the Germans gave their worried ally had been accurate but its provenance was unknown to the Hungarians, who circulated it.[1] So despite being alerted to a past leak as early as mid-December, its nature was unclear, and Britain had no reason to look into espionage at the embassy.

Knatchbull-Hugessen became aware of how much his German adversary seemed to know by early January. In a telegram at that time he informed London that Papen had more knowledge of things than he should: Menemencioglu had just met with the ambassador to discuss Papen's démarche over the building of radar stations in European Turkey. The foreign minister's discomfort meant that he himself had not divulged the British proposal; apparently Papen had acquired some secret source of accurate information about the talks. Sir Hughe continued to wonder why his negotiations with Turkey caused so little open reaction from the Germans; such complacency too suggested some extended leak. Meanwhile others at the embassy had Turkish contacts who relayed similar cautions to them. One example was the statement of a British economic warfare agent that someone close to Turkey's president had alerted him to trouble.[2] That such sympathizers and personal friends would have passed along their observations and concerns is understandable. Rechecking of embassy security was initiated.

Soon evidence came that prompted an even closer scrutiny: an American intelligence officer working in neutral Switzerland had obtained documentary proof of compromise from a German contact. In August 1943 an official of the German Foreign Ministry on a business trip to Switzerland had approached the British legation in Bern with an offer to supply copies of important Foreign Ministry papers he had brought from Berlin. A high-ranking British official rebuffed him without investigating or referring him to intelligence specialists, committing an inexcusable error.[3] Fritz Kolbe found a much different reception when he contacted the Americans: Allen Dulles was then the chief representative of the OSS in Bern, and he recognized the value of what Kolbe offered. As the principal assistant to Karl Ritter, the Foreign Ministry's liaison official with the Military High Command (OKW), Kolbe screened all cable traffic for distribution. His opposition to the regime led him to extract, summarize, or copy reports and documents that he thought important. Dulles gave the new source the code name "George Wood," and he got a second batch of items in October. Although he could not always travel or send his material, Kolbe for more than a year kept in touch with Dulles, eventually supplying him with about two thousand documents or abstracts.[4] Due to their volume and for security reasons Dulles often divided the information with the British for radio transmission to their respective capitals.[5]

Kolbe again handed over a large number of papers late in December. Using the 24 December date of one item he carried and Dulles's telegram analyzing some of the documents transmitted on 29 December, it is possible to bracket the time of Kolbe's visit. Dulles first reported to Washington the content of recent telegrams that Papen had dispatched to Berlin: nos. 1804 (12 December), 1811 (14 December), 1842 (18 December), 1863 (22 December), and 1875 (24 December). The German messages covered a number of developments—the 15 February British target date, delivery times for war supplies, troubles in Anglo-Turkish talks—but these were not specifically identified with Cicero's work. Kolbe's material also included some items dating from an earlier period that clearly noted the existence at that time of a spy being called "Cicero." Dulles may have delayed inspecting that group of papers because most bore older dates from early November, but he soon realized what they meant. The telegrams showed that the Germans had a new source in Britain's embassy whose true name was unknown. On 1 January Dulles reported having given his local MI6 counterpart, Frederick Vanden Heuvel, the Papen telegrams revealing the spy for quick transmission to London: nos. 1576, 1600, and 1603, dated 3 to 5 November 1943. In his message to his superiors Dulles mentioned having still other items as well: the Foreign Office memorandum of 7 October on long-range policy toward Turkey, Sir Hughe's list of questions for Eden at Cairo, and Papen's telegram no. 1642 to Berlin (10 November) about the enemy's current aims. Kolbe himself was never able to provide more data about Cicero.[6]

Dulles's telegram alerted the head of his agency, General William Donovan, who passed the incoming report directly to Roosevelt. On 15 January the president informed Churchill that an OSS agent had acquired German papers showing that Berlin had documents from their recent Cairo Conference. One was Churchill's minute of 6 December to the Chiefs of Staff about Operation Saturn, or using Turkey's airfields. Roosevelt pointed out that the information had been attributed to an agent working for Berlin. Undoubtedly London had already been alerted by its Bern operative; by the time the prime minister acknowledged the president's telegram, four days after its receipt, an official inquiry had been ordered.[7] That the reports produced profound concern is evident from official messages.

Churchill's alarm led him to pose a sharp question to Eden: "Do you think that the leaky condition of the Angora [Ankara] Embassy reflects seriously upon the Ambassador?" In his answer the foreign secretary acknowledged that "some very bad leakages" existed and called the situation "so serious and disturbing" that special officers were being sent to investigate. He offered as the likely explanation that Menemencioglu "tells nearly everything" to Papen, but he thought an embassy leak was possible.[8] Nevertheless, there was general confidence that the security specialists would provide a sound answer and take whatever steps were necessary.

A means by which Britain is often said to have discovered the espionage was the decoding of German messages that mentioned the spy's work. London's ability to decipher wartime radio transmissions that its enemy considered safe had indeed long been a carefully guarded secret, with the code designation "Ultra." References in the Ultra information appear to have revealed only that a breach in security at Ankara had been effected; nothing in the intercepted messages, however, allowed identification of the source. This dramatic manner of learning about the espionage long seemed plausible and attractive, given that details were lacking, but the authors of the semiofficial history of wartime intelligence accorded it scant importance.[9]

Other sources from which the British may also have become aware of Cicero have been offered: an American informant belonging to Papen's staff—Moyzisch's new assistant secretary who reported his activities to the OSS—or an Abwehr defector to the British side. There are problems with respect to such assertions, beyond the presumption that Anglo-American cooperation through personal ties or the coordinating Ankara Committee was prompt and complete, for no timely information came from the sources indicated. The secretary's reports referring to existence of a spy did not begin until about mid-January; jealousy and friction produced such strained relations between the OSS and MI6 that Britain did not know about her findings for several months; and the Abwehr employee refused as a matter of principle to discuss in detail his intelligence work. Moyzisch's secretary thought her British interrogators had not yet heard the name Cicero when she was subjected to questioning in April after defecting to the Americans.[10] Of course the particular team who listened to her account may have known nothing of the espionage affair until then. The employee of the Abwehr had probably only heard of the Germans' spy through his colleagues. In any event neither defector could name or describe the agent. At most such late reports confirmed what by then was already known.

* * *

The organization of Britain's intelligence and security services in the 1940s fostered independent action. Only at the very highest level, the Joint Intelligence Committee (JIC)—formed in 1936 and during World War II headed by William Cavendish-Bentinck—were all the efforts brought together. The two main organizations, MI5, or the Security Service, responsible for countering subversion and espionage at home, and MI6, or the Secret Intelligence Service (SIS), charged with gathering and analyzing foreign intelligence, came under separate authorities. MI5 worked closely with the Home Office; MI6 became associated with the Foreign Office. The initials, standing for "military intelligence," were misleading; each military service maintained its own intelligence branch. The new Special Operations Executive (SOE), a wartime addition with the task of sabotage and disruption in enemy territory, came under the Ministry of Economic Warfare.

Two aspects of the structure have a significant bearing on the handling and interpretation of the spy affair. Security at all diplomatic missions was the Foreign Office's own responsibility, and MI6's Section V protected the facilities against incursions and spies. Other representatives of MI6, working from embassies and consulates, conducted Britain's basic field operations.[11] The secrecy enveloping all the activities of MI6 long obscured the organization's possible role in the Cicero affair and allowed for widely conflicting claims. In time there were useful clarifications, as outspoken critics of the SIS charged the service with concealing its wartime and postwar failings.

Lieutenant Colonel Montague Chidson was listed as assistant military attaché in Ankara, but he worked for MI6. He acted quickly to recheck and tighten all security, but Chidson had apparently had some sort of difficulty with Knatchbull-Hugessen; they were barely on speaking terms.[12] Their friction may well have arisen over issues of how to safeguard papers. During the period when a leak of information was first indicated, British officials at the embassy and in London believed the security breach was among the Turks, a past situation that might not have recurred. Precautions were nevertheless taken to make certain that embassy papers and work areas were safe, however, and a careful search was made for listening or recording devices.[13] The thorough rechecking of embassy security led Sir Hughe to affirm his belief that Turkish sources were responsible for the presumed leaks. He reported that conclusion about the same time that London got evidence from Kolbe that an enemy agent had gained access to documents. The Foreign Office hurriedly conveyed its awkward discovery to Sir Hughe.[14] Due to the seriousness of the situation, London sent two experts to conduct an investigation.

Sir John Dashwood was assistant to the Foreign Office's head security officer; Chief Inspector Cochrane was drawn from the Special Branch's roster of detectives.[15] Anxious to protect his source, Dulles had wanted any inspection to look like a periodic check of conditions at Ankara, an appearance hard to manage, but in fact the enemy never sensed that any problem on its own side lay behind the sudden security survey. During their stay the investigators pursued their twofold task, trying to find exactly how the Germans had obtained the British papers referred to in their dispatch, and also reexamining and tightening all aspects of security. The team knew only that some documents, many weeks before, had by uncertain means reached enemy hands. They eventually concluded that the problem arose from a personnel leak.[16]

Reviewing physical security in the embassy and the residence posed few problems. Although various changes had already been effected, the experts made further improvements, trying to ensure the safekeeping of papers. Of particular concern were making certain that there were no hidden microphones, altering locks and combinations for secure storage, and attaching a new electric alarm system for the safe in the ambassador's home office. The inspectors felt that such measures collectively rendered impossible any further threat of espionage. (Bazna, even though aware of greater difficulties and danger, would continue activity until early March, though as he later admitted his efforts became less frequent and productive.)

Dashwood had to proceed "with considerable tact" in dealing with Knatchbull-Hugessen. One of his objectives was to ascertain from Sir Hughe and others the routines followed in handling the embassy papers mentioned in enemy telegrams. Knowing the documents' whereabouts in the days preceding the German messages would help the investigators in pinpointing the leak. The valet later recalled the ambassador's displeasure with the inquiries, his annoyance and nervousness, as the specialists probed into embassy procedures and staffing: "He seemed to disapprove of these secret service methods; he had too much delicacy of feeling for this world."[17] Sensitivities could not, however, impede the investigation.

For a time the team was misled into thinking the papers had been secretly copied aboard a train. Certain British documents known to be in German hands had been carried by Knatchbull-Hugessen on the special train taking Turkey's president and other officials to Adana on the first leg of their trip to Cairo at the beginning of December. One particular item, headed by Sir Hughe "What I want to know from the Foreign Secretary," had appeared in his own handwriting. The ambassador admitted leaving his dispatch case in his compartment during lunch, and it was learned that one of Inönü's staff sympathetic to Germany had left the lunch for a brief time; suspicion thus developed that the aide had taken the opportunity to photograph the papers.[18] The explanation seemed plausible, if unprovable.

Meanwhile, the investigators had undoubtedly discovered the ambassador's habit of keeping official papers overnight in his residence, but observing and questioning all the household servants produced no results. The valet, having been forewarned of their arrival and purpose by Mara, handled the queries without trouble and avoided their simple traps meant to catch him in lies about his languages. Summoned to the ambassador's study, where he found the security experts examining the safe, he was instructed to bring coffee for everyone. Sir Hughe asked him in French how long he had been working, to which he replied three months; the diplomat told the investigators in English that he was satisfied with Bazna. They nevertheless tried to trick him, one asking in English for more milk, which the valet gave him, and then in German for some sugar, a trap he managed to avoid. Bazna informed them in French that he understood little German except some memorized *Lieder*. His own narrative stressed his cleverness, but in the end Bazna appears to have been dismissed as a suspect largely because he was thought rather stupid and not able to understand or read English well. Apparently it was assumed that any spy would be a professional, accomplished in using a camera and fully aware of the content of documents he was copying. Dashwood like so many others was fooled by the abject manner that Bazna could adopt. Inwardly the valet was nevertheless tense and most uneasy, but throughout the security review he watched and listened as best he could and kept his contact informed.[19]

Disagreement over the investigation's effectiveness added to the controversy. One view, represented by Dulles, thought it fully successful. He felt his warning had had "direct practical value of the very highest kind," in that it ended the spying.[20] Yet he and those drawing similar conclusions assumed their stand on faith. A second idea has held that the spy was identified, though quite late, and used for some brief period to deceive the enemy. A former intelligence official and respected historian, Hugh Trevor-Roper, hinted at that explanation in later years; other analysts noted the possibility but skirted endorsing it.[21] The original and still prevailing view, which has also been set forth in the semi-official history of British wartime intelligence, holds that Cicero was never identified until after the war and ceased spying only because of a growing risk of imminent discovery.[22]

The principal investigator remained far from personally satisfied with the situation. Upon his return to London Dashwood reportedly wrote a "withering condemnation" of conditions Sir Hughe had allowed to exist at Ankara.[23] He apparently also studied carefully all the documents received from Kolbe and eventually spotted a small but key discrepancy in their texts. An embassy typist who had made a mistake in a telegram about Churchill's visit to Tehran had corrected the error in all copies but the one for the ambassador. The presence of the mistake in the document obtained by the Germans identified the diplomat's own copy as the enemy's source.[24] By the time the investigator perhaps concluded that Bazna was the culprit, however, the valet had resigned his position.

That lax security had been tolerated at the embassy was primarily the responsibility of the ambassador and senior staff. Too often such old-school, senior diplomats, regarding the world of diplomacy as one of gentlemen and not criminals, disdained tight safeguards and resented outside help. In addition, the Foreign Office's insistence on exclusive authority over security at all its facilities, exceptional wartime challenges notwithstanding, make it answerable as well for the serious and unsolved problem Sir Hughe had caused. When awkward situations arose it was not unusual for the Foreign Office to be accused of concealing its shortcomings and shielding its personnel. Thus it is hardly surprising that some observers have felt that Sir Hughe's later career and honorable retirement were a notable example of the Foreign Office closing ranks to avoid public embarrassment and to protect its own.[25]

* * *

In the mid-1970s a major controversy arose following publication of Anthony Cave Brown's *Bodyguard of Lies*, a history of deception schemes during World War II. His argument that the Cicero operation had in fact been part of a successful British trick brought quick denials and criticism, but a few supporters welcomed what they considered acceptable proof of a deception, and they added their own views. The claims and contentions are too significant to ignore, because they permeate so much of the more recent literature and commentary on the affair. Some background explanations are necessary, however, especially concerning the frictions in wartime intelligence and the nature of deception.

Obviously the decentralized structure of intelligence was confusing; "organizations were riddled with wartime factionism and rivalry," and criticism of some services and individuals abounded. A principal source of dismay was the SIS, or MI6, because of untrained personnel and poor work. Although its ineptitude and inefficiency had been evident to some prewar insiders, there remained many who "believed the myth that SIS was the best intelligence service in the world," unaware of problems that left "its few successes overshadowed by its disasters."[26] General Sir Stewart Menzies headed the service; by custom he was called "C" in MI6 and Britain. He was blamed by many during and after the war for the SIS's failings, because he had chosen its top staff and set the standards, but the Foreign Office also must be held responsible for the awkward record of the controversial Menzies and MI6. To a sizable extent the debate over the Cicero case followed the division between supporters of MI6 and its critics.

The art of deception involves creation of a false and misleading picture by feeding the opponent bits of information, slowly and carefully through what appear to be trusted channels and sources, until enemy analysts, sifting and arranging the pieces, gradually reach the deceivers' intended conclusions. Obviously a successful process of misdirection must be geared to specific goals, conducted with patience and subtlety, and designed to point to options and plans that seem plausible or likely. In the European theater the broad Allied objective was to confuse the enemy, keeping Berlin guessing about the time and location of coming attacks, making its strategists leave major forces dispersed and reserves uncommitted.[27] During late 1943 the overall deception effort carried the code name "Jael," but by 1944 the planned spring invasion of Normandy had brought adjustments in deception; the term "Bodyguard," drawn from a remark by Churchill, was now used.[28] Therefore Cave Brown entitled his book about deception *Bodyguard of Lies*.

Cave Brown claimed that Cicero had been controlled by Menzies and MI6 as a part of Jael and then Bodyguard. Having himself long believed such an explanation, he now cited as affirmation a statement by Menzies during an interview not long before his death: "Of course Cicero was under our control."[29] Cave Brown and others who accepted the declaration immediately speculated on the possible methods used to manage Cicero. Certain publications beyond Cave Brown's are especially noteworthy: David Mure's *Practise to Deceive* (1977) and *Master of Deception* (1980), drawing upon his own wartime service, and Constantine FitzGibbon's *Secret Intelligence in the Twentieth Century* (1977). FitzGibbon had translated Moyzisch's narrative into English. Claiming to have had a degree of skepticism even while working on the project, he concluded that the spy had really been a double agent, part of an unpublicized hoax managed by the intelligence service.[30] Only the most significant aspects of their contentions—timing and methods— need be reviewed to show the evidential difficulties.

Deception theorists sought to show official knowledge of the espionage at an early stage; to argue that detection had occurred quite soon reduced potential losses and overall embarrassment. Dates ranging from late October to early 1944 were cited. One opinion even held that Cicero must have been a deliberate plant, but the most common view maintained that only later did he come under control, that he had been a genuine spy whom the British unmasked and forced to work, or to whom they fed information while he remained unaware of being used. Especially noteworthy is Cave Brown's suggestion of a possible December date for discovery: he posited that Kolbe may have delivered his documents earlier than is now established and that Dulles had acted quickly.[31] In such a case the spy's continued activity itself would indicate that he was acting under direction. Both this contention and its evidence lack credibility, however, and the subsequent criticism seems fully justified.

Attempts to identify intelligence personnel who could have supervised such a deception relied heavily on hearsay and failed to be convincing. Mure recalled a visit to Cairo in late December by Brigadier Dudley Clarke, London head of "A" Force or "Deception" during 1941–

1945; Clarke, he said, had told him "A" Force was using Cicero to mislead the Germans. He claimed that other officers in Egypt involved in spreading fear among the enemy of impending attacks in the Balkans also thought the spy a conduit. But no one explained who had falsified or modified papers, how approvals of content and lines of control were managed, or whether the spy was an active collaborator or dupe. Certainly there was no acceptable rationale of why a vital code name like Overlord had not been deleted from papers consciously leaked to the enemy. By the time he wrote Mure may have misremembered facts or confused later claims about Cicero with events he had actually observed.[32]

Chidson was assigned a major role in the deception theory, because he worked for MI6. Postulating that Chidson would have run a careful prehiring check on Bazna, perhaps discovering enough information to suggest using him for deception from the outset, Cave Brown concluded that the valet at some point fell under Chidson's close control—direct or indirect, depending on the spy's awareness or ignorance of his role. He thought it likely that the control had become direct; he cited the appearance of his finger on one of the photographs as indicating that the valet had had guidance and help. Supposedly Chidson chose the items the spy would be instructed or allowed to copy, with Sir Hughe's cooperation. An essential element in the scenario is a contention that Bazna had formal espionage training that helped him play his part convincingly. Cave Brown suggested that he may have received espionage instruction at some earlier time from the Italians. A few others concurred that Chidson must have handled the spy.[33]

There were nevertheless strong objections to such reasoning and views. Chidson never said anything about a role in the affair before he died in 1957. Also, his family recalled that his posting to oversee security matters at the embassy in Ankara had in fact been a sinecure while he was recuperating from a nervous breakdown; MI6 work for many reasons had continued to be directed from the station in Istanbul.[34] Under the circumstances it seems that Chidson's involvement was illusory, asserted only to show that Menzies's claim of control had been correct.

Supporters of the deception premise could not avoid dealing with the argument that any sustained intelligence effort would have required the ambassador's knowledge and cooperation. Nevertheless, the nature of his supposed involvement was seldom made clear. Knatchbull-Hugessen himself may have caught his valet spying, according to some theorists, but he certainly helped exercise control over him. "For all Sir Hughe's grandeur, he was not a fool," as Cave Brown had observed.[35] That the ambassador was not reprimanded at the time and that his career did not suffer were cited as cogent evidence of his awareness of a deception scheme. These arguments forgot the investigator's report, so critical of Sir Hughe's lax security, and the 1950 public declaration that he had indeed been responsible for losses. Surely a victimized man would have defended himself or been vindicated by friends and colleagues.

Equally untenable was the role that deception advocates assigned to Bazna, in disregard of the personal qualities he revealed about himself. Reading his memoir shows that he was simply the wrong man to cast in the part which some accounts have scripted for him. Nothing would have pleased him more than the idea that he had been a trained operative and a double agent who had engaged in a clever and dangerous game with both sides. His ego could not have resisted such an assertion had it been true. The man showed no modesty about his importance and accomplishments and no hesitation to embellish and romanticize his feats. In addition, if the grasping Bazna had ever realized or suspected that he had cooperated even unwittingly with the British, he would certainly have demanded compensation.

There remains a final but fundamental question: Had the elderly Menzies been truthful or been accurately understood in the remark upon which Cave Brown built his theory? His record of wartime stewardship of intelligence operations had been badly marred when a trusted subordinate, Harold "Kim" Philby, and two other government employees were identified as communist agents who had gone undetected for years.[36] A number of former intelligence officers and respected analysts thought that perhaps an embittered Menzies in his last years imagined or invented successes to bolster his damaged reputation. They wondered too whether his declaration had been misconstrued or if some other error had been made in rendering it in print. In any case the statement attributed to him that Cicero had been under control was widely rejected.

Strong criticism of the position taken by Cave Brown had arisen even before his book appeared. Two interviewees who disputed the author's interpretation were Sir John Lomax, an economic warfare agent in Turkey during the period of spying, and General Sir Colin Gubbins of the Special Operations Executive; both thought that Menzies had belatedly sought to manufacture a success. Lomax described Menzies's claim as an attempt to "whitewash the stupidity of his service at Istanbul and Ankara." In a lengthy review of Cave Brown's book, another former intelligence official, Trevor-Roper, also objected to Menzies's statement and to the author's whole argument.[37] FitzGibbon met a similar rebuttal, from Cavendish-Bentinck. Having read the account in manuscript, the former security executive in the Foreign Office and chairman of the Joint Intelligence Committee firmly denied the author's deception claim. His comments were incorporated in the book: "I think you have allowed your imagination to run riot. Operation Cicero was certainly not mounted by the S.I.S." He clearly believed Sir Hughe had been careless. FitzGibbon modified but did not abandon his view concerning Cicero.[38]

The controversy ended with the appearance of several authoritative publications refuting the existence of any deception. In 1984 Nigel West, in a book dealing with World War II spy myths (entitled *Unreliable Witness* in Britain and *Thread of Deceit* in its American edition), showed that Britain and the SIS never controlled the spy or learned Cicero's identity. His previous studies of MI5 and MI6 gave his assessment weight. In the following years several volumes in the semiofficial history *British Intelligence in the Second World War* finally confirmed what so many well-informed analysts had long maintained. Of particular significance were the comprehensive volumes by F. H. Hinsley and C.A.G. Simkins on security and counterintelligence, and by Michael Howard on the operations and achievements in strategic deception. All the contributors' conclusions were clear: Cicero had indeed been a successful spy and had never been caught by the British.[39]

* * *

That investigators were unable to identify the spy is less surprising than appearances suggest. British suspicions of some leak involving Anglo-Turkish relations were not aroused until mid-December. Certainly the conjecture that a Turkish source was responsible seemed reasonable. Even the evidence received in mid-January confirmed only a loss much earlier. Were those documents copied during some single lapse in protection? Had an enemy agent active at that time subsequently ceased to spy? London had no real proof that any spying had occurred beyond December. The OSS eventually acquired such proof, but due to strained relationships and a determination to strengthen its case it withheld the information from the British.

The local and special investigators were both competent and conscientious, but Dashwood misjudged the crafty Bazna, a skillful performer when he chose to play the obsequious servant. He apparently also had difficulty with an overconfident Knatchbull-Hugessen over the issue of conformance with security regulations. That the valet could photograph at least some papers even after the inspection shows that the diplomat learned little from the spy alert. Other British officials remained uneasy but nevertheless thought that they had overcome the Ankara problem. Because of the ambassador's attitude and carelessness, however, tightened physical security had limited effect.

For many years an unwillingness to believe the spy could possibly have escaped detection fed unsupported claims of an official success never made public. With the closing of information gaps by the admissions in several recent publications, debate over the deception theory has also ended, for the uncertainties and ambiguities allowing that interpretation have been largely resolved. As a result, some key points are no longer in doubt: the spy's activity lasted from late October until the beginning of March, a period that exceeded four months; every item of information that he supplied to the enemy was genuine; the responsibility of Sir Hughe and the Foreign Office was in time realized but never acknowledged. Yet the presence of the security experts and the improvements they effected, combined with new factors, greatly limited the valet's access to documents and finally ended his espionage.

British officials visiting Turkey: Sir Hughe Knatchbull-Hugessen and Foreign Secretary Anthony Eden flanked by General Azim Gündüz and Foreign Minister Sükrü Saracoglu, who later became premier (Imperial War Museum).

Elegantly attired for a singing concert, Elyesa Bazna projects the worldly image he pursued as Cicero, only to have his dreams shattered (Droemer Knaur Verlag).

The German embassy's intelligence officer, Ludwig Moyzisch, who was responsible for handling Cicero (The Wiener Library).

Franz von Papen upon his arrest by the Americans at his country estate in April 1945 (National Archives).

Joachim von Ribbentrop working at his desk in the Foreign Ministry just before the start of World War II (National Archives).

Numan Menemencioglu carefully steered his country's foreign policy to avoid direct military involvement in the Second World War (National Archives).

Winston Churchill confers with Sir Hughe Knatchbull-Hugessen at Adana in early 1943: their efforts failed to persuade Turkey's leaders to enter the war (Imperial War Museum).

Old rivals face the same justice: Joachim von Ribbentrop addressing the war crimes court at Nuremberg. Franz von Papen is fifth from the right in the second row; just to the right of the speaker is Ernst Kaltenbrunner (National Archives).

Ex-SD officials waiting to testify at Nuremberg: from left to right, Alfred Naujocks, Viktor Lischka, Wilhelm Höttl, and Walter Schellenberg (National Archives).

A diver retrieving quantities of counterfeit British notes dumped into a lake by the Nazis to conceal their secret forgery operation (The Wiener Library; Copyright Ernst Grossar/*Stern*).

Elyesa Bazna in his later years, now much heavier, nearly bald, and without money—hardly like the once daring Cicero (The Wiener Library; Droemer Knaur Verlag).

11   Cicero's Last Achievements

Anglo-Turkish relations reached their lowest point after the military mission left on 3 February. Deliveries of supplies and equipment ceased immediately, and no further personnel arrived; trade sanctions and an oil embargo were both considered for a while. London had nevertheless already decided against a complete break in formal ties and therefore rejected a proposal by Stalin to withdraw ambassadors. Still hoping for some compromise, Britain wanted a diplomat available in Ankara. There was little official contact between Sir Hughe and Menemen-cioglu, however, until they had a chilly conversation on 28 February, just before the diplomat left the country for three weeks. Before his departure for Cairo the ambassador described as "little short of an in-sult" the stories circulating in Turkey that its airfields might be seized by force. During this critical period the Foreign Office instructed its missions in the region to remain "aloof" and let Turkey and the enemy alike worry about what the Anglo-Turkish breakdown in relations might mean.[1]

Cicero resumed his spying on a reduced level during February. Germany nevertheless failed to profit from its knowledge, gained from British documents, that any large-scale Anglo-Turkish military operation in the Balkans had been abandoned. Berlin still questioned whether there might be renewed pressure on Turkey, and it realized from the spy and other sources that the Allies planned some major action in the west for the late spring. Scholarship on both issues—Germany's man-power commitment to the Balkans and what it learned through Cicero about the plans for Overlord—has often been misleading. Meanwhile, a local incident with far-reaching repercussions diminished the Germans' satisfaction with the end of the immediate threat to their position.

* * *

At the beginning of February the defection of an Abwehr employee stationed in Istanbul brought a profound crisis. Magnified in importance by other current circumstances, the Vermehren incident became the catalyst of the Abwehr's fall, setting up a situation long awaited by its enemies. To the old claims that it had been inefficient in its intelligence mission were now added new charges that it harbored defeatism and outright treason. Angered by the Abwehr's pessimistic military assessments and by speculation about the Vermehren case, Hitler gave in to the SS, whose RSHA division chiefs had long coveted added control at the Abwehr's expense. Already Gestapo investigations of its personnel and methods had disrupted and almost paralyzed Abwehr activities; now Hitler ordered a unification of the intelligence system and assigned its administration to the RSHA departments. Schellenberg had triumphed over Canaris.

While the Vermehren episode and its consequences remained peripheral to the Cicero affair, officials and operations in Turkey came under intense scrutiny, and Papen for weeks found himself hard pressed to satisfy Berlin about the case. For Cicero there was deep anxiety that the defector might have compromised him and his work. Bazna's worry stemmed from his unfamiliarity with how Germany ran its intelligence services and their networks in Turkey.

Security restrictions and sensationalized versions have clouded the events with uncertainties and controversies, but the outline of what happened is clear. Erich Vermehren was a young idealist married to the former Countess Elisabeth von Plettenburg. Both the Vermehrens had close contacts with resistance elements, he through a young Foreign Ministry friend, Adam von Trott zu Solz, she through prominent Roman Catholic circles, all together a diverse group of anti-Nazi leaders. Frau Vermehren was also distantly related to Papen. Trott used his influence to get Vermehren assigned to military intelligence in Turkey. His posting came just as the couple faced grave danger: friends were being arrested and questioned. The situation precipitating the Vermehrens' defection had occurred earlier. A Berlin social gathering attended by an unsuspected Gestapo informant had exposed an elite anti-Nazi group. During the ensuing four-month investigation of the guests, countless other individuals, private citizens, and officials, became implicated, including many close friends and associates of the couple.[2] When mid-January brought mass arrests, Vermehren made contact with British authorities.[3] London's policy of discouraging defections apparently did not apply to the Vermehrens, the couple managed to reach the local SIS man, Nicholas Elliott, and MI6 quickly got them to safety. Speed in removing them from the country was essential lest Turkey request that they be surrendered and thereby embarrass the ambassador.[4]

On 26 January the Papens had begun a trip to Bursa for treatment of his rheumatism, stopping first at Istanbul for two days and timing their stay in Bursa to avoid participating in Nazi anniversary celebrations on 30 January. They were still there on 4 February when an embassy official arrived to say that Vermehren and his wife were missing. The staff had alerted Berlin on 2 February of their disappearance, but the Germans expected no success in locating them despite requests for Turkish help. The Papens quickly returned to Istanbul.[5] Soon everyone was busy trying to ascertain the damage and explain how the defections could have occurred.

The Abwehr's Istanbul office, under Paul Leverkühn, handled Middle East operations. Trained in law and widely experienced in foreign service, Leverkühn had apparently been chosen for the post because Canaris thought he could channel peace feelers to the Americans, but the secret police knew he made such contacts. Himmler had therefore already told Hitler of security questions about Leverkühn. Thus the defection of the Vermehrens and thereafter three more people fueled Himmler's charges against the local supervisor. Leverkühn soon returned in disgrace to Germany.[6]

Meanwhile Papen tried to calm Berlin's worries. The principal cause of anxiety was fear that Vermehren had revealed Abwehr activities and names of agents and informants. Speculation and rumors added to the confusion and embarrassment. Britain then exacerbated the situation, by informing the press of the defection, once the Vermehrens were safe, and by exerting other forms of pressure in order to undermine Papen. It hoped the affair might lead to his recall. Yet neither contemporary nor later reports that a top-ranking intelligence officer had fled with vital secrets and done incalculable harm are supported by the facts. Vermehren had not held a major position, and the data to which he had had access were probably already known to the British. In the end the couple was not willing to talk about his work, and Vermehren shed no light on Cicero.[7] That Berlin nevertheless worried so much shows how little it knew of the enemy's widespread penetration of Abwehr ranks.

In a succession of telegrams Papen urged upon Berlin the wisdom of silence and restraint. Turkey's secret service wanted to avoid public revelation of the countries' cooperation against the Allies; the ambassador doubted that much information of value had been compromised; Britain would probably exercise moderation for fear of jeopardizing its own stalled courting of Ankara. Papen used such arguments to caution against giving the incident undue weight or harmful publicity.[8]

A special problem involved explaining how Frau Vermehren had gotten permission to travel abroad. The situation suggested careful plan-

ning, possible collusion, and some rather odd decisions. Almost immediately a Foreign Ministry official prepared a memorandum explaining
how Frau Vermehren had got both travel documents and funds: in November 1943 she had come to him as recommended for foreign employment and as approved by the Abwehr, and he had provided her a minor
commission to justify her travel to Istanbul. In fact the Abwehr had
opposed the journey, and German army officers had stopped her in Bulgaria: it was then that she had obtained the Berlin official's help to
proceed. He supposedly knew nothing of a travel ban when he had let
her continue by courier plane. His request to Papen's embassy to persuade her to return to Berlin was still pending.[9]

Understandably Papen distanced himself from the Vermehrens' defection. Among his first reports to Berlin was his version of events: the
family relationship was acknowledged but quite remote; he had not
known her before 22 November 1943, when they met in Berlin's Hotel
Esplanade soon after a bombing raid; the ministry had certainly been
asked to recall her; Berlin had cited health reasons to let her remain
temporarily in Turkey. His account omitted or concealed a great deal:
their meeting had come just when she applied for foreign employment,
his statement about her delay in returning home contradicted the ministry official's memorandum, and he later admitted in his memoirs to
facilitating her travel. After the war Papen also claimed that "party
officials were quick to accuse me of having organized the whole affair,"
that "the party was clamouring for me to be brought to trial," and that
a secret plan had been conceived "about this time" to send SS men "for
the purpose of kidnapping me." Obviously the danger was real, even if
his account seems melodramatic.[10]

Throughout the crisis Ribbentrop felt pressured to demonstrate firmness, especially after the arrests of some of his ministry's personnel for
alleged ties to suspect Abwehr staff and activities. Papen answered
repeated questions about Leverkühn and others working in Turkey.[11]
Though anxious to be informed and reassured, Ribbentrop appeared to
support Papen, their past discord notwithstanding. That he took this
approach suggests how seriously Ribbentrop viewed the RSHA's determined move into the area of foreign affairs. Thus with help from
Ribbentrop, along with speedy action, deft arguments, and a few falsehoods, Papen survived the crisis. Undoubtedly his close connection with
the Cicero operation and the recent presence of the British military
mission had proven an advantage.

Moyzisch had been urgently summoned back from Bursa when officials reported the flight of the Vermehrens. He knew the defector
slightly and considered Leverkühn a good friend; their offices were in
regular touch; some thought Cicero himself might be compromised by
the couple. While Moyzisch had never divulged particulars about the

spy, he remained sure that information of "great value" had been delivered to the enemy, although no actual complications arose through the Vermehren case. Moyzisch nevertheless also worried whether the "considerable sensation" over events might scare off Cicero.[12] Both he and the ambassador thought that the combination of recent developments could bring the espionage to an end. For Moyzisch, the difficulties over the defection became a foretaste of his own miseries when his secretary deserted to the Americans two months later.

Meanwhile, the Abwehr was dissolved. Hitler's reaction to events in Turkey reflected long exasperation with Canaris. Having misforecast a number of military developments and having let his agency drift without strong leadership, Canaris had been in trouble all during 1943, though at first the military had shielded him, keeping his opponents from forcing a showdown. Hitler had himself remained steadfastly opposed to turning over intelligence operations to Himmler. In February, however, Hitler vehemently rejected a new intelligence analysis of the Russian military front. Hitler raged about Canaris's pessimistic assessment of the situation and also the relatively minor Vermehren incident in Turkey. In his wrath and frustration he ordered the Abwehr placed under RSHA supervision but left it intact as a unit. The Abwehr's downfall clearly resulted from its own failings, in both poor intelligence work and careless security, and the Vermehren case underscored the criticisms which ended its existence.

Dissolution of the Abwehr had far-reaching repercussions. Until mid-1944 military intelligence remained a separate entity within the RSHA structure; the subsequent failure of the 20 July assassination plot let Schellenberg assume full control. In the wake of the abortive coup the German resistance was crushed by mass arrests and executions.[13] Meanwhile Abwehr operations deteriorated, as agents abroad were recalled or defected, just as the war was entering a new phase with the Normandy landings. Certainly German intelligence operations in Turkey suffered heavily; Papen sent home about a dozen staff members connected to the Abwehr, while the Allies increased pressure on Turkish authorities. Consequently at least eight hundred known Axis agents and informants were soon compromised.[14]

* * *

Cicero became active again during February. After a period of caution when the British first improved their security, he regained some confidence upon discovering how to circumvent the alarm system; still, conditions made Bazna's access a matter of chance. Some items he copied had little value. With the departure of the British military mission at the beginning of the month, the coldness in relations with Turkey left the ambassador less busy. Changes in physical safeguards were accompanied by more careful handling of papers: important documents were kept under tighter control and less often stored overnight in the residence. With an extended absence of the ambassador, a leave encouraged by London to underscore its annoyance with Turkey's refusal to help, the valet had nothing to photograph. Thus the cessation of his espionage work resulted from lack of opportunity to produce more films. Cicero made his final delivery early in March, of photographs he had taken just before his employer's departure; by the time the ambassador returned later that month, Bazna had decided to give notice to Sir Hughe. It was a quiet ending to his role.

Moyzisch reacted with silent disbelief to the spy's "highly involved stories" about "complicated safety measures" being taken by the British. Still convinced that the valet knew English despite all his earlier denials, the intelligence officer listened without comment to the spy's account of overhearing his employer and the experts discuss how the new protective devices worked, taking pride in having caught Cicero contradicting himself. He labeled a similar claim of having observed how the alarm system functioned "an extraordinarily unlikely tale," because the specialists would never have allowed a foreign servant to stand nearby. In the end he concluded that the elaborate stories about his cleverness were the spy's preparation for seeking more money. Indeed, the valet asked for £20,000 per roll, guaranteeing at least fifteen exposures; he rejected the proposal, noting that he had already paid some £200,000 before the break in deliveries. It was his belief that "the feeling of power" now kept the spy going.[15]

Actually, there was a motive beyond manipulation and money: Bazna's fascination with the impressionable Esra. Unable to control his ego as first protector and then lover, he displayed his daring to her despite the dangers, reflecting the tension in a return to his former mood swings. "I was conceited, shameless, sentimental, cynical, superstitious, ugly, and full of complexes. I was burning with ambition, and felt very sorry for myself."[16] In part he went on taking risks to be a hero in her eyes.

Bazna later described how he overcame the safeguards installed by the British. One day the power failed as he was pressing the ambassador's clothing; Esra had been instructed to remove all the fuses while some men worked on the alarm for Sir Hughe's safe. He spoke to the embassy official assigned to watch the workers, explaining that he needed current to carry on with his duties and suggesting that only the fuse serving the study need be removed. He and the young woman saw which fuse the man did not reinstall. The following day they confirmed how to cut electric power to the alarm.[17] But he also had a scare.

On an occasion when Sir Hughe and his secretary were away during midday, Bazna took papers from the safe and copied them in his room, holding the camera by hand since his makeshift stand was at the rented house, and letting the eager Esra think that keeping watch was really necessary. Concealing the papers under his livery to return them and leaving Esra to replace the fuse after five minutes, he unexpectedly ran into the ambassador's wife, who asked when his relative would be leaving and requested tea to relieve a cold. Despite the delay he restored the papers to the safe without incident, discovering with relief that the alarm was still deactivated, but he could not readily dispel the nervous panic that had seized him. Relaying to another servant the order for tea, he suddenly vented his rage upon his helper, whose trouble with the fuse had saved him, telling the confused young woman that she must leave the residence at once.[18] Whatever the extent of truth in this particular tale, perhaps very little, he obviously took risks getting papers to copy.

Cicero resumed his sales of film during the first week of February. Moyzisch must have just been called back from his stay at Bursa to deal with the crisis created by the Vermehrens. He had probably taken the rare leave because the spy had been inactive for a while. It is also possible that his brief absence and the defection rumors caused the valet anxiety: this was perhaps the occasion when Bazna agreed to a meeting at Moyzisch's office despite his dislike of going there. Using the same precautions and access through the fence as on his initial visit, he spoke with Jenke, supposedly telling the diplomat what more he had learned about the enemy's war plans, until the busy Moyzisch could see him. The valet later claimed that Jenke had told him that Hitler planned to reward him with a villa.[19] Although Bazna used the story to magnify his importance, perhaps inventing the visit just to mention the minister and house, it had certainly become essential to the Germans to reassure him. Papen had indeed sent two telegrams on 10 February to alert Ribbentrop that they could soon lose Cicero: he might decide he had enough money or be frightened by the dangers.[20]

There were a number of other deliveries, stretching over about four weeks, but access to papers now depended too greatly on luck: neither the volume nor content of the photographs matched past efforts. While he considered some items to be quite interesting, Moyzisch called the material "nowhere near" the "former standard" set by Cicero; still, he hoped that better information might arrive. If statements made by Moyzisch about his payment records are correct, there were in all perhaps ten rolls, although it is unlikely Cicero would have exhausted each spool's capacity.[21] Given the need for timely delivery and the uncertainty about filming opportunities, not to mention his greed, he undoubtedly marketed whatever exposures he had as quickly as possible. Nor would Moyzisch's rejection of higher payments for a guaranteed minimum of shots have precluded his acceptance of partial rolls that

Berlin could use. Actually, during this period Moyzisch refused payment for one roll, with more exposures than usual, showing a list of British outlays for petty embassy expenses. Berlin soon overruled his judgment, however, ordering him to compensate Cicero.[22] Moyzisch cited the incident to show both the spy's trickery and how much poorer his material was in February.

Cicero made his final delivery—reportedly the code word Overlord again appeared in one of the papers—at the beginning of March. He gave no indication of ending his activity, even implying that there would be more photographs later, but the ambassador had already gone on leave. Cicero appeared a few days later to collect money still owed him and arranged one or two further meetings with Moyzisch, but he had nothing more to sell. In his own account Bazna ignored his employer's three-week absence, mentioning only that curiosity kept him prying into Sir Hughe's papers for a while. Yet that could only have been in late March or the first week of the following month. He stopped even that practice upon realizing that Ankara's then-improving relations with London exposed him to his own government's ire if he were caught. The story of unprofitable snooping lacks a semblance of truth, however, and it was probably added to sustain an image of daring. Moyzisch dated the spy's last contact as just before 6 April, the "ghastly" day his secretary defected to the Allied side; Cicero thereafter feared that she could identify him to the British.[23] That development was later seized upon by both men independently to provide an exciting close to their respective narratives of the spying—that in fact had already reached an undramatic end.

It is impossible to determine the exact number of documents that were copied during the spy operation, because the evidence is sketchy and the participants cited different counts. There is no official record of how many rolls of film were bought or supplied; nor would the majority of the spools have been fully exposed. Discrepancies in the subsequent recollections therefore arose from mixed references to rolls and photographs. Not even those figures, however, reveal the extent of loss: with multipage items requiring two or more shots, the count of exposures would have exceeded the number of documents. Some general indicators are nevertheless available. Moyzisch spoke of a total of forty to fifty rolls of film and said that he bought "in all some four hundred photographs" in his dealings with Cicero. An average of about ten exposures per roll was well within reason. The German translator of the material throughout the period, Maria Molkenteller, estimated that she had worked on some 130 to 150 telegrams. That figure too is compatible with other information about the number of spools and photographs. Not every message had an exceptional value; many dealt with commercial and trade issues.[24]

Bazna reviewed his personal arrangements during the quiet weeks of March, but a deepening fear of being caught dictated his next actions. Believing himself to be enormously rich, with £300,000 sterling, or 2.3 million in Turkish pounds, he finally solved his storage difficulties. Moving notes from under the carpet in his embassy room first to the hiding place under the basement steps and then to his suburban house had been only a temporary measure. With private safe-deposit space in a bank already rented for the "greater part" of his funds, he now packed the notes into a suitcase, which the loyal Esra then brought to him by taxi when he finished work one day. He took the money to the bank. About the same time he smashed the strong light bulb and the camera, throwing the camera and quadripod pieces into a river, thereby removing from his quarters any signs that he might have been spying.[25]

One reason for transferring the notes was his decision to give up the house. Not only did he associate it with the spy activities he was now abandoning, realizing it represented an unnecessary risk, but also he wanted to separate his intended life from his humble past. Esra also had to go, not because she knew he was a spy but because she knew he had been a *kavass*. He established her first in a hotel and later in a small apartment; he claimed also to have paid her university fees. When he left the ambassador's employ, he rented for himself a fashionable flat in the city's Maltepe area. A shapely but modestly talented singer of Greek origin, Aika, became Bazna's mistress as long as his money lasted. They were already together in early June when news came of the Normandy landings that opened the western front.[26]

Bazna's resolve to quit his position brought worries that giving notice might alert the British. He may have chosen to inform the ambassador about 20 April because Sir Hughe then seemed preoccupied with his duties and other problems: amid the flurry of official visits and messages accompanying newly improved Anglo-Turkish relations, he supposedly accepted the valet's resignation with little concern. Instructed to settle financial matters with the butler, Bazna was also told to turn over his duties to Zeki. As usual, later he dramatized the brief exchange: that he had taken out his handkerchief to dry his nervous hands, and as the ambassador walked away out fell the duplicate key to the black box. The diplomat did not see it but would have recognized it at once. Another servant saw it fall but assumed it belonged to Esra's place in the city, an error the valet confirmed. Afterward he threw his keys into a canal. Whether the whole key incident really occurred is, of course, doubtful. Sir Hughe was working and had asked not to be disturbed when the valet left the building for good on 30 April. "My departure could not have been more unobtrusive. . . . I walked down the empty street with my attaché case, unnoticed by anyone, a short, thickset man, beginning to grow bald."[27]

Had he quit or was he fired? Questions and difficulties exist because of the alleged dates of his notice and departure. On 6 April the young secretary in Moyzisch's office defected to the Americans; later she informed the British of a servant's spying activities. She may have first told the British her story in Cairo, due to trouble between the local OSS and MI6 units, but British officials would have alerted Sir Hughe at once to the danger. The warning would explain his postwar comment that there had been a minor incident involving a servant dismissed for spying. Perhaps there was even some brief attempt, as some have claimed, to use him to deceive the enemy. Because his espionage had already stopped, there could be no evidence. Whether the awkward situation was handled by accepting the suspect valet's already proffered resignation or by firing him remains unknown. Bazna may also have departed well before 30 April. In any case, clearly he was able to leave without trouble.

Germany had meanwhile been unable, due to its own problems and the uncertainties of Hitler, to profit substantially from the British failure to get Turkey's cooperation by the beginning of February. Coinciding with the departure of the British military mission had come the embarrassment of the Vermehren case and its attendant turmoil. Papen also discovered before long that the extent of Turkish isolation was causing concern and rethinking in Ankara. Despite his efforts to build good will and exploit the difficulties in Anglo-Turkish and Turco-Soviet relations, he knew that his country's long-range prospects had not improved. Meanwhile Berlin's secret knowledge gave it little advantage, political or military, because officials did not act upon Cicero's reports. Hitler in particular still expected some British operation that might endanger the Balkans. By preventing reassignment of troops to other areas—Italy, France, and Russia—he fulfilled a secondary aim of his opponents.

Papen conveyed an aura of satisfaction and confidence in his signals to Berlin. Still, his efforts to exacerbate the enemy's difficulties and solidify German gains met with little success, and he was too shrewd not to realize that Turkey's policy would not last. Soon after the withdrawal of the British military group came some hints. On 8 February, when Papen entertained the cabinet with a concert by pianist Walter Gieseking, he saw that the political awkwardness had much disquieted Menemencioglu. The minister indicated that relations with the Allies could not be allowed to deteriorate further. On 11 February the ambassador summarized another official conversation with Menemencioglu. Patently aiming to reassure his superiors, he stressed that Germany had prevailed for the moment in the struggle over Turkey's joining the war, a victory the enemy was admitting. Ankara had accepted the immediate effects of Allied annoyance and feared no direct coercion by London, due to British weakness in the Aegean. Papen kept to himself the possibility of some placating Turkish gesture, like limiting German trade. Meanwhile he reported that the Soviet Union must be relieved and that Menemencioglu foresaw no change in relations. While apparently wanting Ankara to join the war, Moscow would not welcome a military buildup in Turkey or the presence of RAF installations so near. The Turks in the ambassador's opinion remained deeply concerned about the unstated postwar ambitions of their Soviet neighbor.[28] If time indeed confirmed Ankara's suspicion that Stalin still adhered to his country's old territorial aims, especially to control the Straits, its leaders would be proven wrong in believing Britain might be working secretly with Moscow to undermine their rights. Papen was correct in thinking that the Turks' main focus was fixed on Moscow.

Turkey's unwillingness to help develop a southern front in the Balkans served in the end to increase the danger that Soviet troops would in time overrun and then dominate eastern Europe. Papen still hoped to avoid communist expansion, through negotiation or even capitulation to the West. "It had become absolutely clear to me, as a result of reading all the Cicero telegrams, that I must do everything I could to hasten the end of the war." Once again he had his friend Kurt von Lersner contact George Earle about terms of peace; it is obvious that Papen and others exaggerated the American agent's influence and did not grasp Roosevelt's commitment to wartime unity. Earle forwarded an outline peace proposal, which Roosevelt rejected; he referred all such queries to Eisenhower. Flying to Washington, Earle argued in vain that the West was in effect giving all eastern Europe to the Russians. Papen meanwhile also requested assistance from the Vatican.[29]

In other instances Papen used the Turks' good will as leverage to mitigate policies. Thus he managed to convince an annoyed Ribbentrop that Ankara would assert the right of its embassy in Budapest to grant asylum to Hungarian leaders who sought such protection. Also, he successfully opposed Berlin's order to strip many émigrés of their citizenship. Alerted by Jewish contacts to proposed deportations from occupied southern France of thousands of Ottoman Jews long living there in exile, Papen approached Menemencioglu, who let him inform Berlin that any such action would create a public sensation and severely damage Turco-German relations. "This démarche succeeded in quashing the whole affair." Citing such interventions in his memoirs was intended to bolster his reputation: "I mention these incidents only to demonstrate that it was possible . . . for a person in my position to exercise normal instincts and refuse to obey such unprincipled orders."[30]

The quiet diplomatic scene during February and March reflected a time of readjustments. Britain's withdrawal into a dignified coolness,

deepened by Sir Hughe's long absence, strongly underscored the isolation of Turkey. Its leaders realized that they must soon reach some
accommodation with the Allies; Papen correctly sensed that the Turkish concession would involve curbing deliveries of raw materials to Germany. While privately recognizing his country's dwindling prestige and
lack of bargaining power, he exerted his influence in Ankara to delay
any such decision, hoping that use of the spy's information might improve military conditions. In that vital regard he erred.

Germany failed to react as might have been expected to what had
become clear by February: abandonment of any Anglo-Turkish campaign or cooperation. That timely knowledge of the frustrating of Britain's military aims in southeastern Europe gave no advantage to
German defense strategists arose from Hitler's caution and new developments on the eastern front. During the second half of 1943 the Germans had responded to the rapidly changing regional situation—Italy's
collapse and invasion. Britain's attacks in the Aegean, pressure on Turkey—by increasing from about seventeen to twenty-five the number of
divisions stationed in the region. The new question was whether Berlin
could now risk shifting some of those troops and resources from the
Balkans to areas under greater threat. Such advice was given, but fragments of evidence show that Hitler resisted his generals' views.

Schellenberg related some insights to attitudes in Germany. His staff
concluded, based on early analyses of Allied talks at top-level conferences, with "a certainty of 60 per cent that Churchill had not been able
to maintain his plan for a second front through an invasion of the Balkans." Schellenberg despaired when political leaders in Berlin thought
in terms mainly of having weathered a crisis and refused to see how
the Allies' mounting strength and firm determination spelled their nation's impending doom. The fault lay not with his reports, for "our evaluating commentaries were simple and straightforward, and there was
no mistaking their meaning." Himmler supposedly fell into a "state of
uncertainty" under the influence of Schellenberg;[31] Ribbentrop, however, still harbored misgivings about information from Cicero and along
with Goebbels welcomed only comforting stories of Allied tensions.[32] In
all likelihood such party loyalists used their access to Hitler to reinforce
his instincts about how to conduct the war.

Military analysts had meanwhile weighed continually and carefully
all data affecting their existing and projected needs. After integrating
the spy's material circulated by Schellenberg with other sources of intelligence, they no longer expected a major British assault or effort in
the southeastern region: nothing in the reports from aerial reconnais-
sance and listening posts indicated any significant shifting of combat
units or assembling of naval craft. In February an entry in General
Alfred Jodl's diary showed that the head of the OKW's Operations Staff

felt that "results from Cicero" had now made clear that they need fear no imminent British attack in the eastern Mediterranean. Instead, Britain intended only to maintain a challenging posture while the Allies prepared for a spring invasion along the western European coastline. That conclusion suggested that troops could be released to other current and expected fronts.[33]

On 13 February the OKW proposed that two divisions from the Balkans be chosen for transfer to France or the Italian lines. Fifteen days later a further assessment of Fremde Heere West (Enemy Armies West) agreed that given the stand Turkey had now taken, neither the Mediterranean nor the Balkans need be considered under threat for the present. Also, early in March Field Marshal Maximilian von Weichs confirmed the High Command's belief that Allied action in Thrace or Turkey was most unlikely.[34] The troop transfers thought feasible by the German defense planners were delayed, however, for Hitler did not trust the intelligence reports.

Hitler had been briefed regularly on the data from Cicero. Thus, in a conversation on 27 December he had told General Kurt Zeitzler, the army chief of staff, that Britain wanted "to force Turkey into the war by 15 February." He wondered how much Ankara's policy would be determined by Soviet military advances north of the Black Sea, as well as by the old issues: was Turkey still so deeply fearful of Russian expansion to the south and designs on the Straits that it would resist the Allies' aims?[35] While subsequent reports seemed to be reassuring, new material in mid-January from Cicero showed enemy intentions to maintain some kind of regional threat—a much too ambiguous and troublesome phrase. Did it mean the appearance of a challenge, some sort of feint, or the mounting of an assault or landings? Nor was it certain that Turkey would stand firm under new pressure. Some sort of enemy operation made sense to Hitler, because of the advantages it would offer: attacks by guerrillas in the Balkans would increase in number and severity, vital ore and oil deliveries to Germany would be disrupted or cut, and the small satellites linked to Berlin would desert to save themselves. With the intensified fighting in Italy after the mid-January Anzio landings, a new Allied attack would further strain his defenses. Because southeastern Europe held an important place in his strategic thinking and he instinctively distrusted spies, he hesitated to reduce the size of the Balkan force. Hitler and Ribbentrop nevertheless used the spy's reports ruling out any immediate operation to calm the jittery leaders of Bulgaria and Hungary.[36]

Time ran out before troops were moved. Any question of transferring two divisions westward became moot starting in March, when strong new Soviet drives on the Ukrainian front gained momentum and threatened to overrun the region. All available units were needed in the vain effort to check the Soviet advances that swept south and west during the rest of the year. What the effect might have been on the Italian fighting or on the later French front cannot be determined, but Germany failed to shift the divisions, based on the Cicero data; the secondary British aim of worrying the enemy about the Balkans and tying down forces was achieved.

The most sensational claim concerning the information that Cicero gave the Germans maintained that it included details of the secret preparations and schedules for "Overlord," or the Allied invasion of the continent planned for late spring. (A soothing corollary to the admissions of leakage has usually been that little or no actual harm resulted, because the enemy's distrust of the spy led it to consider the data a trick and therefore to disregard it. Such stories, however popular, are untrue.) The claims originated with Moyzisch's exaggerated description of the information he handled, became part of the legend as the case acquired fame, and gained dramatic definition when the film *Five Fingers* reached world audiences. Sir Hughe never escaped the stigma created by such extravagant accounts of his valet's exploits; the misinformation was revived in their obituaries when both principals died in the early 1970s.[37] His stature and key post brought access to many special documents and analyses, and the general code name itself was indeed mentioned in various papers, but Sir Hughe would not have received details of plans for D-Day. The code word is all that the Germans ever learned through the spy.

Moyzisch maintained that the term Overlord represented the "one considerable success" achieved by Cicero in his cautious efforts during February.[38] The information, hinting at an important new operation, aroused immediate interest among his superiors. Schellenberg even claimed that it was from the Cicero films that Berlin first discovered that the invasion of France was codenamed Overlord. That eventual wartime conclusion resulted from correlation of many reports and inquiries, however, rather than from any specific document. By implication, Moyzisch and Schellenberg attributed far greater importance to Cicero's contributions and consequently to their own than is warranted. Papen remained much closer to the truth, however, stressing only knowledge of the word Overlord. In contrast, of scarcely any value are Bazna's inflated claims on the subject. Noting that the term often appeared in documents, Bazna would write that he realized even then that it represented the second front demanded by Moscow, an assertion clearly based on egoism and later insights.

Identifying the general meaning of Overlord was less difficult for the Germans than ascertaining the significant details. Knowing the enemy's broad operational plans from the body of copied documents, and examining items where the term appeared for contextual clues, analysts soon linked the code designation with the expected attack in the west. Schellenberg asserted that the high-frequency impulses of the cable between Britain and America had been recorded and that "by an incredibly complicated process" the sounds and messages had been deciphered. The military buildup clearly pointed to an impending invasion. Thus in February General Jodl made a diary entry headed "Results from Cicero" and listed the code name: "Overlord=Major invasion from Britain."[39]

Meanwhile, the quest for information took a number of forms. In addition to conferring with General Thiele's cryptography section of the High Command, whose experts he asked to search all Allied signals for use of the code term, Schellenberg alerted his agents, like Moyzisch, to question their sources about the designation. Moyzisch attempted in vain to get the spy to seek out references to Overlord: "As usual, it was no use giving him orders." The intelligence officer had to be satisfied with the spy's ordinary pace. Nevertheless he watched for mention of Overlord in all deliveries of new photographs. At about this time Moyzisch's recollection of having seen before a document saying that some issue in Anglo-Turkish negotiations had to be fully resolved no later than 15 May caused him great excitement. The deadline might suggest the timing for launching the attack. He explained his reasoning in a report, but he received a bland reply that called his theory "possible but hardly probable." Perhaps the story is untrue. Moyzisch was passing himself off as a diplomat and criticizing Ribbentrop: "It seems ironic that the last piece of invaluable information supplied by Cicero should have been treated by Berlin with exactly the same lack of comprehension as all the others."

Papen proposed talking publicly about Overlord. "I repeatedly suggested that in order to deceive the enemy into thinking that we knew its details, our propaganda should give the impression that we possessed considerable knowledge." Instead, silence was preserved to prevent the enemy from discovering that its secret term had become known.

There is no doubt that appearance of the word Overlord in the Cicero films helped German analysts gain insights to their opponents' plans. Whether the first knowledge of the term came from those documents remains less clear, because the evidence comes from self-serving claims. In any case, Berlin obtained no details concerning Overlord through Cicero, because none were available to Sir Hughe. He eventually learned the invasion date, but that fact was never at risk, for by then the espionage had ceased.[40] It must also be remembered that the term Overlord was generally superseded, as the Allies chose new names for each component of planning.[41] Unfortunately the inflated claims publicized by Moyzisch and other sensationalists about the Overlord plans produced decades of avoidable misunderstanding. In view of the gravity of such false representations, it is surprising that the British government in acknowledging the espionage in 1950 failed to clarify that point, in order to minimize embarrassment and prevent further speculation.

* * *

The outcomes and trends of events during February and March meant disappointment for all the nations involved. Britain recognized the thwarting of its ambitious military plans and bided its time, awaiting new developments; Germany failed to benefit significantly from its enemy's setback and experienced its own troubles over the Abwehr; Turkey realized with discomfort the extent and consequences of its isolation from the war's likely winners. The spy too wanted a change; Cicero delivered his last photographs at the beginning of March. The great issues and excitement at the turn of the year had given way to quiescence and doubts. But there remained a drama yet to surface.

Throughout the closing months of the Cicero affair an intelligence operation controlled by American agents sought to identify the spy: a young assistant secretary newly employed in Moyzisch's office reported whatever information she could learn. These parallel espionage efforts remained separate, however, until the young woman's defection finally exposed the connection and danger. That her sudden disappearance later enabled both Moyzisch and Bazna to end their narratives sensationally is misleading: the valet's spying had in fact already ceased for other reasons. Yet an examination of both her unsuspected role and the OSS's months of concealed activity in the Cicero case is essential for understanding all dimensions of the affair.

12   An American Spy

A romantic tradition in espionage literature, both in fiction and true stories, prescribes the involvement of an intriguing woman. Usually she is mysterious, beautiful, and quite dangerous. In Moyzisch's narrative and later in Bazna's as well the role fell to Moyzisch's new, young office assistant. Cornelia Kapp had been born into a respected family in Berlin but had spent many formative years in the United States. The attractive daughter of a German consular official, she was not infiltrated into her job, but the Americans acquired much information through her. Only years later did she speak of her wartime activity, however, and her statements drew little attention despite the new insights they afforded.

Moyzisch's book is unreliable on the Kapp episode due to his limited knowledge, unwarranted suppositions, and his highly colored treatment of Kapp's part in what finally happened to Cicero. Certainly he refused to admit her espionage. He used her story only to create a dramatic thread and climax for his narrative and to conceal awkward truths and implications that he must have suspected. That he was capable of deception is clear from his pose as a diplomat; that he had to concoct a plausible defense stemmed from difficulties with his superiors. In consequence his version of events became so misleading that it must be disregarded. Among the needed corrections is the dropping of the pseudonym "Elisabet," which he introduced and many writers repeated over the years.[1]

Kapp's postwar fate remained unknown until the early 1960s, when the collaborator in Bazna's memoir, Hans Nogly, traced her by engaging a journalist to check records. G. Thomas Beyl located her through friends in Chicago and then interviewed her in California.[2] The statements that she and others made to him were quoted at length in the book. While the framework of her account appears sound, she clearly exaggerated certain points, both to enhance and explain her past actions. It is doubtful that she was as calculating as she claimed, for instance, or that her nervous outbursts were entirely a clever act. Yet her comments supplied facts and connections missing from Moyzisch's narrative and revealed another dimension of the spy operation. Therefore no study of the Cicero affair can be complete or balanced without noting her months of intelligence work and the Americans' secret efforts to identify the spy.

* * *

Karl Kapp appears to have been a conscientious servant of Nazi Germany. In 1936, after a posting at Bombay, he became consul-general in Cleveland, remaining until mid-summer 1941. While two sons, Torald and Peter, remained in their native land, the couple brought their daughter, Cornelia or "Nele," who was seventeen. The family settled in suburban Shaker Heights, and Nele Kapp attended first the private Laurel School and then Flora Stone Mather College of Western Reserve University, through her junior year. Her comfortable life and youthful experiences would change her outlook. In particular she fell in love with a young Clevelander, whom she would later meet again when he was working in intelligence. Meanwhile, an American government order in July 1941 suddenly closed all German consulates, and the Kapp family departed for Germany the same month. Their expulsion had resulted from a sweeping crackdown on Germans deemed to be subversives or threats to security.[3]

Certainly the consul-general had been active and outspoken in behalf of his country's regime. Press reports said that he had followed the Nazi line "tenaciously" while in Cleveland and had served the regime with open pride: he had displayed a life-size portrait of Hitler in his office, flown the swastika flag at his residence, and badgered the German community with speeches and slogans at rallies. In more confidential work Kapp supplied his nation's military attaché, General Friedrich von Boetticher, with data and clippings about Cleveland industries and civil defenses.[4] His outlook and record suggest how much his daughter's later flight must have upset him.

After the family's return home, Kapp was posted to Italy. Cornelia studied nursing in Germany, though she soon joined her parents. In July 1943 she accompanied them when her father was reassigned to Bulgaria, and she became an embassy secretary in Sofia. She later said that within a month she was approached by the Americans to undertake intelligence work. The offer originated in Turkey and was readily accepted.

Years later Kapp explained her decision: "I worked exclusively for the American secret service. . . . I was never paid for what I did," since "my chief motive was my desire to return to America, and that was promised me as the reward. . . . I was never really at home in Germany, . . . I made all my friends in the United States, and I remained in Cleveland until the war broke out. . . . A young love affair dating from my Cleveland days played a big part in making me willing to work for the American secret service." She met the man again in Ankara, where he served with the OSS, but in her postwar interviews would not identify him. Kapp claimed that "it was no accident that I went to Ankara."[5] Perhaps she meant only that her commitment to spy and defect had been made consciously well before her move, or she may have romanticized the facts a bit. Other sources indicate that she could not have foreseen her transfer to the specific place or job.

That agents of American intelligence in Turkey recruited Kapp when she reached Sofia is not surprising. Once aware of her presence, and using the young Clevelander whom she loved as leverage, they would have thought it a worthwhile gamble. Kapp later gave no particulars about the initial contact or any spying in Sofia. She denied seeing her friend again until after her transfer to Ankara, and tales about lovers who had worked together are fanciful.[6] Because her relocation to a neutral country would have mutual advantages, American agents probably suggested ways in which she might broach and pursue the idea. She admitted inducing her father to help, making use of her reactions to recent air raids, and before long the stratagem brought results.

Accounts differ on how Kapp came to work for Moyzisch, with access to his secrets. Overly dramatic writers have implied a deliberate plant, but there is no foundation for such claims, the evidence revealing only broad intent and then opportunity. Kapp sought transfer to any country from which she could defect; Moyzisch's staffing needs and a friend's help led to specific employment. But her new position exposed Kapp to unexpected stress and danger.

Moyzisch had a heavy workload of reports for the SD. He had to follow the local press, whether in Turkish or other languages, forwarding translations of significant articles, and to inform his superiors about all important people and developments. His responsibilities for the SD required quantities of information rather than detailed analyses, for which Berlin had its own specialists. With additional burdens from the Cicero operation, which required his personal attention, the harassed Moyzisch needed more office help. His problem was exacerbated by a mishap. Moyzisch's regular secretary was ordinarily so efficient that embassy colleagues had nicknamed her "Schnürchen," loosely "Clockwork." But for many months she could not type well, because in early September she had caught and injured her thumb in the heavy safe door.[7]

In mid-December the press attaché, Moyzisch's friend Seiler, traveled to Sofia to purchase supplies. Staying at the Bulgari Hotel, reserved for Germans, he happened to meet the Kapps. The diplomat asked Seiler about employment for his daughter, at Istanbul or Ankara, because she was so nervous during air raids. It seemed evident to Seiler that the Kapps thought her high strung. He later insisted that the inquiry came from Kapp, that the young woman herself sat quietly. The long-haired blonde was attractive, "very well dressed," and skilled in the normal office procedures. So he mentioned an opening, one requiring complete discretion, that might be available. Seiler would remain positive that he never used the name Cicero in reference to the work in Ankara. His account confirms Moyzisch's claim that Kapp arrived by chance.[8]

Moyzisch believed that he had discovered help for Schnürchen. The young woman seemed ideal—a respected family, diplomatic background, several languages, and office experience. Thus he was determined to hire her. Arranging a transfer nevertheless required joint approvals. Neither Papen nor the ministry raised any objections, but his own superior did, the crafty Kaltenbrunner supposedly suggesting a male aide. Moyzisch knew that any such person would undermine his position, by acting under orders from Berlin.[9] Finally his own choice was accepted.

When Kapp arrived about the first week of January 1944, both Seiler and Moyzisch met her train at Ankara's station. The pretty and carefully groomed person Seiler had met was now disheveled and overwrought. Neither man could understand her appearance and mental state. According to Seiler, "she looked appalling. She was a bundle of nerves. Her hair was hanging down over her face, and her hands and finger-nails were filthy." Moyzisch was unprepared for Kapp: "Her eyes were dull, with a sort of glazed expression. Her skin was greasy and had an unhealthy grayish tinge. She was altogether a most unattractive sight." He left her at a hotel he had chosen, but the following day found her seriously ill, so he moved her to the home of friends, to whom she was, he claimed, rude and ungrateful. Ten days passed before she started to work. Kapp herself said nothing later about being sick upon arriving in Ankara.[10]

Various possibilities may explain her appearance and behavior. Full realization of her position, her irrevocable commitment to spying and eventual defection, may have produced uncontrollable panic, aggravated by fatigue and perhaps some viral infection. There remains too a suspicion that Moyzisch and Seiler later exaggerated the facts for personal ends: portraying a distraught and irritating woman, trouble from the outset, made their misjudgments seem less blameworthy. Her own assertion of simple "play-acting" is the least credible interpretation. Such conscious efforts may have occurred later, when she sought to redirect attention from her secret work, but her distress upon arrival was probably real.

Kapp's nearly three months of spying presumably went unsuspected even after her defection; they were certainly not acknowledged or described by Moyzisch. That his version of events, with its evasions and misrepresentations of issues and facts, has so often been repeated is especially unfortunate. The story emerging from Kapp's statements is much different.

Her initial duties involved preparing routine translations. Moyzisch described her work as careless, probably the effect of nervousness and anxiety. Even though not handling sensitive items, and kept under a certain degree of surveillance, she soon pursued her secret purpose.[11] Security was minimal. She had Moyzisch fooled—"he fell for all my play-acting"—so "he made my work for the Americans easy. . . . After only four days I had a key to his safe and copied out secret documents." Although Kapp never explained about the key, she most likely did as Bazna had done, that is, got a good copy made with her contact's help. She later claimed to have obtained a quantity and variety of materials, all given at night to her contact man, her remarks giving a flattering picture of both her control and achievements. Yet her basic success cannot be denied.

At some point the OSS instructed her to identify the spy Moyzisch would meet at night. "The Americans had known for some time that a man known as Cicero really existed in flesh and blood. It was my task to establish his identity." Attempts to learn about him by watching Moyzisch may account for the earlier car pursuit: "The Americans once nearly caught sight of the man. . . . That was on the evening when Moyzisch and Cicero only just managed to get away after a wild chase through the whole of Ankara." On several occasions Kapp spoke with Cicero without learning anything. Bazna remembered talking to the new secretary with the "bright, pleasant voice" when he telephoned to arrange an appointment with Moyzisch. She tried to question him. Her curiosity and efforts persisted in their later conversations, in which "Pierre" said she "giggled" at times; he liked to engage her in flirtatious banter. Kapp later claimed that she once caught a glimpse of Cicero: "One night he went to Moyzisch's rooms. I kept watch in front of the house, and I saw him in the distance, but it was too dark." Thus when Kapp at last faced him she could not identify him: "I did not know what Cicero looked like."[12]

Shortly before her defection Kapp and Cicero met by chance in an Ankara shop called the ABC, where both ordered clothing. Despite past conversations neither had recognized the other's voice. Moyzisch too was present, to help his assistant with Turkish, but Kapp wanted custom-made lingerie, for which Moyzisch's Turkish failed him. They soon attracted Cicero's notice. Moyzisch would recall that Cicero was ordering special silk shirts, a display Moyzisch thought careless; Cicero approached them offering in French to help. He and Kapp chatted amiably while Moyzisch hid his discomfort in silence. Moyzisch had always believed the spy was Albanian and was surprised to hear Cicero addressing the clerk in "perfect Turkish." Bazna would recall that his purchase had been not a shirt but a dress for Esra. Despite the risk in patronizing an expensive shop, "the thrill of playing with danger held me in its grip." He especially liked making his contact uneasy, thinking that he had caught him buying lingerie for a girl friend. Bazna learned that the lady was German.[13] Neither guessed the role that each played in the other's life.

Moyzisch never admitted knowing that his assistant had been a spy, but he did describe two security lapses that occurred in March. With Schnürchen absent for illness, her aide carried the load, for once earning Moyzisch's praise. Only her forgetfulness worried him. One evening when she worked late to finish items for the courier, he left his safe key with her, returning a while later having become concerned that she might misplace it. Finding her typing and therefore questioning nothing, he took the key and sent her home, clearly resentful of his implied distrust of her. An occurrence that, he acknowledged, let her learn about Cicero happened "toward the end of March," when he was away and his secretary was still out. Kapp handled the items from Berlin. On this occasion SD headquarters had not printed the usual notice directing to him alone the envelope with Cicero materials. "She had done quite right in opening it, since I had given her no instructions not to do so." Upon his return Kapp asked him who Cicero was, a question he thought casual but troubling, for "the message in question made it clear to anyone who read it that Operation Cicero referred to something going on inside the British Embassy." Since she continued to work alone, he conceded that she became "more or less well informed" about the spy operation, though insisting that "she knew nothing of the details" that mattered most, a conclusion he reached on faith.[14]

Kapp had information never suspected by Moyzisch. "I knew about Cicero before it became my task to open the mail. . . . As I worked alone and undisturbed, I had plenty of time to copy out documents from Berlin which made it clear that Cicero was to be sought in the British Embassy itself. I handed over the copies to the Americans every evening." She thought the spy was a servant but did not know his name. Kapp considered her task finished by the start of April: "I had gained all the information about Cicero that it was possible to obtain."[15] For other reasons too she wanted release. Pressure was more intense than ever. With Schnürchen's return the routine work fell to Kapp again.

Moyzisch recalled getting an especially poor translation, venting his temper when she complained that he no longer trusted her, and suggesting that she return to Sofia. She reportedly cried, ran from the room, and then apologized. At a dinner party in his home she barely ate or drank, as if she feared being poisoned or drugged. Seiler thought that she seemed "out of her mind" by early in April: "She was having a nervous breakdown."[16] Given the mounting tensions and general prospects, clearly it was time for the Americans to let her withdraw; the likelihood of problems outweighed further gains.

The decision to have Kapp disappear was soon made. Every day that she now continued, frightened and distraught, meant a greater risk of discovery. She perhaps also sensed that Moyzisch was now scheming against her. Obviously she was exhausting his patience, and he might take some action too quickly to be counteracted. For such reasons her withdrawal could not be delayed.

By mid-March the tired but unsuspicious Moyzisch had resolved on his own that Kapp must go. When he discussed his predicament with the ambassador, Papen was annoyed but acquiesced in arranging a quiet solution. They would inform Berlin that she had to leave Turkey for health treatment. Papen knew her father and in a private letter asked him to escort his daughter back to Sofia. In a belated answer Herr Kapp reported his hurried transfer to Budapest during a recent crisis: German forces had occupied Hungary in the third week of March to bolster the Axis. He could not leave Budapest until after Easter but would come then.[17] No one objected to the delay.

Cornelia Kapp and the Americans had meanwhile planned her disappearance for the weekend of Easter Sunday, on 9 April. A fictitious trip to see her parents was suggested to cover any excitement or last-minute preparations. On Monday she requested permission to visit Budapest over the holiday, since one of her brothers would be on leave, and a secretly delighted Moyzisch saw how to dismiss Kapp tactfully: he and Papen would ask her father to keep her there. It was agreed that she would work until Thursday, take the overnight train to Istanbul and then the courier plane on Friday, Papen being so relieved that he guaranteed a seat. Moyzisch bought her ticket to Istanbul. A second letter to her father would travel in the diplomatic bag aboard her train and plane. Meanwhile Kapp and her employer each kept up the pretense of her 12 April return.[18] During the following days she seemed much happier, spending time shopping, but foolishly she packed all her belongings in trunks. Fortunately no one suspected her secret intention.

On the day of departure Kapp went to Moyzisch's office to say good-bye, but he also wanted to verify that she left, so that afternoon he reached the Ankara station at 5:30, in ample time. Nearby, Papen was bidding farewell to Spain's ambassador. As time passed Moyzisch grew increasingly alarmed, checked in vain, and realized that Kapp had not appeared. After the train's departure, Moyzisch spoke briefly with Papen, then continued his search. At her apartment he discovered that Kapp had gone at 3:00 that afternoon with all her possessions. He briefed the ambassador and offered to inform Berlin and the police, but the angry Papen advised that he wait, since telling the Turkish police would alert the press and cause embarrassment. Moyzisch searched again and had the train rechecked at Istanbul but was unable to find any trace of Kapp. He asked a senior official in the Interior Ministry for assistance without a leak to the press, then he notified Berlin that Kapp had apparently defected.[19] Not unexpectedly, it became Moyzisch's own inquiries, however circumspect, that aroused Ankara's ever-active rumor circuit. The soon rampant tales claimed that Kapp had fled to the British and added other false details.

During this time Kapp stayed in hiding. "I went to the man I had known since my Cleveland days, the man who was now working for the American O.S.S." It was essential to conceal Kapp's whereabouts, not only from her embassy and its many informants but also from Turkey's police and secret service. Already difficult relations required avoiding unneeded complications.

Despite his influence on her decisions and life, the identity of Kapp's friend from Cleveland has remained uncertain, but she never held him responsible for anything. Kapp later implied also that he was not her regular contact in Ankara. Bazna claimed to have seen the couple together, however, and to have learned that his name was something like Sears. He recognized the young woman from the clothing shop incident; he supposedly remembered the man from the dramatic car chase. Following them to a hotel dining room, he acquired the name from the concierge, who was unsure of the man's nationality. Bazna attempted to reach Moyzisch, because he thought the woman might be a German agent deceiving a Briton, and he continued to investigate. It is difficult to judge the extent of truthfulness in his tale.[20]

Full realization that Kapp had bolted made Moyzisch fear his superiors' wrath: he would certainly be held accountable for her disloyalty and flight. There quickly followed an "avalanche of excited signals" with questions and demands. Five days after Kapp's disappearance he was ordered to Berlin by the next courier plane. Initially he obeyed, leaving for Istanbul the next day, but then he reconsidered. A plane arrived on 13 April with more messages from Kaltenbrunner and a warning from a friend: he faced arrest. Risking looking guilty but thinking of his family, he decided to plead illness, so he returned by train to Ankara.

Within a few days of the defection Moyzisch had received a telephone call from Cicero, who was anxious to arrange a meeting. Bazna later recalled that he sneaked into the compound to enter Moyzisch's office, but the latter recorded that they went to Seiler's. Nor did they agree in their respective recollections on the spy's manner: Bazna portrayed himself as under control; Moyzisch emphasized that he was in a panic. Cicero had confirmed the secretary's defection and told Moyzisch where he thought she was staying, in Ankara. During the preceding days he had sought to learn all he could about her, claiming some success, but was still unsure whether she might know his identity or his exact job. Moyzisch confided that she had stolen no photographs but knew his code name, "perhaps more," and under the circumstances he advised that the highly nervous spy quickly leave Ankara. "He stood in front of me, his expression tense, acute anxiety written all over his face." Once again he had been biting his nails. "Now he seemed a beaten man with no resilience left in him. There was cold fear in his dark eyes." For the first time they shook hands, Cicero saying, "Au revoir, Monsieur," and then leaving the building. At the time he described this scene so melodramatically, Moyzisch did not know what had become of him; the two would not meet again until Moyzisch was asked many years later to identify him.

Papen had suggested that the attaché avoid the embassy, rest, and await quietly some further contact by Berlin. But worry made him genuinely ill, and no word came until after he resumed work some two weeks later. He then learned that an official inquiry had been opened to ascertain his degree of guilt, and perhaps bring severe punishment. Yet nothing happened to him, either because investigators found no proof of culpability, or because conditions soon changed. Meanwhile Moyzisch was himself approached by people who he believed worked for British intelligence. In that regard he was correct: awareness of his difficulties had prompted agents to solicit his own defection. His account made the enemy contacts sound highly dramatic, befitting the climax of the narrative, but stressed his refusals to show his loyalty.[21]

Britain's security officers in Turkey appear to have been told nothing of Kapp's activities until mid-April. The chill and rivalry between the British and American intelligence services operating in Istanbul and Ankara had had varied causes and a long gestation. In spring 1942 the new OSS had opened a headquarters at Cairo to cover the whole region. The Istanbul office was established in April 1943, but it focused on the Balkans; Washington forbade the gathering of data on Turkey itself. The inexperienced eagerness of the American personnel proved serious handicaps, however, creating amateurishness and major problems with security. Too many of the Americans' local contacts were either Axis agents or officers of Eminyet, the respected Turkish secret service, pro-German in sympathy and reporting on American efforts to their superiors and friends. The leakage was such that British officials and representatives of the SIS would not risk sharing data. Relations that were already decidedly cool had by February 1944 broken down almost completely, amid further recriminations. American acceptance of three further defectors after the disappearance of the Vermehrens had helped to provoke the Germans into reorganizing their intelligence service by replacing the weak and ineffective Abwehr.[22] The highly strained atmosphere undoubtedly explains why the OSS decided to keep silent about its discovery of a spy in the British embassy until it could somehow maximize the embarrassment.

Local OSS agents flew Kapp to Cairo for British questioning—probably with a measure of smugness, given the rivalries involved. Kapp later described British reaction to her Cicero story. She thought that the interviewers had never heard the spy's cover name, noting their expressionless faces as she spoke. "I have no idea whether they believed me or not," she said, for "it was a slap in the face" to them. Possibly she misinterpreted the stoic, professional reserve, or perhaps her individual interrogators had lacked knowledge. Afterward the OSS seems to have taken her back to Ankara for processing. There Kapp's new appearance added to the confusion, for she now had short black hair, and she wore a British uniform. Bazna later claimed that spotting her convinced him, and probably Moyzisch in consequence, that the secretary had defected to Britain.[23] But whether Bazna had indeed seen Kapp is uncertain. His story lacks corroboration of any sort.

About two weeks passed before the international press carried the first and often incorrect stories of her disappearance.[24] The stories, coming just two months after the Vermehren case, portrayed a crumbling German system. Still, the incident held little significance for anyone not involved in the espionage affair.

"We had no idea she was working for the other side." Seiler's comment many years later summarized the Germans' surprise when they finally learned about Kapp. Moyzisch had considered any question about her loyalty before the defection as "unthinkable."[25] Initial lack of suspicion, compounded by subsequent false assumptions, distorted how he reported things: he erred in explaining her motives, in estimating her information, and in concluding where she sought refuge. He had some interesting reasons for misdirection.

Because Moyzisch never admitted suspecting her real role, he insisted that his criticisms had caused Kapp's flight. Noting her "disastrous" impact on the Cicero affair, he blamed himself: "She would probably never [have] become involved in it at all, at least certainly not in the role she ultimately assumed, if she had liked me." She had obviously "hated" him. After first foreshadowing her defection—"on n'est trahi que par les siens," "a small pebble can start a landslide"—he told of alienating her. But by focusing on personal issues—her appearance, performance, and behavior—he minimized the basic security question. He cited her grooming as one problem: "she remained incredibly slovenly, even dirty" in matters like her hair. Suggestions for improvement prompted sullen anger, and one particular reprimand produced what he asserted was hatred. But friction built also over her duties. "Her work proved thoroughly unsatisfactory, full of mistakes and oversights and very untidily presented." He found her lethargic, inattentive, and bored with routine. Still, he was right about one point: "She seemed starved for trust above all." Only under such conditions could she pursue her secret work. Moyzisch disliked especially the emotional outbursts so common with Kapp. He recounted instances of sobbing and crying, characterized her as a "neurotic creature" given to hysterical scenes and petulant and irritating ways. Seiler reinforced Moyzisch. Although in time she relaxed somewhat, controlling her responses, the abrupt mood swings still occurred. Her loyalty itself went unquestioned. Reports of the Vermehrens' defection provoked convincing patriotic remarks, for instance, and association with two Luftwaffe deserters aroused no concern.[26]

The emphasis on behavioral problems was not all invention. Kapp did not deny the stories but came to describe her conduct as wholly a ruse to mislead Moyzisch. "My hysterical behavior was no more than a diversionary manoeuvre on my part. I acted hysteria to disguise my perpetual fear of being caught." Yet her incidental remarks cast doubt: she admitted taking strong drugs, their names or types unknown, which suggests major problems. She also acknowledged having considered using poison provided by the intelligence service.[27] Such information belies her assertion of giving throughout a controlled and adroit performance. Clearly the truth about her moods and behavior lies between Moyzisch's stress on emotional instability and Kapp's contention that she had merely been play-acting for him.

A second area of error in Moyzisch's book involved the extent of losses. That he minimized the amount of information Kapp obtained followed from not understanding her aim. While admitting that she learned something of his spy operation, he cited only isolated, late incidents, when she often worked alone, as when she opened the unmarked envelope. Even that slip was called Berlin's fault rather than his own. Adding that she might have copied a few papers and could remember some things, he never gave details or any summary of leakage. Moyzisch's third mistake lay in combining circumstantial factors and unsound suppositions to involve the British. "It is certain, though, that once the suspicions of the British were aroused, they made intense efforts to find out where the German Ambassador was getting his information. These efforts culminated in the behavior of my own secretary, Elisabet." British counteraction of some sort seemed inevitable to

Moyzisch, and his misconception received strong reinforcement from Bazna. Apparently both believed in some British connection until Nogly's investigator got her statements.[28]

The various stories and arguments presented in Moyzisch's book conveyed both sincerity and surface plausibility. Yet the expectation of an official investigation had undoubtedly led him almost immediately to formulate a more or less believable defense. Its elements had to exclude any implication of espionage, minimize the loss of information, and emphasize personal factors. An emotionally unstable secretary who had defected might be explainable; an undetected enemy agent working in his office was indefensible. So he argued that he could not have known what to expect from her. "From the moment I met her," Kapp "was an enigma to me. She still is." Her strange behavior was therefore made the decisive point, and one of the Luftwaffe deserters was also given a role in accounting for why she had changed sides. That he suspected that there were more serious facts behind her disappearance may be inferred from occasional hints in his narrative. He was certainly capable of deliberate misrepresentation, as in identifying himself as a diplomat, and one important inconsistency merits special note. Early in his text he acknowledged that she had played a "very subtle, psychological game with us," implying purpose and control, but the concept of such a deception never resurfaced in any later discussion.[29] Nor did he explain his lack of any curiosity about other possible causes for his secretary's taut nerves and odd moods. Instead, he chose discreet silence on such subjects.

Conditions became unexpectedly harsh for Kapp during the remaining months of the war. Bazna even claimed that discovery of her difficulties made him empathize with Kapp: "I found a perverse consolation in not being the only one ill-treated by fate." Once beyond protection by people in Ankara, she was regarded as a troublesome alien; after reaching Washington, she faced more screening before being interned. Kapp "felt terribly insulted after all I had done for America." But in detailing her complaints—of having been imprisoned in the capital with prostitutes, "kept under observation and treated like a criminal," "subjected to terrible shock treatment" like the mentally ill, and placed in a North Dakota detention camp—she also revealed special problems.[30] Given her behavior prior to defection, she probably displayed disturbing signs, perhaps more hysteria or sudden depression.

Following her release at the end of hostilities, Kapp boarded with a family of German origin named Coutandin and became a waitress in Chicago, where friends described her as nervous and unhappy. She told them how much she loved her father, who had spoiled her, and also how much she missed the old times. Kapp blamed herself for his death and went to pieces when the news reached her in 1947. The Coutandins recalled that "she talked continually about a young man, the love of her youth, whom she had met in Ankara," and how she had left there only reluctantly because of him. Another blow was discovering that he was dead. FBI agents visited her weekly while she stayed with the Coutandins.

In Chicago she married and then moved to California. The Coutandins' daughter later visited her there, finding her with lively children and an attractive house near the coast, and calmer than in Chicago. She participated in an alcohol treatment program and had become quite religious. Her marriage ended in divorce.[31] Without doubt, her decision to switch loyalties and spy during the war had exacted a lasting and painful price.

* * *

Reconstruction of the events and importance of the Kapp episode depends upon two sources of uneven reliability. Moyzisch's account offers little insight to her real activities and much questionable and false information about Kapp. She in turn misremembered her state of mind, enhanced her service, and erred in her recollection of some details.[32] Yet the narrative of each person is essential to a full and balanced understanding.

One point stands out. The Kapp story confirms that the OSS knew about Cicero's espionage activity, presumably through the documents that Dulles had obtained, and instructed American agents in Ankara to discover who he was. Kapp came to share that assignment by mid-January. While learning valuable details for the expanding dossier, almost certainly being first to report that he must be an embassy servant, she and the others could never identify him. It is remarkable that the OSS said nothing of its vital discovery. Her defection closed any prospect of further espionage, however, since the spy was regarded as fully compromised. In fact, his operation had already come to an end. The great importance attached to her flight by both Moyzisch and Bazna served primarily to add further drama to their narratives. Kapp's spying caused little other damage to Berlin. Although she passed on some useful information, her access had been limited, and any losses would have been readily absorbed. Regardless of such considerations, however, Kapp had completed a successful mission.

13   Dénouement and Aftermath

During the troubling period following withdrawal of Britain's military mission in February, the government of Turkey came to realize the dangers of isolation. German forces retained control of southeastern Europe and the Aegean; relations with both the West and Moscow were marked by friction; Allied leaders like Churchill now criticized rather than courted Ankara; and conquest of the entire Balkans by Soviet troops seemed increasingly likely. The prospect of facing alone a powerful Moscow posed a dilemma of the utmost seriousness; realism therefore dictated earning Western support through expedient concessions. Turkish officials nevertheless proceeded with caution, monitoring the military developments, adjusting policies gradually, and breaking diplomatic relations, but remaining neutral until early 1945. By then the declaration of war had only symbolic value. Yet each step in its realignment improved rapport with the West, and Turkey ensured itself of backers and protectors in postwar conflicts.

Meanwhile the participants in the Cicero affair had gone separate ways. The ambassadors, who had been determined antagonists for over five years, departed at nearly the same time. Papen returned home when diplomatic ties were severed in August 1944; Sir Hughe was reassigned the following month to newly liberated Belgium. Moyzisch, who delayed his repatriation until travel became impossible, was comfortably interned in Turkey. Bazna for a while lived quietly, then played the businessman in bold style, spending the fortune received from Berlin. Still, the early postwar years brought difficulties to everyone: interrogations and imprisonment for many, embarrassing public criticism for another, and an embittering shock—poverty—to the spy.

* * *

Turkey's final break with Berlin came in stages amid diminishing fear of Germany and increasing alarm over the prospect of Soviet control of the Balkans. That outcome seemed certain as the fighting approached the region: the Soviet drive had by spring reached the border of Romania. Leaders in the Axis satellites—Romania, Hungary, and Bulgaria—considered German ties a liability. Hungary's wavering even led the Germans to occupy it in March. Yet it soon became clear that Germany had to abandon the Balkans or see all its units there trapped. For Turkey, the situation brought such anxiety over Soviet aims that Ankara knew it must accommodate its powerful Western friends. Therefore, Menemencioglu quietly informed the Germans of impending changes in Turkish policy.[1]

Ankara's first concession to the Allies ended chromite deliveries to Germany. Allied planners had decided to apply twofold pressure against the Turks: destruction of Balkan rail lines and curtailment of Turkey's oil imports. On 26 February 1944 the State Department notified the OSS that the Western ambassadors in Turkey were urging the sabotaging of rail bridges; in coordinated actions, special OSS teams attacked targets along the Greek and Bulgarian routes on 29 and 30 May.[2] While the operations were successful, they came too late, since shipments had already ceased. Under the Allies' threat of an oil embargo, Turkey had yielded. On 20 April the foreign minister told Papen that chromite deliveries would stop on 1 May.[3] Using extra rolling stock assembled in advance, Berlin, which had expected the move, managed to transport the available ore supply. The final shipments increased its reserve. Armaments supervisor Albert Speer had nevertheless warned that "the war of matériel would be decided by the ending of deliveries of chromium" from Turkish ore suppliers. In September 1944 he estimated that current production levels would deplete stockpiles by June 1945. After that, weapons factories would shut down as they exhausted final allocations.[4] Only minor diplomatic repercussions followed the stoppage. Ribbentrop ordered the ambassador to report home and then announced that Papen would temporarily remain in Germany. Papen's opposition to his recall or any counteraction annoyed Ribbentrop, and it led to a joint appearance before Hitler. Unwilling to exacerbate the problem, Hitler backed Papen, who was instructed to return. Nevertheless, Papen found that he could generate no discussion of what the Cicero information had revealed about the enemy's mounting strength and the Germans' plight.[5]

Despite his fear that southeastern Europe would fall to communism, Churchill continued to criticize Turkey, emphasizing that future Western support depended on present cooperation. In a speech during late May he made clear the choices. Churchill recalled the previous autumn's "great disappointment" when military control of the Aegean had been attainable "but for an exaggerated attitude of caution on the side of Turkey . . . the Turks magnified their danger. . . . Their military men took the gloomiest view of Russian prospects . . . and demanded huge supplies, . . . so the Allies had ceased the arming of Turkey."[6] Implicit in his sharp remarks was notice that Ankara must break with Germany if it expected treatment as a true friend.

Soon Germany itself caused Menemencioglu's fall. Its navy wanted to send some small vessels southward through the Straits, declaring that they were not warships and carried no naval personnel; Allied diplomats made strong official protests when the first ship reached the area. Menemencioglu sought Papen's personal word that the vessels were not being misrepresented; the ambassador had his naval attaché investigate and then reassured Menemencioglu. But the Turks checked the next ship and discovered both arms and a German naval crew. The embarrassed foreign minister resigned on 15 June, and Saracoglu temporarily took over his rival's duties. Even Sir Hughe could sympathize with Menemencioglu, but the cabinet change was welcomed.[7]

During subsequent weeks, as Allied invasion forces in France became stronger and a Soviet drive into southeastern Europe seemed daily more imminent, a compromise emerged: Turkey would stay neutral but sever ties with Germany. Churchill urged patience with Ankara when he told Stalin about developments on 11 July. Stalin voiced contempt: given Turkey's past "evasive and vague attitude" in negotiations, he found "no benefit" in any "half-measures" now offered, saying Ankara should be ignored and lose "special rights." Moscow was by then certain of its ability to control the postwar fate of Turkey. Nonetheless, on 2 August the plan proceeded. Saracoglu asked the legislature to honor a British request, which America backed, that Turkey now end all formal relations with Germany. The assembly voted unanimously, and Churchill reported the news that night.[8]

An angry Ribbentrop told his ambassador to leave Turkey at once. Papen therefore paid Inönü a final visit and accepted the "sorry end" to his work in Ankara. It was a bad time to return home, and many thought his life in danger. On 20 July 1944 a resistance group had nearly killed Hitler with a bomb at his headquarters in East Prussia. Immediately, party fanatics had clamored for mass revenge against all the regime's enemies: eventually thousands would be arrested and often brutally executed in a wholesale purge. Jenke and other staff members had persuaded Papen to affirm their collective loyalty to Hitler.[9] But words would not keep him safe. Papen left Turkey on 5 August with his granddaughter, using a private railway car provided by Turkey for the journey to Sofia. Frau von Papen had meanwhile returned to Germany. As his train neared the German border, he wondered if arrest was imminent, for the Nazis were pursuing all leads, and he might have been compromised. Nothing occurred at the German frontier. However, an official delegation welcomed him in the capital, and Hitler expected him the following day. At headquarters he found Ribbentrop in an indignant rage. Papen considered him "quite incapable of conducting a logical conversation concerning the general situation after our break with Turkey." Hitler took the loss calmly and even presented a medal to Papen. The two men never met again.[10]

Turkey meanwhile grew increasingly apprehensive about the Balkans. During the summer, Romania collapsed under heavy attack and in August switched sides to fight the Germans. But Sofia had vacillated until it was too late; Soviet forces reached the country's borders by 3 September, and Bulgaria was quickly overrun and subdued. To avoid being trapped, the Germans withdrew from Greece during early October, and soon Belgrade too fell. Budapest came under Soviet attack in November. Thus within several eventful months the Turks saw Soviet forces triumph everywhere to their immediate north.

Knatchbull-Hugessen noted with satisfaction the new cooperation with Ankara: "In proportion as Turkey took action against Germany our relations mended." They were fully restored by a final step. Despite the Turks' reluctance to enter the conflict so late, Ankara declared war on Germany and Japan during late February 1945, a requirement for gaining a role in Allied peace planning.[11] Yet difficulties with the Soviet Union grew more ominous. In March Turkey received from Moscow the required six months' advance notice that would terminate the 1925 nonaggression treaty in November. Stalin offered another pact if Turkey would surrender the disputed Kars and Ardahan areas and give Moscow special privileges in the Straits. As such intimidation continued, the West increased its presence and protection. Thus Turkey became one of the first pawns in the Cold War.

Just a month after Papen returned home, Knatchbull-Hugessen took a new post. Sir Hughe left Turkey to become ambassador to Belgium on 9 September. Because his reassignment occurred suddenly, the telegram request arriving on 31 August with departure for Brussels scheduled as soon as possible, the situation later inspired fanciful conjecture. Bazna sought to dramatize the sequence of a hasty summons, transfer, and then retirement as a face-saving arrangement for Knatchbull-Hugessen. The former valet implied that the diplomat's negligence must have been discovered but then suppressed; he stood watching in the street as the ambassador's car left the embassy compound. It was fully in character for the ex-spy, of course, to risk such a brazen public appearance, and his attempt to give the events some hidden meaning was affectation. Turkey and its policy now simply held less importance for London, whereas the freeing of Belgium made British representation there a top priority. Two weeks after Brussels' liberation, Sir Hughe assumed his new duties. Knatchbull-Hugessen held the post until his retirement in 1947.[12] By then he had been in the service nearly four decades.

When two years later he published his memoirs, *Diplomat in Peace and War*, there was no mention of the espionage case, though he must by then have heard about it from the postwar questioning of enemy officials. He also put the best possible interpretation on Turkey's policy of noncommitment during the critical war years. Sir Hughe denied personal credit for keeping Turkey neutral, saying Ankara had always been pro-Allied and would never have joined the Axis side, and in fact Turkish policy had ultimately helped the Allies: had the country fought a German invasion, it might have lost, increasing Western liabilities in the region. Thus neutrality had provided a protective block.[13] The suspicion arises that some of his sympathetic reasoning was influenced by the need for Turkish support in the intensifying postwar struggle to contain communism in that strategically vital area.

Undoubtedly surprised by the publicity that arose in 1950 when Moyzisch's book appeared, Sir Hughe offered his sole comment about Cicero, acknowledging that Moyzisch had indeed reported the basic elements of a wartime incident. He declared that the affair had lasted only about six weeks, after which the spying had been ended, and that the valet involved had been quickly dismissed and had seemed to vanish. Because the explanation was so misleading, probably unintentionally, it added substantially to later confusion. Most painful for the former ambassador must have been Foreign Secretary Bevin's sharp public rebuke during parliamentary questioning in the autumn; no such espionage would ever have been possible had Sir Hughe conformed to the established rules about custody of documents. Asked for his response to the foreign secretary's statement, he said only that "I must have time to think about it." The retired diplomat then and afterward maintained a dignified silence about the affair, but in private conversations he continued to minimize its importance. Knatchbull-Hugessen died just days before his eighty-fifth birthday, in early spring 1971.[14]

By that time only a few people still doubted the Cicero story, major obituaries noting as simple fact that his valet had photographed documents and sold the films to the enemy, but British critics of that conclusion were soon urging a different view. As already seen, they believed the spy had been used in a deception scheme that had long been kept secret. The ambassador's role played little part in their theorizing, though successful establishment of their concept would have vindicated him.

* * *

Nearly all the Germans who had figured in the espionage and counterfeiting affairs faced postwar charges stemming from their other activities during the Nazi regime and conquests. Even the two bitter antagonists who had portrayed themselves as conventional diplomats became codefendants before a court: Papen and Ribbentrop appeared in the dock together during the major war crimes trial at Nuremberg in 1945–1946. Having lived quietly during the war's final winter, Papen was arrested in April 1945 by the advancing Americans. He was quite outraged at being detained for any reason. Because he had held ambassadorial posts since 1934 and had not been directly involved in the war or genocide, Papen was acquitted at Nuremberg, although he remained in difficulties until the late 1940s as a result of lesser charges brought against him. In all he spent four years in various types of detention. Soon afterward he completed the memoirs that recounted his career in such self-serving terms; in later years he sued for a military pension based on his early service. Papen died as he neared his ninetieth birthday, in 1969.[15] His reputation has remained that of a manipulative, wily, and untrustworthy player in many key events.

In consequence of his deep ideological commitment to Nazism and unquestioning support of even its most extreme policies, Ribbentrop was found guilty in 1946, his death sentence as a war criminal causing little criticism from jurists and finding wide support among the public. The shallow but pretentious man who had headed the Foreign Ministry for seven crucial years was hanged in October 1946 along with the dictatorship's other condemned top leaders.

Moyzisch continued in the last months of the war to use his cover status as a diplomat, busied himself with special tasks, and managed to avoid a return to wartime Germany. During spring and summer 1944 he helped evacuate the sizable German colony, its last members leaving in August aboard a series of special trains, since Turkey would intern any Germans who remained at the month's end. Moyzisch planned to take the last train from Ankara, but it never left, Soviet troops having cut rail lines in the Balkans. He and his family joined others interned on the embassy grounds; only a few sentries and some barbed wire sealed off the compound. He felt that "again I was lucky" in new delays. A plan for repatriation on a Swedish ship proved impossible until spring, when the *Drottningholm* picked up the detainees. The ship was still in the Mediterranean when the war ended, and it proceeded to Liverpool, where Moyzisch was formally held, undergoing months of British questioning about his work in the intelligence field. But he had never known Cicero's real name, nor could he shed much light on the bogus funds, and in October he was finally sent home. Although later questioned further and summoned by the Allies to testify in several trials, Moyzisch lived quietly in his native Austria, eventually publishing his book about Cicero and working for a private business firm.[16] Sixteen years after the war he was sought to identify Bazna as the wartime spy he had known and helped make famous.

Jenke too had been repatriated aboard the *Drottningholm*, but by 1950 he had resumed his contracting business in Turkey. Soon he was approached by Bazna for help with mounting debts. His wartime diplomatic service to please his brother-in-law had not been entirely pleasant or helpful to him, and he certainly saw no reason to give the former valet the money now demanded. Jenke died of shock and heart failure in July 1951, when a sailboat capsized with him on board in the Sea of Marmara.

In principle, all the top SS leaders who survived the war, including the Gestapo and SD department heads, were held accountable for the Nazis' reign of terror and crimes. Only some, however, could be brought into court. Himmler committed suicide while in British military custody in late May 1945. Kaltenbrunner's rank earned him a place among the major figures tried at Nuremberg; following his conviction he was hanged in October 1946. Two of his most important subordinates could not be found. Müller disappeared in late April 1945 when Soviet troops took over Berlin, and the fate of the vicious head of the Gestapo has never been determined with any certainty.[17] Adolf Eichmann escaped from internment by the Americans. As administrator of the RSHA's Department IV B4, he had been responsible for the murdering of Europe's Jews in the "Final Solution." Not until 1960 was he finally located in Argentina; in 1962, upon conviction in Israel he was executed.

The most severe punishments meted out to various high officials of the SD stemmed from activities and crimes committed during special assignments in occupied lands. Those who remained in office positions or intelligence outposts faced few or no charges. Schellenberg ended the war as a brigadier general in the SS, sharing the final disgrace of his protector, Himmler. Together they had sought a separate peace in the West and had suffered the wrath of diehards and old enemies. Kaltenbrunner had dismissed Schellenberg from his positions at the end of April 1945, but Schellenberg had been sure he would be reinstated when Himmler succeeded Hitler. The fantasy was doomed. Schellenberg was apprehended by the Allies and tried in one of the subsidiary cases at Nuremberg. Both his ambition and closeness to Himmler made him responsible for policy. In 1949 the court sentenced him to six years' imprisonment, but he was released in late 1950 when his health began to fail. He completed his memoirs before his death in 1952. He died proud of the "series of relatively impressive improvisations" achieved by his department: "The surprisingly high average of the service's effectiveness can only be accounted for by the ruthless expenditure that went on of human life and resources."[18] But his victory in creating a single intelligence agency under his own control had been a hollow one.

Two of his old adversaries, Ohlendorf and Jost, had been condemned to death. Ohlendorf was hanged in June 1951. In addition to his post with the SD and work on economic issues, Ohlendorf had commanded a special SS extermination squad in the Soviet Union during part of 1941–1942, rising to become an SS lieutenant general while still in his late thirties. Jost too was marked for execution for ordering mass killings in Russia, but his sentence was commuted, and he was released in 1951. Naujocks escaped from a camp for accused war criminals in 1946 and disappeared into the confusion of postwar Germany. By the time he emerged from obscurity, no one was pursuing the old charges.

* * *

Bazna, for a while, lived the coveted life of a Turkish man of means.[19] He later claimed to have given Mara funds for a dowry, helped put Esra through university, and provided a new mistress named Aika with an apartment. Money also went to his ex-wife and four children. He was not the type to handle a secret fortune with discretion or make it untraceable, however, and his increasingly open and ambitious business ventures in time led to a catastrophe others might well have avoided. "I had believed myself to be in possession of unimaginable wealth, which I hoarded and squandered, because I had been a poor man for too long to be able to deal with it rationally and sensibly." Actually, though, his downfall came not from squandering the money but from assuming he could spend it at will. Other participants in the affair assumed that Cicero had been clever enough to disappear quickly. Yet something in his character seemed to demand the local display of wealth in foolish disregard of the need for caution and secrecy.

After a brief period of inactivity, he began dealing in used cars, a safe business of small investments, but he still made the Ankara Palace Hotel lobby a sort of office. Noticing a newspaper item offering a used car for sale and recognizing Busk's telephone number, he reportedly approached his former employer about buying the vehicle. Bazna, concluding that the diplomat knew nothing about his spying, paid £300 for the car in £5 notes, perhaps all counterfeit money he had received from the Germans. (In retrospect he would find the irony quite amusing.) He next formed a partnership for construction projects, Bazna & Oztemel, for which the source of his finances went unquestioned. When the firm prospered, even winning some public contracts, his ambitions also grew. Bazna dreamed of creating and owning a luxury hotel in the spa city of Bursa: the Çelik Palace would have five stories, 150 rooms with baths and telephones, and a "magnificent" lobby area. He was certain that the hot springs and nearby skiing would make it a success. Because his partner thought the venture too risky, they parted ways. A new associate had to be found: Niyazi Acar, who helped form Bazna & Acar. Given the project's size, the government too invested funds in the hotel. Work had progressed scarcely beyond the ground floor when the first word of trouble was received; currency being used to pay construction bills had been called counterfeit.

A cautious merchant had sent notes to a Swiss bank, which asked the Bank of England to check them; London had reported back for relay through channels that the notes were forgeries. In Turkey alarm spread quickly upon the news that bogus British currency was in circulation; the Turkish police began investigations and soon charged an Istanbul businessman, Ismail Karaali, with passing such notes. Karaali, however, proved that he had received the money through work on the unfinished Çelik Palace Hotel. The government, fearing a scandal as a backer of the project, acted promptly; it seized all assets of Bazna & Acar and charged it with fraud.[20] Acar telephoned from Istanbul to inform Bazna. The latter, he would later recall, collapsed. His mistress, Aika, cleared out. Accused of distributing false currency and deception, he underwent years of questioning and court prosecutions; criminal action against him was ultimately abandoned, although he remained responsible for repaying all victims. The ex-spy claimed to have been destroyed by years of legal proceedings. Yet despite his problems, he married a young woman, Duriet, and eventually the couple had four children. He thought the image of an "adventurer" with eight children was rather funny.

For over two decades Bazna struggled to survive and settle his debts, trying various occupations and unusual schemes, including attempts to force Germany to pay him some sort of compensation. He lived in Istanbul during those years. At times he gave singing lessons, tried a small export-import business, and dealt again in used cars, but creditors took whatever he made. Bazna's troubles drew some publicity in the early 1950s. Upon hearing of location shooting for the film about his exploits, he approached the director, expecting either a screen role or a consulting fee. The filmmaker, who thought him shabby, refused him any part or payment. Probably hoping to capitalize on the film's publicity, Bazna organized a singing recital in February 1952 at a rented cinema in Istanbul, having placards printed to announce the special program. The baritone performed various works—songs by Handel, Verdi, Bizet, and others—before a small but pleased audience. But a creditor saw the advertisements, appeared with a bailiff, and confiscated all the cash proceeds. The singer walked home in his borrowed evening clothes. His humiliation increased when press coverage complimenting his performance included accounts of the seizure of the receipts.[21]

Bazna also pursued his claim for either reimbursement or a pension from the Germans. In 1950 he tried to see Jenke. Having observed the foreigner on the street, he supposedly visited his house seeking a substantial loan, but the businessman would not admit him. Bazna was angry, because the man knew that he had been cheated by Berlin. Jenke related a less attractive version of the approach: that Bazna had sent his daughter to demand £15,000 and Jenke had "sent her back empty-handed." Bazna next went to the German consulate-general in Istanbul, but he saw only a junior official, who asked for written proofs that he could not produce and dismissed him as a trickster. In April 1954 Bazna sent a carefully drafted letter to Chancellor Konrad Adenauer. Reviewing his special service, and saying sympathy for Germany had prompted his spying, he petitioned for assistance. "It was a long, detailed, servile letter, dictated by bitter need." Many months later the German Foreign Ministry wrote rejecting his claim.[22]

Apparently, soon after publication of Moyzisch's book Bazna started preparing his own manuscript. He recounted his story in a green children's exercise book: the handwriting was ornate, the tone self-flattering and vain, the content ill organized. In 1961 Bazna took the account to Munich and arranged to meet Hans Nogly in the lobby of the Vier Jahreszeiten Hotel. Clearly his taste for elegant living, enjoyed vicariously by sitting in fashionable hotels, had been undiminished by the passing of time. Nogly found the man nondescript and touchy, and initially he neither liked nor trusted the stranger. He portrayed Bazna as looking rather "elderly"; in fact he was not yet sixty. Only the visitor's eyes showed much animation as he insisted that he had been the famous spy and wanted income from publishing his narrative to finance court action against the government. The collaborator took on the project but had the former spy pass an identification test: the meeting with Moyzisch. Bazna described their encounter at Innsbruck: "We smiled coolly, and each of us looked inquisitively at the other to see what life had done to him. We felt no particular sympathy for each other. Our great adventure had rewarded neither."[23]

Nogly later set up a press conference for the author in early November. Bazna, wanting to publicize both his forthcoming book and the planned lawsuit, claimed that his espionage had been prompted in part by his wartime sympathy for Germany. The publication was far from a success, however, and it failed to bring much financial gain. Interest in the affair nevertheless led to its coverage in a documentary series aired on regional television. Bazna's book ended with a description of his new family's "very ordinary flat" on an upper floor of an inconvenient building in Istanbul. His unreliable income came from buying merchandise for resale. He lamented that when he and his wife visited the completed Çelik Palace Hotel, they sat in the lobby and could not afford any refreshments. He did pursue legal action against the German government for some sort of settlement or pension: at the outset he asked for a total of 1.7 million marks but later sought only a small monthly sum. A more astute person would have known that the lawsuit and pleas would fail. Still, Bazna chose to stay on in Germany and, reportedly, worked as a night watchman in Munich before he died there in December 1970. He was sixty-six years old.[24]

* * *

For countless people worldwide, the introduction to the Cicero case came through a feature film, *Five Fingers* (1952), a critically praised and highly popular production made from Moyzisch's book soon after the affair became public.[25] Darryl F. Zanuck had quickly acquired motion picture rights for Twentieth Century–Fox, assigning Michael Wilson to create a screenplay and Joseph Mankiewicz to direct, with James Mason and Danielle Darrieux heading a superb cast. That the film emerged as a work of superior craftsmanship and exciting entertainment is nevertheless based in large part upon artistic liberties its creators took with both the plot and the characters.

In 1951 Mankiewicz enjoyed enormous professional prestige, having just garnered four Oscars for writing and direction, especially for *All about Eve* (1950). Mankiewicz nonetheless had difficulties with Zanuck, and he planned to let his studio contract lapse after a final project to fulfill its terms. Then he received Wilson's script for comment. On 12 May he replied that he was "most enthusiastic" about the screenplay, with the working title *Operation Cicero*. He thought that it had "a last act as good as any I know" and required only "some tightening and a little more ingenuity" in certain places and in the dialogue. "It needs humor, sex and excitement. I think I could supply it in a very short time." Zanuck allowed him to take over the film if he received no screen credit for writing and agreed to keep Otto Lang as producer.[26]

Wilson knew the project was linked to the studio's semidocumentary features from the 1940s. He had therefore used sober voice and title declarations to establish the context, truth, and significance of the espionage story that had recently come to light. Specially photographed scenes of Turkey lent further verisimilitude. Thereafter a narrator joined together the reenactments. Yet the story unfolded with lightness and mocking humor. All the known ironies were carefully heightened, and new ones added through fictional characters and twists. The director's deft reworking of dialogue continued throughout the filming and added to the script's resonance and levels of appeal.[27]

Permeating the screenplay was the theme of deception and betrayal, shown not only through the espionage activity but also in frustration of sexual promise, theft from a benefactor and coconspirator, and payment for dangerous work and secrets in counterfeit notes. Each act of duplicity seemed magnified, because the material stakes or personal expectations were so high. The human folly behind the situations was handled as satire: everything became part of a contest in guile and deceit, one in which the assorted players sought repeatedly to outwit their opponents, only to be defeated by some unforeseen turn of fate.[28]

Despite its opening claims, the film did not deal truthfully with events. The screenplay glamorized the servant-spy, introduced a titled adventuress, treated espionage as gamesmanship, and exaggerated the stolen papers' importance. Characters were modified or invented. Sir Hughe became Sir Frederic. Nothing about the valet called Diello—his easy charm, worldly knowledge, polished diction, and urbane manner—was derived from the real Cicero. Bazna had nothing in common with Mason.[29] Countess Anna was pure invention. Her creation allowed social satire and a romantic variation of the betrayal theme: Anna's flight with all his money forced the last dangerous theft by Diello. Other characters added humor through contrast and by slight overplaying: Moyzisch was drawn as a bumbling comic figure, for instance, while vague ineptness marked a counterpart named Travers.[30] Such supporting portrayals tended to make Cicero and Anna seem more sympathetic, because they had personal style. The film's ironic ending was therefore necessary in order to convey a sense of ultimate justice.

In its most significant untruth, *Five Fingers* reinforced a misconception that Moyzisch's book had first rendered popular: that Diello photographed the Allies' invasion plans for Overlord. Disaster is averted when a German official destroys the photographs, mistakenly believing that the British had planted worthless documents. Such a climactic act of espionage and an exciting escape proved irresistible in terms of commercial filmmaking. Equally fanciful was the production's closing scene, set in Rio de Janeiro, when Cicero learns that his whole fortune consists of counterfeit banknotes. Multitudes of viewers over the years must surely have been convinced that such fictional incidents were historically accurate.

Mankiewicz spent about seven weeks in Turkey during the early summer of 1951 planning and filming on location, mostly for a chase sequence in which doubles stood in for the actors. News of his activities led Bazna to seek money from him. Agreeing to a discreet meeting, held in a hotel garden that Bazna had chosen for its privacy, the filmmaker had snapshots taken secretly. They were part of the dramatic slant Mankiewicz gave to their entire contact; calling the ex-spy "the most obvious-looking villain I've ever met" was another. One of the secret photographs appeared in *Life* in spring 1952, when the magazine reviewed the completed film. Still, the impoverished former spy contributed nothing the director could use and received no fee. When he later saw the finished production he was said to have remarked, "I thought it exciting—but untrue."[31]

Studio production began in late summer.[32] Changes in dialogue continued during the shooting, but otherwise things went smoothly. Lang worked well with Mankiewicz.[33] Yet the old personal friction between Mankiewicz and Zanuck resurfaced over the film's final editing. The former contended that Zanuck had recut "the last two reels of the film with his polo mallet" after Mankiewicz had left the studio. They exchanged angry messages; the director remained annoyed even after the film won praise.[34]

The title was puzzling; Zanuck's choice of "Five Fingers" was never fully explained. He thought a number linked the production to such past semidocumentary hits as *The House on 92nd Street* and *13 Rue Madeleine*, and he visualized a clutching hand as symbolic of theft and greed. While the advertising trailer showed such a hand, the film did not, and the title has been widely regarded as meaningless. That was Mankiewicz's own view.[35] Yet the title has a certain intriguing appeal, appropriate to a mystery, that the straightforward book title could not match.

Sir Hughe was given a special showing of *Five Fingers*. A delegation from the Foreign Office had already viewed it privately, concerned about official handling of the public reaction to its awkward content, and shortly afterward Sir Hughe was also able to judge its approach. He acknowledged to a journalist, "I think it's a very good film," but he noted its artistic license. Asked about the portrayal of his own character, he remarked with humor. "I suppose there are ambassadors and ambassadors." But he avoided a query about the plot situation, a "very delicate" field; he adhered to his policy of polite silence.[36]

Five Fingers enjoyed highly favorable reviews upon its domestic release on 22 February 1952. Bosley Crowther was representative when he called it "literate entertainment" and a "full-flavored adventure tale" in his influential review for the *New York Times*. Critical reception in Britain followed similar lines: the *Daily Sketch* called it "an absorbing and wonderfully entertaining film," and *The Times* noted that "its particular contribution to the legend is unfailingly entertaining."[37] Both Mankiewicz and Wilson earned Oscar nominations for their work, and the Mystery Writers Guild presented its coveted "Edgar" to Mankiewicz.[38] The film brought in substantial profits for the studio, despite competition from television and films in color.[39] Film scholars over the years have continued to praise the production's quality and appeal. While earlier postwar spy films had been somber and instructive, attempting realism, here was espionage done with lightness and an ambiguous message.[40] Mason too remained pleased with *Five Fingers*. Years afterward he thought it clearly the best of the "sensible" spy films that had been made up to that time.[41]

Because *Five Fingers* so cleverly mixed actual events with rumors and fanciful notions, influencing public opinion through its attractive packaging and timely appearance, the film came to figure prominently in the controversies about the Cicero case. Those who refused to believe that anyone had so easily stolen British secrets resented both the film's content and the attention it gained. They argued that its inventions and changes illustrated how the entire affair had been distorted and blown out of proportion to further special interests.[42] At the same time, many viewers who knew the basic story to be factual may also have thought that all the film's details were sound. But the film was intended as popular, albeit superior, entertainment, free to manipulate the material to enhance the story. Completion of *Five Fingers* closed a brilliant period in Mankiewicz's film career. In a succession of later projects he rarely displayed the gifts that had distinguished his earlier films.[43]

14   The Affair in Retrospect

Cicero's daring feats made him the most successful spy of World War II. He managed to photograph a substantial number of valuable British documents during some four months of espionage, a critical period in the mid-winter of 1943–1944 when the military showdown was drawing near. His information gave the enemy insights to Allied conferences on strategic planning and also to important local negotiations. Without question, the spying represented an extraordinary breach of security that carried the possibility of wreaking immeasurable harm. But despite the impressive quantity and nature of their losses the British sustained little actual damage, because German leaders failed to use their secret knowledge more widely and effectively. Nor did the spy himself get to enjoy his gains for long.

It is hardly surprising that such a remarkable story has given rise to varied reactions and conflicting views. Popularizers have exaggerated the facts and made sensational claims; embarrassed officials have obscured and minimized events and losses. The true character and dimensions of the espionage have become generally clear, however, and an objective profile of the operation's important features is long overdue. Few issues remain concerning the spy and his working methods, the processing of the data, the duration of the spying, or the number and kinds of papers that were copied. Several other questions—how the spy managed to escape discovery, what he was paid, and why his efforts had minimal impact—still present difficulties. In view of the available evidence, however, many misconceptions can be resolved or narrowed.

* * *

In basic respects the spying was an amateurish and old-fashioned affair, espionage carried out by an individual who lacked intelligence training or previous experience and whose operating methods were simple—elements that troubled and misled both wartime investigators and some later interpreters. Only with reluctance did Berlin finally accept the valet's stories and explanations; only too late did security specialists from Britain realize what had happened. It seemed incredible to intelligence professionals both that circumstances had permitted a house servant opportunities for sustained spying and that anyone as unimpressive as the obsequious valet could accomplish such remarkable results. But it was indeed an operation conceived and executed by just one cunning man, with German help only in copying special keys, and with an occasional timely warning or minor assistance from a mistress.

Who was the spy, and what sort of man was he? His personality and pretensions make an intriguing study—the ambitiousness, manipulations, fantasies, vanity, insecurities, and extravagance—but they had little importance in the spy operation. Nevertheless, a few matters that have caused errors must be clarified. Bazna's own claims started his persistent misidentification as an Albanian, even though he clearly considered himself to be Turkish. His tendency to embellish his background with fanciful tales and to dramatize his life explains too the various names he used with employers: Ilya, Diello, Elias. In dealing with Moyzisch he thought "Pierre" a good cover name. He seems to have tailored names to suit his changing self-image and roles. Bazna was also much younger than thought by Moyzisch: at the time he began spying, he was not quite forty. His unfamiliar type and growing baldness had obviously misled his contact. Moyzisch formed an astute understanding of the valet's character and motives, however, emphasizing the social ambitions and overriding greed that drove Cicero. There can be no question or doubt whatsoever that he spied only for the money. Certainly the motives that he himself later cited, such as wanting to keep his country neutral and safe, were mere rationalizations, designed to improve his reputation.

A notable characteristic of the spying was its technical simplicity. The affair depended on neither sophisticated planning nor scientific gadgetry. Instead, a competent amateur photographer, working hurriedly with only a good camera and standard film, aided by an improvised stand and an ordinary light bulb, produced material of satisfactory legibility. It is understandable that the Germans had doubts about his ability and the procedures he described; experimentation would nevertheless have lessened their concerns, by showing that Cicero's results were in fact feasible. In the end, they accepted what he told them. Later writers, however, questioned how he had managed alone.[1]

Absent from the affair were any of the physical confrontations so often associated with stories of espionage: the very success of the valet's activities meant that they proceeded and concluded without personal violence. No shots were fired; no one was hurt. The major participants indeed later thought it necessary to add exciting incidents to their narratives, because psychological tension and suspense alone might not have sufficient appeal. Creators of the film version surpassed them by inventing a final entrapment and thrilling escape. Such dramatic conflicts and satisfying climaxes, however popular, misrepresented the espionage affair's true character.

The Cicero operation resulted from chance and owed nothing to German planning. Berlin neither planted nor recruited the spy; nor could it control or direct Bazna. He was not an agent answerable to the Germans but rather an independent opportunist who looked upon Germany as the most logical market for his wares. That he also knew a high-ranking official in its embassy helped to decide his course of action. Had Berlin declined his offer or not satisfied his greed, however, he surely would have taken his films somewhere else—most likely, as he had indicated, to the always suspicious Russians. In his own mind he was proceeding as would any clever businessman who wanted the best terms and maximum profit. The novelty of his initial contact, and their own caution, nevertheless aroused the Germans' suspicions and delayed their placing full trust in the windfall. In any case, Papen's later statement about "the documents that fell by mere chance into our hands" accurately described the Germans' luck.[2]

Cicero's success and survival are explained by both the initial handling of his offer and the nature of power struggles in Germany. While his past contact with Jenke had provided the means of obtaining a hearing for his proposal, the subsequent decision to refer him to Moyzisch and not the Abwehr was critical to his acceptance and safety, for the SD leader's ambitions and its tight security meant he would be welcomed and protected. Had an arrangement been established with the less loyal Abwehr, he undoubtedly would have been compromised through its leaks. Germany was also fortunate in that Moyzisch proved capable. Such a relationship is always difficult and sensitive, requiring a balance of firmness with flexibility, and of reserve with reassurances appropriate to the contact, both especially hard tasks given this spy's personality traits. Despite his lack of training and experience in field operations, Moyzisch in general acquitted himself well.[3] His two major failings lay in not arranging a safe method to reach Cicero if necessary and in not discovering more about the man through discreet inquiries.

The justifications and obvious pretensions in his book reflect an uneasy recognition of these shortcomings. Yet it is important also to remember that Moyzisch and his demanding superiors in Berlin could neither control nor direct Cicero, and that they remained subject to his pace and pleasure. Moyzisch rightly stressed the information over the individual and feared antagonizing the wary Cicero.

For his part, Schellenberg worked from the outset with dispatch and thoroughness to process the items received from Ankara. He had the credibility of both the spy and his information carefully investigated, reached satisfactory terms with the foreign minister's aides for payments to the valet, arranged for top experts to examine the documents in the vain hope of unlocking the enemy's codes, and oversaw the preparation and distribution of précis and analyses of the data. Schellenberg had basic and continuing problems with Ribbentrop's ministry over control of the information, however; in disobedience to clear instructions, Moyzisch showed the newly developed photographs to Papen. Thus the material reached the Foreign Ministry through the ambassador's own reports. In procedural terms using the dual channels created no difficulties—it even resulted in a partial record of documents from the ministry's surviving files—but disagreements over the application of the data were harmful at the time. Schellenberg remained frustrated, because his intelligence reports had little impact and because he could not personally advocate his ideas before Hitler. Nonetheless, his processing of the material was both comprehensive and sound.

Although the main period of the spy's activity is well defined, stretching from later October 1943, when he approached the Germans, until the end of February 1944, when filming stopped, there are unresolved questions about both its beginning and final stages. Little credibility attaches to Bazna's claim that while working for Busk he copied valuable documents. The habitually prying servant probably did find an opportunity to photograph some sort of papers, however, later exaggerating their content and suggesting that he had carefully planned all his spying. Bazna implied that his initial offering included some photographs from the Busk household and that such material had helped to impress the Germans. Also, his mistress allowed him continued access to the Busks' home; however, he appears to have made no further practice of filming. The implication is that he could find nothing there that was worth photographing.

Both the causal circumstances and date when the espionage was abandoned have been subjects of confusion. Moyzisch and Bazna sought to dramatize the ending by linking it to the defection of Kapp early in April. In fact, the spying did not last over five months: the ambassador's absence during the first three weeks of March cut off

Bazna's access to official papers and effectively ended his spying. A resumption of activity after the diplomat's return would have been possible but unlikely; satisfied with his accumulated wealth and having weighed the growing risks, the valet discontinued his espionage. When and under what conditions he left the embassy, however, is not clear. Bazna told of giving notice and quitting on or after 20 April. Some have maintained that he was dismissed when he fell under suspicion, or that he became briefly an unwitting channel for deceiving the Germans. Dates as early as the beginning of March have been cited in efforts to fit Cicero's departure with such views of the affair. Still, the most important points, that his spying ended after February and that Bazna had walked away without trouble, seem to be well established.

Available information about the documents copied by Cicero allows resolution of some points of contention: whether the British papers and their content were indeed genuine, how many items may have been photographed, what secrets were revealed through the spying, and whether Britain's losses were substantial and serious. As already seen, the question of the documents' authenticity created a belated stir when deception theorists in the 1970s claimed that Cicero had fallen under control after about two months and subsequently had fed doctored material to the enemy. Their assertion limited the real losses to the early period. The notion of a successful deception, however, resting as it did on doubtful statements and hearsay, ignored the evidence and cannot be sustained. The conclusion must remain that the items the valet photographed throughout his months of spying were indeed fully genuine in origin and text.

Both the quantity and content of the compromised papers can be determined, within certain limits, from the surviving sources. In the absence of records indicating the number of documents involved, the recollections of those who handled the material provide the next best information, although there are differences in their descriptions and counts to be reconciled. Again as noted, Moyzisch thought that he had purchased forty to fifty rolls of film, or some 400 photographs, in his dealings with Cicero. While the average number of exposures per spool is reasonable, the figure for the rolls is perhaps high, judging from his own calculations of the total compensation paid. The woman in Berlin who translated the photographed documents estimated that she had worked on some 130–150 telegrams in all. Many important items studied by the ambassador would have required several shots, of course, so her testimony is compatible with the total number of photographs. In any case, the quantitative extent of the espionage is considerably less significant than the information in the documents.

The range of topics covered in the compromised reports and messages varied widely, but much of the material dealt with inter-Allied problems and with future strategy in the war, reflecting the nature of issues discussed at the series of high-level conferences. Sir Hughe was always kept exceptionally well informed by the Foreign Office. The ambassador also kept abreast of other developments and activities, both routine and special, so he regularly monitored papers drawn from many sources. Thus some documents were concerned with economic and trade questions. On any given day, chance alone determined the quantity and quality of the papers he might have. The items he retained overnight may well have been among the most significant ones, however, if their import or complexity made necessary such a quiet and considered review.

In two areas the documents contained solid coverage of Allied aims and gave enemy analysts critical facts and insights. On the level of broad policy for prosecuting the war, the reports on the Allied conferences showed the general lines of future plans and revealed tensions among the powers; of more immediate use was the material dealing with the current efforts to bring Turkey into the war, or at least obtain its cooperation concerning airfields and radar installations. Rarely was an event like the Sofia air raid foretold in the photographs; the sensational claim persisting over the years that Cicero had stolen the secrets of Overlord is a gross exaggeration. The only thing that the Germans learned was a code word. That enemy intelligence eventually connected the term with some major Allied operation being planned for northwestern Europe resulted from subsequent careful analyses of data from many sources. By then, all the essential components of the invasion bore separate designations, which were new and safe. Both the location and date of the landings remained secret until the event.

It is easy either to overstate or underestimate the worth of the intelligence the enemy got through the spy. The former distortion was exemplified by Moyzisch and Bazna in order to magnify their roles; the latter approach has been adopted by some British writers to minimize their country's losses. But clearly the intrinsic value of the information cannot be conveniently dismissed by arguing that the Germans' failure to believe it or adjust their policies accordingly deprived the material of real importance. A similar rationale has held that the enemy essentially learned only what was already obvious or what it might probably have acquired through other means. Such contentions serve to obscure the issue of the secrets' inherent worth by invoking the fortunate outcome that the lost information had little impact. Yet the lack of enemy use of the espionage windfall neither excuses the seriousness of the security breach nor reduces the harm the spying might have done. Britain was merely lucky that the valuable secrets were not used effectively by Berlin.

* * *

Bazna's secret role was known to only a few people in Turkey. Aside from some conspicuous spending, his own caution and the limited external awareness of his activities shielded him from exposure through betrayal or loose talk. For his part, the artful Bazna made certain that he always performed his duties well and never called attention to himself, conveying the image of a dullard and managing not to arouse any suspicions in Sir Hughe about his work or conduct. Neither of the valet's successive mistresses, though each knew he was a spy, ever presented a serious threat. Among the Germans, only a small group of discreet individuals—the Jenkes, Moyzisch, and Papen—had enough knowledge about Cicero to endanger him and his efforts. With Kapp's arrival, the tight containment of information about the affair was breached, however—although her involvement and reports had belated impact due to the Americans' silence. The restricted number of people who knew of his existence protected the spy and helped make possible the duration and success of his espionage.

That neither the ordinary police nor the efficient Turkish internal security service seems to have discovered Bazna's spy activities or sudden wealth is not really surprising. There was little likelihood of disclosures by informants or of entrapment through casual surveillance of Moyzisch. The Turkish police were evidently not responsible for the nocturnal pursuit of Moyzisch's car. Bazna's expensive tastes and shopping also failed to draw the special attention so feared by Moyzisch. No one appears to have questioned his habits and purchases or the source of his money in a city newly crowded with officials and businessmen from many places. Once again Bazna was lucky. Had the local authorities possessed any information or suspicions about him, they surely would have moved quickly, for his espionage was inimical to their interests.

The spying would obviously have been impossible without Sir Hughe's disregard of the prescribed standards of security. As a representative of his country, he was dedicated, able, and conscientious in carrying out his highly demanding duties. As a person, he possessed a sense of humor and charm much admired by those who knew him. But despite his responsibility for a wartime mission in a notorious center of intrigue, especially at a time of key negotiations, he adhered to outmoded notions of security and exercised poor judgment in personal habits. By working in his residence and retaining papers overnight he permitted an opportunity for espionage that under proper conditions no members of the domestic staff would have had. The spy profited too from the diplomat's customary air of detachment, deep preoccupation with bargaining difficulties, and perhaps by a reliance on the use of sleeping aids. Some evidence suggests that the ambassador even ignored warnings by security advisers about the dangers inherent in his work patterns, and that instead he trusted in the adequacy and effectiveness of existing and improved safeguards without realizing how his own conduct and complacency undermined them.

Over the years, few observers have found much purpose in elaborating upon Foreign Secretary Bevin's statement to Parliament in 1950 noting that Knatchbull-Hugessen had made it possible for the valet-spy to photograph embassy papers: "He would not have been able to do this if the Ambassador had conformed to the regulations governing the custody of secret documents." Subsequent judgments of the unfortunate diplomat have generally registered brief concurring comments and tactful silence.[4] Sir Hughe himself handled the distressing revelations about the affair with a quiet dignity and reserve that he steadfastly maintained until his death in 1971.

The failure of wartime officials to discover and close the security leak after becoming aware of such a possibility in January reflects both the rather tenuous nature of the evidence brought to their attention and the authority of the willful ambassador. Reports from Dulles revealed only that papers dating from early December had reached German hands; it seemed just possible that a Turkish official traveling with Sir Hughe had photographed them on a train; a Turkish source might also have given Papen details about allowing the British new air bases. Also, neither careful checks by embassy personnel nor investigations by outside specialists located any current breach of security on the premises or in procedures. Yet the experts were vaguely dissatisfied, and they worried that the ambassador's work routine posed a threat. Despite observing and questioning the residence servants, the investigators found nothing to arouse their suspicions, believing the valet too stupid for espionage. If indeed spying of some type and extent was finally acknowledged, with indications pointing to the ambassador's papers and his unprepossessing servant, such awareness came too late to limit the damage or catch the culprit.

In the affair's later stages, the OSS played a hidden and strange role. Dulles was wrong in thinking that his warnings to MI6 in Switzerland had brought about the exposure or turning of Cicero; the search for a spy had failed. Meanwhile, American pique stemming from jealousies and disagreements induced the local OSS representatives to withhold important knowledge from British colleagues. Friction existed at several levels: American political and military views concerning the region differed sharply from the bold aspirations of Churchill; Allied diplomats did not always work in harmony in Ankara; MI6 agents had curtailed cooperation when their fledgling counterpart allowed leaks to the Germans. The American intelligence agents, in their early eagerness to build contacts and show results, had come to rely too heavily on local officials and informants, who were careless or not entirely sympathetic to the Allied cause. Thus an unfortunate atmosphere of professional rivalry and distrust kept the local OSS from informing the British immediately that one of their embassy servants appeared to be an enemy spy.

The OSS did not initially understand what was apparently its first encounter with Cicero. In her postwar statement about the car chase, Kapp asserted that an American agent had been involved; the subsequent claim by Bazna that he had seen and later recognized the pursuer is nevertheless nonsense. It appears that the whole incident arose by chance, however, not from special surveillance of the car or driver. That the occurrence was isolated and produced no immediate problems therefore gives it slight importance.

Far more significant were Kapp's secret role and knowledge. Her opportunity to work in Moyzisch's office came about by accident, for she would have taken any posting to reach her goal, and how much information the Americans got through her remains uncertain. She did learn and report, however, that there was a spy. Kapp apparently surmised that he was a servant but knew little beyond his code designation as "Cicero." Untrained and emotionally unsuited for the dangerous role she played, Kapp must have created great difficulties for her contact in the OSS; her nervous outbursts were genuine rather than a clever act. In the end she appears to have been a victim of her youth and dreams. Nevertheless, Kapp gave an extraordinary advantage to American intelligence. It seems certain that the OSS had enough bits of information from Kapp by some point in February to give immediate warning to the British to search for a spy. The foolish decision to keep silent while awaiting further developments suggests the seriousness of the strained relations between the services.

What occurred after Kapp's defection in early April has never been clear. Were the Americans so resentful that they decided to bypass their local British rivals? If she told her story to MI6 before being flown to Cairo, the British must have learned of the spy before Bazna left the embassy. If they first heard her account in Cairo, however, the British had little time to react and make plans. Certainly, with her information, the spy could have been identified. Was there even a brief attempt to test her claim by feeding him false data in the few days before he quit his job? Such a step would help to explain later comments that he was caught and used. By that point he had stopped spying, however, and nothing could be gained or proven, but Sir Hughe's coolness when the valet left may have had reasons that Bazna never guessed.

For more than four months the spy's good luck had held. He had managed to escape notice and cope with tightened security and investigations, which reduced but never fully stopped his work. In the end, it was his lack of access to documents during most of March and his growing fear of being caught that caused him to cease spying. The existence and length of the Americans' secrecy about their knowledge of a spy were inexcusable, however, endangering for apparently petty reasons the security of the Allied cause and plans for new operations. That their intelligence officials probably underestimated what information a personal servant could compromise scarcely mitigates their irresponsibility and actions.

* * *

Uncertainties about financial aspects of the Cicero affair involve three areas of disagreement. Were payments made primarily in British pounds sterling, or in Turkish pounds of considerably less value? How much in all was the spy paid? What proportion of the money consisted of British notes produced in the secret counterfeiting scheme? Answering such questions is complicated by missing records, conflicting testimony, varying calculations, and efforts to minimize the currency issue. Conclusions will always be tentative.

Moyzisch's assertion that he had generally paid the spy in British pounds received from Berlin was not challenged in the subsequent comments of other Germans, nor did Bazna ever deny that he himself had asked for payment in British money. Nevertheless, a few British accounts of the affair have explained the unusual sums by suggesting that Turkish pounds were used.[5] The notion has had the twofold appeal of making unnecessary any mention of the enemy's successful forgery project and of lessening the monetary value and importance of the information lost. Still, the evidence and circumstances do not support that interpretation. The SD had no reason to deny the request made by Cicero; its supply of bogus notes was more than adequate, the valet would be constrained not to endanger himself by calling early attention to his large amounts of foreign money, and the transactions could be kept simple and secret. Moyzisch personally would have had to make any conversions into the local currency, arousing unwelcome suspicion and probably exposing the counterfeit notes to immediate careful scrutiny, conditions clearly fraught with risks and repercussions for the embassy staff and Germany. His problems obtaining even relatively small amounts of dollars and gem stones would have seemed minor in comparison. Certainly, Bazna would never have experienced his postwar legal difficulties except for having spent British counterfeit notes.

Cicero received what was undoubtedly the highest amount of cash ever paid to a spy in the history of espionage up to the 1940s. The total figure remains in controversy, however, and different sums have been reported; Moyzisch himself appears to have given a range of figures, under questioning by the Allies. Most analysts have cautiously accepted Moyzisch's published statement that he paid the spy roughly £300,000 sterling, or about $1.2 million at the prevailing exchange rate, in either British notes or occasionally some special substitute.[6] In one consignment alone he claimed to have received £200,000 in notes from the SD to be expended as needed for his purchases of film. Undoubtedly he was required to account carefully for his transactions, and he ought therefore to have remembered the total disbursement. Schellenberg concurred that the figure involved had been about £300,000.

There is no agreement among the suppliers themselves about how much counterfeit money was used, but it appears that the SD acquired sizable sums from the Foreign Ministry, through the occasional transfer of Reichsmarks to meet the operation's cost. That the intelligence service kept as much of that money as it could while paying the spy in its own worthless notes cannot be doubted. Schellenberg nevertheless recorded that about half of all payments had consisted of authentic notes and that the counterfeit portion had therefore been perhaps £150,000.[7] Bazna apparently accepted that breakdown, since his lawsuit asked the German government to reimburse him in the amount cited by Schellenberg. On his own he had no way of determining how many false notes he had been paid. Nonetheless, given the ready supply of bogus notes, it seems unlikely that sound money had been used for half the payments. In retrospect Moyzisch thought that only £35,000, $20,000, and $2,000 worth of diamonds given to Cicero were genuine.[8] That he had in fact realized even at the time that the new notes arriving from Berlin were counterfeit can hardly be doubted, despite all his later denials.

Bazna's greed and overconfidence always blinded him to the manner in which he was being regularly cheated by the Germans. Never did he realize that anything was wrong: he questioned neither the origins nor the number and new condition of the notes. He took none of the sensible precautions that less trusting and more intelligent people would have thought wise. He made no attempt to convert or exchange the money quickly and secretly in order to dissociate himself from it and the spying; and there was no effort to seek anonymity by relocating to another country where the profit from his activity could be enjoyed in peace. The ambitious servant's dream of living with wealth and position in a familiar setting proved too compelling. For a man who prided himself on his cleverness, he was rather easily deceived by people who were smarter. His futile postwar efforts to obtain compensation from the German government show how profoundly victimized he felt.

The factors that shaped the affair's financial character and produced its ultimate ironies emerged largely through chance and time. Bazna set a high initial price, because he had no way of knowing at the outset how long he might be able to deceive Sir Hughe. Even he seemed surprised by the capital that he acquired over the passing months. He was also fortunate that Germany agreed to buy the photographs. Certainly a more modest scale of payments would have prevailed had Bazna been forced to turn to Moscow. Nor would even Berlin have continued to meet the mounting cost of the operation had it not already possessed an unsuspected means to accommodate Bazna, that is, bogus notes. Its reasons for later reducing his payments represented self-protection and prudence rather than any shortage of funds. Had it been required to provide such large amounts in a genuine foreign currency, or in jewels or gold, it would undoubtedly in time have insisted upon more stringent adjustment in the purchase price.

* * *

Although Turkey played no direct role in shaping the development or outcome of the spy episode, its government never discovering the valet's espionage, both local conditions and the nation's strategic importance were essential factors in the Cicero affair. The opportunities to be found in the neutral country, with its heady wartime atmosphere and pervasive intrigues, intense competition among representatives of the warring powers for useful intelligence about enemies and friends alike, and potential for mischief by any daring adventurer, provided just the milieu for a spy case. Moreover a significant aim of both sides in the conflict was to influence Ankara's decisions about entering the war and agreeing to military cooperation. Turkey was not only the guardian of vital shipping routes through the Straits; it also lay at a juncture of three great power blocs—the Soviet Union to the north, Axis forces in the Aegean region and the Balkans, and the Western Allies to the south. Permitting Germany to frustrate Britain's efforts to win cooperation from Ankara was a major use of Cicero's information.

Churchill was the driving force behind Britain's efforts to obtain support from Turkey. Having long taken too much for granted in dealing with his nation's ally, he now once again ignored the practical obstacles to his plans, pressing ahead with a vision that others thought had slight chance of success. The events and timetable on which the prime minister based his plans added to the troubles: British forces had failed in their autumn campaign to seize and hold islands in the Aegean; Allied troops in Italy were unable to advance as quickly as predicted and to take Rome early in 1944; Britain faced looming deadlines for the shifting of resources needed for coming operations in western Europe. Churchill's hope of carrying significant fighting into the Balkans was highly unrealistic, given both British weakness and the inability of London to meet the minimum terms expected by Ankara. Britain simply had little or nothing to offer Turkey. Under the circumstances, only his deep concern about expansion of Soviet power can explain Churchill's persistence in pursuing his objectives over so many frustrating weeks.

The failure of its negotiations led to the lowest point in Britain's wartime relations with Turkey and caused British leaders to reconsider both their plans and policy. An immediate consequence of Turkish intransigence was cancellation of Balkan operations as once envisioned. Yet it is doubtful whether many besides Churchill were really upset by the outcome: other officials continued to stress the planned invasion of France as the top priority for men and supplies. Large numbers of Axis troops remained tied down in the Balkans, however, though not because of any British threat. Also, Britain took a much firmer stand in its dealings with Turkey. Political concerns no longer prevented the application of overwhelming pressure in order to achieve the aims of economic warfare, for instance, and the potential effects of the neutral's choice of isolating itself from the Western democracies were quickly made apparent. The new approach soon brought results, but the abrupt switch represented an acknowledgment that previous policies had largely failed.

Throughout the period of mounting tension, Cicero provided Germany with valuable insights to the problems. Nevertheless, it is clear that neither his spying nor any action taken by Papen using the secret knowledge played much part in prompting or shaping them. The information served essentially as reassurance that the enemy was making no substantial progress in its negotiations.

Turkish leaders considered their caution in international affairs to be justified, and they were determined not to endanger or weaken their country by any precipitate commitments just to accommodate Britain. Ankara's insistence on resisting military involvement until it had been satisfied about its role, including expected benefits, and also about the protection of its sovereignty has been aptly described in French as *attentisme*, a "wait and see" policy. Through its temporizing the suspicious government hoped in particular to discover what promises Moscow might have received and why it maintained an ominous silence on regional issues. Certainly, it was not difficult for Turkish leaders to use inflated demands for arms and contrived but plausible arguments on other problems to prolong the discussions with the British until such matters could be clarified. Following the December meetings in Cairo, they also perceived that Roosevelt and other Americans would be understanding.

Obviously there were elements in the Turkish policy that were expedient and insincere.[9] British officials made Menemencioglu the principal target of their criticism, even though there was tacit recognition that the foreign minister was only a spokesman for a policy that clearly had widespread support among Turkish leaders in 1943–1944. Sir Hughe and others understood that point far better than did Churchill. Deeply committed to serving his country, Menemencioglu acted as he did not out of regard for Nazi Germany but to safeguard his nation's interests. He sought to maintain a balance in part by telling Papen certain things about the negotiations in which he was engaged; nevertheless, he gave a specific and timely warning to the British that the enemy ambassador had some secret source of information.

Ankara's wariness of commitment became too entrenched, however, and its prolonged indecision favored the Germans. The Turkish leaders grasped too late how deeply they had exasperated their ally and how greatly the course of the war had undermined their power to affect Allied plans. Their subsequent steps to relieve political pressures and avoid economic sanctions were embarrassing to them. In the end, Ankara's initial hopes for gaining some advantage or territory during the confusion of World War II came to naught; at the conflict's end, Turkey faced a Soviet threat from the Balkans as well as along its northern coast and border.

* * *

A basic tenet in the intelligence field holds that the real value of information about an opponent's plans or capabilities lies in its advantageous use. Assessing objectively the amount of actual benefit the Germans derived from the Cicero affair requires looking at specific situations and results. It is as misleading to accept Moyzisch's unqualified contention that the secret knowledge was disregarded as it is to believe Papen's exaggerated claims about its impact.[10] For some purposes, the material was of limited use. Documents being studied by the ambassador seldom contained intelligence that affected the current fighting (the reference to the bombing of Sofia had clearly been an exception). Nor was possession of British texts a help to the Germans in breaking major codes. In three areas the items of information had been extremely valuable, however, and their significance with respect to developments requires more specific review. Of local and immediate importance were insights to British aims in Turkey at a time of critical negotiations and planning. There were also documents that helped clarify where the Western Allies might launch their expected invasion of the continent. At the broadest level, the mounting evidence revealed the Germans' waning prospects of victory, given their enemies' strength and resolution.

Papen gained a substantial advantage from following, through the enemy's own documents, its efforts to win military cooperation from Turkey. Still, the approaches he employed to keep Ankara neutral and to maintain vital deliveries of chrome, including playing on old fears of Soviet expansion and threatening that Turkish cities might be exposed to bombing, at most underscored the existing determination of the Turkish leaders to avoid any commitments for the present. On one occasion it appears that Papen so badly misjudged the degree of danger, thinking Turkey might yield to British pressure, that in his forceful protest to Menemencioglu he revealed that he had secret knowledge. The intervention was in fact unnecessary, given Ankara's attitude, and it might have destroyed the spy operation had British rechecks of embassy security discovered the leak. Papen felt justified in taking the risk, however, and resented the later criticism of it by Moyzisch. Nevertheless one conclusion is inescapable: the spy material benefited Papen only because Ankara itself was resolute in temporizing. In his postwar assertions, the former ambassador plainly overstated the significance of the information and his own influence on events.[11]

It seems clear in retrospect that the photographs taken by Cicero did not give Germany any great advantage through insights to its enemies' military plans. Clarification of the basic question that worried German leaders, whether the British and Americans would mount their next assault in the west or in the Aegean and Balkan region, developed slowly and failed to produce substantial benefits. The knowledge that ruled out any immediate threat of invasion in southeastern Europe was overshadowed by unrest in the satellites and an unstable eastern front; the realization that the next important operation would be launched in northwestern Europe was unaccompanied by specific data allowing a concentration of defensive forces. In both situations the spy's information, however valuable, had only a limited impact.

German leaders remained uncertain during the early winter of 1943–1944 about what enemy action to expect in the Balkans. Insights to the Allies' secret conferences showed that Churchill continued to urge operations in the area despite Britain's military defeat in the Aegean that autumn. The spy's photographs let Berlin follow closely the British efforts to obtain Turkey's cooperation in new joint plans. But could documents indicating Turkish resistance to continued British pressure really be trusted? Even if they were reliable, would Ankara maintain its firmness and not alter course? Not until the beginning of February did intelligence analysts in Germany rule out any immediate threat, and military staff experts thought it safe to shift at least two divisions from the Balkans to other fronts. Still, action was delayed, in part because Hitler worried about controlling his restive satellites and protecting the southern end of his long eastern front. Further developments soon made the transfers impossible. Thus while the information from Cicero had finally been accepted as trustworthy, other factors and considerations lowered its value, producing no major reduction of Germany's military strength in the southeast. The tying down of those forces, London's fall-back aim in its talks with Turkey, occurred despite data from the spy.

The widespread belief that the valet's espionage provided the Germans with vital information about the Allied plans for invasion of northwestern Europe is traceable to early exaggerations that found frequent repetition. Moyzisch introduced the sensational claim in his book, by overstating the significance and results of having obtained documents containing the word "Overlord." Upon that limited fact and his postwar knowledge he built the implication that valuable details about the enemy landings had been learned. The contention appealed to the imagination of popularizers, who copied and perpetuated it. In particular, the worldwide success of the purportedly factual film *Five Fingers* made the misconception a durable part of the accepted lore. Awareness of the code name was only part of the intelligence puzzle, which would still be unsolved when the attack came. The actual gain through the espionage was in fact minor.

In Berlin the impact of the documents was delayed by uncertainties about their genuineness and tempered by the doctrinaire thinking of Nazi leaders. That the material had initially aroused doubts and suspicion was understandable, of course, but even eventual acceptance of its authenticity failed to alter attitudes. Hitler's own view set the pattern for his coterie of sycophants like Ribbentrop. While items pointing to tensions and difficulties within the opponents' coalition were seized upon eagerly, since they sustained visions of ultimate triumph, the regime wasted an opportunity to exploit enemy distrust and disagreements for its own advantage. The information about discussions and decisions at Tehran and other conferences remained largely a curiosity.[12]

German intelligence had an unimpressive record of accomplishments in World War II. Its overall failure reflected not only the poor quantity and quality of the information being gathered but also the narrow ideology and distorted attitudes that impaired the decisions of the nation's leaders. The inefficiency of the Abwehr was discovered only slowly, partly because early victories concealed the inadequacy and unreliability of its data about the enemy, but especially because the German military shielded the faltering service. Meanwhile, Schellenberg schemed to have his SD gain control of foreign intelligence efforts and to obtain support for his continuing intrigues to remove Ribbentrop as head of the Foreign Ministry. Such bitter antagonisms precluded careful consolidation of all incoming information and enabled Hitler to avoid facing reality by choosing to disregard unwelcome reports and analyses. In the end, the combined characteristics of the regime—its authoritarian structure, power struggles, overlapping jurisdictions, rigid thinking, and delusional outlooks—undermined the role and influence of its intelligence efforts. The Cicero operation represents the greatest intelligence success of the war, but it also illustrates the dictatorship's unwillingness to absorb information that was incompatible with Nazi dreams.

* * *

The British leaders and public were understandably reluctant to accept the Cicero story when the first rumors and reports circulated early in 1950. Nevertheless, that autumn the foreign secretary admitted that an investigation had confirmed the essential truthfulness of the published account of wartime spying at the embassy. Such espionage should never have occurred, of course, but the unexpected had indeed happened. Thereafter the embarrassing situation was minimized or ignored; a purposeful effort to control the damage shielded the individuals, Foreign Office, and intelligence services. A face-saving impression that the case as publicized had been misconstrued, was much less important than some claimed, and had involved still-secret elements, was nurtured and encouraged in a number of ways over the years. Not even the alleged theft of Overlord details was denied quickly and firmly. Full discussion of the espionage affair would undoubtedly have raised too many other awkward issues, especially the counterfeiting scheme but also the failures in both wartime foreign policy and military operations in the region. Soon the Foreign Office and intelligence services faced new and greater difficulties, in the scandal emerging from the disloyalty of Kim Philby and his friends. Thus the extended official silence allowed distortions and speculations concerning the Cicero episode to grow and eventually permeate much of the literature about it. Two volumes published in 1990, in the series entitled *British Intelligence in the Second World War*, made clear that Cicero acted independently and was never caught. A suspicion remained that many people would still prefer to play down the affair, however, and to let the record on some points contain a certain amount of confusion and doubt.

For various reasons, the fame of the Cicero affair came to transcend the historical facts. There were simply too many elements in the story— its roster of players, the setting, circumstances, and results, its turnings of fortune—that imbued the episode with a wide public appeal. Mere chance and luck, both good and bad, played a clear role. The ironic twists that turned all the participants' various hopes and expectations into frustrations or chagrin have given the overall situation the image by which it is best remembered. The war's most successful and most highly paid spy profited little from his dangerous work; a country justly proud of its other wartime intelligence work was embarrassed that an unimpressive servant could have stolen its secrets so simply; the government that acquired the information proved incapable of using it to much advantage. It is hard to find winners in such a tale—but it is easy to see the lessons to be learned.

Notes

REFERENCES AND ABBREVIATIONS

In references to Britain's Foreign Office files, the broad designation "FO 371" for documents in the Public Record Office has been omitted; the category is common to all items in the citations. Only the file and document numbers are noted: for example, 37479/R13545. In a few instances there is just one document in a file, and no item number is cited.

German Foreign Ministry documents have been cited using the microfilm copies available in the United States National Archives. Record Group 242 includes items from the years 1920–1945 and constitutes part of Microfilm Publication T120. Roll 52 covers German relations with Turkey during the period from November 1943 through April 1944. The roll and frame numbers are separated by a slash mark—for example, 52/41937–41939—and are comparable to references to Volume IX of *Akten des Politischen Archivs im Auswärtigen Amt*.

Newspaper citations not identifying a page number are based on copies of articles obtained through clipping and archival services that did not record page information.

The following abbreviations have been used for convenience in note citations:

FM   German Foreign Ministry
FO   British Foreign Office

CHAPTER 1. THE "NOTORIOUS" CASE

1. Ludwig C. Moyzisch, *Operation Cicero*, postscript by Franz von Papen, trans. Constantine FitzGibbon and Heinrich Fraenkel (New York: Coward-McCann, 1950). The original title, *Der Fall Cicero: Es geschah in Ankara—Die sensationellste Spionageaffäre des Zweiten Weltkriegs* (Frankfurt: Die Quadriga, 1950), was more flamboyant. FitzGibbon later became convinced that the spy had been a double agent working for the British. His views are discussed

at a later point. An abridgment of Moyzisch's book appeared in *High Stakes and Desperate Men: Classics of Espionage* (Pleasantville, N.Y.: Reader's Digest Association, 1974), pp. 87–178. Excerpts were also published by Allen Dulles and Graham Greene in their spy story anthologies. Citations of Papen's postscript are so identified. A prefatory note in the French-language edition of Moyzisch's book said that many editors in France and elsewhere hesitated to publish it. See *L'Affaire Ciceron*, trans. Suzanne Belly (Verviers, Belgium: Gérard, n.d.), p. 5. The British publisher also questioned Moyzisch's tale. See Nigel West, *A Thread of Deceit: Espionage Myths of World War II* (New York: Random House, 1985), pp. 99–100. West's book was first published in Britain by Allan Wingate under the title *Unreliable Witness*.

2. Moyzisch, *Operation Cicero*, pp. 1–7, 18–19, 25, 30–32, 59, 70–71, 138–39, 201–202. On pp. 3–5 he describes the various competing intelligence services in Nazi Germany without ever acknowledging his status with the SD. Moyzisch's equivalent rank reportedly was that of a lieutenant colonel, or Obersturmbannführer. See, for example, *Die Zeit*, 28 Dec. 1970, p. 5. He joined the Nazi Party very early but in his book denied having been in the SS. Apparently he could not prove that his racial background was satisfactory.

3. Papen, postscript to Moyzisch, *Operation Cicero*, pp. 207–209.

4. Robert M. W. Kempner, "The Highest-Paid Spy in History," *Saturday Evening Post*, 28 Jan. 1950, pp. 17–19 and continuations.

5. Papen, postscript to Moyzisch, *Operation Cicero*, pp. 207–209; Franz von Papen, *Der Wahrheit eine Gasse* (Munich: Paul List Verlag, 1952). See also his *Memoirs*, trans. Brian Connell (New York: E. P. Dutton, 1953), pp. 509–10. The translation was slightly abridged, but the editing did not affect Chapter 28, "Operation Cicero," pp. 506–28.

6. Walter Schellenberg, *The Labyrinth: Memoirs of Walter Schellenberg*, trans. Louis Hagen, intro. Alan Bullock (New York: Harper & Brothers, 1956), pp. 336, 338, 341. The book has also been published as *Hitler's Secret Service*.

7. Sir Hughe Knatchbull-Hugessen, *Diplomat in Peace and War* (London: John Murray, 1949). Three excerpts appeared in February–April 1949 before the book itself. The third segment dealt with Turkey in the last prewar months: "Ambassador in Turkey," *Fortnightly* 171 (Apr. 1949), pp. 228–35. For Sir Hughe's first comments on the spy affair see John Prebble, in *Sunday Express*, 15 Jan. 1950, p. 4. Sir Hughe's anger in the later remarks was prompted by details in the article by Kempner. He was holding a copy of the magazine as he spoke. See *Sunday Chronicle* (London ed.), 5 Feb. 1950.

8. Great Britain, *Parliamentary Debates (Hansard)*, Fifth Series, Vol. 478, *House of Commons, Official Report*, Session 1950, 24 July–26 Oct. 1950, cols. 2023–2024 (London: His Majesty's Stationery Office); *Times* (London), 19 Oct. 1950, p. 7; *Daily Telegraph & Morning Post* (London), 19 Oct. 1950, p. A–7. Stories of the same date in the *Daily Express* and *News Chronicle* took the same line in covering the statement.

9. Anthony Cave Brown, *Bodyguard of Lies*, 2 vols. (New York: Harper & Row, 1975). In this edition the pages are numbered continuously, so no volume is cited.

10. F. H. Hinsley and C. A. G. Simkins, *Security and Counter-Intelligence* (New York: Cambridge Univ. Press, 1990), pp. 213–15. The work is volume 4

of F. H. Hinsley et al., *British Intelligence in the Second World War*, 5 vols. (London: Her Majesty's Stationery Office, 1979–1990).

11. For full particulars concerning the production see the filmography. The film is available on videocassette.

12. Elyesa Bazna, with Hans Nogly, *Ich war Cicero: Die Bekenntnisse des grössten Spion des Zweiten Weltkriegs* (Munich: Kindler Verlag, 1962); *I Was Cicero*, trans. Eric Mosbacher (New York: Harper & Row, 1962). Nogly described his involvement in the project and Bazna's first comments in his introductory note on pp. v–vii.

13. The nature and location of the diplomatic documents are described in the bibliography. Two publications that summarize many of the communications and may be more readily accessible are Henry M. Adams and Robin K. Adams, *Rebel Patriot: A Biography of Franz von Papen* (Santa Barbara, Calif.: McNally & Loftin, 1987), and Lothar Krecker, *Deutschland und die Türkei im zweiten Weltkrieg* (Frankfurt: Vittorio Klostermann, 1964).

CHAPTER 2. TURKEY AND THE POWERS

1. Atatürk renounced revenge and expansionism after World War I. İnönü was more pragmatic and more ambitious for Turkey. He and others saw the war as presenting good opportunities for a degree of adventurism at perhaps a small cost.

2. W. N. Medlicott, "Economic Warfare," in *Survey of International Affairs, 1939–1946: The War and the Neutrals*, ed. Arnold Toynbee and Veronica Toynbee (London: Oxford Univ. Press, 1956), pp. 30–31, 81–83. Germany's 50-percent share of Turkey's prewar trade fell to 10 percent by 1941, but other nations often acted as conduits. Before the war, Turkey supplied about a third of Germany's need for chromite. Frank G. Weber, *The Evasive Neutral: Germany, Britain, and the Quest for a Turkish Alliance in the Second World War* (Columbia: Univ. of Missouri Press, 1979), pp. 35, 129–31, 150–51; George E. Kirk, "Turkey," in Toynbee and Toynbee, eds., *The War and the Neutrals*, pp. 351–52; Knatchbull-Hugessen, *Diplomat*, p. 172.

3. Sir Hughe traced the family's history in his book *Kentish Family* (London: Methuen, 1960).

4. Knatchbull-Hugessen, *Diplomat*, pp. 1–26, 129–46; *Current Biography* (Mar. 1943), pp. 391–93.

5. Knatchbull-Hugessen, *Diplomat*, pp. 26–27, 93–128; *New York Times*, 23 Mar. 1971, p. 19. Japan expressed "deep regret," and the British Parliament voted him £5,000.

6. Appendices to his memoirs give examples of official correspondence and of his poems that the items inspired. Knatchbull-Hugessen, *Diplomat*, pp. 243–61. His chapter of reflections on diplomatic service also reveals humor and wit (pp. 28–40).

7. Photographs of two watercolors and several drawings appear in his memoirs. *Times* (London), 23 Mar. 1971, p. 19; *Daily Telegraph* (London), 23 Mar. 1971, p. 14. Cave Brown, *Bodyguard*, p. 437, reported that "he was said to have played very badly."

8. Knatchbull-Hugessen especially praised Saracoglu as being "whole-heartedly with us" but said Inönü too was pro-British. Knatchbull-Hugessen, *Diplomat*, pp. 179–80, 201–202.

9. Ibid., pp. 178–80. Geoffrey Lewis, *Turkey*, 3d ed. (New York: Praeger, 1965), p. 119, notes that most of the press was pro-Allies. Turkey had two newspapers published in French that stressed international affairs: *La République* favored German views, and *Le Journal d'Orient* the Allied cause.

10. Knatchbull-Hugessen, *Diplomat*, pp. 169–94; Winston Churchill, *The Hinge of Fate*, vol. 4 of *The Second World War* (Boston: Houghton Mifflin, 1950), pp. 715–16; Weber, *Evasive Neutral*, pp. 161–68. Before the meetings, Churchill had told President Roosevelt's friend Harry Hopkins that he would threaten not to oppose Moscow's control of the Straits if Ankara did not cooperate. Robert E. Sherwood, *Roosevelt and Hopkins: An Intimate History* (New York: Harper & Brothers, 1950), p. 683. Soon after the meetings Sir Hughe stated publicly that "absolute harmony prevailed" between Inönü and the prime minister. *Times* (London), 4 Feb. 1943. He was counteracting early reports of difficulties. Churchill did persuade the Turks to seek better relations with Moscow. Papen lacked foreknowledge of Inönü's secret conference with Churchill.

11. Papen, *Memoirs*, pp. 15–52, 68–85.

12. André François-Poncet, *The Fateful Years: Memoirs of a French Ambassador in Berlin, 1931–1938*, trans. Jacques LeClercq (New York: Harcourt, Brace, 1949), p. 24.

13. Knatchbull-Hugessen, *Diplomat*, pp. 150–51.

14. Ibid., pp. 146–51. The former ambassador, Wilhelm Keller, retired due to age. Ribbentrop claimed that he and Hitler believed that Papen could induce Ankara not to join the Allies. Joachim von Ribbentrop, *The Ribbentrop Memoirs*, trans. Oliver Watson (London: Weidenfeld and Nicolson, 1954), p. 164n.

15. Weber, *Evasive Neutral*, pp. 146–61. The treaty doomed the visit that month of Roosevelt's special emissary, Wendell Willkie, who discovered Ankara had little interest in the ideas he proposed. German officials had no illusions about Turkey. Joseph Goebbels had summarized the situation in spring 1942: "Ankara no doubt has the intention of deciding in favor of one side or the other only when victory for that side is absolutely sure." The minister considered Papen "the best horse in our stable" there. Joseph Goebbels, *The Goebbels Diaries, 1942–1943*, ed. and trans. Louis P. Lochner (Garden City, N.Y.: Doubleday, 1948), entries for 19 Mar. 1942, p. 128; 11 Mar. 1943, p. 293; 23 May 1943, p. 392. For Goebbels's meddling in Turkey see Moyzisch, *Operation Cicero*, pp. 7–9.

16. Weber, *Evasive Neutral*, pp. 170–72. Jenke was one of two ministers at the embassy in Ankara. He handled the spy's material when the ambassador was absent.

17. Germany had acquired the legation property with its absorption of Czechoslovakia.

18. Ibid., pp. 126–37. Soviet agents have also been blamed for the attempt to kill Papen. For Papen's contacts with the enemy see ibid., pp. 151–61, 167–71; Anthony Cave Brown, *The Last Hero: Wild Bill Donovan* (New York: Times Books, 1982), pp. 359–81; and Papen's memoirs. Moyzisch and Schellenberg

confirmed that the Nazis watched Papen. Moyzisch, *Operation Cicero*. pp. 10–11; Schellenberg, *Labyrinth*, pp. 301, 305, 311.

19. Knatchbull-Hugessen, *Diplomat*, p. 150.

20. Ibid., pp. 191–94. Coolness existed in Turkish-American relations as well.

21. The thorough analysis of the campaign by Peter C. Smith and Edwin Walker, *War in the Aegean* (London: William Kimber, 1974), has been used for most of this information.

22. Italy needed to protect the large island of Rhodes and also the Dodecanese ("Twelve") islands, acquired from Turkey in 1912 after the Italo-Turkish War. All the islands were inhabited primarily by Greeks, and Greece acquired them after the war.

23. Smith and Walker, *War in the Aegean*, p. 269.

24. Marshall L. Miller, *Bulgaria during the Second World War* (Stanford, Calif.: Stanford Univ. Press, 1975), pp. 169–70.

25. U.S. Department of State, *Foreign Relations of the United States, Diplomatic Papers, 1943: The Conferences at Cairo and Tehran* (Washington, D.C.: Government Printing Office, 1961), p. 210.

26. Miller, *Bulgaria*, pp. 166–67, 169–70.

CHAPTER 3. THE VOLUNTEER SPY

1. For Bazna's background and life see *I Was Cicero*, pp. 3–10. It is impossible to know how truthful his account is, but he probably overstated his family's importance.

2. An example of errors about the spy was a statement William Cavendish-Bentinck reportedly made to Constantine FitzGibbon: "I knew 'Cicero' when he was Horace Rumbold's valet at the Lausanne Conference in 1922–1923. He was an excellent valet and was of very good presence (as was required of footmen and valets)." Constantine FitzGibbon, *Secret Intelligence in the Twentieth Century* (New York: Stein and Day, 1977), p. 264n. The man could not have been the spy.

3. For Bazna's account of his early spying see *I Was Cicero*, pp. 8–9, 13–18, 20–23, 26–28, 31–32, 41–42, 47, 186.

4. Bazna claimed that the letters he read were from Ribbentrop. Ibid., p. 46.

5. Busk joined the diplomatic service in 1929 and held various posts before Ankara. He enjoyed a long and successful career and was knighted. Busk never published his memoirs but discussed his field in *The Craft of Diplomacy: How to Run a Diplomatic Service* (New York: Praeger, 1967). Among those "erstwhile senior colleagues" to whom he dedicated the book was "H. K. H.," or Sir Hughe.

6. The intelligence officer was Nicholas Elliott. See his memoir, *Never Judge a Man by His Umbrella* (Salisbury, U.K.: Michael Russell, 1991), p. 135. He thought that the ambassador had not listened to the embassy's security officer. For Sir Hughe's comment see the Prebble interview, *Sunday Express* (London), 15 Jan. 1950, p. 4. Bazna implied that he began working for the ambassador in September or October, but one account placed his hiring as early as July. Hinsley and Simkins, *Security*, p. 214. The earlier date raises the question of why he waited so long to shoot any film.

7. Two of Busk's colleagues in Turkey have discredited Bazna's story about copying his official papers, even though both thought Cicero had indeed filmed Sir Hughe's documents. The assertion about a list of British agents met with particular scorn. Elliott, *Never Judge*, pp. 135–36; Frank Brenchley, interview with author, London, 21 Dec. 1995. Brenchley is a retired ambassador who then served in the embassy at Ankara. Bazna also described at length an early occasion when he read but did not copy a file of papers brought home by Busk. *I Was Cicero*, pp. 14–18. The photography in the kitchen supposedly took place the night before he started working for the ambassador. See pp. 31–34. For the 25 October photography see pp. 41–42.

8. Ibid., p. 42. In order to impress his contact with his resourcefulness, Bazna claimed to have planned his spying two years in advance. Ibid., p. 71; Moyzisch, *Operation Cicero*, p. 110.

9. Papen, *Memoirs*, pp. 509–10. The former ambassador referred to the "rather puzzling way" the spy had approached the embassy; Papen's account is plausible and compatible with Moyzisch's book. Moyzisch would not have known why the diplomats directed the spy to the SD. He regarded the foreign minister's sister as a charming woman but quite ambitious. See *Operation Cicero*, p. 14. Later, Frau Jenke died from Parkinson's disease. Papen also denied speculation in the weekly *Die Zeit* on 14 December 1950 that Germany had planted the spy in the embassy. See *Memoirs*, p. 518. A similar conjecture held that after Jenke had caught him prying, the Germans had forced the valet to spy. See Charles Wighton, *The World's Greatest Spies: True-Life Dramas of Outstanding Secret Agents* (New York: Taplinger, 1965), p. 259.

10. See Bazna, *I Was Cicero*, pp. 42–52.

11. For his account see Moyzisch, *Operation Cicero*, pp. 23–38, 72, 84; see also Papen, *Memoirs*, pp. 510–12. Moyzisch joined the Nazi Party in 1932, as member no. 1,307,980. In 1942 he was refused membership in the SS. David Kahn, *Hitler's Spies: German Military Intelligence in World War II* (New York: Macmillan, 1978), pp. 341, 620.

12. Schellenberg, *Labyrinth*, pp. 335–36, 338, related what happened in Berlin.

13. Nearly all analysts concur that the first payment was genuine currency. See also Moyzisch, *Operation Cicero*, p. 39, where he describes the mixed, small-value notes. Certainly Berlin would have been foolish to jeopardize relations with a potentially valuable spy by offering him bogus British notes.

14. For Bazna's early spying in the residence see *I Was Cicero*, pp. 27–30, 35–36, 39–41, 53–57, 59–60.

15. The explanation about the altered building functions came from the Brenchley interview, 21 Dec. 1995. One of the ambassador's daughters worked as a cipher clerk in the embassy and lived with her parents.

16. Busk, *Craft of Diplomacy*, pp. 17–18, described the Italians' plight at the reception: neither the Germans nor the Allies wanted them. Neutral guests separated enemy delegations.

17. Moyzisch, *Operation Cicero*, pp. 34–38; Bazna, *I Was Cicero*, pp. 52–53, 60–64. Both authors give the texts of the Ankara-Berlin telegram exchange covering the offer. Moyzisch perhaps got more help from the professional photographer than he acknowledged. Prior to the second delivery, he also bought

an instruction book. Moyzisch, *Operation Cicero*, p. 61. See also Kempner, "Highest-Paid Spy," p. 103.

18. Moyzisch implied that the spy got no five-pound notes, but Bazna said he received some from the Germans. Bazna, *I Was Cicero*, p. 193.

19. For their feelings in approaching the first sale see ibid., pp. 56–60, and Moyzisch, *Operation Cicero*, pp. 38–41.

20. Information on Bazna's motives was drawn from *I Was Cicero*, pp. vi, 9, 12–13, 15–18, 32–34, 39, 54, 62–63, 65–66, 69–71, 73–74, 76–78, 80–81, 101–102, 127, 132, 149, 181–82, 189. See also Moyzisch, *Operation Cicero*, pp. 61–62, 75, 109–11, 148, 191.

21. Bazna identified his father as Hafiz Yasar. *I Was Cicero*, pp. 13, 74. In explaining the story of his father's killing, he said of Moyzisch, "I played on his credulity." See pp. 72–73, 80–81. Schellenberg recalled a different version from that of Moyzisch. See *Labyrinth*, p. 339. But he had misremembered what he heard.

CHAPTER 4. SELLING THE SECRETS

1. Moyzisch, *Operation Cicero*, pp. 41–48; Bazna, *I Was Cicero*, pp. 60–64. Kempner reported that the spy asked for £5,000 per document and offered four items for £20,000. He also thought that the first meeting occurred in a park. "Highest-Paid Spy," p. 103. Kempner got such information from Moyzisch, but it is clear that Moyzisch related things he did not actually know and protected himself by telling various stories during questioning by the Allies after the war. It is often hard to know which of his tales to believe.

2. Moyzisch, *Operation Cicero*, p. 68. He supposedly admitted in postwar interrogations that he had processed most photographs so quickly that he rarely noticed the content. Hinsley and Simkins, *Security*, p. 215.

3. Moyzisch, *Operation Cicero*, pp. 48–59, 61–62; Papen, *Memoirs*, pp. 510–12; Bazna, *I Was Cicero*, p. 42. Kahn, *Hitler's Spies*, p. 341, reported fifty-six photographs from the first two rolls.

4. Churchill in a minute to the Foreign Office on 23 April 1945 again rejected new names like Ankara. "As for Angora, long familiar with us through the Angora cats, I will resist to the utmost its degradation to Ankara. . . . As long as I have a word to say in the matter Ankara is banned, unless in brackets afterwards." Winston Churchill, *Triumph and Tragedy*, vol. 6 of *The Second World War* (Boston: Houghton Mifflin, 1953), pp. 752–53.

5. Bazna, *I Was Cicero*, pp. 64, 66.

6. Moyzisch, *Operation Cicero*, pp. 63–69; Bazna, *I Was Cicero*, pp. 63–66. Both men said the camera was a Leica and not a Minox, as has at times been reported. Bazna, pp. 56, 63; Moyzisch, pp. 64, 132.

7. Moyzisch, *Operation Cicero*, pp. 65–66; Bazna, *I Was Cicero*, p. 76.

8. Bazna, *I Was Cicero*, pp. 51–52, 63, 65; Moyzisch, *Operation Cicero*, pp. 64, 108, 125.

9. Moyzisch, *Operation Cicero*, pp. 72–76, 108.

10. Papen, *Memoirs*, p. 512. Jenke handled the spy's material during absences of Papen. See Moyzisch, *Operation Cicero*, pp. 15, 61–62.

11. Schellenberg, *Labyrinth*, pp. 336–38; Moyzisch, *Operation Cicero*, pp. 72, 84. Schellenberg's shipment of money had been approved by Kaltenbrunner. Some writers have maintained that Moyzisch exchanged the forged notes for Turkish pounds before paying the spy. Supposedly the valet got a monthy stipend, a price per roll, and a bonus for one achievement. In all, he received 700,000 Turkish pounds, or about £150,000 in the sterling equivalent. Hinsley and Simkins, *Security*, p. 214. The idea has influenced others (see Elliott, *Never Judge*, p. 138), but it disregards too much testimony—Bazna, Moyzisch, Schellenberg, and Papen—and creates other difficulties as well. Making an embassy employee regularly convert large quantities of counterfeit notes would have been extremely risky and potentially disastrous. Also, Bazna's postwar financial ruin and prosecutions showed that he had acquired British notes. Had he been paid in his own country's money, he would have been safe. Moyzisch apparently told conflicting stories about the payments and forgery operation under questioning by the British. There has also been lingering reluctance by some British writers to accept the magnitude of the counterfeiting scheme. Another troublesome question involves the Foreign Ministry's financial contributions to the operation. Kempner thought that eventually the SD got the equivalent of $500,000. A photograph accompanying his article showed a ministry order dated 24 February 1944 authorizing transfer of 250,000 Reichsmarks (about $100,000) to the SD "for purposes of the 'Cicero' operations." Ribbentrop's complaints about getting little credit for the espionage affair reportedly got some funds returned by the SD. "Highest-Paid Spy," p. 103. But the document suggests how the SD obtained sound money while using bogus British notes to pay the spy.

12. Bazna, *I Was Cicero*, pp. 59–60, 65–66; Papen to Ribbentrop, 3 and 5 Nov. 1943, nos. 1576 and 1603, 52/41708–41711 and 52/41722-41724. The 7 October document, "Long-Term British Policy towards Turkey," may be found in Foreign Office records: 37517/R9970. Nearly all of Sir Hughe's questions for Eden dealt with Turco-Russian relations. For Papen's use of rumors in the war of nerves see Knatchbull-Hugessen, *Diplomat*, pp. 178–80.

13. Papen, *Memoirs*, p. 511; Moyzisch, *Operation Cicero*, pp. 57, 76; Schellenberg, *Labyrinth*, p. 337.

14. Moyzisch, *Operation Cicero*, pp. 50–51, 56–57, 69, 76.

15. Bazna, *I Was Cicero*, pp. 14–18.

16. Ibid., pp. 33–34, 41, 58–59.

17. Ibid., pp. 36–38. For the description of the black and red leather-bound boxes, the author is indebted to Sir Donald Hawley, retired British diplomat.

18. William Sholto Douglas and Robert Wright, *Combat and Command: The Story of an Airman in Two World Wars* (New York: Simon & Schuster, 1966), pp. 543–44. Douglas became Marshal of the RAF and Lord Douglas of Kirtleside. Knatchbull-Hugessen's year-end report dated the visit described as 11–15 March 1943.

19. Bazna, *I Was Cicero*, pp. 27–30, 34–35, 39, 56–57, 77–78, 89–90, 128, 150, 165, 168. Bazna's wariness of Sir Hughe's wife was shared by Elliott: "My relationship with her went through certain vicissitudes." He noted that Mrs. Elliott found her "alarming and spent a considerable part of our visits keeping out of the way," for on one occasion the hostess "rebuked her severely." *Never Judge*, pp. 118–19.

20. For the piano question see Bazna, *I Was Cicero*, pp. 35, 99–100, and Knatchbull-Hugessen, quoted in the *Sunday Chronicle*, 5 Feb. 1950; for the pills see Bazna, pp. 29–30, 38, 91, and Knatchbull-Hugessen, in the Prebble interview, *Sunday Express*, 15 Jan. 1950, p. 4. Brenchley recalled that there was indeed a piano at the residence in Ankara. Interview with author, 21 Dec. 1995.

21. Some writers have claimed that the spy sought a large bonus for getting the safe key. Bazna, *I was Cicero*, pp. 40, 56, 73, 80, 84; Moyzisch, *Operation Cicero*, pp. 126–27, 131. See also Kempner, "Highest-Paid Spy," pp. 103–104.

22. Bazna, *I Was Cicero*, pp. 38–38, 56–57, 59–60. Bazna claimed that he used the improvised quadripod in his room as early as 30 October.

CHAPTER 5. GERMANY'S INTELLIGENCE LABYRINTH

1. Joachim Fest, "On Remembering Adolf Hitler," *Encounter* 41 (Oct. 1973), p. 32.

2. SS is an abbreviation for Schutzstaffel. Himmler became head of all police in 1936.

3. Heinz Höhne and Hermann Zolling, *The General Was a Spy: The Truth about General Gehlen and His Spy Network*, trans. Richard Barry (New York: Coward, McCann & Geoghegan, 1972), p. 318. Kahn, *Hitler's Spies*, pp. 57–62, has a brief account of the SD's growth.

4. The creation of the RSHA made Heydrich a top leader. He no longer feared Karl Wolff, Himmler's chief of staff of the SS, a rival who often thwarted Heydrich. Schellenberg, *Labyrinth*, pp. 51, 294.

5. See Kahn, *Hitler's Spies*, pp. 251–55, on Jost's career.

6. Schellenberg, *Labyrinth*, pp. 12–13, 16–17, 51. Even after the war he praised Heydrich's skills and work for the regime.

7. Ibid., pp. 141–43, 202–204, 208–15.

8. Ibid., pp. 142–43, 208–209. In the 1930s the odd studies pursued by the SD's many previously unemployed university graduates gave the organization a "bizarre atmosphere of pedantry." William L. Shirer, *The Rise and Fall of the Third Reich: A History of Nazi Germany* (New York: Simon & Schuster, 1960), p. 273. See also Kahn, *Hitler's Spies*, p. 254.

9. Schellenberg, *Labyrinth*, pp. 190–97, 209–10, 214–15, 235–36, 261–62. He described with pleasure fortifying his office and installing gimmicks in his car; he also liked theatrics, like carrying poison in an artificial tooth and ring.

10. Ibid., pp. 231–32, 236, 293–98, 377. Schellenberg's youth and restricted interests meant that he posed no immediate threat to Himmler.

11. For the quotation see Gilles Perrault [Jacques Peyroles], *The Secret of D-Day*, trans. Len Ortzen (Boston: Little, Brown, 1965), p. 126. Kaltenbrunner had been head of the police in Vienna. He was doctrinaire, vicious, and frequently drunk. Late in April 1945, when Himmler was in disgrace, he deprived Schellenberg of all posts, but even then Schellenberg expected Himmler to succeed Hitler and restore his power. Schellenberg, *Labyrinth*, pp. 275–76, 287–89, 331–34, 404.

12. The German army created the Abwehr on 24 November 1919. For its

structure early in World War II see Wilhelm Höttl, *The Secret Front: The Story of Nazi Political Espionage*, trans. R. H. Stevens (New York: Praeger, 1954), p. 19. Höttl directed SS intelligence operations for southeastern Europe from his headquarters in Vienna.

13. There seems no doubt that Canaris did leak valuable information to the Allies, through various personal channels. Himmler had an SS attorney, Walther Huppenkothen, investigate Canaris and the Abwehr.

14. See Höhne and Zolling, *The General Was a Spy*, App. A; Schellenberg, *Labyrinth*, pp. 345–54; and Karl Bartz, *The Downfall of the German Secret Service*, trans. Edward Fitzgerald (London: William Kimber, 1956), pp. 69–72.

15. Schellenberg, *Labyrinth*, p. 354; Bartz, *Downfall*, pp. 96–111.

16. Dohnanyi was the brother-in-law of pastor Dietrich Bonhoeffer and knew most of the leading anti-Nazis. On 5 April 1943 both men were arrested; they were executed on 9 April 1945. Bartz, *Downfall*, pp. 86–88.

17. Schellenberg, *Labyrinth*, pp. 354–56. Other writers find nothing to support this claim. Himmler always seemed well disposed toward Canaris. See Bartz, *Downfall*, pp. 26, 112–29. He also took care not to let subordinates overcome his sense of caution.

18. Schellenberg had to be pragmatic in 1941. He could not wrest a communications intelligence unit from Göring; Goebbels attacked him repeatedly in ways he described as vicious. Schellenberg, *Labyrinth*, pp. 211–14, 254–55, 361–67, 369.

19. Ibid., p. 143. After his first long interview with the foreign minister, Schellenberg said that he lost "all my illusions" about cooperation "in any way on any issue." He said of Ribbentrop: "His vanity and narrowness of mind really shocked me." Ibid., pp. 245–51.

20. Ibid., pp. 29–32, 34, 114, 200–202, 256–60, 271. Martin Luther was severely punished for his charges against Ribbentrop. Ibid., pp. 301, 305, 308–15, 322–33.

21. Kaltenbrunner had continued the old pressure to place more RSHA agents in missions still maintained by the Foreign Ministry. Even the total of seventy-three RSHA agents in nineteen missions in October 1943 was soon increased. Problems like those between Moyzisch and Papen occurred elsewhere as well. Kahn, *Hitler's Spies*, p. 62. Kaltenbrunner supported Schellenberg against Ribbentrop. Schellenberg, *Labyrinth*, p. 338.

22. Baron Steengracht von Moyland invoked an agreement from August 1941 and reported Kaltenbrunner's reaction to Ribbentrop on 7 November 1943. Paul Seabury, *The Wilhelmstrasse: A Study of German Diplomats under the Nazi Regime* (Berkeley: Univ. of California Press, 1954), p. 130.

23. In 1944 a new agreement affirmed existing procedures—"The foreign intelligence that comes from the RSHA will, insofar as it is of interest to the Führer, be submitted by the foreign minister to the Führer as RSHA material"—while still letting Himmler tell Hitler about reports. Kahn, *Hitler's Spies*, p. 62.

24. Papen, *Memoirs*, p. 511. How the spy's films and information were handled remained a source of complaints. See Papen to Berlin, 3 Dec. 1943, no. 644, 52/41789; 13 Dec., no. 1803, 52/41825; 18 Dec., no. 1845, 52/41849–41850; 23 Dec., no. 1870, 52/41859; and 10 Feb. 1944, no. 218, 52/42008.

25. Telegram from Ribbentrop to Papen, 17 June 1944, printed in Seabury, *The Wilhelmstrasse*, p. 131.

CHAPTER 6. QUESTIONS AND DOUBTS IN BERLIN

1. Allen W. Dulles, *The Craft of Intelligence* (New York: Harper & Row, 1963), p. 153.

2. On the exaggerated image of Britain's intelligence services see Richard Deacon [Donald McCormick], *A History of British Secret Service* (London: Granada, Panther Books ed., 1980), pp. 320, 353.

3. Moyzisch, *Operation Cicero*, pp. 59, 62, 191–92.

4. Ibid., pp. 1, 32, 35; Bazna, *I Was Cicero*, pp. 9, 44, 46, 65–66; Schellenberg, *Labyrinth*, p. 336. Bazna thought that Jenke chose not to remember him in order to avoid questions about whether Bazna had spied against Germany. Moyzisch thought the valet had worked for Jenke in Istanbul; Bazna said it was after Jenke joined the embassy in Ankara.

5. Moyzisch, *Operation Cicero*, pp. 74–75, says that the spy specifically told him he was Albanian. He never questioned that.

6. Ibid., pp. 85–86, 170. Bazna was thirty-nine, having been born in July 1904. Bazna, *I Was Cicero*, pp. 12–13.

7. Moyzisch, *Operation Cicero*, p. 51; Schellenberg, *Labyrinth*, pp. 344, 392.

8. The same issues that produced the Germans' doubts fueled postwar claims by some Britons that the spy must have been controlled. They too refused to believe that he had acted without help or direction. See, for example, Cave Brown, *Bodyguard*, pp. 443–44.

9. Moyzisch, *Operation Cicero*, pp. 26, 62–63, 134–35, 151–53; Schellenberg, *Labyrinth*, p. 339. Moyzisch exaggerates the language question to show he outwitted Cicero. He was not qualified to judge the spy's language skills. The latter's own words seem truthful: noting that besides Turkish he spoke French and Serbo-Croat, plus a little Greek, and some German from his singing, Bazna said he read and understood English in simple forms but that he had difficulty speaking it. Bazna, *I Was Cicero*, pp. 11–12, 99–100, 103. Given the frequent contention that he was Albanian, it is noteworthy that Bazna did not claim to know that language. Any exchanges he had with Moyzisch in English must have used conventional phrases. Nogly too said that Bazna spoke very poor English. They switched to French in their talks. Ibid., p. v.

10. Moyzisch, *Operation Cicero*, pp. 64–65, 122.

11. Ibid., pp. 53, 83, 90. In his account the author refers on p. 90 to 112 documents but probably meant exposures. He was speaking of the number of rolls and prints.

12. Ibid., pp. 132–34.

13. Ibid., pp. 59, 64–65, 82–83, 132–35; Schellenberg, *Labyrinth*, pp. 340, 344, 392. Kempner said the spy's photographs became so poor that he agreed to come to the embassy for lessons from an SD expert. Kempner, "Highest-Paid Spy," p. 103. Kempner relied on records of postwar questioning of Moyzisch, but none of the memoirs mention the point.

14. Moyzisch, *Operation Cicero*, pp. 69–71. He knew he might be assigned to a fighting unit if he did a poor job. See pp. 18–19.

15. Ibid., pp. 76–79, 102, 105–106. Moyzisch said that his plane reached Istanbul too late on 24 November for the night train but that he left the next evening and reached Ankara early on the 26th. For Jenke's report see Jenke to FM, 15 Nov. 1943, no. 1668, 52/41752-41753.

16. Moyzisch, *Operation Cicero*, pp. 76–103. The following paragraphs are based on his narrative. See also Schellenberg, *Labyrinth*, p. 338. Moyzisch's pretense that he knew little of the feuds in Berlin is belied by his own words, in places like pp. 9–10.

17. Schellenberg had to approve outlays that exceeded 15,000 Reichsmarks (about $6,000), and Kaltenbrunner those in excess of 50,000 Reichsmarks (about $20,000). Kahn, *Hitler's Spies*, p. 297.

18. Papen to Ribbentrop, 12 Dec. 1943, no. 1801, 52/41824; Papen, *Memoirs*, p. 518.

19. Papen, *Memoirs*, p. 518.

20. Spellman had no official mission but made the extensive trip for Roosevelt. Robert I. Gannon, *The Cardinal Spellman Story* (Garden City, N.Y.: Doubleday, 1962), pp. 212–14; Papen, *Memoirs*, pp. 498–500; Moyzisch, *Operation Cicero*, pp. 92–94. Moyzisch described the affair more dramatically than did Papen. He did not identify the lawyer, but Paul Leverkühn is suggested by the ambassador's memoir. Leverkühn headed the Abwehr office in Istanbul.

21. See also Michael Bloch, *Ribbentrop* (London: Bantam Press, 1992), pp. 388–90. Likus was a former journalist who directed a private intelligence office for Ribbentrop.

22. Schellenberg, *Labyrinth*, pp. 338–40.

23. Moyzisch, *Operation Cicero*, pp. 102–103.

24. Ibid., pp. 70–71, 98–101, 106. Moyzisch thought that many offices had started files on Cicero. Ribbentrop himself apparently discussed the spy with Oshima. David Irving, *Hitler's War* (New York: Viking, 1977), p. 880, note for p. 584. See also Bazna, *I Was Cicero*, pp. 109–10.

25. Schellenberg, *Labyrinth*, p. 339.

26. Kempner, "Highest-Paid Spy," p. 103. Irving located some records in Cabinet office file AL 2656, secret Foreign Ministry files (serial 1553), and Steengracht's file on Turkey (serial 61). Irving, *Hitler's War*, p. 880, p. 584.

27. Goebbels, *Diaries*, 13 and 20 Nov. 1943, pp. 510–11, 518. His 8 November entry noted that Turkey resisted the British at Cairo: "I am therefore firmly convinced that Ankara is not thinking of yielding to English wishes." See p. 501. The minister appears to have based the entry on the spy's information.

28. Irving, *Hitler's War*, p. 880, note for p. 584; Hans Speidel, *Invasion 1944: Ein Beitrag zu Rommels und des Reiches Schicksal* (Tübingen: Rainer Wunderlich Verlag, 1949), p. 18.

29. Papen, *Memoirs*, p. 507. Papen spoke with Hitler in mid-November, after Menemencioglu's return from Cairo. Bazna, *I Was Cicero*, p. 110.

30. Auswärtiges Amt, Politisches Archiv, Inland II, *geheim*, 464:296166. The conference statement appears in Helmut Heiber, ed. *Hitlers Lagebesprechungen: Die Protokollfragmente seiner militärischen Konferenzen, 1942–1945* (Stuttgart: Deutsche Verlags-Anstalt, 1962), pp. 440–41, and in Kahn, *Hitler's Spies*, p. 344. Heiber and others have agreed that Hitler had been referring to the Cicero documents.

31. Irving thought that "the authenticity of Cicero's documents was accepted at every level right up to Hitler." *Hitler's War*, p. 880, note for p. 584. Kahn agreed that in time nearly everyone lost doubts about Cicero. *Hitler's Spies*, p. 343. Cave Brown felt, however, that the information was never fully trusted by Hitler himself. *Bodyguard*, p. 442.

CHAPTER 7. OPERATION BERNHARD

1. Origins of the name "Andreas" have not been determined. Anthony Pirie, *Operation Bernhard* (New York: William Morrow, 1962), pp. 6–7.

2. Shirer, *Rise and Fall*, p. 519. Gerald Reitlinger, *The SS: Alibi of a Nation, 1922–1945* (New York: Viking, 1957), p. 122, called Naujocks a "garrulous bully." He helped stage the incident with Poland that was used as an invasion pretext. A biography by Günter Peis, *The Man Who Started the War*, foreword by Alfred Naujocks (London: Odhams Press, 1960), was based on many interviews.

3. Ibid., pp. 154–57, 163; Pirie, *Operation Bernhard*, p. 6.

4. Vincent Duggleby, *English Paper Money*, 4th ed. (London: Spink and Son, 1990), pp. 62–63, 84–87, 123.

5. Peis, *Man Who Started*, pp. 157–68; Schellenberg, *Labyrinth*, pp. 367–68; Pirie, *Operation Bernhard*, pp. 12–19, 49, 208; Kahn, *Hitler's Spies*, p. 300; George J. McNally and Frederic Sondern, Jr., "The Great Nazi Counterfeit Plot," *Reader's Digest* (July 1952), p. 28; Duggleby, *English Money*, p. 123. Bazna later found it ironic that the linen used to make his bogus notes came from Turkey. Bazna, *I Was Cicero*, p. 194.

6. Pirie, *Operation Bernhard*, pp. 6–21, 48–49; Schellenberg, *Labyrinth*, pp. 367–68; Peis, *Man Who Started*, pp. 113, 167–69.

7. Peis, *Man Who Started*, pp. 149–54, 167–86; Pirie, *Operation Bernhard*, pp. 19–20; Kahn, *Hitler's Spies*, pp. 280–81.

8. Heydrich's car was attacked by guerrillas in Prague in late May 1942, and he died of his wounds in early June. The German retaliation against the town of Lidice became a symbol of Nazi barbarism.

9. Pirie, *Operation Bernhard*, pp. 7, 22–23, 43; Höttl, *Secret Front*, p. 19; Kahn, *Hitler's Spies*, p. 281. The technical support section was "F" and its subsection for documents was "4."

10. Peis, *Man Who Started*, p. 160; McNally, "Counterfeit Plot," p. 28; Pirie, *Operation Bernhard*, pp. 23, 29, 115; Kahn, *Hitler's Spies*, pp. 299–300. Naujocks' operation had been housed in a residential part of Berlin. The Sachsenhausen camp was earlier known as Oranienburg.

11. Pirie, *Operation Bernhard*, pp. 44, 58, 115. Schellenberg usually communicated delivery orders directly to Krüger.

12. Ibid., pp. 23, 29, 43–45, 49, 56, 58–59, 81–87, 115–16, 119–20.

13. Ibid., p. 58; McNally, "Counterfeit Plot," pp. 28–29.

14. Pirie, *Operation Bernhard*, pp. 149–51, 161–64.

15. Ibid., pp. 210–12, 221, 232–34, 267–68; Höttl, *Secret Front*, p. 87. There were difficulties getting paper, ink, and plates of suitable quality. An imprisoned master counterfeiter, Solly Smolianov, was located and transferred, but

his new and superior plates were never used. McNally, "Counterfeit Plot," pp. 29–30.

16. Apparently Krüger got along well with the political prisoners and Jewish workers. Pirie, *Operation Bernhard*, pp. 119–20.

17. Nigel West [Rupert W. S. Allason], *MI5: British Security Service Operations, 1909–1945* (London: Bodley Head, 1981), p. 120, noted that German radio broadcasts in summer 1940 warned the British public about counterfeit pounds. Schellenberg, *Labyrinth*, p. 368, said the lack of planes and fuel prevented dropping the notes over Britain.

18. The SD got small sums from the Foreign Ministry. Höttl, *Secret Front*, p. 85.

19. Pirie, *Operation Bernhard*, pp. 22–34, 45–49, 54–56, 100, 122–23, 139, 153–54, 187–89, 196–97, 219, 222–29, 269–76. Schwend survived the war and moved to South America. See also Höttl, *Secret Front*, p. 86.

20. Ibid., pp. 86–87; Schellenberg, *Labyrinth*, pp. 368–69; Pirie, *Operation Bernhard*, pp. 22–26, 29–34, 47–48, 50–54, 59–80; McNally, "Counterfeit Plot," p. 29.

21. McNally, "Counterfeit Plot," pp. 25–27; West, *MI5*, pp. 224, 320–23; Kahn, *Hitler's Spies*, p. 300.

22. Höttl, *Secret Front*, p. 86; Pirie, *Operation Bernhard*, pp. 36–42.

23. Schellenberg, *Labyrinth*, p. 368.

24. C. B. Josset, *Money in Britain: A History of the Currencies of the British Isles* (London: Frederick Warne, 1962), App. 4, "Printed Note Issues in Great Britain," pp. 199–200; Duggleby, *English Money*, pp. 62, 123.

25. It seems clear that subsequently the SD kept any sound currency received from the Foreign Ministry and expended its own forged notes. See Höttl, *Secret Front*, p. 85.

26. Höttl moved his office to Vienna and then Hungary to escape trouble with the Gestapo. In summer 1944 he reportedly got Kaltenbrunner to restore Operation Bernhard after a disruption the Gestapo had caused. Pirie, *Operation Bernhard*, pp. 26–27, 35–36, 122–23, 153–54, 167, 187–89.

27. Moyzisch, *Operation Cicero*, pp. 114–16.

28. An unanswerable question is whether Moyzisch got notes with sequential serial numbers. It seems doubtful that notes were thoroughly mixed in the bundles. Similar questions arise about the telltale newness of the bogus notes.

29. McNally, "Counterfeit Plot," p. 30; Pirie, *Operation Bernhard*, pp. 232–43. Redl and Zipf are small communities, often linked in name, between Linz and Salzburg.

30. McNally, "Counterfeit Plot," p. 30; Pirie, *Operation Bernhard*, pp. 250–51.

31. McNally, "Counterfeit Plot," pp. 30–31; Pirie, *Operation Bernhard*, pp. 242–44, 246–47, 250–59, 261–62.

32. See Simon Wiesenthal, *The Murderers among Us: The Simon Wiesenthal Memoirs*, ed. Joseph Wechsberg (New York: McGraw-Hill, 1967), pp. 92, 109.

33. McNally, "Counterfeit Plot," pp. 25–31. McNally had investigated counterfeiting as a Secret Service agent before entering the army in 1942. Ibid., pp. 25, 27; Pirie, *Operation Bernhard*, pp. 252–55, 261–62, 266–67.

34. Sources agree about the number of notes printed—Kahn gives an exact

figure of 8,965,080—but not on their monetary or face value. McNally's team estimated £140 million, Pirie reports about £150 million using Skala, and Kahn cites £134,610,810. Nor is there consensus on the dollar equivalents: McNally's figure is $564 million, while Kahn's is $645 million. McNally, "Counterfeit Plot," p. 31; Bazna, *I Was Cicero*, pp. 195–96; Pirie, *Operation Bernhard*, p. 268; Kahn, *Hitler's Spies*, p. 300. From 1939 to 1949 the exchange rate was £1=$4.03. McNally's figures conform to that ratio; Kahn's different rate is unexplained. See Douglas Jay, *Sterling—Its Use and Misuse: A Plea for Moderation* (London: Sidgwick & Jackson, 1985), pp. 109, 115, 122.

35. The Allied troops reportedly recovered about £20 million from the Traun river sites. Bazna, *I Was Cicero*, p. 195. The deep lake's layer of submerged debris made diving dangerous and proved to be impenetrable, but the boxes were found fourteen years later. Pirie, *Operation Bernhard*, pp. 266–68, 278–79.

36. McNally, "Counterfeit Plot," p. 31.

37. By the early 1960s no notes used in the mid-1940s remained legal tender. Josset, *Money in Britain*, pp. 199–200; Duggleby, *English Money*, pp. 62–63, 87; Schellenberg, *Labyrinth*, p. 369; Bazna, *I Was Cicero*, p. 196; Pirie, *Operation Bernhard*, pp. 196, 290.

38. Wolfgang Löhde was the principal investigating reporter for *Stern*. The expensive equipment included an underwater television camera. Pirie, *Operation Bernhard*, pp. 279–88; Wiesenthal, *Murderers among Us*, p. 281. In 1984 divers recovered a wartime rocket launcher but no further money or other valuables. *Plain Dealer*, 18 Nov. 1984, p. 11-A.

CHAPTER 8. CICERO'S OUTSTANDING PERIOD

1. Moyzisch, *Operation Cicero*, pp. 117, 147.

2. See Bazna, *I Was Cicero*, especially pp. 78, 149–50.

3. Ibid., pp. 99–100, 102; Knatchbull-Hugessen's statement, *Sunday Chronicle* (London ed.), 5 Feb. 1950, p. 5. Some accounts say that Sir Hughe kept a room in the city where he practised: Elliott, *Never Judge*, p. 139; Kempner, "Highest-Paid Spy," p. 104; James Mason, *Before I Forget: Autobiography and Drawings* (London: Hamish Hamilton, 1981), p. 224. Mason heard that version in 1951.

4. Bazna, *I Was Cicero*, pp. 131, 137–38; Moyzisch, *Operation Cicero*, p. 131. Moyzisch placed the occurrence about mid-December. Bazna had told him of singing for Sir Hughe and said Moyzisch asked him to sing to test his veracity.

5. Gossip about a homosexual connection lacked any basis. But see Ladislas Farago, *The Game of the Foxes: The Untold Story of German Espionage in the United States and Great Britain during World War II* (New York: David McKay, 1971), pp. 415, 482–83. Joseph Mankiewicz heard such tales in Turkey when he was filming *Five Fingers*. Kenneth L. Geist, *Pictures Will Talk: The Life and Films of Joseph L. Mankiewicz* (New York: Scribner's, 1978), p. 214.

6. Bazna, *I Was Cicero*, pp. 84–89; Knatchbull-Hugessen's statement to Prebble, in *Sunday Express* (London), 15 Jan. 1950, p. 4.

7. Schellenberg, *Labyrinth*, pp. 340–41; Moyzisch, *Operation Cicero*, pp. 122, 126–27, 147. Hinsley and Simkins, *Security*, p. 214, stated that the spy asked for 50,000 Turkish pounds as a bonus for getting the key impressions.

8. Moyzisch, *Operation Cicero*, p. 106. He was probably not away for two weeks as he claimed, but if he left Berlin on 22 November he was still there after Papen himself had arrived.

9. Ibid., pp. 105–11. Bazna later claimed that he had in fact received the gun from Moyzisch. The latter might well have concealed the point. In any case, the gun was never used. Moyzisch worried too about his own fate if anything ever happened to Cicero. Kempner, "Highest-Paid Spy," p. 104.

10. Moyzisch, *Operation Cicero*, pp. 64, 113–16, 119, 122, 132–35; Schellenberg, *Labyrinth*, pp. 339–40; Bazna, *I Was Cicero*, pp. 31, 63.

11. Moyzisch, *Operation Cicero*, pp. 116–17, including Papen's postscript, p. 208.

12. Ibid., p. 131.

13. Ibid., pp. 120–22; Bazna, *I Was Cicero*, pp. 78–80, 92–93.

14. For Britain's policy just before Churchill's new efforts see 37517/R9969, "The Immediate Aims of British Policy in Turkey," and R9970, "Long-Term Policy towards Turkey," both dated 7 October 1943. Germany obtained the latter document through Cicero. Churchill later explained his regional goals in *Hinge of Fate*, pp. 696–716.

15. The Moscow meetings between 19 October and 3 November included planning for the Tehran Conference of the three Allied leaders. Churchill summarized the developments, main Soviet aims, and his messages to Eden dated 20 and 23 October. See Winston Churchill, *Closing the Ring*, vol. 5 of *The Second World War* (Boston: Houghton Mifflin, 1951), pp. 284–89, 334–35, 346, 430–31. For the Anglo-Russian agreement on Turkey see also 44065/R1088. American officials had little interest in bringing Turkey into the war, despite the efforts by the British. See Harry N. Howard, *Turkey, the Straits, and U.S. Policy* (Baltimore: Johns Hopkins Univ. Press, 1974), pp. 161–209, and Department of State publications of diplomatic papers listed in the bibliography.

16. For a Foreign Office minute of the Cairo talks during 5–8 November see 37476/R12407. Sir Hughe was also at Cairo. General Hastings Ismay attended in his capacity as chief of staff to Churchill. For Eden's comment see his memoirs, *The Reckoning*, vol. 2. of *The Memoirs of Anthony Eden* (Boston: Houghton Mifflin, 1965), pp. 485–86; see also Churchill, *Closing the Ring*, pp. 334–35. For Turkey's written response see Knatchbull-Hugessen to FO, 15 Nov. 1943, no. 2016, 37475/R11777, and no. 489, 37476/R12329.

17. For Sir Hughe's views on the policy see *Diplomat*, pp. 194–97. A former Foreign Office colleague confirmed their common disagreement with Churchill's risky aim. Sir George Rendel, letter to *Times* (London), 31 Mar. 1971, p. 16. Knatchbull-Hugessen had stressed at the time that Russian participation in any negotiations might raise demands that no Turkish government would accept. Knatchbull-Hugessen to FO, 22 Nov. 1943, no. 2062, 37475/R12117.

18. FO to Knatchbull-Hugessen, 19 Nov. 1943, no. 1594, and Sir Hughe's response, from 37475–37476; Papen, *Memoirs*, pp. 512–13, quoting an article by Paul Schwarz in the *New Yorker Staats-Zeitung*, n.d. Bazna claimed that he photographed the exchange of telegrams. See *I Was Cicero*, pp. 70–71.

19. Stalin too was impatient with the Turks: "We ought to take them by the scruff of the neck if necessary." Discussion of Soviet postwar naval and shipping rights was avoided at Tehran, to prevent problems. Churchill, *Closing the Ring*, pp. 352–58, 381.

20. Churchill admitted "not hesitating to repeat the arguments remorselessly" at Tehran. Ibid., pp. 346, 367–68, 371–72, 389–94, 404. Turkey was the subject of points 2 and 3 in the three leaders' five-item document summarizing their decisions (reproduced in Churchill).

21. Eden sent the invitation in Churchill's name: Eden to Knatchbull-Hugessen, 1 Dec. 1943, no. 33, 37476/R12548. Sir Hughe cautioned his superiors about the domestic pressures influencing Inönü. Knatchbull-Hugessen to Churchill and Eden at Cairo, 3 Dec. 1943, no. 407, 37477/R12707.

22. Churchill, *Closing the Ring*, pp. 415–18. He reprinted the ten-point proposal for Operation Saturn from his telegram to Ismay for the Chief of Staff Committee, 6 Dec. 1943. See also 44065/R1294. An official record of the Cairo talks appears in 44066/R1600.

23. Knatchbull-Hugessen met twice with Menemencioglu on 11 December. A morning talk was so unsatisfactory that he visited the minister's home that evening. The foreign minister considered the 15 February deadline to be an ultimatum. Knatchbull-Hugessen to FO, 11 Dec. 1943, nos. 515 and 516, 37479/R13922 and R13923; Knatchbull-Hugessen to FO, 12 Dec. 1943, nos. 2183 and 2184, 37477/R13067 and R13068. French text of Turkey's 12 December reply in Knatchbull-Hugessen to Eden, 13 Dec. 1943, no. 518, 37479/R13924, and English translation in telegram to FO, 13 Dec. 1943, no. 2191, 37478/R13144. The answer included a long list of equipment deemed essential before any action could be taken.

24. A Foreign Office minute called the Turkish reply an "outrageous affair." See 37477/R13069 and also Churchill to Eden, 15 Dec. 1943, no. 485, 37478/R13265. Bazna noted Sir Hughe's anger. *I Was Cicero*, p. 135. Eden nevertheless gave a highly optimistic report on the situation in Parliament. Text of his remarks of 14 December, FO to Knatchbull-Hugessen, 15 Dec. 1943, no. 1714, 37517/R13478.

25. Churchill, telegram to Eden, 13 Dec. 1943, in *Closing the Ring*, pp. 422, 430–31. The prime minister went to Morocco for recovery; not until 14 January did he leave there. For Sir Hughe's conclusion see *Diplomat*, pp. 194–97.

26. Papen, postscript in Moyzisch, *Operation Cicero*, p. 208; Seabury, *Wilhelmstrasse*, p. 195, n. 28, citing a ministry memorandum of 12 May 1944 reporting that Moyzisch had shown Papen nearly all the material. Possibly excepted were a few reports on strictly military matters. See also Jenke to FM, 15 Nov. 1943, no. 1668, 52/41752–41753. Jenke again handled the Cicero items when Papen went to Bursa during late January 1944.

27. Papen, *Memoirs*, pp. 512–13, 517. Papen identified the British exchanges as FO telegram no. 1594 of 19 Nov. 1943 and Sir Hughe's telegram as no. 875. The Turkish security police also supposedly told Moyzisch what Turkey's ambassador in Moscow had learned of Allied talks. Irving, *Hitler's War*, pp. 584–85.

28. Papen to Ribbentrop, 5 Nov. 1943, no. 1603, 52/41722–41724.

29. Papen to FM, 7 Nov. 1943, no. 1623, 52/41728–41729.

30. Papen to FM, 11 Nov. 1943, no. 1648, 52/41741–41742, and 12 Nov., no. 1654, 52/41747; Jenke to Berlin, 15 Nov. 1943, no. 1668, 52/41752–41753. See also Papen, *Memoirs*, pp. 506–07, and Irving, *Hitler's War*, pp. 584–85. For Sir Hughe's report on the Menemencioglu-Papen talks see Knatchbull-Hugessen to FO, 10 Nov. 1943, no. 1991; 11 Nov., no. 1996; and 12 Nov., no. 2000, 37475/R11583, R11638, and R11695, respectively.

31. Papen, *Memoirs*, pp. 507–09. On 17 November he visited Hitler's headquarters in East Prussia. His other discussions were in Berlin. Hungarian leaders were already wavering in their support of Germany. Papen's memoirs describe his efforts to explore peace arrangements during 1943–1944.

32. Papen from Istanbul to FM, 3 Dec. 1943, no. 644, 52/41789; 4 Dec., no. 1766, 52/41790; 6 Dec., no. 1769, 52/41791. Papen noted that the Soviet ambassador had left with Inönü and wondered who might represent Moscow at Cairo. Due to travel problems the Russians took no part in the meetings.

33. Papen to FM, 7 Dec. 1943, no. 1774, 52/41792–41793, and 13 Dec., no. 1804, 52/41826–41830.

34. Moyzisch, *Operation Cicero*, pp. 120–22; Papen, *Memoirs*, pp. 514–15. The Cairo meetings mentioned by Moyzisch were apparently those with Chiang Kai-shek before the Tehran Conference. For the British statement see Hinsley and Simkins, *Security*, p. 215.

35. Papen to FM, 9 Dec. 1943, no. 1789, 52/41814–41818. Menemencioglu quickly reported the gist of this conversation to Sir Hughe. See Knatchbull-Hugessen to FO, 9 Dec. 1943, no. 2161, 37477/R12997.

36. Papen to FM, 12 Dec. 1943, no. 1801, 52/41824, and 14 Dec., no. 1811, 52/41832–41833. Sir Hughe acknowledged his receipt of the Cairo records in a telegram on 10 Dec. 1943, no. 2167, 37477/R13000. Details of the meetings were therefore available. See also Papen to FM, 13 Dec. 1943, nos. 1804 and 1805, 52/41826–41830 and 41831.

37. Papen to FM, 18 Dec. 1943, nos. 1842 and 1845, 52/41845–41848 and 52/41849–41850. The Soviet official mentioned was not a participant in the Cairo meetings.

38. See Knatchbull-Hugessen to FO, 13 Dec. 1943, no. 2195, 37478/R13147.

39. Moyzisch, *Operation Cicero*, pp. 111–12. The draft may have been part of an analysis sent by Sir Hughe to Eden, 1 Dec. 1943, no. 505, 37478/R13218; more likely, it was a portion of his seventy-six-page annual report sent to London on 1 Jan. 1944, no. 5, 44137.

40. General Fevzi Pasha was a World War I hero, later known as Marshal Fevzi Çakmak. Allied leaders thought him too pro-German. At first Kazim Orbay replaced his deputy and then succeeded Çakmak himself. An important issue was progress in modernizing the army. The changes pleased the British but also misled them: there was no immediate shift in views. Knatchbull-Hugessen to FO, 1 Dec. 1943, no. 368, 37476/R12547, and Papen to FM, 4 Dec. 1943, no. 1766, 52/41790.

41. Moyzisch, *Operation Cicero*, pp. 122–27, 129.

42. Bazna, *I Was Cicero*, pp. 81–84.

43. Moyzisch, *Operation Cicero*, pp. 129–31; Bazna, *I Was Cicero*, pp. 85, 88–92.

44. Churchill, *Closing the Ring*, p. 346, but see also pp. 218–19, 334–35, and *Hinge of Fate*, p. 716.

CHAPTER 9. THE CONTEST FOR TURKEY

1. Regarding Moscow's refusal to give Turkey assurances see 44064/R17; for the Soviet failure to criticize Turkey's neutrality see 44159.

2. Knatchbull-Hugessen to FO, 11 Dec. 1943, no. 515, 37479/R13922; FO minute, 15 Dec. 1943, 37478/R13354; Knatchbull-Hugessen to FO, 7 Jan. 1944, no. 34, 44064/R338. Churchill claimed Britain had already transferred to Turkey military equipment and American arms worth £25 million. *Closing the Ring*, pp. 390, 392. Another British study put the figure at £30 million. Llewellyn Woodward, *British Foreign Policy in the Second World War*, 5 vols. (London: Her Majesty's Stationery Office, 1970–1976), vol. 4, p. 178n. Turkey had long been unable to absorb all the supplies being sent by Britain. See 37517/R6787. British training officers also despaired at the poor care of equipment given to Turkey. "The Anatolian plateau became scattered with military vehicles and tanks that had broken down because no one had topped up the oil in their engines or serviced them properly." Elliott, *Never Judge*, pp. 117–18.

3. Knatchbull-Hugessen to FO, 15 Dec. 1943, no. 2189, 37477/R13142.

4. Knatchbull-Hugessen to FO, 18 Dec. 1943, no. 2243, 37478/R13408, and 24 Dec. 1943, no. 2279, 37479/R13689; military attaché, Ankara, to Commander-in-Chief, Middle East, 25 Dec. 1943, no. 5163, and report to FO, 25 Dec. 1943, 44064/R35. See also the Foreign Office analysis of the issue in 37479/R13481. Britain had continued work on airfields and training of Turkish pilots under joint programs that had begun before 1943. A mid-year report on the airfields appears in 37505/R337.

5. For Knatchbull-Hugessen's reports of meetings with Menemencioglu see 44064/R395 and 37479/R13500–13501; see also Knatchbull-Hugessen to FO, 21 Dec. 1943, no. 2257, and 22 Dec., no. 2269, 37479/R13545 and R13551, respectively; Turkey's terms were forwarded by the ambassador to General Sir Henry Maitland-Wilson, 27 Dec. 1943, no. 931, 44064/R357.

6. Eden to Knatchbull-Hugessen, 21 Dec. 1943, nos. 264 and 1753, 37479/R13522; Knatchbull-Hugessen to FO, 20 Dec. 1943, no. 2249, 37478/R13448, and FO minute, 23 Dec. 1943, 37479/R13547.

7. FO to Knatchbull-Hugessen, 21 Dec. 1943, no. 1751, 37479/R13527; Churchill, *Closing the Ring*, pp. 430–31.

8. Sir Hughe summarized the situation in his seventy-six-page annual report for 1943. Knatchbull-Hugessen to FO, 1 Jan. 1944, no. 5, 44137.

9. Churchill's minute to Eden, 7 Jan. 1944, 44065/R1327; Knatchbull-Hugessen to FO, 6 and 7 Jan. 1944, nos. 34 and 36, 44064/R338 and R403; FO to Knatchbull-Hugessen, 11 Jan. 1944, no. 59, 44064/R587.

10. İnönü and others must have found it painful to ease out their old friend Çakmak, but the step had been foreseen when Orbay had been appointed as his deputy. Britain seemed satisfied with Orbay. Knatchbull-Hugessen to FO, 14 Jan. 1944, no. 72, 44133/R789.

11. Knatchbull-Hugessen to FO, 5 Jan. 1944, no. 27, 44064/R295. The code

word "Overlord" had also appeared in the Foreign Office's telegram to the ambassador dated 21 December, already cited.

12. Letters from Menemencioglu to Knatchbull-Hugessen, 16 Jan. 1944, 44066/R1612, and 24 Jan. 1944, reported in Knatchbull-Hugessen to FO, 25 Jan. 1944, no. 127, 44067/R2045. For Sir Hughe's answer to the first letter on 19 Jan. 1944 see 44066/R1844.

13. For Eden's comment see FO memorandum, 4–5 Jan. 1944, 44064/R395. On the continuing frustration with Menemencioglu see 44068/R4548 and 44133/R9321 and R10541.

14. See Knatchbull-Hugessen's letter of 4 Jan. 1944 in 44065/R858. The American ambassador, Laurence Steinhardt, was regarded as temperamental and egotistical; one Foreign Office official, G. L. Clutton, called him a "thoroughly unsatisfactory character. . . . He is a cross we have to bear." FO minute, 6 Oct. 1944, 44202/R15806. Sir Hughe considered Steinhardt uninformed and ill mannered. See Weber, *Evasive Neutral*, p. 217. Papen reported that Steinhardt had allegedly called Inönü "dimwitted" and "another Franco." Papen to FM, 13 Dec. 1943, nos. 1804 and 1805, 52/41826–41830 and 41831. Britain could not get Moscow to reassure Ankara. See British embassy in Moscow to FO, 30 Dec. 1943, no. 1652, 44064/R17.

15. Knatchbull-Hugessen to FO, 17 Jan. 1944, no. 91, 44065/R874; Churchill's minute to Eden, 24 Jan. 1944, and FO to Knatchbull-Hugessen, 30 Jan. 1944, nos. 136 and 137, 44066/R1345 and R1366; Knatchbull-Hugessen to FO, 27 Jan. 1944, no. 132, 44066/R1425. Sir Hughe notified the foreign secretary that the military mission would depart on 3 February: telegram, 1 Feb. 1944, no. 164, 44066/R1684.

16. Knatchbull-Hugessen, *Diplomat*, pp. 198–200; also Papen, *Memoirs*, pp. 514, 521.

17. The quotation appears in Moyzisch, *Operation Cicero*, p. 10. Papen had many contacts among Turkish officials friendly to Germany. For example, Turkey's ambassador to Berlin, E. Hüsrev Gerede, assured him that "an overwhelming majority" of the nation's leaders wanted to avoid a break with Germany. Papen, *Memoirs*, pp. 519–20.

18. Papen to FM, 18 Dec. 1943, nos. 1842 and 1845, 52/41845–41848 and 52/41862–41864. For Turkey's territorial aspirations and internal politics during this period see Weber, *Evasive Neutral*, pp. 172–76, 188–90, 201–204, 206–208. Menemencioglu learned about Papen's peace efforts through Turkey's secret police. It is clear the Germans did not trust him. Kempner quoted a report in which Moyzisch complained that the foreign minister was "slippery as an eel" and that the Germans should be wary of him. Kempner, "Highest-Paid Spy," p. 104. Papen too always welcomed verification of the foreign minister's assurances by documents copied by Cicero.

19. Papen had already reported how the foreign minister said he dealt with the West: he gave no straightforward answers and always introduced new arguments. Papen to FM, 12 Dec. 1943, no. 1804, 52/41826–41830. For their 18 December conversation see Papen to FM, 18 Dec. 1943, no. 1842, 52/41845–41848; Papen, *Memoirs*, pp. 514, 516.

20. Papen to FM, 24 Dec. 1943, no. 1875, 52/41862–41864, and 29 Dec. 1943, no. 1898, 52/41879.

21. Papen reported his intervention with Menemencioglu in Papen to FM, 30 Dec. 1943, no. 1911, 52/41885–41886. On 2 January he again spoke to Menemencioglu. Papen to FM, 3 Jan. 1944, no. 1, 52/41895. See also Moyzisch, *Operation Cicero*, pp. 135–37; Papen, *Memoirs*, pp. 511–12. Moyzisch implied that the main concern was infiltration of military personnel; Papen identified the specific issue as construction of radar stations. A Cicero document noted in a German telegram suggested that Menemencioglu probably spoke to Sir Hughe on 31 December. Ribbentrop to Papen, 6 Feb. 1944, no. 208, 52/41973–41974. Hinsley and Simkins, *Security*, p. 213, dated the ambassador's message to London as early January. See also p. 215. In 1995 the author could not locate the ambassador's telegram in the Public Record Office (file 37477). Papen learned from a Cicero document that after his discussion with the foreign minister, Knatchbull-Hugessen had ordered a security check of the embassy but had concluded that a Turkish source was responsible for the leak. See Papen to Ribbentrop, 19 Jan. 1944, no. 83, 52/41942–41943.

22. Moyzisch, *Operation Cicero*, pp. 138–39.

23. Papen, *Memoirs*, pp. 511–12, 515–16; Papen, postscript in Moyzisch, *Operation Cicero*, pp. 207–208.

24. Papen to FM, 30 Dec. 1943, nos. 1910 and 1911, 52/41884 and 52/41885–41886. See also Kahn, *Hitler's Spies*, pp. 344, 591.

25. FM to Papen, 10 Jan. 1944, no. 53, 52/41910.

26. "Bigot" was used to restrict access to leaders allowed to know about Overlord. The British document was a telegram, FO to Knatchbull-Hugessen, 21 Dec. 1943, no. 1751, 37479/R13527. Papen to FM, 6 Jan. 1944, no. 15, 52/41898–41899. See also Kahn, *Hitler's Spies*, pp. 344, 591.

27. Papen to FM, 6 Jan. 1944, no. 25, 52/41900–41901.

28. Evidence of Papen's worry appeared in the 18 January entry of his wife's diary. Adams, *Rebel Patriot*, p. 416. See also Papen to FM, 19 Jan. 1944, no. 81, 52/41937–41939.

29. FM telegrams to Papen, 27 Dec. 1943, unnumbered, 52/41868-41872, and 18 Jan. 1944, no. 111, 52/41933.

30. Papen to FM, 19 Jan. 1944, no. 81, 52/41937–41939.

31. Papen to Ribbentrop, 19 Jan. 1944, no. 83, 52/41942–41943.

32. Ribbentrop to Papen, 22 Jan. 1944, no. 124, 52/41949–41950, and Papen to Ribbentrop, 25 and 26 Jan. 1944, nos. 113 and 125, 52/41951 and 52/41953–41954, respectively.

33. Bazna, *I Was Cicero*, p. 100.

34. Miller, *Bulgaria*, pp. 166–67; *Times* (London), 15 Jan. 1944, p. 4; *New York Times*, 15 Jan. 1944, pp. 1, 4. Moyzisch gave the date of the raids as 14 January (*Operation Cicero*, pp. 148–49) but both the *New York Times* and Miller gave 10 January as the date. The first attack occurred at midday and a second about midnight. There were an estimated 3,000–4,000 casualties in the raid. Heavy bombings came again on 16 March and 29–30 March. The latter was a firebomb attack and especially destructive. See Miller, pp. 168–69.

35. Moyzisch, *Operation Cicero*, pp. 133, 148–49, and Papen's postscript, p. 208; Papen, *Memoirs*, pp. 511, 518; Schellenberg, *Labyrinth*, p. 344. Bazna had not known that there were doubts about him in Berlin. Bazna, *I Was Cicero*, p. 117.

36. Even some advocates of the deception theory, that British intelligence used the valet to trick German leaders, suggested the raid had validated the spy. They were nevertheless hard pressed to explain why, if he was under control, such vital military data had been leaked. Their views are discussed later.

37. Schellenberg, *Labyrinth*, pp. 337–38, 340; Moyzisch, *Operation Cicero*, pp. 52, 111; Kahn, *Hitler's Spies*, p. 343; Hinsley and Simkins, *Security*, p. 215; Jozef Garlinski, *The Enigma War* (New York: Scribner's, 1980), pp. 68–69, 152; David Kahn, *The Codebreakers: The Story of Secret Writing* (New York: Macmillan, 1967), pp. 451–52.

38. Bazna, *I Was Cicero*, pp. 68–69; Moyzisch, *Operation Cicero*, pp. 118–20.

39. Moyzisch, *Operation Cicero*, pp. 118–19.

40. Ibid., pp. 131–32.

41. Bazna, *I Was Cicero*, pp. 96–97.

42. For material about Mara see ibid., pp. 2, 30–32, 41–42, 64–66, 68–70, 87–88, 90, 93–96, 100–101, 117–18, 129, 133–34, 136, 192. See p. 72 for Bazna's claim that he knew the Germans called him "Cicero."

43. Concerning Esra see ibid., pp. 93–94, 97–99, 118–24, 127–28, 132–33, 148–49. The former spy referred to her as his "niece," but their family tie was in fact distant.

44. Ibid., pp. 128–31.

45. Papen, *Memoirs*, pp. 517–18; for the comment about the battle for Turkey see Papen to FM, 11 Feb. 1944, no. 222, 52/42011–42013.

CHAPTER 10. SEARCHING FOR AN AGENT

1. The approximate date of the warning can be established from a telegram, British embassy in Cairo to FO, 20 Dec. 1943, no. 2887, 37478/R13466, requesting an investigation of what the Americans learned from the Hungarians in Sweden. For details of how the information was obtained see British embassy in Washington to FO, 30 Jan. 1944, no. 467, 44066/R1599, and 3 Feb. 1944, no. 37, 44067/R2213.

2. Knatchbull-Hugessen warned London in early January: FO file 37477. For his concern about the Germans' lack of worry see his telegram to the FO, 21 Jan. 1944, no. 110, and FO minute, 31 Jan. 1944, 44066/R1683 and R1565. Sir John Lomax received the warning from an aide to Inönü: see report of his interview, Cave Brown, *Bodyguard*, pp. 445–46.

3. He was the military attaché, Colonel H. A. Cartwright, according to one informed source. Elliott, *Never Judge*, p. 136. His action has been called "a real blunder" by Deacon, *British Secret Service*, pp. 418–19.

4. Allen W. Dulles, *The Secret Surrender* (New York: Harper & Row, 1966), pp. 22–23. See also his introduction to the affair in his book *Great True Spy Stories* (New York: Harper & Row, 1968); War Department, Office of Strategic Services, *War Report of the OSS (Office of Strategic Services)*, intro. Kermit Roosevelt (New York: Walker, 1976), p. 278; West, *Deceit*, pp. 100–101; Cave Brown, *Bodyguard*, p. 447; Jock Haswell, *Spies and Spymasters: A Concise History of Intelligence* (London: Thames and Hudson, 1977), pp. 148–49.

5. Colonel Claude Dansey was assistant director of MI6 in London. Pro-

foundly jealous of Dulles, and having given the Kolbe material only a cursory check, Dansey dismissed it. "This incident was to precipitate the beginning of the end of Dansey's Secret Service career." Deacon, *British Secret Service*, p. 419. All data from Kolbe were identified by Dulles using the designation "Kappa" in his reports. Other code terms were employed: for example, Yellow=Turkey, Milit=Papen, Penni=Menemencioglu, Harem=Saracoglu, Zulu=British. Cicero, however, remained Cicero. Neal H. Petersen, ed., *From Hitler's Doorstep: The Wartime Intelligence Reports of Allen Dulles, 1942–1945* (University Park: Pennsylvania State Univ. Press, 1996), editor's note, p. 183.

6. Ibid., Dulles to OSS, 29 Dec. 1943, no. 1466–1476, doc. no. 2–101, pp. 183–85; Dulles to OSS, 1 Jan. 1944, no. 1503–1505, doc. no. 2–108, pp. 189–90. For Kolbe's inability to identify the spy see Dulles to London, 10 Jan. 1944, no. 335–336, p. 591, and Dulles to OSS, 21 Feb. 1944, no. 2137–2142, doc. no. 3–24, p. 226. Vanden Heuvel's name has also been spelled Vanden Huyvel.

7. Dulles, *Secret Surrender*, p. 23, and *Spy Stories*, pp. 30–31. Churchill's minute of 6 December had been given to Inönü and Sir Hughe during the meetings with Turkey's president at Cairo. Roosevelt's telegram no. 442, 15 Jan. 1944, and Churchill's telegram no. 548, 19 Jan. 1944, CAB 170/711.

8. The Foreign Office discussed the security breach in a telegram to Ankara, 19 Jan. 1944, no. 99; Churchill's minute was dated 21 Jan. and Eden answered it quickly: see 44148/R1518.

9. Hinsley et al., *British Intelligence*, vol. 3, part 2, p. 43n. An example of the belief that Cicero quit after British "intercepts of German direct cypher telegrams from Ankara to Berlin which quoted the stolen material" may be found in Phillip Knightley, *The Second Oldest Profession: Spies and Spying in the Twentieth Century* (New York: W. W. Norton, 1987), p. 143.

10. The OSS unit in Turkey was not established until spring 1943 and was considered amateurish by MI6 in Turkey. Elliott, *Never Judge*, p. 120. That judgment appears sound: Robin W. Winks, *Cloak and Gown: Scholars in the Secret War, 1939–1961* (New York: William Morrow, 1987), pp. 116–65. See Cave Brown, *Bodyguard*, pp. 446–47; Kapp, in Bazna, *I Was Cicero*, p. 179; Hinsley and Simkins, *Security*, p. 214.

11. Members of MI6 or SIS were often carried on embassy staffs as passport control officers. The practice was widely known. One former MI6 officer has described the crowding of intelligence operatives into the big, old Istanbul embassy. Elliott, *Never Judge*, p. 120. The counterespionage work of Section V was exceptional, because MI6 otherwise dealt in collecting information.

12. Chidson was a career army officer with a distinguished record who served at the embassy during 1943 and 1944. "Unfortunately the Ambassador was barely on speaking terms with the British security officers." Ibid., p. 135.

13. Frank Brenchley was a signals officer working with the military attaché in Ankara. He helped with the additional security checks to rule out any physical weaknesses, such as bugs. Interview with author, London, 21 Dec. 1995.

14. Papen reported the British ambassador's conclusion about a Turkish leak after reading one of Sir Hughe's telegrams to London. Papen to Ribbentrop, 19 Jan. 1944, no. 83, 52/41942–41943. See also Hinsley and Simkins, *Security*, pp. 213, 215.

15. William Codrington was head of security in the Foreign Office. During

1943–1944 Dashwood was Vice-Marshal of the Diplomatic Corps. One instance of misidentifying an investigator must be noted. Sir Hughe's obituary prompted a letter from the British military attaché at Ankara after the war, Major General Charles R. W. Swynnerton, who claimed the Foreign Office learned of the leak in 1943 and had dispatched Knox Helm. In fact, Helm had been there for other reasons in June 1942. *Daily Telegraph* (London), letters from Swynnerton and Sir John Lomax, 13 April 1971, p. 9, and 26 April 1971, p. 7. See also West, *Deceit*, p. 103. Hinsley and Simkins, *Security*, p. 213, stated that the Foreign Office official was joined by an SIS man from Istanbul.

16. Brenchley interview, 21 Dec. 1995; Nigel West, *MI6: British Secret Intelligence Service Operations, 1909–45* (London: Weidenfeld & Nicolson, 1983), p. 200; Hinsley and Simkins, *Security*, pp. 213–14. Dusko Popov later recalled that MI5 started investigating everyone who had access to the British papers concerning the Tehran Conference. Dusko Popov, *Spy/Counterspy*, foreword by Ewen Montagu (New York: Grosset & Dunlap, 1974), pp. 251–52. The size of the wartime embassy staff complicated the investigators' task. See Knatchbull-Hugessen, *Diplomat*, p. 183. The conclusion in Woodward's book is inaccurate. After mentioning that Papen knew details about the December meetings in Cairo, he stated that "no subsequent leakages are known to have taken place," the Foreign Office thinking that Menemencioglu had told Papen all about Cairo. *British Foreign Policy*, vol. 4. pp. 171n, 178n.

17. Elliott, *Never Judge*, p. 136; Bazna, *I Was Cicero*, pp. 103, 105. Elliott worked at the time for MI6 in Istanbul and was a friend of Knatchbull-Hugessen. The remark about Dashwood's tact is his.

18. See Elliott, *Never Judge*, p. 137; Hinsley and Simkins, *Security*, p. 213.

19. Bazna, *I Was Cicero*, pp. 101–105; Moyzisch, *Operation Cicero*, pp. 147–48. Elliott had met the valet on visits and thought he was "illiterate." *Never Judge*, pp. 136–37. See also Hinsley and Simkins, *Security*, pp. 213–14.

20. Dulles, *Secret Surrender*, pp. 24–25. See also his *Craft of Intelligence*, pp. 152–53, and *Spy Stories*, pp. 30–31. In compiling the Dulles telegrams and reports, Petersen perpetuated Dulles's error about having stopped Cicero. *Hitler's Doorstep*, pp. 9, 16.

21. Hugh Trevor-Roper, review of *Bodyguard of Lies*, Anthony Cave Brown, *New York Review of Books*, 19 Feb. 1976, p. 16. Kahn too thought that the spy had been used quite briefly by the British. See *Hitler's Spies*, p. 370. A fanciful story held that Dashwood had finally caught Bazna in the act of spying. "Not long after this" the valet gave notice and quit. Fitzroy Maclean said the story came from Dashwood. See his *Take Nine Spies* (New York: Atheneum Press, 1978), p. 220.

22. Hinsley et al., *British Intelligence*, vol. 3, part 2, p. 43n.

23. West, *Deceit*, p. 107. In *MI6* West reported that Dashwood's report to Eden concluded that Bazna had spied on Sir Hughe. The valet by then had resigned. West's quotation from the Dashwood report about the ambassador's negligence is quite similar to Bevin's postwar statement to Parliament. See *MI6*, pp. 200–201.

24. Ibid., and Kahn, *Hitler's Spies*, pp. 369–70, 593n. Kahn learned the story from Sir Edward Peck, the embassy's third secretary during 1943–1944, in an interview on 23 February 1974. See also Hinsley and Simkins, *Security*,

pp. 213–14. Some accounts say the error was spotted in enemy radio transmissions.

25. Deacon, *British Secret Service*, pp. 19, 316–17, 451; West, *Deceit*, p. 107.

26. Knightley, *Second Oldest Profession*, pp. 142, 114–15, 153–54. Lord Dacre (Trevor-Roper) had been "appalled by the quality of the prewar recruits" to MI6. See the quotation from "The Profession of Intelligence," Part 2, BBC Radio 4, 12 Mar. 1980, on p. 87. Knightley was the espionage expert for the *Sunday Times* and a consultant on espionage for BBC. See also Deacon, *British Secret Service*, pp. 437–40, 445–51, on MI6's troubles.

27. Five ideas or deceptions were emphasized: that Allied forces might not invade France at all in 1944 and certainly not before July; that the Pas de Calais was the chosen site for Allied landings; that Britain already had overwhelming ground units with further large reinforcements coming from America; that the Norwegian coast would be attacked in spring, with the aid of Russian forces; that Allied plans included invading southeastern Europe in 1944 with a major campaign in the Balkans.

28. Plan "Jael" was completed in October 1943. Regarding wartime secrets, the prime minister had stated, "Truth is so precious that she should be attended by a bodyguard of lies." Cave Brown, *Bodyguard*, p. xi. Michael Howard gave the outline of Plan "Bodyguard," as finally set on 23 January 1944, as Appendix 5 of his book. See *Strategic Deception* (New York: Cambridge Univ. Press, 1990), pp. 247–53. The work is the fifth volume of *British Intelligence in the Second World War*.

29. Cave Brown, *Bodyguard*, p. 449.

30. FitzGibbon, *Secret Intelligence*, pp. 261–64n. Maclean too seemed uncertain and ended his account of the case on an ambiguous note in 1978. See *Take Nine Spies*, p. 221.

31. Cave Brown, *Bodyguard*, p. 447. The author explained how the events allegedly occurred. Vanden Heuvel speedily notified London and three days later appeared at Dulles's office. He "quite literally begged" Dulles to take no steps about Cicero or the situation in Ankara. London was supposedly "aware" of the German agent; therefore Dulles knew that Cicero was part of a "game." Cave Brown claimed that he learned about the hurried visit from Dulles in an undated interview before his death in early 1969. But why would Dulles have suddenly altered his published accounts? Was London trying to conceal the serious problem it knew existed in Turkey? See also David Mure, *Practise to Deceive* (London: William Kimber, 1977), pp. 106, 108–10, 115, 253, and *Master of Deception: Tangled Webs in London and the Middle East* (London: William Kimber, 1980), p. 229.

32. Mure, *Deceive*, pp. 15, 106–107, 109–14, 253; *Deception*, pp. 19, 38–39, 230. Mure said he based his first book "on the little I was told at the time and the more I have learned since" about the wartime spy case. Thus he noted that Colonel Michael Crichton had also claimed deception. Colonel (later Brigadier) Croft-Constable, or "Galveston," was Senior Deception Officer in the Mediterranean. Galveston had concurred about an alleged deception but could not identify the mechanics of any operation involving Cicero. In his second book Mure admitted that using the word Overlord was a bad slip. See *Deceive*, pp. 111, 183, 193, and *Deception*, p. 230.

33. *Times* (London), 4 Oct. 1957, p. 13; Cave Brown, *Bodyguard*, pp. 400, 444–45. The notion that Bazna had Italian training reportedly came from ex-MI6 official Wilfred Dunderdale. See also West, *Deceit*, caption to photograph following p. 88. Jock Haswell, *D-Day: Intelligence and Deception* (New York: Times Books, 1979), p. 104, also thought Chidson controlled Cicero.

34. West, *Deceit*, pp. 106–107.

35. Cave Brown, *Bodyguard*, p. 444.

36. The defections to the Soviet Union of Guy Burgess and Donald Maclean in May 1951 led to long investigations. Philby was in time implicated and fled to Moscow. Menzies retired in the early 1950s.

37. Lomax's and Gubbins's rejections of his views were acknowledged by Cave Brown, *Bodyguard*, p. 445. Trevor-Roper's review of *Bodyguard of Lies* appeared in the *New York Review of Books*, 19 Feb. 1976, pp. 13–16. He found many problems with the book but reacted most strongly to Menzies's claim of controlling the spy: "It was this last remark which was finally too much for me." He was certain that it was inaccurate. See p. 16.

38. FitzGibbon, *Secret Intelligence*, pp. 261–64n. In a hastily added note, FitzGibbon explained that his views about Cicero were at best only guesses. His account has various errors. Cavendish-Bentinck later became the Duke of Portland. Mure also modified his interpretation of the affair by 1980. See also West, *Deceit*, p. 105, and *MI5*, p. 73 and note.

39. It has been suggested that West used official records by special permission. *British Intelligence in the Second World War* is a multivolume publication of Her Majesty's Stationery Office. The view of the contributors was clear: the leak was realized in January 1944, "but neither investigation in the embassy nor such diplomatic and Sicherheitsdienst traffic from Ankara as was decrypted disclosed the source," which was identified only after World War II. See Hinsley et al., *British Intelligence*, vol. 3, part 2, p. 43n. Howard pointed out that the deception planners of A Force could never convince German leaders to focus their attention on southeastern Europe. Cicero's information instead confirmed that the major Allied blow expected in 1944 would come in the West and not the Balkans. Howard, *Strategic Deception*, pp. 104–105, 145.

CHAPTER 11. CICERO'S LAST ACHIEVEMENTS

1. On stopping deliveries and trade issues see 44067/R2043 and 44068/R3918. London at this stage did not consider trade sanctions to be an effective weapon against the Turks. On Stalin's proposal see FO to Knatchbull-Hugessen, 3 Feb. 1944, no. 149, 44066/R1684; letter from British ambassador in Moscow to V. M. Molotov, 8 Feb. 1944, 44068/R4530. On his meeting with Menemencioglu and absence see Knatchbull-Hugessen to FO, 28 Feb. 1944, no. 279, and 22 Mar. 1944, no. 409, 44068/R3976 and R4697. The comment about an insult appeared in Sir Hughe's letter to the FO, 23 Feb. 1944, 44068/R3838. For Britain's attitude see FO to Beirut embassy, 2 Mar. 1944, no. 116, and FO memorandum, 9 Mar. 1944, 44163/R3255 and R3753. Eden also declined to make any statement to Parliament. Sir Hughe was out of Turkey from 28 February to 20 March 1944. Menemencioglu later told Papen that his absence was

in effect Britain's breaking of friendly relations with Ankara. Papen to FM, 13 Apr. 1944, no. 571, 52/42180. Examples of Turkish criticism of Britain in such newspapers as *Vatan* and *Aksam* are quoted in Kirk, "Turkey," p. 360.

2. The guests at the September 1943 tea party hosted by Hanna Solf, widow of an ex-ambassador to Japan, included Otto Kiep, a former diplomat connected to the Abwehr and to the Vermehrens. The Gestapo seized over seventy people on 12 January 1944. Other arrests followed. Nearly all the accused were executed except Frau Solf and her daughter, who survived because bombings destroyed their files.

3. Reports differ about when Vermehren first contacted the British and when he and his wife disappeared. Vermehren may have acted by late December. See West, *MI6*, pp. 198–99, and Heinz Höhne, *Canaris*, trans. J. Maxwell Brownjohn (Garden City, N.Y.: Doubleday, 1979), pp. 549–50.

4. Turkey was in fact not interested in the Germans. See Weber, *Evasive Neutral*, pp. 199–200. British policy opposed any actions that might prompt changes in the ineffective Abwehr. See John C. Masterman, *The Double-Cross System in the War of 1939 to 1945* (New Haven: Yale Univ. Press, 1972), p. 152. The reason for Vermehren's exception was past service: he was connected to Dusko Popov's spy ring financed by the Abwehr but secretly controlled by Britain to deceive the enemy. Vermehren's code name was "Junior." See West, *MI5*, pp. 197–209, 239–42, and *MI6*, pp. 197–99; Popov, *Spy/Counterspy*, pp. 71–72, 261. Masterman mistakenly reports that Junior had defected in November 1943. See pp. 152–53. Elliott's rather casual memoir, *Never Judge a Man by His Umbrella*, did not mention the Vermehrens.

5. Martha von Papen's diary, in Adams, *Rebel Patriot*, pp. 417–18; Fritz von Twardowski to Papen at Istanbul, 2 Feb. 1944, no. 68, 52/41960–41961.

6. Paul Leverkühn in *Der geheime Nachrichtendienst der deutschen Wehrmacht im Kriege* (Frankfurt: Verlag für Wehrwesen Bernard & Graefe, 1957), p. 175, mentioned the defection without naming the Vermehrens. On his peace efforts see Papen, *Memoirs*, especially pp. 499–500. Leverkühn also conceived the armed forces' propaganda magazine, *Signal*. Three part-time informants, journalist Karl Kleczkowski, his wife, and businessman Wilhelm Hamburger, also soon defected. American acceptance of the defectors further dismayed the British.

7. Vermehren has wrongly been called the second in command in Istanbul, but his assignment to assist Leverkühn provided ready access to information. Initial reports that he revealed secrets and delivered code books were untrue. Ian Colvin, *Master Spy: The Incredible Story of Admiral Wilhelm Canaris* (New York: McGraw-Hill, 1951), pp. 217–18. Dulles mistakenly thought Vermehren might help the British to identify Cicero. Dulles to OSS, 24 Feb. 1944, no. 2173–2175, in Petersen, *Hitler's Doorstep*, doc. no. 3–28, p. 228. Ribbentrop had also been concerned that Vermehren might know key facts about Cicero. See Papen to Ribbentrop, 10 Feb. 1944, no. 219, 52/42009–42010.

8. Papen to FM, 6–22 Feb. 1944, nos. 77, 192, 199, 201, 231, 232, 244, and 288, and ministry file note, 20 Feb. 1944, 52/41976–42064 (various locations for items noted).

9. Trott had apparently introduced her to sympathetic officials—Baron Gustav Steengracht von Moyland and especially Baron Adolf Marschall von

Biberstein. The importance of their key roles at several points suggests that they knew something of the couple's intent. Trott was later arrested with others in the resistance and was executed by the Nazis. FM, Marschall memorandum, 5 Feb. 1944, 52/41970–41971.

10. Papen to FM, 7 Feb. 1944, no. 78, 52/41988; Papen, *Memoirs*, pp. 520–21. That he faced recall and punishment was widely rumored. See Weber, *Evasive Neutral*, pp. 200–201.

11. Ribbentrop to Papen, 8 and 10 Mar. 1944, nos. 368 and 389, 52/42104 and 42114, respectively, and Papen to Ribbentrop, 8 and 11 Mar. 1944, nos. 361 and 385, 52/42105 and 42122, respectively.

12. Moyzisch, *Operation Cicero*, pp. 153–54, 157. He neither named the defector nor mentioned his work.

13. Schellenberg justified his long campaign to supplant the Abwehr: *Labyrinth*, pp. 345–60. Under an agreement of 14 May 1944 between Himmler and the OKW, the Abwehr was soon dissolved. For the new structure see Höttl, *Secret Front*, p. 19, and Kahn, *Hitler's Spies*, pp. 267–71. By the war's end Canaris and the other top Abwehr leaders had all been executed.

14. Papen to FM, 22 Feb. 1944, no. 288, 52/42064. For the figure on the compromised German agents and informants see *War Report of the OSS*, vol. 3, pp. 52–53, and West, *MI6*, p. 201.

15. Moyzisch, *Operation Cicero*, pp. 148–51.

16. Bazna, *I Was Cicero*, p. 118.

17. Ibid., pp. 120–21. His claim that the fuse was removable was accurate. Brenchley interview, 21 Dec. 1995.

18. Bazna, *I Was Cicero*, pp. 124–26, 128–31.

19. Moyzisch, *Operation Cicero*, p. 153; Bazna, *I Was Cicero*, pp. 131–32. See also Kahn, *Hitler's Spies*, p. 345, suggesting that Moyzisch and not Jenke mentioned the villa.

20. Papen to FM, 10 Feb. 1944, nos. 218 and 219, 52/42008 and 52/42009–42010, respectively.

21. The possible figure of ten rolls is based on Moyzisch's statements with respect to two accountings he had prepared. He reported total payments before the resumption of deliveries early in February of £200,000 and then of £300,000 in April, when he decided the operation had probably come to a close. Prices were £10,000 per roll. See Moyzisch, *Operation Cicero*, pp. 148, 166.

22. Ibid., pp. 149, 152–53, 163, 203; Bazna, *I Was Cicero*, p. 116. Moyzisch said of his superiors' order to pay Cicero, "In fact they bought a worthless roll of film with worthless pieces of paper" (p. 203).

23. Moyzisch, *Operation Cicero*, pp. 165–66; Bazna, *I Was Cicero*, pp. 150–52, 181–83; Schellenberg, *Labyrinth*, p. 344. The date given by Schellenberg for the last contact with Cicero is a little early.

24. Moyzisch, *Operation Cicero*, p. 203; Hinsley and Simkins, *Security*, pp. 214–15. Papen's reports allow no estimate of the amount of material reaching Berlin. The total of four hundred photographs is widely accepted, but the occasional figure of four hundred *documents* is wrong.

25. Bazna, *I Was Cicero*, pp. 116, 156–57, 162–64.

26. Ibid., pp. 167–68, 188–89.

27. Ibid., pp. 182–88. Bazna said that he explained that he wanted to join

his family and had a job in Istanbul. A British account maintained that he left Sir Hughe's employment in late February but got a salary after that, but it also said that Molkenteller translated the spy's material until April. Hinsley and Simkins, *Security*, p. 214. Bazna would have had no valet duties during the ambassador's absence in the first three weeks of March, but there is no indication that he was dismissed before the ambassador left. Nor does he appear to have taken more photographs.

28. Papen, *Memoirs*, p. 521. The ambassador reported with satisfaction incidents of British military personnel causing trouble in public. Papen to FM, 16 Feb. 1944, no. 250, 52/42045. For his meeting with Menemencioglu see Papen to FM, 11 Feb. 1944, no. 222, 52/42011-42013; Papen, *Memoirs*, p. 521. Both Ankara and Moscow were considering what might happen when their December 1925 Friendship Pact expired in November 1945.

29. Lersner headed the German Orient Society in Turkey; Earle advised his friend Roosevelt about southeastern Europe. See Papen, *Memoirs*, pp. 516–17, 522–24; Earle's comments in the *Philadelphia Enquirer*, 30 Jan. 1949; Schellenberg, *Labyrinth*, p. 339. At Easter 1944 Papen, on a trip to Istanbul, met a visiting papal official, Cardinal Angelo Roncalli (later Pope John XXIII), and asked him to encourage the Allies to distinguish between the Nazis and ordinary Germans. See also Colvin, *Master Spy*, p. 216.

30. Papen, *Memoirs*, pp. 521–22.

31. Schellenberg, *Labyrinth*, pp. 342–43.

32. Papen, *Memoirs*, p. 518; Papen to FM, 27 Dec. 1943, unnumbered, 52/41868–41872, and 18 Jan. 1944, no. 111, 52/41933; Moyzisch, *Operation Cicero*, pp. 117–18, 205.

33. Wehrmacht, High Command (OKW), *Kriegstagebuch des Oberkommandos der Wehrmacht (Wehrmachtführungsstab). 1940–1945*, ed. Percy Schramm et al., 4 vols. in 7 parts plus 2 supplements (Frankfurt: Bernard & Graefe Verlag für Wehrwesen, 1961–1969), vol. 4, pp. 93–94; Jodl's diary, entry probably for 10 Feb. 1944, in National Archives, Collection of World War II War Crimes Records, Record Group 238, War Diaries and Correspondence of General Jodl, Microfilm Publication T989. See also Kahn, *Hitler's Spies*, pp. 344–45, 591.

34. Howard, *Strategic Deception*, p. 145. British intelligence had generally accurate figures on enemy forces in the Balkans. Churchill, *Closing the Ring*, pp. 367, 370.

35. Walter Warlimont, *Inside Hitler's Headquarters, 1939–1945*, trans. R. H. Barry (New York: Praeger, 1964), pp. 390, 394–95. As its deputy head, General Warlimont supervised the Operations Staff's daily activities. From early 1944 the Germans in Bulgaria watched the Turkish border closely. Hitler thought that Turkey would remain neutral only as long as his armies held the Russians in the Balkans. See p. 468.

36. Hitler worried that defection or collapse of his satellites would undermine the southern flank of his front against the Russians. Ribbentrop tried to reassure the client states that there would be no invasion in southeastern Europe. The foreign minister spoke of having reliable intelligence that Ankara was resisting all Britain's pressures and thus not considering joining the conflict. Andreas Hillgruber, ed., *Staatsmänner und Diplomaten bei Hitler: Ver-*

trauliche Aufzeichnungen über Unterredungen mit Vertretern des Auslandes, 1939–1945, 2 vols. (Frankfurt: Bernard & Graefe Verlag für Wehrwesen, 1967–1970), vol. 2, p. 360.

37. Elliott said of his friend Sir Hughe and the story about Overlord secrets, "It caused sorrow, I know, both to him while still alive, his family and his friends." *Never Judge*, p. 139. For examples of press statements decades later see *New York Times*, 25 Dec. 1970, p. 32; *Daily Telegraph* (London). 23 Mar. 1971, p. 14; *Die Zeit*, 28 Dec. 1970, p. 5.

38. For their comments on the Overlord question in the following paragraphs see Moyzisch, *Operation Cicero*, pp. 163–65; Schellenberg, *Labyrinth*, pp. 266, 340, 343; Papen, *Memoirs*, pp. 515, 518; Bazna *I Was Cicero*, pp. 75–77, 124–25, 148, 150. Papen seems to have first seen the code word in January. Papen to FM, 6 Jan. 1944, no. 15, 52/41898-41899. In his message he or the encoder spelled the word "Overlook," or else the photograph from which he worked was unclear.

39. West, *Deceit*, p. 104.

40. Elliott revealed that he as an SIS officer in Istanbul and Sir Hughe both knew Overlord was to take place on 4–5 June. They waited together in Ankara for the news reports, but the landings were delayed a day due to the weather. *Never Judge*, pp. 134–35.

41. By early 1944 "Overlord" referred only to general Anglo-American strategy in northwestern Europe. Germany never learned where or when Allied landings would take place in France. See the excellent chapter entitled "The Ultimate Failure" in Kahn, *Hitler's Spies*, pp. 479–520. For a specific British acknowledgement that the term Overlord had been revealed through the Cicero espionage see Hinsley and Simkins, *Security*, p. 215. A curious view of how the Cicero affair affected dropping the name Overlord appears in Cave Brown, *Bodyguard*, pp. 448–49.

CHAPTER 12. AN AMERICAN SPY

1. To protect her family, Moyzisch and Papen concealed her true name. Moyzisch, *Operation Cicero*, pp. 17–18; Papen, *Memoirs*, p. 512. Even when her surname became known, "Elizabeth Kapp" still appeared in some books.

2. Moyzisch, *Operation Cicero*, p. 201; Bazna, *I Was Cicero*, pp. 114–15, 145, 178–80. Bazna had transcriptions of the taped interviews with Kapp. He implied that he also had written statements from her.

3. Kapp said she was six when she first visited the United States. The length of that visit is not known. Bazna thought that she was twenty-three while working for Moyzisch, but university records show she was born 31 July 1919 and thus nearing twenty-five when she defected. (Professor Emerita Marion C. Siney kindly obtained the information from Case Western Reserve University.) For the Kapps' activities in Cleveland see *Plain Dealer*, 24 Apr. 1944, p. 1, reporting her defection, and Robert T. Stock's feature story on 21 Sept. 1972, p. 7–E.

4. Kapp appeared often at the German Center in suburban southwest Cleveland. He reportedly led audiences in Nazi *Sieg Heils!* and the Horst Wes-

sel Song on at least two occasions. In 1940 he assured an audience of certain victory under Hitler. Ibid.; see also Kahn, *Hitler's Spies*, pp. 69, 345; William B. Breuer, *Hitler's Undercover War: The Nazi Espionage Invasion of the U.S.A.* (New York: St. Martin's, 1989), p. 176; Farago, *Game of the Foxes*, p. 570.

5. Kapp, in Bazna, *I Was Cicero*, pp. 107–109, 179, 203.

6. Cave Brown made a number of mistakes about Kapp: he claimed she and the young Clevelander had first met while working in Sofia and that they married at some point. See *Bodyguard*, p. 446. But Kapp did not reach Sofia until mid-summer 1943, when Bulgaria was already at war with the United States. Lauran Payne even called Kapp the lover of Roosevelt's friend George Earle in his book *German Military Intelligence in World War II: The Abwehr* (New York: Stein and Day, 1984), p. 17. See also Bazna, *I Was Cicero*, p. 112, concerning Earle's alleged role.

7. *Schnürchen* means "little string," but things described as going *am Schnürchen* are being run "like clockwork." She gained the nickname by using the phrase herself and insisting on an orderly office. Moyzisch referred to her only as "Schnürchen." See *Operation Cicero*, pp. 6–18, 106, 121.

8. Seiler was interviewed in the early 1960s by journalist Hans Schwarz to verify data in the account by Bazna. The talks were taped, and excerpts were printed in the book. Seiler, in Bazna, *I Was Cicero*, pp. 137–43, 152; Moyzisch, *Operation Cicero*, pp. 139–40. There is some question about when Seiler met the Kapps: a German official in Sofia later recalled a mid-January date and thought that Kapp left a week or so later. Beckerle to FM, 19 Apr. 1944, nos. 563 and 569, 52/42223 and 42224. His recollection after several months may have been faulty. Moyzisch and Bazna both recorded that she was in Ankara early in January.

9. Moyzisch, *Operation Cicero*, pp. 140–41; Seiler, in Bazna, *I Was Cicero*, p. 143.

10. Seiler, in Bazna, *I Was Cicero*, pp. 141–43; Moyzisch, *Operation Cicero*, pp. 139, 141–43, 201–202. Moyzisch said she was "a typical German of what we call the 'Gretchen' type." Cave Brown, *Bodyguard*, p. 146, reported that she arrived with an OSS agent named Ewart Seager. While an agent may have been present, for security reasons and further instructions, he would not have been an obvious escort. Kempner erred in saying she had arrived in October. See "Highest-Paid Spy," p. 103.

11. See Kapp, in Bazna, *I Was Cicero*, pp. 107–109, 178–79.

12. Ibid., p. 158; see also pp. 104, 106–107, 150–51. Bazna dated their first conversation at 7 January, but Moyzisch said that she was not yet working in early January. The place where Kapp reported glimpsing Cicero was Moyzisch's office building.

13. All three described the incident: Moyzisch, *Operation Cicero*, pp. 167–70; Bazna, *I Was Cicero*, pp. 155–58, including Kapp's statements. Seiler had heard of the encounter from Moyzisch: see pp. 155–56.

14. Moyzisch, *Operation Cicero*, pp. 159–61, 167–68, 173–74.

15. Kapp, in Bazna, *I Was Cicero*, pp. 109, 178–79. She never claimed to have learned the spy's name. See also Hinsley and Simkins, *Security*, p. 214.

16. Moyzisch, *Operation Cicero*, pp. 174–77; Seiler, in Bazna, *I Was Cicero*, pp. 152–54.

17. Moyzisch, *Operation Cicero*, pp. 162–63, 168, 170–71; Seiler, in Bazna, *I Was Cicero*, pp. 154–55.

18. Moyzisch, *Operation Cicero*, pp. 177–80.

19. Ibid., pp. 178–85; Seiler, in Bazna, *I Was Cicero*, pp. 175–78; Papen, *Memoirs*, p. 518. Moyzisch said of Papen (p. 181): "I have seldom, if ever, seen him so angry." Papen erred in saying she defected on 4 April. See also Kahn, *Hitler's Spies*, p. 591, note for p. 345, for a report of her defection in the files of the Foreign Ministry, Inland, *geheim*, 106, for 8 April 1944.

20. Kapp, in Bazna, *I Was Cicero*, pp. 108, 179, and Bazna's statements, pp. 159–62, 168–75. In *MI6* West identified Ewart Seager as her Cleveland friend, but Cave Brown disagreed. West, *MI6*, p. 200; Cave Brown, *Bodyguard*, p. 446. Despite similarity in the names, Sears and Seager, they may have been two people. The spy's claims are suspect: he had barely glimpsed the car's driver. Would employees of enemy countries have risked being identified together in public? See also Kahn, *Hitler's Spies*, p. 345.

21. Bazna, *I Was Cicero*, pp. 173–75; Moyzisch, *Operation Cicero*, pp. 183, 185, 190–92, 197, 202. Moyzisch attributed all the contacts to the British: telephone calls at his Istanbul hotel and offers conveyed through two Luftwaffe deserters and an old acquaintance. Elliott confirmed MI6's calls to Moyzisch at the Park Hotel. See *Never Judge*, p. 137.

22. For the friction between the intelligence services see Winks, *Cloak and Gown*, pp. 137–38; R. Harris Smith, *OSS: The Secret History of America's First Central Intelligence Agency* (Berkeley: Univ. of California Press, 1972), pp. 124–26; *War Report of the OSS*, vol. 2, pp. 47, 51–52, 269–70.

23. Kapp, in Bazna, *I Was Cicero*, pp. 179–80, said she wore the uniform of the Women's Royal Naval Service (WRNS). Ibid., pp. 168–78; Moyzisch, *Operation Cicero*, pp. 201–202.

24. See, for example, *Times* (London), 21 Apr. 1944, p. 2; *Plain Dealer*, 24 Apr. 1944, p. 1. The Associated Press dispatch from Ankara was dated 23 April. The *Times* said Kapp had left Turkey on 17 or 18 April.

25. Seiler, in Bazna, *I Was Cicero*, p. 153; Moyzisch, *Operation Cicero*, p. 168.

26. For his foreshadowings see Moyzisch, *Operation Cicero*, pp. 39, 143–45; for his complaints see pp. 18, 142–45, 155–59, 161–63, 171, 174–76. Seiler confirmed his views about Kapp. See *I Was Cicero*, pp. 143–44, 152–55. Seiler stated, "Her hysteria was sometimes practically unbearable."

27. Ibid., Kapp's statements, pp. 108, 145, 178–79.

28. Moyzisch, *Operation Cicero*, pp. 19–22, 139, 145, 184–85; Papen, *Memoirs*, p. 512; Bazna, *I Was Cicero*, pp. 107–8, 112–15, 137. Moyzisch's false ideas about Britain's role appeared in Papen to FM, 15 Apr. 1994, no. 485, 52/42195, and in Kempner, "Highest-Paid Spy," pp. 104, 106. Many later books repeated the error.

29. Moyzisch, *Operation Cicero*, pp. 17–18, 142. He imagined a romance with one of the Luftwaffe deserters and claimed that he must have subverted her: "One of them was to have a decisive influence on the final shaping of events." It had taken the embassy many weeks to establish that they were deserters and had not made an emergency landing in the neutral country. Moyzisch gave much space to their story, but they had no part in the Cicero affair. See pp. 19–22, 144–45, 171–74, 193–94. Paul Rengers and Johannes Beyer disappeared

on 14 April: Papen learned that they went to Syria. Papen to FM, 14 Apr. 1944, no. 580, 52/42188.

30. Bazna, *I Was Cicero*, pp. 112, 205. Kapp was interned in a camp at Bismarck. Some of her postwar friends were interviewed and their statements published. Ibid., p. 203. Violet Kyle knew Kapp in Chicago.

31. Ibid., statements by Kyle, Mr. and Mrs. Hugo Coutandin, and Ruth Coutandin, pp. 114, 203–205. Seiler reported that her father had "died of grief" over his daughter's defection. Ibid., p. 142. Kyle said that Kapp married an FBI agent. Ibid., p. 114. Kahn identified him as William Gorman and interviewed him in May 1977. The couple was by then divorced. Kahn, *Hitler's Spies*, pp. 591 (note for p. 345), 629.

32. Two examples of her errors may be cited: she spoke of a daily courier from Berlin and of meeting her American contact nearly every evening. Overstating the frequencies made her work seem substantially more important.

CHAPTER 13. DÉNOUEMENT AND AFTERMATH

1. Papen to FM, 7 Mar. 1944, no. 360, 52/42100–42101, and a Foreign Ministry report, distributed 10 Mar. 1944, 52/42114–42119.

2. Sabotaging the rail lines was proposed in autumn 1943, but its effectiveness was questioned. The new suggestion of action won support. Cave Brown, *Donovan*, pp. 437–42; Weber, *Evasive Neutral*, pp. 204–208.

3. On 14 April the British and Americans presented identical notes stating that Turkey would face supply stoppages unless it ceased deliveries to Germany of chromite and other products. Inönü then prevailed over Menemencioglu. Germany had not been forewarned but expected such a decision by Ankara. Weber, *Evasive Neutral*, pp. 204–206; Kirk, "Turkey," p. 361. The Turkish announcement came, ironically, on Hitler's birthday.

4. Speer in November 1943 reported that "the element in shortest supply is chromium" and that the current supply was only 21,000 tons. Germany's monthly use was running at 3,751 tons, but due to continued and extra shipments, by September 1944 there was a reserve sufficient for eight months. Albert Speer, *Inside the Third Reich: Memoirs*, trans. Richard and Clara Winston (New York: Macmillan, 1970), pp. 316–17, 405–406; Papen, *Memoirs*, p. 524; Knatchbull-Hugessen, *Diplomat*, p. 200.

5. Papen, *Memoirs*, pp. 524–26. Papen afterward went to Paris to visit a convalescing son and found deep pessimism about stopping Allied landings in France. He had another fruitless talk with Hitler before returning to his embassy post.

6. Churchill's speech, 24 May 1944, quoted in Lewis, *Turkey*, p. 122.

7. Knatchbull-Hugessen, *Diplomat*, p. 201. The Turkish cabinet had reportedly argued hotly over the German ships. See Weber, *Evasive Neutral*, pp. 208–11. Hasan Saka became foreign minister in September 1944.

8. Exchange of telegrams, 11 and 15 July 1944, quoted in Churchill, *Triumph and Tragedy*, pp. 79–81; text of his speech, *Times* (London), 3 Aug. 1944, pp. 4, 7; Knatchbull-Hugessen, *Diplomat*, p. 201. Weber, *Evasive Neutral*, p. 211, stated that Sir Hughe had been caught off guard by the Turks' break

with Germany. Stalin no longer cared about Turkey's joining the war, because with control of the Balkans he could intimidate Turkey. Ankara had noted the change of attitude in March. See Papen to FM, 7 Mar. 1944, no. 360, 52/42100–42101.

9. Papen, *Memoirs*, pp. 527–528. Papen said the telegram he drafted for Berlin was too formal to satisfy Jenke. Churchill had told Parliament on 2 August that Papen might "meet the blood bath" he had escaped in 1934. *Times* (London), 3 Aug. 1944, p. 7. Papen was offered protection by some countries if he chose not to return to Germany. His memoirs characteristically explained his decision as a matter of loyalty and gentlemanly honor.

10. Turkey's ambassador to Germany was on leave in Ankara during early August. Berlin's official radio statement had an angry tone and said Papen had flown out of the country on 1 August. *Times* (London), 3 Aug. 1944, p. 3. The medal was the Knight's Cross of the Military Order. Papen could not return to reclaim furniture and other belongings left at the embassy until late 1951. Papen, *Memoirs*, pp. 519, 529–32.

11. Knatchbull-Hugessen, *Diplomat*, p. 202. Turkey declared war on 23 February 1945, with an effective date of 1 March.

12. Bazna, *I Was Cicero*, pp. 189–91; Knatchbull-Hugessen, *Diplomat*, pp. 204–206, 216–42. Brussels was liberated on 3 September 1944, and Knatchbull-Hugessen arrived there on 20 September.

13. Knatchbull-Hugessen, *Diplomat*, pp. 201–204. Sir Hughe even expressed admiration for the ill but dedicated Menemencioglu.

14. Sir Hughe had presumably learned of the spy affair from the postwar interrogations of Moyzisch. For his response to Bevin's statement see *Daily Express* and *News Chronicle*, 19 Oct. 1950. See representative obituaries in *Daily Telegraph* (London), 23 Mar. 1971, p. 14; *Guardian* (Manchester), 23 Mar. 1971; and *Times* (London), 23 Mar. 1971, p. 19.

15. In 1964 a Mannheim court awarded Papen, then eighty-four, $13,750 and a monthly pension of $170. West German pension laws recognized his military service during 1896–1919. *Newsweek*, 22 June 1964, p. 44.

16. Turkey's repatriation of all German nationals did not affect refugee Jews. Moyzisch's wife and children spent the immediate postwar months in Sweden. Moyzisch, *Operation Cicero*, pp. 103, 199–201; Bazna, *I Was Cicero*, pp. vii, 201–202.

17. Schellenberg thought Müller went over to the Soviet Union in 1945. He believed he died soon afterward. *Labyrinth*, p. 321.

18. Ibid., pp. 42, 404. Himmler was stripped of all his powers on 6 May 1945. Schellenberg became a defendant in Case 11 at Nuremberg, the so-called "Ministries Case," *United States of America v. Ernst von Weizsaecker et al.* (January 1948–April 1949). He was acquitted of all but two charges—leadership of the SS and of the SD. His sentence ran from the war's end but was shortened due to his liver disease.

19. For Bazna's later life, see *I Was Cicero*, pp. 191–202.

20. Ibid., pp. 197–200. Bazna had arranged with the proprietor of a small establishment, the Hotel Çelik, to develop adjoining land and create the Çelik Palas or Palace Hotel. Guests could still use the old part, but work on the new project was halted for some time. In recent years the five-star hotel has been

further enlarged. The author is grateful to Zeki Ozdilekcan and to the Çelik Palas Hotel for information about it. Letter, 2 Jan. 1996. Even in the mid-1950s, courts ruled against Bazna in fraud cases. In April 1955 an Istanbul court ordered him to pay a recipient of bogus notes the equivalent of about £1,000 sterling. *Daily Telegraph* (London), 29 Apr. 1955.

21. Geist, *Pictures Will Talk*, p. 213; "Miseries of a Master Spy," *Life*, 7 Apr. 1952, pp. 139–40.

22. Jenke talked with a reporter from *Vatan* about a week before his death in summer 1951. The newspaper included his statements in its account of his fatal mishap. They are quoted here from Papen, *Memoirs*, p. 519; see also Bazna, *I Was Cicero*, p. 209.

23. Nogly, introductory note, ibid., pp. v–vii; for Bazna's statement see p. 202.

24. For coverage of the press conference see *Süddeutsche Zeitung*, 8 Nov. 1961, reported by Wolfgang Wehner, and *Die Zeit*, 9 Nov. 1961. The television program about the Cicero affair was shown several times during 1963–1964. See *Die Zeit*, 19 Sept. 1963, for one review. Kempner reported that the former spy visited his law office in Frankfurt and asked him to handle his legal action against the Germans. The attorney refused. Robert Kempner, *Ankläger eine Epoche* (Berlin: Ullstein Verlag, 1983), p. 375. Bazna died on 21 December 1970 and was buried in Munich's Perlacher Forst Cemetery. *New York Times*, 25 Dec. 1970, p. 32; *Die Zeit*, 28 Dec. 1970, p. 5.

25. See the filmography for details about the production and for a synopsis of the screenplay.

26. Zanuck thought he himself deserved more credit for works like *All about Eve*. He had expressed his irritation on 20 December 1950 in a memorandum to the director. Geist, *Pictures Will Talk*, pp. 211–13; Mel Gussow, *Don't Say Yes until I Finish Talking: A Biography of Darryl F. Zanuck* (Garden City, N.Y.: Doubleday, 1971), pp. 155–56, 159. Lang had been Zanuck's ski instructor at Sun Valley.

27. Wilson had shared an Academy Award for 1951 for cowriting *A Place in the Sun*. In a 1972 letter he asserted that Mankiewicz had changed only twenty-five to thirty lines. But the director apparently rewrote nearly all the dialogue. Geist, *Pictures Will Talk*, pp. 219–20, 339.

28. No violence or sex appeared on screen, since the director disliked sensationalism. Some critics objected to Mankiewicz's preference for subtle scenes. They felt his approach did not make best use of the film medium.

29. Mason had signed a two-year contract in order to play Field Marshal Erwin Rommel in *The Desert Fox*. He recalled that "there was not a moment's hesitation" about playing the spy. *Before I Forget*, pp. 223–24.

30. Oskar Karlweis was excellent as Moyzisch. The character of Travers was an amalgam of Britain's security officers.

31. "Miseries of a Master Spy," pp. 139–42. Of the article's seven photographs, four were stills from the film, while three depicted its preparation. The lead photograph showed the director and ex-spy in conversation. The pictures were taken from a tree and a window. Geist, *Pictures Will Talk*, pp. 213–14. For Bazna's remark see *New York Times*, 25 Dec. 1970, p. 32.

32. Production began on 17 August and was completed by 23 October. Meanwhile, on 27 September the studio announced Mankiewicz's departure.

33. Gussow, *Don't Say Yes*, p. 159.

34. Geist, *Pictures Will Talk*, pp. 217–18. The incident apparently occurred in February 1952, upon the production's public release. Gussow, *Don't Say Yes*, p. 159, said Mankiewicz tried to retrieve his "angry letter" after the *New York Times* praised *Five Fingers*. The director apparently wanted more of the extensive footage he had shot on location used in the final editing.

35. Zanuck reportedly rejected using the word "Cicero" because viewers might think of the Chicago suburb, notorious for violence since the 1920s. Geist, *Pictures Will Talk*, p. 213; Mason, *Before I Forget*, p. 224. Both the trailer and the film showed a book with a made-up title: "Five Fingers: The Story of Operation Cicero." The advertising trailer is included with the film in the videocassette release. A television series called *Five Fingers* from 1959 to 1960 was not about Cicero.

36. *Daily Express*, 19 Feb. 1952, p. 4, and *The Standard*, 1 Apr. 1952, p. 4.

37. Bosley Crowther, 23 Feb. 1952, in *New York Times Film Reviews*, vol. 4, p. 2592; *Variety*, 13 Feb. 1952, in *Variety Film Reviews, 1907–1980*, vol. 8, *Time*, 10 Mar. 1952, pp. 100–104. A few critics voiced minor reservations about the amount of fictional material. The *Film Daily*'s annual poll of reviewers gave tenth place to *Five Fingers*. The *1953 Film Daily Year Book of Motion Pictures*, ed. Jack Alicoate (New York: Film Daily, 1953), p. 173. For British reviews see *Times* (London), 4 April 1952, p. 6, and numerous excerpts in Clive Hirschhorn, *The Films of James Mason* (Secaucus, N.J.: Citadel, 1977), p. 101.

38. Geist, *Pictures Will Talk*, p. 395. The "Edgar" is a small bust of the writer Poe. In 1951 Wilson refused to cooperate with the House Un-American Activities Committee. He was blacklisted and did mostly uncredited writing for many years.

39. "Top Grossers of 1952," *Variety*, 7 Jan. 1953, p. 61.

40. See for instance Alan R. Booth, "The Development of the Espionage Film," in Wesley K. Wark, ed., *Spy Fiction, Spy Films, and Real Intelligence* (London: Frank Cass, 1991), p. 146, and James R. Parish and Michael R. Pitts, *The Great Spy Pictures* (Metuchen, N.J.: Scarecrow, 1974), pp. 179–81.

41. Hirschhorn, *Films of James Mason*, p. 101; Mason, *Before I Forget*, pp. 224–25. The actor called it "such a good film" that little comment about it was necessary. "I still admire it; in fact it is one of the few films in which I appear which can be relied on to hold my attention throughout."

42. For example, even years later Major-General C. R. A. Swynnerton referred to *Five Fingers* as "the silly film on the subject." Letter to *Daily Telegraph* (London), 13 Apr. 1971, p. 9.

43. See Geist, *Pictures Will Talk*, pp. 218–19. Mankiewicz was honored for his lifetime achievement at a special tribute two years before his death in 1993.

CHAPTER 14. THE AFFAIR IN RETROSPECT

1. Arguments that he must have had assistance contributed to the theory that the spy became part of a deception. Cave Brown, *Bodyguard*, pp. 438, 444.

2. Papen, postscript in Moyzisch, *Operation Cicero*, p. 208.

3. Papen and a former agent of MI6 in Turkey agreed that Moyzisch was competent in handling Cicero. Papen, *Memoirs*, p. 510; Elliott, *Never Judge*, p. 137.

4. Elliott, in acknowledging his friend's negligence, noted that a head of mission would today be instantly dismissed for the lack of security allowed by Sir Hughe. *Never Judge*, p. 133. A fictional treatment is also interesting. In his 1980 book entitled *Dirty Tricks*, writer Chapman Pincher has his character Sir Mark Quinn, head of SIS, observe that ever since the "phenomenal success" of Cicero "it had been standard practice for the M16 men on the spot to keep close check on the activities of all foreign servants employed in the ambassadorial residences." Checking the chanceries was not enough. *Dirty Tricks* (London: Sidgwick and Jackson, 1981), p. 198.

5. Moyzisch may well have deliberately misled his questioners about the financial arrangements during his early interrogations in Britain. Dissembling would have been a prudent course, since his isolation had left him unaware of how much might have been discovered about the counterfeiting scheme and his part in the distribution of bogus currency.

6. Moyzisch, *Operation Cicero*, p. 166; see also p. 148. Moyzisch's figure is more or less compatible with the number of film rolls he reported buying from Cicero. Hinsley and Simkins, *Security*, p. 214, cited an estimate of £150,000 sterling, based on payments of 700,000 Turkish pounds; Kempner, "Highest-Paid Spy," p. 103, thought that Cicero received about £125,000 sterling, or $500,000 plus some additional payments; the *New York Times*, 25 Dec. 1970, p. 32, offered a range of $840,000 to $1.5 million in British pounds.

7. Krecker, *Deutschland*, p. 239n, quoting Schellenberg's German-language memoirs, p. 322.

8. Moyzisch, *Operation Cicero*, p. 203. Moyzisch seems to have over-estimated the spy's wartime spending; he thought that the valet had preserved only about £40,000. That estimate seems extremely low given the amount he received and his later business ventures.

9. Thus the author of one study has stated, "Turkish diplomacy during the war was a brilliant accomplishment by all standards except those of honesty and integrity." Weber, *Evasive Neutral*, p. 219.

10. Moyzisch claimed that he had foreseen the fate of Germany. Looking backward from the results of a catastrophic defeat, he insisted that Berlin's knowledge of its enemies' growing military strength and of Allied plans should have mandated an early peace. The ambassador thought the documents were of "priceless value," because they had revealed the enemy's strategy: "We were thus able to appreciate the intentions of our enemies in a way that can hardly have a parallel in military history." He noted various ways in which the information impressed him. But in most instances Papen could not show how the Germans benefited from the data. See especially Moyzisch, *Operation Cicero*, pp. 51–52, 199, 203–204; Papen's postscript in Moyzisch's book, pp. 208–209; Papen, *Memoirs*, pp. 512, 515–18.

11. Self-serving hindsight also figured in his arguments. Thus Papen claimed that his knowledge of enemy plans "certainly helped to achieve a goal of historic importance to both sides" in that he was therefore able to keep Tur-

key neutral. Through the preservation of their nation's strength during the war, the Turks had become a bastion of anticommunism in the postwar world. Papen, postscript in Moyzisch, *Operation Cicero*, p. 209.

12. Ibid., pp. 208–209; Moyzisch's statements, pp. 199, 204. The conclusion by Moyzisch was clearly wrong: "In the long run all that the German leaders learned from those documents was simply this: they were about to lose the war." In fact they refused to see that end.

Filmography

FIVE FINGERS

Twentieth Century-Fox, 1952. Black-and-white photography. Running time: 108 minutes. Released in 1994 as Fox Video Studio Classic no. 1384, with original 1952 advertising trailer.

Production Team

Produced by Otto Lang
Directed by Joseph L. Mankiewicz
Screenplay by Michael Wilson
Art direction by Lyle Wheeler and George W. Davis
Photography by Norbert Brodine
Music by Bernard Herrmann
Special effects by Fred Sersen
Edited by James B. Clark

Principal Cast

Ulysses Diello/Cicero	James Mason
Countess Anna	Danielle Darrieux
George Travers	Michael Rennie
Sir Frederic	Walter Hampden
Ludwig Moyzisch	Oscar Karlweis
Colonel von Richter	Herbert Berghof
Franz von Papen	John Wengraf

Advertising Trailer

The first image shows a man's hand, palm upward, fingers moving, while a narrator explains what it symbolizes: the fate of nations and the lives of many people lie within its grasp. Then narration and visual titles declare that the man described in the bestselling *Operation Cicero* was the highest-paid spy in history and that the film will depict his exploits: that he revealed decisions of the Cairo, Moscow, and Tehran wartime conferences to the enemy; that he learned the secret designation "Overlord" used for the second front; that he obtained the date of Allied D-Day landings in Normandy and passed on the information. Various cuts from the film underscore the seriousness of the situation and illustrate the participants' game of guile and deceit. The advertisement announces that exteriors were filmed in Turkey and promises audiences an accurate dramatization of events: "It's True—Every Startling Moment."

Plot Summary

The following synopsis emphasizes depiction of the espionage activities for comparison with the actual events, but it scarcely conveys the film's many subtleties and rich texture.

Opening devices and settings quickly establish a tone of realism, an unseen narrator informing viewers about the story's background, with other scenes underscoring the seriousness of the spy case. The semidocumentary approach, though not sustained throughout the film, retains an effective hold. In depicting the spy's working methods, the screenplay adhered to the published account, adjusting only a few minor details. Cicero's activities are nevertheless condensed to a relatively short time in spring 1944.

Dramatization begins at a diplomatic reception in Ankara, where Papen shows anti-Nazi humor in private observations about his nation's leaders. His conversation with the beautiful Countess Anna Staviska reveals that she is a French-born Polish aristocrat but now an impoverished refugee. Papen speaks with contempt of spying and turns down her offer to spy for Germany. Upon his return to the embassy, the military attaché, Moyzisch, finds a stranger who offers to sell him photographs. The man conceals his identity but describes information he can supply. His terms are set; he will telephone in three days to learn if they are accepted. Then he returns to the British ambassador's residence, where he is identified as Diello, the diplomat's valet. Comments reveal that he once worked for the countess's husband and that she is desperate for money. A few days later Papen tells Moyzisch that the capital has approved the transaction but warns him to take care, for Papen suspects that Britain had sent the man or that he is a swindler. Papen informs him that Ribbentrop has codenamed him "Cicero."

At their second meeting Cicero delivers two rolls of film, counts the money before it is placed in a wall safe, and waits while a nervous Moyzisch goes to his darkroom. The spy looks at a portrait and bust of Hitler and gets an idea about the safe combination; Diello has opened the safe and taken the money before Moyzisch returns. Cicero explains that he guessed the combination: it was 1–30–33, or the date Hitler came to power, his other choice having been Hitler's birthday. He suggests the combination 6–18–15, or the date of Waterloo, as a new possibility. Subsequently Moyzisch is unable to learn anything from the man except that he works in the British embassy.

Cicero walks after dark to a shabby building to visit Anna. He offers her money to redeem her pawned jewelry and the use of a rented mansion, where he will at times conduct secret business. Later they will travel to South America, posing as a married couple. Sparring, class and sexual, begins. While she accepts the business arrangement, agreeing to hold the funds he cannot keep or put in a bank, she resists a liaison.

In Berlin Kaltenbrunner and Colonel von Richter suspect that the documents are a trap but as a test await the Allied bombing of the Ploesti oil fields, set for 5 April. The next scene shows the fires raging. Papen is angry that Romania was not forewarned and vows to use Cicero's new items without Berlin.

Diello is seen photographing papers just before the return of Sir Frederic. The ambassador notifies London that Papen knows secret information. A security agent named Travers soon comes to investigate. Richter also arrives, to take over dealings with Cicero. At their first meeting Cicero refuses to tell Richter about himself but later tells Anna that he came from Albania and had served at sea. In Britain he had entered service to become a polished Englishman.

A narrator says the spy now has £155,000, but Berlin still does not trust the documents. Travers thinks that there is no spy and suspects a leak through loose talk at a party given by Anna, but he announces that London has broken a code and can decipher Papen's messages to his superiors. At the villa Richter tells Cicero that previous documents had mentioned Overlord plans and consequently offers him £40,000 for the details. Travers informs Sir Frederic that a decoded intercept identifies a spy called "Cicero" in Britain's embassy. Alarms are installed on the safes, but combinations cannot be changed for several days. When the spy fails to appear at a rendezvous Richter declares that it may be time to silence him.

At her old apartment, Cicero and Anna discuss their escape plan. She has purchased false passports, booked their passage to South America on a neutral ship, and had the funds transferred. Cicero says he will not risk further thefts for the extra £40,000. Then he insists that all the money is his alone. She appears to accept his domination, but the look on her face as they embrace suggests that she has plans of her own. At work the next day, Cicero spots a letter to the ambassador in Anna's handwriting, but Travers locks it away for Sir Frederic to read later. Then he casually mentions that Anna has flown to Switzerland with £130,000 she had somehow obtained. The valet at first is shocked but tries in vain to trace her, knowing he is now being watched. Finally he telephones Moyzisch to say that he will steal the invasion plans for delivery in Istanbul and not locally. He knows the grave danger he now faces from both sides.

Cicero checks the wiring and realizes that removing a fuse will silence the safe's alarm installed by the British. After opening the safe he takes the countess's letter and starts photographing in the next room, but he sends away a maid who wants to clean the office so does not realize that she has replaced the fuse in order to vacuum the hall. Despite the alarm sounding as he returns the papers to the safe, he is able to flee, but the security officer orders him killed before he delivers the plans. Both the British and Germans await him at the railway station, but he boards the already moving train; neither side will risk any violence before Cicero reaches Istanbul. Meanwhile Diello reads the letter in which Anna denounced him as a German spy. He tears it up and throws the pieces out the window.

At his destination he tells his German protectors to meet him later at a restaurant, demands £100,000 instead, and offers a film showing part of a British document to convince them to pay. During the subsequent exchange men from both sides wait for the spy to leave. The Germans want to silence him and keep secret their transactions; the British need to find out what he has told the enemy. The latter escort him from the restaurant, but he escapes amid a passing funeral procession. Each group searches the city in vain. As Moyzisch develops the film, Richter gets a note from Papen: the ambassador has received a letter from Anna declaring that Cicero was a British plant and the diplomat believes the information. Moyzisch does not agree but cannot stop the angry Richter; the latter tears up the photographs and throws the pieces out a window overlooking the harbor. There Richter sees a ship leaving; elsewhere Travers too sees it depart. Both are sure Cicero is on board.

In an epilogue set in Rio de Janeiro, an elegant Diello is dining on his terrace. His banker and a government official arrive to inform him that all the pounds he has been spending are counterfeit: Germany's scheme has been discovered by the British. The bogus money has also turned up in Switzerland and been traced to a recently arrived lady. The last scene shows Cicero laughing loudly, saying Anna's name, and throwing useless British notes from his terrace. This recurring image of people throwing away papers once thought important underscores the story's many ironies: Diello's disposal of the countess's letter denouncing him, Richter's destruction of plans he thinks were planted by the British, Cicero's tossing to the wind his counterfeit money.

Selected Bibliography

MEMOIRS AND PERSONAL ACCOUNTS

Bazna, Elyesa. *Ich war Cicero: Die Bekenntnisse des grössten Spion des zweiten Weltkriegs*. Written with Hans Nogly. Munich: Kindler Verlag, 1962.
———. *I Was Cicero*. Written with Hans Nogly. Translated by Eric Mosbacher. New York: Harper & Row, 1962.
Busk, Douglas. *The Craft of Diplomacy: How to Run a Diplomatic Service*. New York: Praeger, 1967.
Churchill, Winston S. *Closing the Ring*. Vol. 5 of *The Second World War*. Boston: Houghton Mifflin, 1951.
———. *The Hinge of Fate*. Vol. 4 of *The Second World War*. Boston: Houghton Mifflin, 1950.
———. *Triumph and Tragedy*. Vol. 6 of *The Second World War*. Boston: Houghton Mifflin, 1953.
Douglas, William Sholto, and Robert Wright. *Combat and Command: The Story of an Airman in Two World Wars*. New York: Simon & Schuster, 1966.
Dulles, Allen W. *The Craft of Intelligence*. New York: Harper & Row, 1963.
———. *Germany's Underground*. New York: Macmillan, 1947.
———, ed. *Great True Spy Stories*. New York: Harper & Row, 1968.
———. *The Secret Surrender*. New York: Harper & Row, 1966.
Eden, Anthony. *The Reckoning*. Vol. 2 of *The Memoirs of Anthony Eden*. Boston: Houghton Mifflin, 1965.
Elliott, Nicholas. *Never Judge a Man by His Umbrella*. Salisbury, U.K.: Michael Russell, 1991.
François-Poncet, André. *The Fateful Years: Memoirs of a French Ambassador in Berlin, 1931–1938*. Translated by Jacques LeClercq. New York: Harcourt, Brace, 1949.
Goebbels, Joseph. *The Goebbels Diaries, 1942–1943*. Edited and translated by Louis P. Lochner. Garden City, N.Y.: Doubleday, 1948.
Höttl, Wilhelm [pseud. "Walter Hagen"]. *Die Geheime Front: Organisation, Personen und Aktionen des deutschen Geheimdienstes*. Linz: Nibelunger-Verlag, 1950.

————. *The Secret Front: The Story of Nazi Political Espionage*. Translated by R. H. Stevens. Introduction by Ian Colvin. New York: Praeger, 1954. (A later reprint spelled the author's name as "Hoettl.")

————. *Unternehmen Bernhard: Ein historischer Tatsachenbericht über die grösste Geldfälschungsaktion aller Zeiten*. Wels: Welsermühl, 1955.

Kempner, Robert M. W. *Ankläger eine Epoche*. Berlin: Ullstein Verlag, 1983.

————. "The Highest-Paid Spy in History." *Saturday Evening Post*, 28 January 1950, pp. 17–19ff. Abridged in *Reader's Digest*, June 1950, pp. 91–95. Abridgment reprinted, pp. 299–303, in *Secrets and Spies: Behind-the-Scenes Stories of World War II*. Pleasantville, N.Y.: Reader's Digest, 1964.

Knatchbull-Hugessen, Sir Hughe. "Ambassador to Turkey." *The Fortnightly* 171 (Apr. 1949), pp. 228–35. Reprinted from *Diplomat in Peace and War*.

————. *Diplomat in Peace and War*. London: John Murray, 1949.

————. *Kentish Family*. London: Methuen, 1960.

Leverkühn, Paul. *Der geheime Nachrichtendienst der deutschen Wehrmacht im Kriege*. Frankfurt: Verlag für Wehrwesen Bernard & Graefe, 1957.

————. *German Military Intelligence*. Translated by R. H. Stevens and Constantine FitzGibbon. New York: Praeger, 1954.

Mason, James. *Before I Forget: Autobiography and Drawings*. London: Hamish Hamilton, 1981.

Masterman, John C. *The Double-Cross System in the War of 1939 to 1945*. New Haven: Yale University Press, 1972.

McNally, George J., and Frederic Sondern, Jr. "The Great Nazi Counterfeit Plot," *Reader's Digest*, July 1952, pp. 25–31. Reprinted as "The Nazi Counterfeit Plot," pp. 507–514, in *Secrets and Spies: Behind-the-Scenes Stories of World War II*. Pleasantville, N.Y.: Reader's Digest, 1964.

"Miseries of a Master Spy." *Life*, 7 April 1952, pp. 139–42.

Moyzisch, Ludwig C. *L'Affaire Ciceron*. Translated by Suzanne Belly. Verviers, Belgium: Gérard, n.d.

————. *Der Fall Cicero: Es geschah in Ankara—Die sensationellste Spionageaffäre des Zweiten Weltkriegs*. Frankfurt: Die Quadriga, 1950.

————. *Operation Cicero*. Postscript by Franz von Papen. Translated by Constantine FitzGibbon and Heinrich Fraenkel. New York: Coward-McCann, 1950.

————. *Operation Cicero*. Abridged ed. In *High Stakes and Desperate Men: Classics of Espionage*. Pleasantville, N.Y.: Reader's Digest, 1974.

Mure, David. *Master of Deception: Tangled Webs in London and the Middle East*. London: William Kimber, 1980.

————. *Practise to Deceive*. London: William Kimber, 1977.

Papen, Franz von. *Memoirs*. Translated by Brian Connell. New York: E. P. Dutton, 1953.

————. *Der Wahrheit eine Gasse*. Munich: Paul List Verlag, 1952.

Peis, Günter. *The Man Who Started the War*. Foreword by Alfred Naujocks. London: Odhams Press, 1960.

Popov, Dusko. *Spy/Counterspy*. New York: Grosset & Dunlap, 1974.

Ribbentrop, Joachim von. *The Ribbentrop Memoirs*. Translated by Oliver Watson. Introduction by Alan Bullock. London: Weidenfeld and Nicolson, 1954.

Schellenberg, Walter. *The Labyrinth: Memoirs of Walter Schellenberg*. Translated by Louis Hagen. Introduction by Alan Bullock. New York: Harper & Brothers, 1956. (Published as *The Schellenberg Memoirs* in Britain and as *Hitler's Secret Service* in a later American printing.)

Schlabrendorff, Fabian von. *The Secret War against Hitler*. Translated by Hilda Simon. Foreword by John J. McCloy. New York: Pitman, 1965.

Speer, Albert. *Inside the Third Reich: Memoirs*. Translated by Richard and Clara Winston. New York: Macmillan, 1970.

Speidel, Hans. *Invasion 1944: Ein Beitrag zu Rommels und des Reiches Schicksal*. Tübingen: Rainer Wunderlich Verlag, 1949.

Warlimont, Walter. *Inside Hitler's Headquarters, 1939–45*. Translated by R. H. Barry. New York: Praeger, 1964.

Wiesenthal, Simon. *The Murderers among Us: The Simon Wiesenthal Memoirs*. Edited by Joseph Wechsberg. New York: McGraw-Hill, 1967.

Winterbotham, F. W. *The Ultra Secret*. New York: Harper & Row, 1974.

OFFICIAL RECORDS

Germany. Foreign Ministry. *Documents: La politique allemande en Turquie (1941–1943)*. Moscow: Éditions en Langues Étrangères, 1949.

———. Foreign Ministry. *Documents secrets du Ministre des Affaires Étrangères d'Allemagne*. Vol. 1, *Turquie*. Translated from Russian by Madeleine and Michel Eristov. Paris: Éditions Paul Dupont, 1946.

———. Foreign Ministry. Office of the State Secretary. *Akten des Politischen Archivs im Auswärtigen Amt*. Vol. 9, Turkey, 1 November 1943–30 April 1944. (See the entry under United States National Archives for the microfilm copies used.)

———. Wehrmacht. High Command (OKW). *Kriegstagebuch des Oberkommandos der Wehrmacht (Wehrmachtführungsstab. 1940–1945)*. Edited by Percy Schramm et al. 4 vols. in 7 parts plus 2 supplements. Frankfurt: Bernard & Graefe Verlag für Wehrwesen, 1961–1969.

Great Britain. *Parliamentary Debates (Hansard)*. Fifth Series, Vol. 478, *House of Commons, Official Report*, Session 1950, 24 July–26 October 1950. London: His Majesty's Stationery Office, 1950.

———. Empire Parliamentary Association. *Report on Foreign Affairs for Months of January, February and March 1944*. Vol. 25, no. 1. London: Empire Parliamentary Association, 1944.

———. Public Record Office. Unpublished Foreign Office and Cabinet documents in Record Groups FO 371 and CAB 170. (In citations to Foreign Office records the group designation has been omitted. The number preceding the slash mark refers to the file; the second number identifies the document in multi-item files.)

Heiber, Helmut, ed. *Hitlers Lagebesprechungen: Die Protokollfragmente seiner militärischen Konferenzen, 1942–1945*. Stuttgart: Deutsche Verlags-Anstalt, 1962. Paperback edition: *Lagebesprechungen im Führerhaupt-*

quartier: Protokollfragmente aus Hitlers militärischen Konferenzen, 1942–1945. Munich: Deutscher Taschenbuch Verlag, 1963.

Hillgruber, Andreas, ed. *Staatsmänner und Diplomaten bei Hitler: Vertrauliche Aufzeichnungen über Unterredungen mit Vertretern des Auslandes, 1939–1944*. 2 vols. Frankfurt: Bernard & Graefe Verlag für Wehrwesen, 1967–1970.

Hinsley, F. H. *British Intelligence in the Second World War*. Abridged ed. London: Her Majesty's Stationery Office, 1993.

Hinsley, F. H., et al. *British Intelligence in the Second World War*. Vol. 3, Part 2, *Its Influence on Strategy and Operations*. New York: Cambridge University Press, 1988.

Hinsley, F. H., and C. A. G. Simkins. *Security and Counter-Intelligence*. Vol. 4 of *British Intelligence in the Second World War*. New York: Cambridge University Press, 1990.

Howard, Michael. *Strategic Deception*. Vol. 5 of *British Intelligence in the Second World War*. New York: Cambridge University Press, 1990.

Petersen, Neal H., ed. *From Hitler's Doorstep: The Wartime Intelligence Reports of Allen Dulles, 1942–1945*. University Park, Penn.: Pennsylvania State University Press, 1996.

United States. Department of State. Historical Office. *Foreign Relations of the United States. Diplomatic Papers, 1943*. Vol. 4, *The Near East and Africa*. Department of State Publication No. 7665. Washington, D.C.: Government Printing Office, 1964.

———. Department of State. Historical Office. *Foreign Relations of the United States. Diplomatic Papers, 1944*. Vol. 5, *The Near East, South Asia, and Africa; The Far East*. Department of State Publication No. 7859. Washington, D.C.: Government Printing Office, 1965.

———. Department of State. Historical Office. *Foreign Relations of the United States. Diplomatic Papers. The Conferences at Cairo and Tehran, 1943*. Department of State Publication no. 7187. Washington, D.C.: Government Printing Office, 1961.

———. Military Tribunals (Nuremberg). *Trials of War Criminals before the Nuernberg Military Tribunals under Control Council Law No. 10*. 15 vols. Case 11: The Ministries Case (*United States v. Ernst von Weizsaecker et al.*), 1947–1949. Vols. 12–14. Washington, D.C.: Government Printing Office, 1950–1953.

———. National Archives. Collection of Seized Foreign Records. Record Group 242, Records of the German Foreign Ministry, 1920–1945, Received by the Department of State. Microfilm Publication T120, roll 52 (Turkey, 1943–1944). (In all citations T120 has been omitted. The numbers identify the roll and then the frame or frames where the document may be found.)

———. National Archives. Collection of World War II War Crimes Records. Record Group 238, War Diaries and Correspondence of General Jodl. Microfilm Publication T989 (2 rolls).

———. War Department. Military Intelligence Division. *German Military Intelligence, 1939–1945*. Frederick, Md.: University Publications of America, 1984.

————. War Department. Office of Strategic Services. *War Report of the OSS (Office of Strategic Services)*. 2 vols. Introduction by Kermit Roosevelt. New York: Walker, 1976.

Woodward, Llewellyn. *British Foreign Policy in the Second World War*. 5 vols. London: Her Majesty's Stationery Office, 1970–1976.

INTERVIEWS AND CORRESPONDENCE

Patricia H. Beall (United States)
Frank Brenchley (Great Britain)
Dirk Douglas (Germany)
Lutz Kempner (Germany)
Zeki Ozdilekcan (Turkey)
Marion C. Siney (United States)

NEWSPAPERS AND PERIODICALS

Christian Science Monitor
Daily Express (London)
Daily Telegraph and Morning Post (London)
Economist
Evening News (London)
Evening Standard (London)
Guardian
Library Journal
Manchester Guardian
New Statesman and Nation (London)
New Yorker
New York Herald Tribune Book Review
New York Times
New York Times Book Review
News Chronicle (London)
News of the World (London)
Newsweek
Philadelphia Enquirer
Plain Dealer (Cleveland)
San Francisco Chronicle
Saturday Review of Literature
Spectator (London)
Standard (London)
Sunday Chronicle (London ed.)
Sunday Dispatch (London)
Sunday Express (London)
Sunday Times (London)
Time
Times (London)
Times Literary Supplement (London)

INTELLIGENCE AND SECRET OPERATIONS

Abshagen, Karl Heinz. *Canaris*. Translated by Alan Houghton Brodrick. London: Hutchinson, 1956.

Andrew, Christopher. *Her Majesty's Secret Service: The Making of the British Intelligence Community*. New York: Viking Penguin, 1986.

Bartz, Karl. *The Downfall of the German Secret Service*. Translated by Edward Fitzgerald. London: William Kimber, 1956.

Bennett, Ralph. *Behind the Battle: Intelligence in the War with Germany, 1939–45*. London: Reed, 1994.

Breuer, William B. *Hitler's Undercover War: The Nazi Espionage Invasion of the U.S.A.* New York: St. Martin's, 1989.

———. *Hoodwinking Hitler: The Normandy Deception*. Westport, Conn.: Praeger, 1993.

———. *The Secret War with Germany: Deception, Espionage, and Dirty Tricks, 1939–1945*. Novato, Calif.: Presidio Press, 1988.

Brissaud, André. *Canaris: The Biography of Admiral Canaris, Chief of German Military Intelligence in the Second World War*. Translated and edited by Ian Colvin. New York: Grosset & Dunlap, 1974.

———. *The Nazi Secret Service*. Translated by Milton Waldman. New York: W. W. Norton, 1974.

Buranelli, Vincent and Nan. *Spy/Counterspy: An Encyclopedia of Espionage*. New York: McGraw-Hill, 1982.

Cave Brown, Anthony. *Bodyguard of Lies*. 2 vols. New York: Harper & Row, 1975.

———. *The Last Hero: Wild Bill Donovan*. New York: Times Books, 1982.

Chalou, George C., ed. *The Secrets War: The Office of Strategic Services in World War II*. Washington: National Archives and Records Administration, 1992.

Colvin, Ian. *Master Spy: The Incredible Story of Admiral Wilhelm Canaris*. New York: McGraw-Hill, 1951. Published in Britain as *Chief of Intelligence*.

Crankshaw, Edward. *Gestapo: Instrument of Tyranny*. London: Putnam, 1956.

Deacon, Richard [Donald McCormick]. *A History of British Secret Service*. Panther Books ed. London: Granada, 1980. First published in 1969 by Frederick Muller.

———. *Spyclopedia: The Comprehensive Handbook of Espionage*. New York: William Morrow, 1987.

Deschner, Günther. *Reinhard Heydrich*. Translated by Sandra Bance et al. New York: Stein and Day, 1981.

Farago, Ladislas. *Burn after Reading: The Espionage History of World War II*. New York: Walker, 1961.

———. *The Game of the Foxes: The Untold Story of German Espionage in the United States and Great Britain during World War II*. New York: David McKay, 1971.

FitzGibbon, Constantine. *Secret Intelligence in the Twentieth Century*. New York: Stein and Day, 1977.

Ford, Corey. *Donovan of the O.S.S.* Boston: Little, Brown, 1970.

Garlinski, Jozef. *The Enigma War*. New York: Scribner's, 1980.

Graber, G. S. *The Life and Times of Reinhard Heydrich*. New York: David Mc-Kay, 1980.

Gunzenhäuser, Max. *Geschichte des geheimen Nachrichtendienstes (Spionage, Sabotage, und Abwehr): Literaturbericht und Bibliographie*. Frankfurt: Bernard & Graefe, 1968.

Haldane, R. A. *The Hidden War*. New York: St. Martin's, 1978.

Hartman, Tom, and Robert Hunt, eds. *Swastika at War: A Photographic Record of the War in Europe as Seen by the Cameramen of the German Magazine "Signal."* Introduction by Gunther Heysing. Garden City, N.Y.: Double-day, 1975.

Haswell, Jock. *British Military Intelligence*. London: Weidenfeld and Nicolson, 1973.

————. *D-Day: Intelligence and Deception*. New York: Times Books, 1979.

————. *Spies and Spymasters: A Concise History of Intelligence*. London: Thames and Hudson, 1977.

Höhne, Heinz. *Canaris*. Translated by J. Maxwell Brownjohn. Garden City, N.Y.: Doubleday, 1979.

Höhne, Heinz, and Hermann Zolling. *The General Was a Spy: The Truth about General Gehlen and His Spy Network*. Translated by Richard Barry. New York: Coward, McCann & Geoghegan, 1972.

Jarl, G. *Das Rätsel Cicero: Eine sensationelle Spionageaffäre*. Berlin: Deutscher Militärverlag, 1966.

Kahn, David. *The Codebreakers: The Story of Secret Writing*. New York: Mac-millan, 1967.

————. *Hitler's Spies: German Military Intelligence in World War II*. New York: Macmillan, 1978.

Knightley, Phillip. *The Second Oldest Profession: Spies and Spying in the Twentieth Century*. New York: W. W. Norton, 1987.

Maclean, Fitzroy. *Take Nine Spies*. New York: Atheneum, 1978.

Manvell, Roger, and Heinrich Fraenkel. *The Canaris Conspiracy: The Secret Resistance to Hitler in the German Army*. New York: McKay, 1969.

Payne, Lauran. *German Military Intelligence in World War II: The Abwehr*. New York: Stein and Day, 1984.

Perrault, Gilles [Jacques Peyroles]. *The Secret of D-Day*. Translated by Len Ortzen. Boston: Little, Brown, 1965.

Persico, Joseph E. *Piercing the Reich: The Penetration of Nazi Germany by American Secret Agents during World War II*. New York: Viking, 1979.

Pincher, Chapman. *Dirty Tricks*. Paperbound ed. London: Sidgwick and Jackson, 1981.

Pirie, Anthony. *Operation Bernhard*. New York: William Morrow, 1962.

Ramme, Alwin. *Der Sicherheitsdienst der SS*. Berlin: Deutscher Militärverlag, 1970.

Reader's Digest Association. *High Stakes and Desperate Men: Classics of Espionage*. Pleasantville, N.Y.: Reader's Digest, 1974.

————. *Secrets and Spies: Behind-the-Scenes Stories of World War II*. Pleasantville, N.Y.: Reader's Digest, 1964.

Rogers, James. *The Secret War: Espionage in World War II*. New York: Facts on File, 1991.

Rowan, Richard W., and Robert G. Deindorfer. *Secret Service: Thirty-Three Centuries of Espionage*. New York: Hawthorn Books, 1967.

Rubin, Barry. *Istanbul Intrigues*. New York: McGraw-Hill, 1989.

Russell, Francis, et al. *The Secret War*. New York: Time-Life Books, 1981.

Seth, Ronald. *Encyclopedia of Espionage*. Garden City, N.Y.: Doubleday, 1972.

Smith, R. Harris. *OSS: The Secret History of America's First Central Intelligence Agency*. Berkeley: University of California Press, 1972.

Trevor-Roper, Hugh. *The Philby Affair: Espionage, Treason and Secret Services*. London: William Kimber, 1968.

————. Review of Anthony Cave Brown, *Bodyguard of Lies*, in *New York Review of Books*, 19 February 1976, pp. 13–16.

Waller, John H. *The Unseen War in Europe: Espionage and Conspiracy in the Second World War*. New York: Random House, 1996.

West, Nigel [Rupert W. S. Allason]. *MI5: British Security Service Operations, 1909–1945*. London: Bodley Head, 1981.

————. *MI6: British Secret Intelligence Service Operations. 1909–45*. London: Weidenfeld & Nicolson, 1983.

————. *A Thread of Deceit: Espionage Myths of World War II*. New York: Random House, 1985. Published as *Unreliable Witness: Espionage Myths of the Second World War* in Britain. London: Weidenfeld & Nicolson, 1984.

Wighton, Charles. *The World's Greatest Spies: True-Life Dramas of Outstanding Secret Agents*. New York: Taplinger, 1965.

Wighton, Charles, and Günter Peis. *Hitler's Spies and Saboteurs: Based on the German Secret Service War Diary of General Lahousen*. New York: Henry Holt, 1958.

Winks, Robin W. *Cloak and Gown: Scholars in the Secret War, 1939–1961*. New York: William Morrow, 1987.

SELECTED STUDIES AND BIOGRAPHIES

Adams, Henry M., and Robin K. Adams. *Rebel Patriot: A Biography of Franz von Papen*. Santa Barbara, Calif.: McNally & Loftin, 1987.

Ansel, Walter. *Hitler and the Middle Sea*. Durham, N.C.: Duke University Press, 1972.

Beitzell, Robert. *The Uneasy Alliance: America, Britain, and Russia, 1941–1943*. New York: Knopf, 1972.

Berber, Friedrich, ed. *Jahrbuch für auswärtige Politik, 1942*. Berlin: August Gross Verlag, 1942.

Bloch, Michael. *Ribbentrop*. London: Bantam, 1992.

Buchheim, Hans. *SS und Polizei im NS-Staat*. Duisdorf bei Bonn: Selbstverlag der Studiengesellschaft für Zeitprobleme, 1964.

De Belot, Raymond. *The Struggle for the Mediterranean, 1939–1945*. Translated by James A. Field, Jr. Princeton, N.J.: Princeton University Press, 1951.

Döscher, Hans-Jürgen. *Das Auswärtige Amt im Dritten Reich: Diplomatie im Schatten der "Endlösung."* Berlin: Wolf Jobst Siedler Verlag, 1987.

Duggleby, Vincent. *English Paper Money*. 4th ed. London: Spink and Son, 1990.

Fest, Joachim. "On Remembering Adolf Hitler." *Encounter* 41 (October 1973), pp. 18–34.

Fodor, Denis J., et al. *The Neutrals*. Chicago: Time-Life Books, 1982.

Gannon, Robert I. *The Cardinal Spellman Story*. Garden City, N.Y.: Doubleday, 1962.

Grunberger, Richard. *Hitler's SS*. New York: Delacorte, 1970.

Howard, Harry N. *Turkey, the Straits, and U.S. Policy*. Baltimore: Johns Hopkins University Press, 1974.

Irving, David. *Hitler's War*. New York: Viking, 1977.

Jay, Douglas. *Sterling—Its Use and Misuse: A Plea for Moderation*. London: Sidgwick & Jackson, 1985.

Josset, C. R. *Money in Britain: A History of the Currencies of the British Isles*. London: Frederick Warne, 1962.

Kirk, George E. *The Middle East in the War*. Introduction by Arnold Toynbee. Issued under the auspices of the Royal Institute of International Affairs. London: Oxford University Press, 1952.

———. "Turkey." In Royal Institute of International Affairs, *Survey of International Affairs, 1939–1946: The War and the Neutrals*. Edited by Arnold Toynbee and Veronica M. Toynbee. London: Oxford University Press, 1956.

"Knatchbull-Hugessen, Sir Hughe." *Current Biography*, March 1943, pp. 391–93.

Krausnick, Helmut, et al. *Anatomy of the SS State*. Translated by Richard Barry et al. Introduction by Elizabeth Wiskemann. New York: Walker, 1968.

Krecker, Lothar. *Deutschland und die Türkei im zweiten Weltkrieg*. Frankfurt: Vittorio Klostermann, 1964.

Kurowski, Franz. *Kampffeld Mittelmeer*. Herford: Koehlers Verlagsgesellschaft, 1984.

Lewis, Geoffrey. *Turkey*. 3d ed. New York: Praeger, 1965.

Lukacs, John. *The Last European War, September 1939/December 1941*. Garden City, N.Y.: Anchor Press/Doubleday, 1976.

McCombs, Don, and Fred L. Worth. *World War II: Strange and Fascinating Facts*. New York: Greenwich House, 1983.

Medlicott, W. N. "Economic Warfare." In Royal Institute of International Affairs, *Survey of International Affairs, 1939–1946: The War and the Neutrals*. Edited by Arnold Toynbee and Veronica M. Toynbee. London: Oxford University Press, 1956.

Miller, Marshall L. *Bulgaria during the Second World War*. Stanford, Calif.: Stanford University Press, 1975.

Onder, Zehra. *Die türkische Aussenpolitik im Zweiten Weltkrieg*. Munich: Oldenbourg Verlag, 1976.

Orlow, Dietrich. *The Nazis in the Balkans: A Case Study of Totalitarian Politics*. Pittsburgh: University of Pittsburgh Press, 1968.

Piekalkiewicz, Janusz. *Krieg auf dem Balkan, 1940–1945*. Munich: Südwest Verlag, 1984.

Reitlinger, Gerald. *The SS: Alibi of a Nation, 1922–1945*. New York: Viking, 1957.

Rhodes James, Robert. *Anthony Eden*. New York: McGraw-Hill, 1987.

Royal Institute of International Affairs. *Survey of International Affairs, 1939–1946: The War and the Neutrals*. Edited by Arnold Toynbee and Veronica M. Toynbee. London: Oxford University Press, 1956.

Seabury, Paul. *The Wilhelmstrasse: A Study of German Diplomats under the Nazi Regime*. Berkeley: University of California Press, 1954.

Sherwood, Robert E. *Roosevelt and Hopkins: An Intimate History*. New York: Harper & Brothers, 1950.

Shirer, William L. *The Rise and Fall of the Third Reich: A History of Nazi Germany*. New York: Simon & Schuster, 1960.

Smith, Peter C., and Edwin Walker. *War in the Aegean*. London: William Kimber, 1974.

Ure, John, ed. *Diplomatic Bag: An Anthology of Diplomatic Incidents and Anecdotes from the Renaissance to the Gulf War*. London: John Murray, 1995.

Weber, Frank G. *The Evasive Neutral: Germany, Britain, and the Quest for a Turkish Alliance in the Second World War*. Columbia: University of Missouri Press, 1979.

Weinberg, Gerhard L. *A World at Arms: A Global History of World War II*. New York: Cambridge University Press, 1994.

Weisband, Edward. *Turkish Foreign Policy, 1939–1945: Small State Diplomacy and Great Power Politics*. Princeton, N.J.: Princeton University Press, 1973.

Weitz, John. *Hitler's Diplomat: The Life and Times of Joachim von Ribbentrop*. New York: Ticknor & Fields, 1992.

Wighton, Charles. *Heydrich: Hitler's Most Evil Henchman*. London: Odhams, 1962.

FILM STUDIES

Booth, Alan R. "The Development of the Espionage Film." In Wesley K. Wark, ed., *Spy Fiction, Spy Films, and Real Intelligence*. London: Frank Cass, 1991.

Geist, Kenneth L. *Pictures Will Talk: The Life and Films of Joseph L. Mankiewicz*. New York: Scribner's, 1978.

Gow, Gordon. *Hollywood in the Fifties*. New York: Barnes, 1971.

Gussow, Mel. *Don't Say Yes until I Finish Talking: A Biography of Darryl F. Zanuck*. Garden City, N.Y.: Doubleday, 1971.

Hirschhorn, Clive. *The Films of James Mason*. Comments by James Mason. Secaucus, N.J.: Citadel, 1977.

Hopkins, Charles. "*Five Fingers.*" In *Magill's Survey of Cinema*. English Language Films, 2d Series, vol. 2, pp. 784–88. Edited by Frank N. Magill. Englewood Cliffs, N.J.: Salem, 1981.

Kay, Eddie Dorman. *Box-Office Champs: The Most Popular Movies of the Last Fifty Years*. New York: Portland House, 1990.

New York Times Film Reviews. 6 vols. New York: New York Times & Arno Press, 1970.

1953 Film Daily Year Book of Motion Pictures. 35th ed. Edited by Jack Alicoate. New York: Film Daily, 1953.

Nogueira, Rui. "James Mason Talks about His Career in the Cinema." *Focus on Film*, March–April 1970, pp. 18–36. Taped interview transcribed by Gillian Hartnell.

Parish, James R., and Michael R. Pitts. *The Great Spy Pictures*. Metuchen, N.J.: Scarecrow, 1974.

Terrace, Vincent. *The Complete Encyclopedia of Television Programs, 1947–1976*. 2 vols. South Brunswick, N.J.: Barnes, 1976.

"Top Grossers of 1952." *Variety*, 7 January 1953, p. 61.

Variety Film Reviews, 1907–1980. 16 vols. New York: Garland, 1983.

Variety Movie Guide. Edited by Derek Elley et al. Foreword by Sir Richard Attenborough. New York: Prentice Hall, 1992.

Wark, Wesley K., ed. *Spy Fiction, Spy Films, and Real Intelligence*. London: Frank Cass, 1991.

Index

About the Author

RICHARD WIRES is Professor Emeritus of History at Ball State University, where he chaired the department and later became Executive Director of the University's London Centre. He holds degrees in European history and law, and he served with the Counter-Intelligence Corps in southern Germany. His recent research interests include early espionage fiction as well as actual intelligence operations.

DATE DUE